PATERNOSTER BIBLICAL MONOGRAPHS

Paul's Understanding of the Church's Mission

Did the Apostle Paul Expect the Early Christian Communities to Evangelize?

PATERNOSTER BIBLICAL MONOGRAPHS

A complete listing of all titles in this series and Paternoster
Theological Monographs will be found at the close of this book.

PATERNOSTER BIBLICAL MONOGRAPHS

Paul's Understanding of the Church's Mission

Did the Apostle Paul Expect the Early Christian Communities to Evangelize?

Robert L. Plummer

Paternoster:
thinking faith

Copyright © Robert L. Plummer 2006

First published 2006 by Paternoster

Paternoster is an imprint of Authentic Media
9 Holdom Avenue, Bletchley, Milton Keynes, MK1 1QR, UK
and
P.O. Box 1047, Waynesboro, GA 30830–2047, USA

12 11 10 09 08 07 06   7 6 5 4 3 2 1

The right of Robert L. Plummer to be identified as the Author of this Work
has been asserted by him in accordance with the Copyright, Designs
and Patents Act 1988.

British Library Cataloguing in Publication Data
A catalogue record for this book is available from the British Library

ISBN 1-84227-333-7

Typeset by Michael D. Carter
Printed and bound in Great Britain
for Paternoster
by Nottingham Alpha Graphics

PATERNOSTER BIBLICAL MONOGRAPHS

Series Preface

One of the major objectives of Paternoster is to serve biblical scholarship by providing a channel for the publication of theses and other monographs of high quality at affordable prices. Paternoster stands within the broad evangelical tradition of Christianity. Our authors would describe themselves as Christians who recognise the authority of the Bible, maintain the centrality of the gospel message and assent to the classical credal statements of Christian belief. There is diversity within this constituency; advances in scholarship are possible only if there is freedom for frank debate on controversial issues and for the publication of new and sometimes provocative proposals. What is offered in this series is the best of writing by committed Christians who are concerned to develop well-founded biblical scholarship in a spirit of loyalty to the historic faith.

Series Editors

I. Howard Marshall, Honorary Research Professor of New Testament, University of Aberdeen, Scotland, UK

Richard J. Bauckham, Professor of New Testament Studies and Bishop Wardlaw Professor, University of St Andrews, Scotland, UK

Craig Blomberg, Distinguished Professor of New Testament, Denver Seminary, Colorado, USA

Robert P. Gordon, Regius Professor of Hebrew, University of Cambridge, UK

Tremper Longman III, Robert H. Gundry Professor and Chair of the Department of Biblical Studies, Westmont College, Santa Barbara, California, USA

This book is lovingly dedicated to my wife, Chandi, and to my two daughters, Sarah Beth and Chloe. May you lead many to righteousness and shine like the brightness of the stars forever (Dan 12:3).

Contents

Preface   **xiii**
Abbreviations   **xv**

Chapter 1
Introduction and Survey of Approaches   **1**
Survey of Approaches   2
   Pre-1950   5
      APOSTLE-CHURCH MISSION CONTINUITY   5
        Gustav Warneck   5
        Roland Allen   8
        Adolf von Harnack   11
        Carl von Weizsäcker   13
        Michael Green   15
      APOSTLE-CHURCH MISSION DISCONTINUITY 16
        Paul Wernle   16
        Ernest Renan and William Wrede   18
   1950-Present   22
      APOSTLE-CHURCH MISSION DISCONTINUITY 22
        Heinrich Greeven et al. 22
        W-H. Ollrog   23
        W. P. Bowers   24
        David Bosch   25
        John P. Dickson   26
        Stephen Chambers   27
      APOSTLE-CHURCH MISSION CONTINUITY   28
        Douwe van Swigchem   28
        Peter T. O'Brien   31
        James Patrick Ware   33

I. Howard Marshall   35
Eckhard J. Schnabel   35
John Piper   37
G. K. Beale   37
Norbert Schmidt   38
Conclusion   41

Chapter 2
The Church's Mission in the Pauline Letters: A Theological
Basis for Apostolic Continuity   43
Definitions   43
   Church   43
   Apostle   45
Theological Basis of the Church's Apostolic Mission   48
The Nature of the Gospel   50
   The Gospel as "Power"   51
   The Dynamic Gospel and Paul's Apostolic Mission   56
   The Dynamic Gospel and the Church's Mission   59
Paul's Theology of Mission within the Broader
New Testament Understanding of the Church's Mission   64
Conclusion   67
Excursus: Discontinuity of Missionary Activity Between
the Old Testament and the New Testament   68
Excursus: Pauline Co-workers   69

Chapter 3
Paul's Instructions to Evangelize   71
Paul's Commands to Witness Actively   72
   Paul's Instructions to the Philippians to Proclaim the Gospel   72
   Paul's Instructions to the Ephesians to Proclaim the Gospel   77
   Paul's Instructions to the Corinthians to Evangelize   81
      FIRST CORINTHIANS 4:16   83
      FIRST CORINTHIANS 11:1   85
      FIRST CORINTHIANS 7:12-16   93
      FIRST CORINTHIANS 14:23-25   94
   The Church's Active Witness: Concluding Thoughts   96
Pauline Commands to Witness Passively   96

Conclusion 105

Chapter 4
Incidental Evidence that Paul Expected the Churches to
Spread the Gospel in the Apostolic Pattern 107
Miracles, Prayer and Teaching in Paul and in the Church 107
   Divine Confirmation of the Gospel through Miracles 107
   Praying for Missions and the Church 111
   Teaching and Building up the Church 117
Suffering in Paul and in the Church 121
   Christian Identity: Why the Apostles and Church Suffered 121
   The Social and Historical Context of Christian Suffering 126
   Patterns of Christian Suffering in the Pauline Letters 128
      SECOND CORINTHIANS 4:7-15 128
      COLOSSIANS 1:24-25 131
      PHILIPPIANS 134
      FIRST AND SECOND THESSALONIANS 135
Conclusion 138

Chapter 5
Conclusions and Implications 141
Conclusions 141
Implications 144

Bibliography 147

Scripture Index 177

Modern Author Index 187

PREFACE

This work is a revision of a dissertation entitled "The Church's Missionary Nature: The Apostle Paul and His Churches," which I completed at the Southern Baptist Theological Seminary in May, 2001. In this study, I examine Paul's letters to discover what the apostle expected from the early Christian communities in regard to missionary labor. It is my prayer that the readers of this book will not only acquire a greater understanding of the selected texts' meanings, but also joyfully submit to the teaching therein.

As with my original dissertation, I want to express thanks to all the persons who have aided me in completing this work. First and foremost, I must thank the Lord, Jesus Christ, for his sustaining grace. Also, as servants of our great God, my professors at Southern Seminary were especially supportive of my research. Worthy of particular mention are Robert Stein, John Mark Terry, and Mark Seifrid. Thanks also to Eckhard Schnabel, who served as the external reader of this work and whose focused criticism improved it. Shortcomings, of which there are no lack, remain my own.

I must also express special gratitude to my friend, Ben Merkle. This study, my teaching, and my spiritual life are better because of his influence. "As iron sharpens iron, so one man sharpens another" (Prov 27:17).

As there are scant rewards for such activity on earth, there must be rewards in heaven for creating book indices. Until then, my assistant, Chuck Hetzler, will have to be satisfied with my deep appreciation and his minimal remuneration. Thanks also to Michael Carter for his invaluable assistance in formatting this manuscript and to Kelly Krebs and Emily Owens for proofreading.

I also want to express gratitude to my parents, who taught me the Scriptures from my childhood (Prov 1:8-9).

Finally, a heartfelt word of commendation is in order for my faithful and loving wife, Chandi. "A wife of noble character is her husband's crown" (Prov 12:4).

Robert Lewis Plummer
Louisville, Kentucky
December 2005

Abbreviations

AB	Anchor Bible
ABD	*Anchor Bible Dictionary*
AMZ	*Allgemeine Missions-Zeitschrift*
AJT	*American Journal of Theology*
AnBib	Analecta Biblica
2 Apoc. Bar.	*Apocalypse of Baruch*
ATR	*Anglican Theological Review*
b.	Babylonian Talmud
Sanh.	*Sanhedrin*
BAGD	W. Bauer, W. F. Arndt, F. W. Gingrich, and F. W. Danker, *Greek-English Lexicon of the New Testament and Other Early Christian Literature*, 2nd ed.
Barn.	*Barnabas*
BBB	Bonner biblische Beiträge
BDAG	W. Bauer, F. W. Danker, W. F. Arndt, and F. W. Gingrich, *Greek-English Lexicon of the New Testament and Other Early Christian Literature*, 3rd ed.
BDF	F. Blass, A. Debrunner, and R. W. Funk, *A Greek Grammar of the New Testament*
BECNT	Baker Exegetical Commentary on the New Testament
BETL	Bibliotheca ephemeridum theologicarum lovaniensium
Bib	*Biblica*
BHT	Beiträge zur Historischen Theologie
BNTC	Black's New Testament Commentaries
BSac	*Bibliotheca Sacra*
BTB	*Biblical Theology Bulletin*
BZAW	Beihefte zur Zeitschrift für die altestamentliche Wissenschaft
BZNW	Beihefte zur Zeitschrift für die neutestamentliche Wissenschaft
CBC	Cambridge Bible Commentary
CBQ	*Catholic Biblical Quarterly*
CGTC	Cambridge Greek Testament Commentaries

2 Clem.	*2 Clement*
CR	Corpus Reformatorum (Halle: C. A. Schwetschke, 1834-1900; reprint, New York: Johnston Reprint Corp., 1964)
CurTM	*Currents in Theology and Mission*
Did.	*Didache*
DPL	*Dictionary of Paul and His Letters*
Ebib	Études bibliques
EDNT	*Exegetical Dictionary of the New Testament*
EKKNT	Evangelisch-katholischer Kommentar zum Neuen Testament
EMZ	*Evangelische Missions-Zeitschrift*
Ep. Aris.	*Epistle of Aristeas*
EvQ	*Evangelical Quarterly*
EvT	*Evangelische Theologie*
ExpTim	*Expository Times*
FRLANT	Forschungen zur Religion und Literatur des Alten und Neuen Testaments
GCS	Die Grieschischen christlichen Schriftsteller der ersten drei Jahrhunderete (Berlin: Akademie, 1897-)
GNC	Good News Commentary
Herm. Man.	*Shepherd of Hermas, Mandate(s)*
Herm. Sim.	*Shepherd of Hermas, Similitude*
HNT	Handbuch zum Neuen Testament
HNTC	Harper's New Testament Commentaries
HTKNT	Herders theologischer Kommentar zum Neuen Testament
HTR	*Harvard Theological Review*
ICC	International Critical Commentary
Ign.	Ignatius
Eph.	*Letter to the Ephesians*
Rom.	*Letter to the Romans*
Trall.	*Letter to the Trallians*
Int	*Interpretation*
IVPNTCS	IVP New Testament Commentary Series
JB	Jerusalem Bible
JBL	*Journal of Biblical Literature*
JETS	*Journal of the Evangelical Theological Society*
Josephus	
Ant.	*Jewish Antiquities*
B.J.	*Jewish War (Bellum Judaicum)*
JQR	*Jewish Quarterly Review*
JSNT	*Journal for the Study of the New Testament*
JSNTSup	Journal for the Study of the New Testament Supplement Series
JTS	*Journal of Theological Studies*

KJV	King James Version
LCBI	Literary Currents in Biblical Interpretation
LCL	Loeb Classical Library
Louw and Nida	Johannes P. Louw and Eugene A. Nida, *Greek-English Lexicon of the New Testament Based on Semantic Domains*, 2nd ed.
Mart. Pol.	*Martyrdom of Polycarp*
MeyerK	H. A. W. Meyer, Kritisch-exegetischer Kommentar über das Neue Testament
MGEG	Mancherlei Gaben und Ein Geist
MHT	Moulton, James Hope, Wilbert Francis Howard, and Nigel Turner, *A Grammar of New Testament Greek*, 4 vols.
MM	J. H. Moulton and G. Milligan, *The Vocabulary of the Greek New Testament*
MNTC	Moffatt New Testament Commentary
MNTS	McMaster New Testament Studies
NAC	New American Commentary
NASB	New American Standard Bible
NCB	New Century Bible
NEB	New English Bible
NewDocs	*New Documents Illustrating Early Christianity*
NIBC	New International Biblical Commentary
NICNT	New International Commentary on the New Testament
NIDNTT	*The New International Dictionary of New Testament Theology*
NIDOTT	*The New International Dictionary of Old Testament Theology and Exegesis*
NIGTC	New International Greek Testament Commentary
NIV	New International Version
NovT	*Novum Testamentum*
NovTSup	Supplements to Novum Testamentum
NRSV	New Revised Standard Version
NSBT	New Studies in Biblical Theology
NTD	Das Neue Testament Deutsch
NTS	*New Testament Studies*
1QM	*Milhamah* (*War Scroll*)
1QS	*Serek hayyahad* (*Rule of the Community, Manual of Discipline*)
RB	*Revue Biblique*
RHPR	*Revue d'Histoire et de Philosophie religieuses*
RNT	Regensburger Neues Testament
RSV	Revised Standard Version
SANT	Studien zum Alten und Neuen Testament

SBL	Studies in Biblical Literature
SBLDS	SBL Dissertation Series
SBM	Stuttgarter biblische Monographien
SBS	Stuttgarter Bibelstudien
SBT	Studies in Biblical Theology
Sib. Or.	*Sibylline Oracles*
SJT	*Scottish Journal of Theology*
SNTSMS	Society for New Testament Studies Monograph Series
SP	Sacra Pagina
SR	*Studies in Religion/Sciences Religieuses*
Str-B	H. Strack and P. Billerbeck, *Kommentar zum Neuen Testament*
T. Benj.	*Testament of Benjamin*
T. Joseph	*Testament of Joseph*
TDNT	*Theological Dictionary of the New Testament*
TDOT	*Theological Dictionary of the Old Testament*
THKNT	Theologischer Handkommentar zum Neuen Testament
TLZ	*Theologische Literaturzeitung*
TNTC	Tyndale New Testament Commentaries
Trin	*Trinity Journal*
TS	*Theological Studies*
TynBul	*Tyndale Bulletin*
TZ	*Theologische Zeitschrift*
UNT	Untersuchungen zum Neuen Testament
WBC	Word Biblical Commentary
WTJ	*Westminster Theological Journal*
WMANT	Wissenschaftliche Monographien zum Alten und Neuen Testament
WUNT	Wissenschaftliche Untersuchungen zum Neuen Testament
ZMR	*Zeitschrift für Missionskunde und Religionswissenschaft*
ZNW	*Zeitschrift für die neutestamentliche Wissenschaft*
ZTK	*Zeitschrift für Theologie und Kirche*

CHAPTER 1

Introduction and Survey of Approaches

The Apostle Paul clearly and frequently makes known his personal evangelistic fervor.[1] On the other hand, Paul rarely, if ever, commands the recipients of his letters to evangelize.[2] In assessing this data, scholars have reached highly divergent conclusions on Paul's expectations of his churches' involvement in the missionary task.[3] The goal of this book is to contribute to the ongoing discussion of Paul's missionary theology by seeking to answer this one question: in what ways, if any, did Paul expect the churches to engage in missionary work? Of course, prior to answering this question, we must clarify what we mean by "missionary work." I will use the terms "missions," "evangelism," and cognate expressions to refer to the attempt to convert non-Christians to the Christian faith, regardless of any geographical or cultural considerations. Thus, for the purposes of our discussion, "missions" is not simply a shorthand for all the expected activities of the Christian church (i.e., as many ecumenical Protestants or Roman Catholics define it),[4] nor is it simply

---

1   E.g., 1 Cor 9:16 ("Woe to me if I do not proclaim the gospel!"). See also Rom 1:1; 15:20; 1 Cor 1:17; 4:15; 9:12; 2 Cor 2:12; 10:16; Gal 1:16, 23; Eph 3:8; 6:19; Phil 1:12–18; Col 1:23; 1 Thess 1:5; 2:2–9. English Bible quotations come from the New Revised Standard Version (NRSV), unless otherwise noted.

2   Even Peter T. O'Brien (who argues that Paul expected his churches to be active missionary entities) is forced to query, "How are we to explain this peculiar situation with Paul, who at every turn is preoccupied with an active mission to the Gentiles, failing clearly to indicate independent responsibility in such a mission for his churches?" (Peter T. O'Brien, *Gospel and Mission in the Writings of Paul: An Exegetical and Theological Analysis* [Grand Rapids: Baker; Carlisle: Paternoster, 1995], 54).

3   Compare for example, these two recent works that discuss the missionary dimension of the Pauline congregations: Eckhard J. Schnabel, *Early Christian Mission*, 2 vols. (Downers Grove: InterVarsity; Leicester: Apollos, 2004), 1459–65, and John P. Dickson, *Mission-Commitment in Ancient Judaism and in the Pauline Communities*, WUNT 2.159 (Tübingen: Mohr Siebeck, 2003), 311–12.

4   Recently, many ecumenical Protestants and Roman Catholics have used both the terms "mission" and "evangelism" to refer broadly to the church's total activity in the world (David J. Bosch, *Transforming Mission: Paradigm Shifts in Theology of Mission*, American Society of Missiology Series 16 [Maryknoll, NY: Orbis, 1991],

cross-cultural or cross-geographical evangelism, as it is often defined in evangelical missiological literature. Rather, I will be asking in what ways Paul expected the early Christians in scattered communities across the Roman Empire to win any outsiders (whether local persons or those separated by geographical or cultural distance) to the same religious commitment that they espoused.

In the remainder of this chapter, I will survey and classify significant works that have addressed Paul's expectations of the churches' missionary activity. Then, in chapter two, I will argue that Paul gives a theological basis for an active missionary church in his letters, but it is not found in Jesus' words of the Great Commission or in a direct appeal to the work of the Holy Spirit. Rather, Paul expects the dynamic, effective word of the Lord (i.e., the gospel) to propel all Christians in witness. In chapter three, we will find that this theological understanding of the church's mission is confirmed by Paul's specific exhortations to evangelize. Then, in chapter four, a study of incidental parallels between the apostolic mission and the church's ministry provides further confirmation that Paul saw the missionary activity of the church in close continuity with the apostles' evangelistic mission.

In the end, this book seeks to show that Paul envisioned himself as an apostle who conveyed the dynamic gospel to his hearers, so that the same effective, self-diffusing word that characterized Paul's apostolic mission also characterized the congregations he began. As extensions of the apostles' ministry, the churches are agents of God's word, which continues to work in and spread through them (e.g., Col 1:5–6; 3:16–17; 1 Thess 1:8; 2:13–16; 2 Thess 3:1). By its very nature, the "apostolic church" must be missionary.

Survey of Approaches

As an initial overview, we can say that the overwhelming majority of scholars in the past century have assumed or argued that Paul expected his churches to engage in centrifugal (outward-directed) missionary work that was in continuity with his own missionary labors.[5] That is, the early churches were not simply to

---

409–12; J. Andrew Kirk, *What is Mission?: Theological Explorations* [London: Darton, Longman, and Todd, 1999], 56–57).

5   The following representative scholars can be listed as agreeing that Paul expected his churches to preach the gospel to non-Christian outsiders: Adolf von Harnack, *The Mission and Expansion of Christianity in the First Three Centuries*, ed. and trans. James Moffatt, 2nd ed. (London: Williams and Norgate; New York: G. P. Putnam's Sons, 1908), 1:74; Nils Alstrup Dahl, *Das Volk Gottes: Eine Untersuchung zum Kirchenbewusstsein des Urchristentums* (Darmstadt: Wissenschaftliche Buchgesellschaft, 1963), 241; Stephen Neill, *A History of Christian Missions*, rev. Owen Chadwick, 2nd ed. (Harmondsworth, Middlesex: Penguin, 1986), 22–23; D. M. Schlunk, *Paulus als Missionar* (Gütersloh:

be passive instruments of attraction, but active evangelistic entities. Beyond this general affirmation of expected continuity, however, prior to the 1950s, few scholars treated our topic with any level of detail. In exactly what missionary tasks does Paul expect the churches to be involved? Which persons within the congregation are to be involved? On what basis does Paul expect this involvement? Proposed answers to these questions, and indeed the questions themselves, are often absent from both early Pauline and missiological studies.

Two broad observations need to be made before we look at particular scholars' views on Paul's missionary expectations of the churches. First, biblical teaching on missions and evangelism has been neglected by the academy. This problem is widely recognized, though few attempts have been made to rectify it.[6] Due to the lack of serious biblical studies on missionary

---

Bertelsmann, 1937), 45; Joseph A. Grassi, *A World to Win: The Missionary Methods of Paul the Apostle* (Maryknoll, NY: Maryknoll, 1965), 139; E. Best, *The Letter of Paul to the Romans*, CBC (Cambridge: University Press, 1967), 168; M. Green, *Evangelism in the Early Church*, rev. ed., (Grand Rapids: Eerdmans, 2004), 361–66; Günther Bornkamm, *Paul*, trans. D. M. G. Stalker (Minneapolis: Fortress, 1995), 54; E. Glenn Hinson, *The Early Church: Origins to the Dawn of the Middle Ages* (Nashville: Abingdon, 1996), 51, 63–64; D. Senior and C. Stuhlmueller, *The Biblical Foundations for Mission* (Maryknoll, NY: Orbis, 1983), 333; J. Ziesler, *Paul's Letter to the Romans*, TPI New Testament Commentaries (London: SCM; Philadelphia: Trinity Press International, 1989), 343; J. Knox, "Romans 15:14–33 and Paul's Conception of His Apostolic Mission," *JBL* 83 (1964): 1–11; Otto Michel, *Der Brief an die Römer*, 12th ed., MeyerK 4 (Göttingen: Vandenhoeck & Ruprecht, 1963), 366–67.

6   Köstenberger and O'Brien note, "Mission has thus far been one of the step-children of New Testament theology. Rarely has this significant biblical theme been given its due in the overall discipline" (Andreas J. Köstenberger and Peter T. O'Brien, *Salvation to the Ends of the Earth: A Biblical Theology of Mission*, NSBT 11 [Leicester: Apollos; Downers Grove: InterVarsity, 2001], 19). Elisabeth Schüssler Fiorenza agrees, "Since for various reasons religious propaganda, mission, and apologetics are not very fashionable topics in the contemporary theological scene, these issues have also been widely neglected in New Testament scholarship" (E. S. Fiorenza, "Miracles, Mission, and Apologetics: An Introduction," in *Aspects of Religious Propaganda in Judaism and Early Christianity*, ed. E. S. Fiorenza [Notre Dame: University of Notre Dame Press, 1976], 1). Senior and Stuhlmueller write, "The agenda of theology and exegesis is set, at least in part, by the experiences and preferences of those who take up these studies. It is not surprising, therefore, that such domestic issues as the evolution of church structures and ministries, or more speculative questions such as Christology, dominate the present agenda. These, in fact, are the issues that many professional exegetes and theologians find more palatable (*Biblical Foundations for Mission*, 3). Also see Andreas J. Köstenberger, "The Place of Mission in New Testament Theology: An Attempt to Determine the Significance of Mission Within the Scope of the New Testament's Message as a

themes, a missions-related "history of research" is difficult to write. A researcher is often left to piece together another scholar's views on a missionary topic from a smattering of incidental references in his or her writings. Furthermore, while it may be shown that particular scholars have similar views, it is often difficult to show clear lines of dependence between them. Because many scholars judged missionary topics as only peripherally important, they apparently saw little need to document prior opinions on the subject.

A second broad observation is that existing studies devoted exclusively to missionary subjects rarely meet the demands of a rigorous biblical theology. Such works are frequently written by missiologists for their peers and/or more popular audiences. David Bosch insightfully comments,

> Even where [missiologists] are sufficiently sophisticated not to use the Bible as a handy reference file of quotations to justify their own group's actions, they do have a tendency to operate with a very large brush. On the one hand, they are inclined to overlook the rich diversity of the biblical record and therefore to reduce the biblical motivation for mission to one single idea or text (for instance, the great commission or, more recently in liberation theology circles, Jesus' appeal to Isaiah in Luke 4); on the other hand, they tend far too easily to read back into the Bible aspects of the missionary enterprise in which they are involved today.[7]

Thus, we see that while New Testament scholars have neglected missionary themes, missiologists have produced mainly more popular works and have failed to construct a well-crafted biblical theology of mission. As we survey the contributions of significant scholars in the following pages, one of the challenges we will face is including the relevant materials from two scholarly disciplines which have not addressed our topic sufficiently. Furthermore, most New Testament scholars have failed to interact with missiologists' insights and vice-versa.[8]

Whole," *Missiology* 27 (1999): 347–62; David J. Bosch, "Mission in Biblical Perspective," *International Review of Mission* 74 (1985): 532, 535; William J. Larkin, Jr., "Introduction," in *Mission in the New Testament: An Evangelical Approach*, American Society of Missiology Series 27, ed. William J. Larkin, Jr. and Joel F. Williams (Maryknoll, NY: Orbis, 1998), 1–2; James Patrick Ware, "'Holding Forth the Word of Life': Paul and the Mission of the Church in the Letter to the Philippians in the Context of Second Temple Judaism" (Ph.D. diss., Yale University, 1996), 4. Christoph Stenschke, however, sees some recent New Testament studies on missions as a hopeful sign ("Mission in the New Testament: New Trends in Research. A Review Article," *Missionalia* 31 [2003]: 355–83).

7   Bosch, "Mission in Biblical Perspective," 532.

8   Ferdinand Hahn's approach is typical; he writes, "In using the work of other scholars I have confined myself mainly to exegetical researches. Works on mission

I will be subdividing the previous research on Paul's missionary expectations of the church into two broad chronological periods: (1) pre-1950 and (2) 1950-present. Within each period, we find scholars that advocate (a) apostle-church mission continuity and (b) apostle-church mission discontinuity. The main difference between the chronological periods is that in the earlier period (pre-1950), both the continuity and discontinuity advocates are generally characterized by more superficial and non-textual arguments (e.g., logical arguments or appealing to the Gospels in arguing that Paul supported church evangelism). While there is no lack of superficial missionary studies in the post-1950 period, we will be focusing on those that apply a more rigorous biblical theological method in an attempt to discern specifically *Paul's* view of his churches' missionary obligation (or lack of obligation). The order of scholars presented within the following subsections is loosely chronological.

Pre-1950

In this earlier chronological period, we will look at several important thinkers who represent major trends in the consideration of Paul's missionary expectations. These persons are: Gustav Warneck, Roland Allen, Adolf von Harnack, Carl von Weizsäcker, Paul Wernle, Ernest Renan, and William Wrede. Though the influential missiologist Michael Green wrote after 1950, his approach clearly reflects pre-1950 methods, so will will consider his writings at this juncture as well.

We will begin by surveying scholars who assume or argue for continuity between Paul's own evangelistic activity and the missionary activity that he expected of his churches. While these scholars appeal to a few texts or logical arguments, their studies lack careful attention to multiple Pauline texts and a convincing over-arching biblical theological synthesis.

As stated above, because the question of Paul's missionary expectations was long-neglected and early scholars rarely cite others' views on the subject, it is nearly impossible to conjecture any linear intellectual development on this issue until more recent days.

APOSTLE-CHURCH MISSION CONTINUITY

Gustav Warneck
Holder of the first chair of "the science of mission" at the University of Halle, Gustav Warneck (1834–1910) is considered the founder of Protestant

---

itself are introduced only occasionally" (F. Hahn, *Mission in the New Testament*, trans. Frank Clarke, SBT 47 [London: SCM, 1965], 9). An equally serious problem is many missiologists' disinterest in their theological heritage.

missiology.[9] Warneck's scholarship is rooted in pietism, and exhibits a very practical orientation in his writing – switching between the biblical context and current situation more frequently than most academic theologians.

Warneck approaches the biblical text with conservative presuppositions as to its authority and historical accuracy. He thus moves freely between biblical authors, ignoring academic questions such as the authenticity of the Pauline letters, the historical reliability of Acts, or to what extent Paul's congregations knew the Gospel traditions.[10] In this practical and canonical approach, one can see the influence of Warneck's neopietistic teacher, August Tholuck, as well as the pietistic tradition of Württemberg.[11]

Warneck posits Jesus' Great Commission (Matt. 28:18–20) as one of two main theological foundations of the church's mission.[12] The apostles (including

---

9   Bosch, *Transforming Mission*, 4, 491. Julius Schmidlin (1876–1944) is considered the founder of Catholic missiology (ibid., 4). Hans Kasdorf comments that Warneck built on the ideas of such predecessors as Karl Graul (1814–64), Friedrich Ehrenfeuchter (1814–78), Hermann Th. Wangemann (1818–94), and Karl H. C. Plath (1829–1901) (Hans Kasdorf, "Gustav Warneck: His Life and Labor," *Missiology* 8 [1980]: 281). For the standard biography of G. Warneck, see Martin Kähler and Johannes Warneck, *D. Gustav Warneck 1834–1910: Blätter der Erinnerung* (Berlin: Martin Warneck, 1911). Also, see Hans Kasdorf, *Gustav Warnecks Missiologisches Erbe: Eine biographisch-historische Untersuchung* (Giessen: Brunnen, 1990).

10 Warneck was certainly familiar with such critical approaches, which had earlier been championed by Wilhelm Martin Leberecht de Wette (1780–1849) and Ferdinand Christian Baur (1792–1860), among others. For example, see W. M. L. de Wette, *An Historico-Critical Introduction to the Canonical Books of the New Testament*, trans. Frederick Frothingham (Boston: Crosby, Nichols, and Co., 1858). This translates the fifth (and last) German edition (1848). Also see F. C. Baur, *Historisch-kritische Untersuchungen zum Neuen Testament*, Ausgewählte Werke in Einzelausgaben 1 (Stuttgart: Friedrich Frommann, 1963).

11 Seppo A. Teinonen, *Gustav Warneckin Varhaisen Lähetysteorian Teologiset Perusteet* [The Theological Basis of Gustav Warneck's Early Theory of Mission], Suomalaisen Teologisen Kirjallisuusseuran Julkaisuja 66 (Helsinki: Savon Sanomain Kirjapaino oy, 1959), 17–80, 240–44, 257–58. Note Warneck's treatment of Pietism and the Moravians in his history of Christian missions text (Gustav Warneck, *Outline of a History of Protestant Missions from the Reformation to the Present Time: A Contribution to Modern Church History*, ed. George Robson, trans. J. P. Mitchell and Campbell M. Macleroy [New York: Fleming H. Revell, 1901], 53–73). This is a translation of the seventh German edition.

12 Similarly, the first chapter of William Carey's famous *Enquiry* is titled "An Enquiry whether the Commission given by our Lord to his Disciples be not still binding on us" (William Carey, *An Enquiry into the Obligations of Christians to Use Means for the Conversion of the Heathens* [Leicester: Ann Ireland, 1792; facsimile, London: Carey Kingsgate, 1961], 7–13). Harry R. Boer documents the

Paul) *and their churches* are assumed to missionize on the basis of Jesus' direct command – an example we should also follow in modern times.[13]

The other theological foundation of the church's mission is the monotheistic and absolute nature of the Christian faith.[14] Christianity alone possesses ultimate truth and salvation. Furthermore, all of humanity is in need of this redemption. It is assumed that the theological foundations of the church's mission are uniform in the New Testament documents.

Addressing missionary concerns of his day, Warneck also proposes "natural" reasons for the church's missionary obligation. He appeals to the universality and superiority of the Christian religion in comparison to other faiths.[15] Christianity's superiority is especially exhibited in modern times by its

---

dominance of the Great Commission in modern missionary thought in chapter one, "The Role of the Great Commission in Modern Missions," of his book (H. R. Boer, *Pentecost and Missions* [Grand Rapids: Eerdmans; London: Lutterworth, 1961], 15–27). Significantly, the Epistles and Acts do not seem to support the idea that the early church was motivated to missionary labors by the Great Commission. See Boer, "The Great Commission and Missions in the New Testament" (ibid., 28–47). Boer thinks the Holy Spirit, as poured out since Pentecost, is the basis of the church's mission. Dean S. Gilliland agrees (D. Gilliland, *Pauline Theology and Mission Practice* [Grand Rapids, Baker, 1983], 187–88).

13   Gustav Warneck, *Evangelische Missionslehre: Ein missionstheoretischer Versuch*, 3 vols. [Gotha: Friedrich Andreas Perthes, 1892–1903]), 2nd ed., 1:91, 183–85. Warneck attacks Ernst Troeltsch (1865–1923) and other liberal scholars who attempt to found the church's mission on moral and humanitarian concerns (G. Warneck, *Missionsmotiv und Missionsaufgabe nach der modernen religions-geschichtlichen Schule* [Berlin: Martin Warneck, 1907]). This booklet originally appeared as separate articles in *Allgemeine Missions-Zeitschrift*. Cf. Ernst Troeltsch, "Missionsmotiv, Missionsaufgabe und neuzeitliches Humanitäts-christentum," *ZMR* 22 (1907): 129–39, 161–66. Chalmers Martin adopts a view similar to Warneck's (C. Martin, *Apostolic and Modern Missions* [New York: Fleming H. Revell, 1898], 27–28). Gustav Warneck's son, Johannes, follows in his father's footsteps in *Paulus im Lichte der heutigen Heidenmission* (Berlin: Martin Warneck, 1913). J. Warneck examines the ministry of the apostle Paul as a basis for evaluating current missiological practice. He concludes that Paul expected his churches to evangelize in obedience to Jesus' Great Commission (Matt 28:18–20; Acts 1:8) and that the modern church should also obey the Lord in missionary service (ibid., 16). Cf. Adolf von Harnack's comment, "Paul . . . knew nothing of such a general [mission] command" (*Mission and Expansion,* 1:41).

14   Warneck, *Missionslehre,* 2nd ed., 1:91–121. See Schärer's discussion of "supernatural" and "natural" missionary foundations (Hans Schärer, *Die Begründung der Mission in der katholischen und evangelischen Missions-wissenschaft*, Theologische Studien 16 [Zollikon-Zürich: Evangelischer, 1944], 3–10).

15   See chapter fifteen ("Die ethnologische Begründung") of Warneck's *Missionslehre,* 2nd ed., 1:278–304; cf. Schärer, *Die Begründung der Mission,* 6–10.

missionary success, adaptability, and the cultural achievements of European society. Warneck says, "Es ist doch gewiß keine zufällige Erscheinung daß die christlich gewordenen Nationen die Träger der Kultur und die Führer der Weltgeschichte geworden sind."[16]

If one were to examine thoroughly Warneck's missionary publications (which run into the hundreds), other theological reasons for the church's mission would be revealed: love toward God and humanity, thankfulness for salvation, compassion for non-believers, direction of the Holy Spirit, and the church's nature.[17] In summary, one notes the "broad strokes" with which Warneck paints (see Bosch's comment above). While Warneck appeals to specific Scriptures (e.g., the Great Commission) and logical arguments (e.g., the monotheistic and absolute nature of the Christian faith), there is a lack of detailed and specific description of Paul's expectation from the apostle's own letters. Indeed, this superficiality is the main characteristic of the pre-1950 investigation of our question.

Roland Allen

The influential English missiologist Roland Allen (1869–1947) is perhaps the first scholar to note a textual (i.e., evidential) problem with the issue of Paul's missionary expectations. In his ground-breaking missiological study, *Missionary Methods: St. Paul's or Ours?* (1912), Allen's concern to apply the biblical message to contemporary missionary practice leads him to take up the question of what Paul expected from his churches.[18] Though practical in orientation, Allen's text shows familiarity with scholarly works and exegetical issues.[19] Allen writes,

---

16 Warneck, as quoted without citation in Schärer, *Die Begründung der Mission*, 24. The son of Gustav Warneck, Johannes, defends a similar thesis in *The Living Forces of the Gospel: Experiences of a Missionary in Animistic Heathendom* [later titled *The Living Christ and Dying Heathenism*], trans. Neil Buchanan (Edinburgh: Oliphant, Anderson & Ferrier, 1909). The original German title of the work is *Die Lebenskräfte des Evangeliums*. Also see Hans-Werner Gensichen, "Evangelisieren und Zivilisieren: Motive deutscher protestantischer Mission in der imperialistischen Epoche," *Zeitschrift für Missionswissenschaft und Religionswissenschaft* 67 (1983): 257–69.

17 Teinonen, *Gustav Warneckin*, 170–77, 253–54.

18 Roland Allen, *Missionary Methods, St. Paul's or Ours? A Study of the Church in the Four Provinces* (London: Robert Scott, 1912).

19 Outside of Scripture, Allen most frequently references Adolf von Harnack's *The Mission and Expansion of Christianity in the First Three Centuries*; Ludwig Friedländer's *Roman Life and Manners Under the Early Empire*, trans. Leonard A. Magnus, J. H. Freese, and A. B. Gough, 7th ed., 4 vols. (London: George Routledge & Sons; New York: E. P. Dutton, 1908–13); and W. M. Ramsay's *St. Paul the Traveller and the Roman Citizen* (London: Hodder and Stoughton; New York: G. P.

One other effect of St. Paul's training is very clear. His converts became missionaries. It seems strange to us that there should be no exhortations to missionary zeal in the Epistles of St. Paul. There is one sentence of approval, "From you sounded out the word of the Lord," [1 Thess 1:8] but there is no insistence upon the command of Christ to preach the Gospel. Yet, Dr. Friedländer is certainly right when he says, "While the Jews regarded the conversion of unbelievers as, at the most, a meritorious work, for the Christians the spread of the doctrine of salvation was the highest and most sacred duty."[20] The Christians of the Four Provinces were certainly zealous in propagating the faith, and apparently needed no exhortation on the subject. This surprises us; we are not always accustomed to find our converts so zealous. Yet it is not really surprising. Christians receive the Spirit of Jesus, and the Spirit of Jesus is the missionary spirit, the Spirit of Him Who came into the world to bring back lost souls to the Father. Naturally when they receive that Spirit they begin to seek to bring back others, even as He did.[21]

Thus, for Allen, the inevitable prompting of the indwelling Spirit results in the early church's evangelistic zeal. The Spirit is the source of mission.[22] One

---

Putnam's Sons, 1896). Ramsay argues that Paul aimed his mission at the major provincial cities and that the well-trod Roman roads assured the Christianization of outlying areas (Ramsay, *Pauline and Other Studies in Early Christian History* [New York: A. C. Armstrong and Son, 1906], 73–78). Cf. William Wrede, *Paul*, trans. Edward Lummis (London: Green, 1907; reprint, Lexington, KY: ATLA Committee on Reprinting, 1962), 45. Wrede, however, does not think Paul expected the churches to carry on his mission, as we will see below.

20 Ludwig Friedländer (1824–1909) also writes, "The example of the first apostles continually inspired an ever-increasing number of imitators, who, in accordance with the teaching of the gospel, distributed what they had amongst the poor, and set out to carry the word of God from one people to another, and whose zeal never wearied nor abated even in the midst of the greatest dangers and difficulties" (*Roman Life and Manners*, 3:186). Friedländer's *Sittengeschichte Roms* was originally published from 1865–71.

21 Allen, *Missionary Methods*, 125–26. The unusual capitalization is Allen's own and typical of all his works. In his later volume, *The Spontaneous Expansion of the Church* (1927), Allen restates his case along similar lines (R. Allen, *The Spontaneous Expansion of the Church and the Causes which Hinder It*, 3rd ed. [London: World Dominion, 1956], 8–9).

22 See John E. Branner, "Roland Allen: Pioneer in a Spirit-Centered Theology of Mission," *Missiology* 5 (1977): 175–84. For a monograph dealing with the Spirit as the basis of the Church's mission, see Harry R. Boer, *Pentecost and Missions* (1961). For a briefer, more recent restatement of this thesis, see Don N. Howell, Jr., "Confidence in the Spirit as the Governing Ethos of the Pauline Mission," *Trin* 17 (1996): 203–21. Supporting his arguments mainly from 1 and 2 Thessalonians, Howell claims, "Paul's post-Damascus life was dedicated to building the new

may query, however, since the Spirit is also the source of ethics, and Paul frequently teaches on Christian living, how then shall we explain Paul's apparent reticence to instruct his churches on evangelism? According to Allen, no command was needed. Incidental references to the church's evangelistic activity are sufficient to convince him that ordinary believers were consistently involved in evangelism.[23] An activity in full-swing has no need of being enjoined. At its most fundamental level, Allen's basis for his Pauline theology of the church's mission is an argument from silence.

According to Allen, another factor which may help explain why Paul frequently included ethical teaching in his letters, but not evangelistic instruction, is a psychological phenomenon exhibited in conversion. Allen claims that a "certain natural instinct" or "instinctive force" led early Christians to proclaim the gospel. Citing the proverbial difficulty of keeping a secret, Allen claims that new believers felt compelled to share the new-found joy that they had discovered in Christ. Archytas of Tarentum's observation, as quoted by Cicero, provides an illustration of this psychological phenomenon for Allen: "If a man should ascend alone into heaven and behold clearly the structure of the universe and the beauty of the stars, there would be no pleasure for him in the awe-inspiring sight, which would have filled him with delight if he had had someone to whom he could describe what he had seen."[24]

Integrating his psychological and spiritual insights, Allen states, "In Christians there is more than this natural instinct. The Spirit of Christ is a Spirit who longs for, and strives after, the salvation of the souls of men, and that Spirit dwells in them. That Spirit converts the natural instinct into a longing for the conversion of others which is indeed divine in its source and character."[25]

Allen does not deny that his experiences as a missionary have influenced his

---

community of God's Spirit-people, who would by the leading of that same Spirit declare God's salvation to the nations still in darkness" (ibid., 221).

23 Allen cites Acts 8:4, Acts 16:3, and 1 Thessalonians 1:8 (*Spontaneous Expansion*, 8–9). Dean S. Gilliland follows Allen and Boer in positing a spontaneous expansion of the church under the guidance of the Spirit. Like Allen, Gilliland thinks Paul often assumed his churches' witnessing activity, rather than commanding it (Gilliland, *Pauline Theology*, 187–88).

24 Allen, *Spontaneous Expansion*, 12; Cicero *De amicitia* 23.88, trans. William Armistead Falconer, under the title, *Laelius On Friendship*, LCL 154 (Cambridge, MA: Harvard University Press; London: William Heinemann, 1923), 195. Because of its greater readability, I have chosen Falconer's translation over Allen's.

25 Allen, *Spontaneous Expansion*, 12. Allen was not the first to note the importance of the Holy Spirit for missions. See A. J. Gordon, *The Holy Spirit in Missions: Six Lectures* (New York: Fleming H. Revell, 1893); Arthur T. Pierson, *The Acts of the Holy Spirit: Being an Examination of the Active Mission and Ministry of the Spirit of God, the Divine Paraclete, as Set Forth in The Acts of the Apostles* (New York: Fleming H. Revell, 1898).

psychological and exegetical conclusions. He confesses

> Many years ago my experience in China taught me that if our object was to establish in that country a Church which might spread over the six provinces which then formed the diocese of North China, that object could only be attained if the first Christians who were converted by our labours, understood clearly that they could by themselves, without any further assistance from us, not only convert their neighbours, but establish Churches.[26]

Thus, we can summarize several characteristics of Allen's distinctive approach: experiential arguments, pragmatic concerns, an emphasis on individual conversion, and a harmonizing exegetical method. A distinctively Pauline basis for ecclesiastical evangelistic activity is notably lacking.

Adolf von Harnack

In 1902, the well-known church historian and New Testament scholar Adolf von Harnack published the original German edition of his *The Mission and Expansion of Christianity in the First Three Centuries*.[27] As pre-eminently a historical work (rather than a theological or exegetical one), Harnack's text reckons with the overwhelming evidence for Christianity's rapid spread.[28] The missionary work of a select group (i.e., "professional" missionaries) will not account for the religion's numerical increase. Thus, Harnack posits the importance of many unnamed laypeople in the spread of early Christianity. He writes, "We cannot hesitate to believe that the great mission of Christianity was in reality accomplished by means of informal missionaries."[29] Like Harnack, other historians who attempt to explain the explosive growth of Christianity are inevitably compelled to credit the masses of ordinary Christians.[30]

---

26 Allen, *Spontaneous Expansion*, 1.

27 This translates the German title *Die Mission und Ausbreitung des Christentums in den ersten drei Jahrhunderten*.

28 See Harnack, "General Evidence for the Extent and Intensity of the Spread of Christianity: The Main Stages in the History of the Mission," in *Mission and Expansion*, 2:1–32.

29 Ibid., 1:368. Elsewhere, Harnack claims, "It was characteristic of this religion [i.e., early Christianity] that everyone who seriously confessed the faith proved of service to its propaganda" (ibid., 1:367).

30 Neill, *History of Christian Missions*, 22, 26; Martin Hengel, *Between Jesus and Paul: Studies in the Earliest History of Christianity*, trans. John Bowden (London: SCM; Philadelphia: Fortress, 1983), 58. K. S. Latourette writes, "The chief agents in the expansion of Christianity appear not to have been those who made it a profession or a major part of their occupation, but men and women who earned their livelihood in some purely secular manner and spoke of their faith to those whom they met in this natural fashion" (Latourette, *The First Five Centuries*, vol. 1 of *A History of the Expansion of Christianity* [New York: Harper & Brothers,

Claiming the historical necessity of the early converts' witness is not a far step from suggesting that the apostles expected their converts to evangelize. Harnack finds such evidence in Paul's letter to the Roman Christians. The apostle writes, "From Jerusalem and as far around as Illyricum, I have fulfilled the good news [πεπληρωκέναι τὸ εὐαγγέλιον] of Christ" (Rom 15:19).[31] Harnack explains, "The fundamental idea is that the gospel has to be preached everywhere during the short remaining space of the present world-age, while at the same time this is only feasible by means of mission-tours across the world. *The fire it is assumed, will spread right and left spontaneously from the line of flame* [my emphasis]."[32] As further evidence that Paul expected the gospel to spread spontaneously from his new congregations, Harnack cites 1 Thessalonians 1:8, Romans 1:8, and Colossians 1:6.[33]

On what basis, though, could Paul expect his congregations to finish his evangelistic task? Had he instructed them to preach to their neighbors? Harnack does not address this question directly, but at points he offers a hint of what might be his answer. In dealing with the Christian mission's indebtedness to Judaism, Harnack claims that Christianity derived from its Jewish roots "the feeling that self-diffusion was a duty."[34] Elsewhere, Harnack states that Jews

---

1937], 116). Also see Pliny *Epistularum* 10.96; Irenaeus *Adversus haereses* 1.10.2; Tertullian *Apologeticus* 1.7; Origen *Contra Celsum* 3.55; Eusebius *Historia Ecclesiastica* 4.7.1.

31   My translation.

32   Harnack, *Mission and Expansion*, 1:73–74. Bornkamm agrees, "Romans 15:19 is therefore anything but adventitious and exaggerated. Instead, it expresses the apostle's amazing confidence that the gospel needed only to be preached for it to spread automatically: starting from the various cities it would reach out to the whole of the country round about and pervade it" (*Paul*, 54). L. J. Lietaert Peerbolte also endorses Harnack's conflagration metaphor (*Paul the Missionary*, Contributions to Biblical Exegesis and Theology 34 [Leuven: Peeters, 2003], 250, 255). Elsewhere, Peerbolte seems to present the Pauline congregations with primarily attractive or supportive evangelistic roles (213, 221, 259).

33   Harnack, *Mission and Expansion*, 1:74 n. 2. Harnack queries whether Paul was the first to conceive of the need for a rapid world-wide mission (ibid., 1:74 n. 1). He assumes that references to a universal mission in the four Gospels are anachronistic interpolations (ibid., 1:41).

34   Ibid., 1:15; cf. ibid., 1:9. In criticism of Harnack, it should be noted that more recent scholarship has claimed that little if any evidence can be found for an outward directed evangelistic campaign in second temple Judaism. See *Salvation to the Ends of the Earth*, 55–71; Ware, "Holding Forth," 22–64. Also, for the uniqueness of the early Christian worldwide mission, see Hengel, *Between Jesus and Paul*, 48–52; Scot McKnight, *A Light Among the Gentiles: Jewish Missionary Activity in the Second Temple Period* (Minneapolis: Fortress, 1991), 48, 115–17; Martin Goodman, *Mission and Conversion: Proselytizing in the Religious History of the Roman Empire* (Oxford: Clarendon, 1994).

felt a logical necessity to spread their religion because of its exclusive claims to a definitive revelation of the creator God.[35] Presumably, because Christianity shared such exclusive theological claims, early believers felt compelled to share their universally-applicable knowledge of the divine.[36]

Like Allen's *Missionary Methods*, Harnack's text remains a standard among missiologists to the present day. Because of its continued prominence and early date, we are warranted in taking a few paragraphs to look at an earlier scholar who influenced Harnack.

In searching for influences upon Harnack's understanding of Paul's mission, one is led to an intriguing comment in the introduction of his text. He writes, "[For a more detailed discussion of missions during the apostolic age] one may turn to numerous works upon the subject, notably to that of Weizsäcker. After his labours, I had no intention of once more depicting Paul the missionary."[37] Two things are notable here – (1) Harnack acknowledges admiration of or agreement with a previous scholar's study of Paul the missionary, and (2) few current scholars show awareness of Weizsäcker's work.

Carl von Weizsäcker

The Weizsäcker of whom Harnack speaks is Carl von Weizsäcker (1822–99), professor of Church History, and later chancellor, at the University of Tübingen, 1861–99.[38] Weizsäcker's *The Apostolic Age of the Christian Church* first appeared in German in 1886 and is duly noted for its detail, originality, and insight.[39]

---

35 Harnack writes, "Proudly the Jew felt that he had something to say and bring to the world, which concerned all men, viz., *The one and only spiritual God, creator of heaven and earth, with his holy moral law.* It was owing to the consciousness of this (Rom. ii. 19 f.) that he felt missions to be a duty" (*Mission and Expansion*, 1:9–10).

36 Cf. Warneck, *Missionslehre*, 2nd ed., 1:91–121.

37 Harnack, *Mission and Expansion*, 1:viii.

38 W. G. Kümmel, *The New Testament: The History of the Investigation of Its Problems*, trans. S. McLean Gilmour and Howard C. Kee (Nashville: Abingdon, 1972), 495.

39 Carl von Weizsäcker, *The Apostolic Age of the Christian Church*, trans. James Millar, 2 vols. (London: Williams and Norgate; New York: G. P. Putnam's Sons, 1894–95). Weizsäcker's second, revised German edition (1892) was translated into a two-volume English set, originally published 1894–95. The original German title of Weizsäcker's work is *Das apostolische Zeitalter der christlichen Kirche*. In light of Weizsäcker's work, Bosch's suggestion that Wernle's *Paulus als Heidenmissionar* is "the first serious scholarly attempt to look at Paul from the perspective of his missionary calling and ministry" will have to be corrected (Bosch, *Transforming Mission*, 124). W. M. Ramsay demonstrates a favorable

Since Harnack cites Weizsäcker's work as the definitive study on Paul the missionary, we are curious as to how he treats Paul's missionary expectations of his churches. Is this where Harnack derives his ideas? Unfortunately, investigation of *The Apostolic Age of the Christian Church* leads one to conclude that Weizsäcker's silence at this point exceeds that of Harnack. Weizsäcker discusses evangelism primarily as the activity of Paul, the other apostles, and explicitly-mentioned apostolic co-workers. In Weizsäcker's treatment of the Pauline churches' relationship with "the outer world," he considers three issues – eating meat offered to idols, being married to a non-believer, and respecting the civil government.[40] In none of these cases does evangelistic concern enter the discussion.

Weizsäcker's examination of the origin of the church in Rome leads him to speculate briefly as to evangelistic activity of ordinary members of the early Christian communities. He says that the Roman church could have been started by Paul's disciples (i.e., "professional" co-workers), or it could have been chartered by Hellenistic Jews (presumably lay-believers) who heard the gospel while visiting Jerusalem.[41] Weizsäcker suggests that such Hellenistic Jews might have been responsible for "preaching the Gospel in Rome" and that the Jewish uproar under Claudius could have been occasioned by their activity.[42]

Regardless of the Roman church's beginning, Weizsäcker discounts the importance of any such explanatory hypothesis as pure speculation. Elsewhere, he writes,

> In the first place, there can be no doubt that the marvellous extension of the faith beyond the limits of Judaism – in other words, Gentile Christianity – was due to Saul, soon now to be called Paul, and to no other. If others contributed in any way to the furtherance of this work, their names are lost to us or have paled behind his. He alone is remembered by its members as the founder of the new Church. He is this not merely because he established his claims to it by his teaching, but also because he was actually the pioneer in the movement.[43]

Like Harnack, Weizsäcker thinks Paul was rushing to complete his world-

---

awareness of Weizsäcker's scholarship (Ramsay, *St. Paul the Traveller and the Roman Citizen*, 86).

40   Weizsäcker, *Apostolic Age,* 2nd ed. (1899), 2:372–79.
41   Ibid., 2:77–79.
42   Ibid., 2:78; Suetonius *Claudius* 25.4. The text reads, "Iudaeos impulsore Chresto assidue tumultuantis Roma expulit." Cf. Acts 18:2.
43   Weizsäcker, *Apostolic Age,* 1st ed. (1894), 1:93–94. By "the new Church," Weizsäcker means the new Pauline Christianity which he differentiates from the Jewish Christian movement (ibid., 1:93).

wide mission before the Lord's imminent return.[44] Unlike Harnack, however, Weizsäcker does not mention Paul's expectation that the churches he began would continue his work, i.e., the apostle's assumption that "the fire . . . will spread right and left spontaneously from the line of flame."[45]

Although the importance of Paul's missionary work can hardly be underestimated, it is doubtful that the author of Acts or the apostle Paul would agree with Weizsäcker's dismissal of others' evangelistic labors. Did the early churches really play such a negligible role in the spread of early Christianity? As noted above, in reckoning with the evidence for early Christianity's rapid spread, historians are driven to highlight the importance of unnamed, lay-witnesses. While not a textual argument, the historical challenge stands: how does one explain early Christianity's rapid spread if only a small group of people were outwardly evangelistic? It is striking that scholarly giants in the study of Paul's mission, such as Weizsäcker, could neglect so completely the question of continuity between Paul's missionary labors and those of his churches. In his scattered assertions and general neglect, Weizsäcker is more properly classified with the next broad category we will discuss (apostle-church mission discontinuity), but we have considered him at this point because of Harnack's appeal to him.

Michael Green

Though I have organized the present chapter into two large chronological divisions, it is important to note that a "pre-1950" (i.e., superficial) approach to a Pauline theology of the church's mission still has many proponents. In the 2004 revision of his classic text, *Evangelism in the Early Church*, Michael Green still essentially follows the dominant pre-1950 method. Thus, I will briefly discuss Green here as a reminder that our chronological distinctions are not exhaustive, but are helpful in noting broad interpretive trends.

Green stresses God's divine wrath against sinners as an impetus for mission. He writes, "[These early Christian laypeople taught by Paul] really believed that those without Christ might suffer eternal and irreparable loss, and this thought drove them to unremitting labours to reach them with the gospel."[46] Green also cites the following factors as inducing evangelism: (1) a sense of loving gratitude to God for his gracious salvation in Christ, (2) the example of Christ, (3) a sense of responsibility and awareness of the coming "day of judgment," (4) a sense of concern for lost persons' present state and their eternal destiny, (5) obedience to the Lord's commands, (6) the prompting of the

---

44 Harnack, *Mission and Expansion,* 1:73–74; Weizsäcker, *Apostolic Age,* 1st ed. (1894), 1:228.

45 Harnack, *Mission and Expansion,* 1:74.

46 Green, *Evangelism in the Early Church,* rev. ed., 382. Green's original study was published in 1970.

Holy Spirit, and (7) an eschatological understanding that the Lord was going to return quickly and the gospel must be proclaimed throughout all the world.[47]

Green offers some reasonably logical arguments for evangelism, but the explicit textual support for his views is sometimes lacking. For example, it seems logical to assume that if one is taught to love one's neighbor and his neighbor is going to suffer eternal punishment, he would do all that he could to persuade that neighbor to repent and be saved. Nevertheless, even a cursory look at existing churches which hold to an exclusivist soteriology demonstrates that belief does not always eventuate in the logically-expected behavior. We should also note that Green's various logical arguments lack the over-arching theological framework needed to explain *what* missionary work Paul expected from his congregations and *why*.[48]

Green's book also exhibits several methodological deficiencies which minimize its usefulness in addressing specifically *Paul's* expectations of the churches' missionary work. For example, while sometimes making comments about a particular New Testament author's emphasis, Green does not provide separate discussions of Paul's letters, Acts, and the Gospels, and simply assumes that Paul and his churches were familiar with Jesus' teaching in the Gospels.[49] Also, Green uses Paul's statements about his own ministry as a paradigm for all believers without adequate justification.[50]

Alongside Green and other scholars who superficially argue for continuity between Paul's missionary labors and his expectations for his churches, we will now consider scholars who superficially argue for the opposite view, i.e., that Paul did not expect his churches to engage in outward mission. We will also include within this grouping scholars whose superficial treatments lead to their wholesale neglect of the question of Paul's evangelistic expectations.

APOSTLE-CHURCH MISSION DISCONTINUITY

Paul Wernle

Born in 1872, Paul Wernle studied at Göttingen before becoming a Privatdozent in New Testament at Basel in 1897. In 1900 Wernle became Associate Professor of Church History and the History of Dogma at the same school, where he served until his death in 1939.[51] While better known for such

---

47 Ibid., 208–10, 273–99, 369–79.
48 Green says, "It is no exaggeration to say that the Word is the prime agency under the Spirit of God for the mission of the Church in evangelism" (ibid., 211). Unfortunately, he leaves these ideas in nascent form (ibid., 208–14).
49 Ibid., 273–99, 356–79; but cf. 211.
50 E.g., ibid., 281–86.
51 Kümmel, *The New Testament: The History of the Investigation of Its Problems*, 496.

works as *Der Christ und die Sünde bei Paulus*, *Die synoptische Frage*, and *Die Anfänge unserer Religion*, Wernle is of interest to us primarily because of a short pamphlet he published in 1899, *Paulus als Heidenmissionar*. This work has been described by David Bosch as "perhaps the first serious scholarly attempt to look at Paul from the perspective of his missionary calling and ministry."[52] In this work, Wernle discusses the historical context of Paul's mission, the apostle's self-understanding, and his message. Oddly enough, Wernle does not consider the missionary role of Paul's churches. Later, in his two-volume work, *The Beginnings of Christianity* (*Die Anfänge unserer Religion*, 1901), the subject is also noticeably absent.[53] Wernle primarily seeks to demonstrate that Paul worked out his theology in light of his mission and that there is a discontinuity between Jesus and Paul.[54] While Jesus taught the brotherhood of humanity and fatherhood of God, Paul required the acceptance of certain dogmatic theological propositions and limited the obligation of love by focusing it within the Christian community.[55] Jesus' universal ideal became parochialized.[56]

When discussing the early Christian churches, Wernle focuses on Paul's moral expectations of the communities he founded. Wernle asserts,

> Scarcely have the Gentiles become members of the Christian community than Paul tries to discover something for them to do. His aim is now to train these masses of men, who had hitherto been for the most part without any kind of

---

52 Bosch, *Transforming Mission*, 124; Paul Wernle, *Paulus als Heidenmissionar* (Freiburg: Mohr, 1899). Indicative of New Testament scholars' disinterest in missions is Kümmel's failure to mention this work in his treatment of Wernle (W. G. Kümmel, *The New Testament: The History of the Investigation of Its Problems*, 288–92, 316–17). The word "mission" does not even appear in Kümmel's subject index.

53 Paul Wernle, *The Beginnings of Christianity*, ed. W. D. Morrison, trans. G. A. Bienemann, 2 vols., Theological Translation Library, vols. 15, 17 (London: Williams and Norgate; New York: G. P. Putnam's Sons, 1903–04).

54 Paul Wernle, *The Rise of the Religion*, vol. 1 of *The Beginnings of Christianity*, ed. W. D. Morrison, trans. G. A. Bienemann, Theological Translation Library, vol. 15 (London: Williams and Norgate; New York: G. P. Putnam's Sons, 1903), 209. Wernle writes, "Fidelity to the Christian conscience implies the clearest and most unflinching criticism of all that contradicts it, even though it be received upon the authority of a St Paul or a St John – *i.e.* the Gospel is to be employed practically as the canon and standard for all its later historical accretions" (ibid., x–xi).

55 Ibid., 84–85, 208–09, 342–43.

56 In his understanding of the apostle Paul as a corrupter of Jesus' teaching, Wernle has been influenced by William Wrede. See "P. Wernle," in *Die Religionswissenschaft der Gegenwart in Selbstdarstellungen*, vol. 5 (1929), 11, as cited in Kümmel, *The New Testament: The History of the Investigation of Its Problems*, 289 n. 358.

discipline, to work for the realization of the Christian ideal . . . . Words of Jesus, texts of the Old Testament, claims of the conscience, rules of Christian custom and discipline, reflections prompted by consideration for the outside heathen world, are all to become one combined motive for moral regeneration.[57]

Although Wernle mentions that Paul expected the church to provide a good example to its pagan neighbors, and that the church looked with some "patronizing compassion" on those outside, Paul and his co-laborers seem to be the only persons directly connected with evangelism in Wernle's mind.[58]

While Wernle thinks Paul distorted Jesus' teaching, he insists that the inheritors of Paul's doctrine committed more egregious errors. These congregations taught by Paul "went so far as to consider all that were without – the unbelievers – as such, for lost, whatever their works and their character might be."[59] Wernle sums up the "true gospel" as a calling to a moral and pious lifestyle, and judges the Christian dichotomizing of "saved" and "unsaved" as a further degeneration of an already adulterated Pauline gospel. In light of these views, it is not surprising that Wernle does not reflect extensively on what Paul expected the churches to do in regards to evangelism. Though Wernle is credited with producing "perhaps the first serious scholarly attempt to look at Paul from the perspective of his missionary calling and ministry,"[60] it seems that his theological biases prevented him from exploring a most natural theological and historical question – the apostle Paul's evangelistic expectations of his churches.

Ernest Renan and William Wrede

Ernest Renan and William Wrede represent scholars with a somewhat more defensible theological bias which likewise causes them to see discontinuity between Paul's mission and the activity that the apostle expected from his churches. Both Renan (1869) and Wrede (1904) believe that Paul only hoped to complete a rushed, representative preaching of the gospel before Christ returned.[61] The imminent parousia prevented the apostle from conceiving of an ongoing mission by his congregations.

Wrede, for example, writes, "If the name of Christ were only preached in every province, then the whole world – which meant in effect, for Paul, the Roman empire – would have heard the gospel."[62] Similarly, Renan remarks,

---

57   Wernle, *Rise of the Religion*, 191. Cf. 207–08, 220–21, 254.
58   Ibid., 315, 346, 350.
59   Ibid., 343.
60   Bosch, *Transforming Mission*, 124.
61   Ernest Renan, *Saint Paul* (Paris: Michel Lévy Frères, 1869), 492–93; William Wrede, *Paul* (1907), 47–48. The German original, *Paulus*, was first published in 1904.
62   Wrede, *Paul*, 48.

"Les premiers chrétiens vivaient de même si renfermés dans leur cercle, qu'ils ne savaient presque rien du monde profane. Un pays était censé évangélisé quand le nom de Jésus y avait été prononcé et qu'une dizaine de personnes s'étaient converties."[63]

Wrede's and Renan's eschatological reading of Paul's missionary expectations are representative of a large stream of missiological thought that continues to flow past our pre-1950 period. C. K. Barrett, for example, comments regarding Romans 15:19–23,

> Paul has already πεπληρωκέναι τὸ εὐαγγέλιον as far as Illyricum, and has no longer any τόπος in the East; that is, by *c.* A.D. 56 the Gospel had already been preached to all the ἔθνη at the eastern end of the Mediterranean, and Paul himself was proposing to deal with the West (Rom 15.23f). [Mark 13:27] must be interpreted similarly; when the parousia happens there will be (small) groups of ἐκλεκτοί all over the world.[64]

Paul Althaus, in like manner, writes (in reference to Romans 15:19), "Die Völker stehen als ganze vor Gott und seinem Gerichte. Sie sind Ganzheiten. Ist einem Volke, diesem seinem Endgeschlechte, auch nur in wenigen seiner Glieder das Wort nahegekommen, so sind damit alle erreicht, das ganze Volk verantwortlich. Mehr hat der Apostel nicht erstrebt. Darum ist er jetzt fertig im Osten."[65] This understanding of Paul's missionary vision was adopted by a number of scholars in subsequent years.[66]

---

63 Renan, *Saint Paul,* 562. Also, in reference to Romans 15:19, Renan writes, "Ainsi se termina cette troisième mission, qui, dans la pensée de Paul, achevait la première partie de ses projets apostoliques. Toutes les provinces orientales de l'empire romain, depuis sa limite extrême vers l'est jusqu'à l'Illyrie, l'Égypte toujours exceptée, avaient entendu annoncer l'Évangile" (ibid., 492–93). On the dedication page of *Saint Paul,* Renan makes a remark about Paul's and Barnabas's fervent eschatological expectations fueling their mission. He writes, "*Sûrement, ces espérances matérielles immédiates donnaient dans l'action une énergie que nous n'avons plus*" (ibid., i).

64 C. K. Barrett, "New Testament Eschatology," *SJT* 6 (1953): 228.

65 Paul Althaus, *Der Brief an die Römer,* 10th ed., NTD 6 (Göttingen: Vandenhoeck & Ruprecht, 1966), 147.

66 E.g., D. Hans Lietzmann, *Einführung in die Textgeschichte der Paulusbriefe: An die Römer,* 5th ed., HNT 8 (Tübingen: Mohr, 1971), 121; C. K. Barrett, *A Commentary on the Epistle to the Romans,* 2nd ed., BNTC (London: Black, 1991), 253; Johannes Munck, *Paul and the Salvation of Mankind,* trans. Frank Clarke (London: SCM, 1959), 48, 51–55, 276–78; Ernst Käsemann, *An die Römer,* 2nd rev. ed., HNT 8a (Tübingen: Mohr, 1974), 377; Roger D. Aus, "Paul's Travel Plans to Spain and the 'Full Number of the Gentiles' of Rom. XI 25," *NovT* 21 (1979): 232–62; Arland J. Hultgren, *Paul's Gospel and Mission: The Outlook from His Letter to the Romans* (Philadelphia: Fortress, 1985), 125–45; Lucien Legrand, *Unity and*

Undoubtedly, a proper understanding of first-century Jewish eschatology is essential for understanding early Christian history.[67] The New Testament evidence, however, will not conform to a monolithic apocalyptic eschatology. Several other scholars previously discussed understand Paul's eschatological views similarly to Wrede and Renan, but they do not allow that point to dictate the contours of Paul's mission in the same way.[68] If Paul was madly rushing to reach as many provinces as possible before the Christ's imminent return, would he have spent three years in Ephesus or one and one-half years in Corinth? Why would Paul have waited more than a decade after his conversion to start his world-wide missionary campaign? It seems more likely that the apostle aimed to establish mature congregations in his steady progress for the gospel.[69] Certainly Paul thought Christ could return at any moment (Rom 13:11–12; 1 Cor 7:26–31; Phil 4:5; 1 Thess 4:13–5:3), but the apostle's appointment of church leaders, among other evidence, shows that Paul was preparing his congregations for possible long-term existence (Phil 1:1; 1 Tim 3:1–13; Acts 14:23).[70] In Philippians 1:20–30, Paul explicitly considers the ongoing existence of the local Christian community after his death, and in Romans 15:28–33, Paul's task of evangelizing Spain is presented as contingent upon future circumstances. In other words, if Paul is not "rescued from the unbelievers in Judea," someone else would conceivably evangelize Spain (Rom

---

Plurality: Mission in the Bible, trans. Robert R. Barr (Maryknoll, NY: Orbis, 1990), 119–21; cf. E. P. Sanders, *Paul, the Law, and the Jewish People* (Philadelphia: Fortress, 1983), 186, 207. That is not to say that some of these scholars do not also acknowledge that the gospel spread through Paul's congregations (e.g., Wrede, *Paul*, 46–47; Munck, *Paul*, 278; Legrand, *Unity and Plurality*, 118), though this secondary spreading was not essential to Paul's missionary vision.

67 Cf. Albert Schweitzer, *Von Reimarus zu Wrede: Eine Geschichte der Leben-Jesu-Forschung* (Tübingen: Mohr, 1906).

68 Harnack, *Mission and Expansion*, 1:73–74; P. Wernle, *Der Christ und die Sünde bei Paulus* (Freiburg: Mohr, 1897), 121; cf. Weizsäcker, *Apostolic Age*, 1:228.

69 Paul Bowers, "Fulfilling the Gospel: The Scope of the Pauline Mission," *JETS* 30 (1987): 185–98. In a recent dissertation, Michael D. Barram provides a more comprehensive study supporting Bowers' contention in this article. See Michael D. Barram, "'In Order That They May Be Saved': Mission and Moral Reflection in Paul" (Ph.D. diss., Union Theological Seminary and Presbyterian School of Christian Education, 2001).

70 For a defense of the historicity of Paul's practice of appointing leaders in his new churches, see E. Nellessen, "Die Presbyter der Gemeinden in Lykaonien und Pisidien (Apg 14, 23)," in *Les Actes des Apôtres: Traditions, rédaction, théologie*, BETL 48, ed. J. Kremer (Gembloux: Ducolot; Leuven: Leuven University Press, 1979), 493–98; Benjamin L. Merkle, *The Elder and Overseer: One Office in the Early Church*, SBL 57 (New York: Peter Lang, 2003).

15:28–33).[71]

C. E. B. Cranfield's summary of New Testament eschatology seems closer to the textual evidence. He writes,

> It is well known that very many scholars regard it as an assured result that the primitive Church was convinced that the End would certainly occur within, at the most, a few decades, and that its conviction has been refuted by the indisputable fact of nineteen hundred years of subsequent history. The true explanation, we believe, is rather that the primitive Church was convinced that the ministry of Jesus had ushered in the last days, the End-time. History's supreme events had taken place in the ministry, death, resurrection and ascension of the Messiah. There was now no question of another chapter's [sic] being added which could in any way effectively go back upon what had been written in that final chapter. All that subsequent history could add, whether it should last for few years or for many, must be of the nature of an epilogue.[72]

Thus, in Wrede, Renan and others who work with similar theological biases, we find pivotal scholars who deny or neglect Paul's expectation of the churches' evangelistic activity. Because of theological biases or simply disinterest, scholars neglect key texts that relate to the missionary dimension of Pauline congregations. The actual investigation of important Pauline materials is absent. Superficial arguments or theological biases have prevented a more rigorous biblical theological approach to the question.

Prior to the 1950s, most scholars assume or argue that the church expanded spontaneously according to Paul's expectations.[73] The minority of scholars that argue for apostle-church mission discontinuity, however, share an interesting commonality with their continuity counterparts – superficiality. Their theses lack strong textual support and a cogent synthesis of the Pauline writings. Undoubtedly, superficial studies continue to be written even today, though, post-1950, they have been surpassed by scholars giving more rigorous attention to the Pauline writings.

---

71 I. Howard Marshall, "Who Were the Evangelists?," in *The Mission of the Early Church to Jews and Gentiles*, WUNT 127, ed. Jostein Ådna and Hans Kvalbein (Tübingen: Mohr Siebeck, 2000), 258.

72 C. E. B. Cranfield, *A Critical and Exegetical Commentary on the Epistle to the Romans*, ICC (Edinburgh: T. & T. Clark, 1979), 2:683. Roughly this same view is shared by John Calvin; note his comment on 1 Peter 4:7, "Praeterea tenendum est illud principium, ex quo semel apparuit Christus, nihil fidelibus relictum esse, nisi ut suspensis animis semper ad secundum eius adventum intenti essent" (John Calvin *Commentarius in epistolas catholicas* [1551] *Epistola Petri apostoli prior* 4.7 [ed. Wilhelm Baum, Eduard Cunitz, and Eduard Reuss, CR 83 [1896]: 274]).

73 See n. 5 of this chapter.

1950-present

Only since the latter half of the twentieth century have scholars begun to produce more precise biblical theological investigations on the question of Paul's missionary expectations of his churches. Like the earlier period, we can break these studies into two broad categories (1) those who deny continuity between Paul's missionary activity and his missionary expectations of his churches, and (2) those who affirm continuity between Paul's mission and the evangelism he expected of his congregations. Both groups have clear precursors in the earlier period, but unlike earlier scholars, they understand the evidential problem and admit that an argument for continuity or discontinuity must be established on firmer textual grounds.

APOSTLE-CHURCH MISSION DISCONTINUITY

We will begin by considering some significant voices that have denied continuity between Paul's own evangelistic labors and the missionary activity he expected from the churches

Heinrich Greeven et al.

Beginning in the 1950s, a number of German scholars took a renewed look at the Pauline writings and found scant evidence for Paul's expectations that the early Christian communities would engage in missionary activity in continuity with his own outward-directed evangelism. Unlike some scholarly predecessors whose overarching theological biases prevented them from taking interest in disputed texts, these scholars scoured the Pauline writings for answers to the congregational missionary question. Because of the resemblance of these approaches, we will quickly survey a number of similar ones. Heinrich Greeven speaks for many in his assertion, "Für den unmittelbaren Auftrag der Gemeinde zur Verkündigung gibt es kaum einen Beleg in den Briefen."[74] Greeven handles this evidential problem by suggesting that the church's missionary obligation is primarily one of attraction.[75] Peter Lippert, in *Leben als Zeugnis* (1968), also emphasizes the centripetal missionary attraction of the Pauline churches.[76] In like fashion, Hans-Werner Gensichen (1971) argues that Paul expected ordinary Christians to be "missionary" ("missionarisch") rather than

---

74 Heinrich Greeven, "Die missionierende Gemeinde nach den Apostolischen Briefen," in *Sammlung und Sendung: Vom Auftrag der Kirche in der Welt*, ed. Joachim Heubach and Heinrich-Hermann Ulrich (Berlin: Christlicher Zeitschriftenverlag, 1958), 66.
75 Greeven, "Die missionierende Gemeinde," 65–66.
76 Peter Lippert, *Leben als Zeugnis: Die werbende Kraft christlicher Lebensführung nach dem Kirchenverständnis neutestamentlicher Briefe,* SBM 4 (Stuttgart: Katholisches Bibelwerk, 1968), 127–28, 164–65, 175–76.

"missionizing" ("missionierend").[77] That is, ordinary Christians had a centripetal and attractive function, which should be distinguished from the apostle's centrifugal, outward-directed missions. Dieter Zeller, in his article, "Theologie der Mission bei Paulus" (1982), claims that the apostle develops a theological understanding only of his own mission, not that of other missionaries or churches. Zeller writes, "Dabei sind wir uns bewußt, daß Paulus zunächst einmal nur ein theologisches Verständnis seiner eigenen Mission entwickelt. Es läßt sich nicht ohne weiteres auf andere Missionare und andere kirchliche Situationen ausdehnen."[78] One must applaud these scholars for asking how the words of the apostle Paul himself inform our understanding of his expectations of the churches' missionary activity. Undoubtedly, the centripetal or attractive missionary function of the churches is a neglected theme in Paul's writings. In addition, none of these German scholars deny the church's missionary role in praying for and financially supporting the apostle's mission; they only reject the thesis that Paul expected his churches to engage in independent, outward-directed evangelism.[79] One must admit that if Paul expected an outward-directed ecclesiastically-based mission there is, at the very least, a paucity of explicit commands in that regard. One must also appreciate these scholars' hesitancy to go beyond the explicit textual data by weak inferences or logical arguments.

W-H. Ollrog

Wolf-Henning Ollrog (1979) is not content to say that Paul envisioned simply *churches* supporting his apostolic mission or an attractive role for his congregations. Ollrog proposes that Paul planned for the congregations to choose persons from among themselves to serve as the apostle's missionary co-workers.[80] It was then, primarily in this way, that the congregations took part in the apostle's missionary campaign – through designated representatives. Again,

---

77 Hans-Werner Gensichen, *Glaube für die Welt: Theologische Aspekte der Mission* (Gütersloh: Gerd Mohn, 1971), 165–86.

78 D. Zeller, "Theologie der Mission bei Paulus," in *Mission im neuen Testament*, ed. Karl Kertelge (Freiburg: Herder, 1982), 164.

79 For the churches' role in supporting Paul's mission, see Greeven, "Die missionierende Gemeinde," 69; Lippert, *Leben als Zeugnis*, 178; Zeller, "Theologie der Mission bei Paulus," 181; Rudolf Liechtenhan, *Die urchristliche Mission: Voraussetzungen, Motive und Methoden* (Zurich: Zwingli, 1946), 87; cf. Douwe van Swigchem, *Het missionair karakter van de Christelijke gemeente volgens de brieven van Paulus en Petrus* (Kampen: Kok, 1955), 23–33.

80 Wolf-Henning Ollrog, *Paulus und seine Mitarbeiter: Untersuchungen zu Theorie und Praxis der paulinischen Mission*, WMANT 50 (Neukirchen-Vluyn: Neukirchener, 1979). Johannes Nissen apparently endorses Ollrog's thesis (*New Testament and Mission: Historical and Hermeneutical Perspectives* [Frankfurt am Main: Peter Lang, 1999], 112).

we see under the influence of a more rigorous biblical theological approach, scholars such as Ollrog began to revive neglected themes in the Pauline writings – i.e., in Ollrog's case, the congregations' participation in the apostles' missionary labors through delegated representatives.

W. P. Bowers

Though the view that Paul expected his churches to be active in mission has been challenged in the past, it has possibly never received such an articulate opponent in the English-speaking world as W. P. Bowers. Bowers claims that *no textual evidence* can be found to support the view that Paul expected his churches to be active in outward-directed evangelism. Rather, in line with Ollrog's conclusions, Paul wanted his churches to support and pray for *his* missionary work (e.g., Rom 15:30–32; 2 Cor 1:11; 11:7–9; Phil 1:5,19; 2:25). Bowers argues that Paul undoubtedly instructed his churches to live exemplary lives and respond to inquirers (i.e., to have an attractive role), but we do not have any evidence that he anticipated their involvement in an independent outward-directed missionary campaign. According to Bowers, the statements we do find support a centripetal (inward-directed) mission of attraction for the local church. The community of believers is to set an example of holy living, so as to draw outsiders into its midst (Col 4:5–6). Bowers writes,

> The most the evidence indicates is that these churches were to facilitate accessions to their community by an attractive behaviour and by a responsiveness to inquiries. But an energetic, aggressive, mobile missionary outreach of the sort prosecuted by Paul himself is not described, expected, or enjoined for his churches. Apparently Paul perceived the missionary role in terms of believing individuals rather than believing communities.[81]

Thus, in Bowers' reading, Paul mirrors the singular role of an Old Testament prophet, while his congregations act as Israel – drawing in outsiders by their exemplary lifestyle.[82]

Bowers claims that Scripture texts used to support an active mission for the Pauline churches have been misinterpreted. For example, "the word of the Lord ringing out" (1 Thess 1:8; cf. Rom 1:8; 2 Cor 3:2) refers to the encouragement *other believers* receive from news of the Thessalonians' faithfulness. Also,

---

81   W. Paul Bowers, "Church and Mission in Paul," *JSNT* 44 (1991): 111. Bowers makes this same argument in a portion of his doctoral dissertation. Bowers, "Studies in Paul's Understanding of His Mission" (Ph.D. diss., University of Cambridge, 1976), 103–21. For a very similar approach and conclusions, see Terence L. Donaldson, "The Absence in Paul's Letters of Any Injunction to Evangelize" (paper presented at the annual meeting of the Society of Biblical Literature, Nashville, TN, November 2000), 1–14.

82   Bowers, "Church and Mission," 109.

Paul's injunctions to imitate him have to do with ethical behavior and intra-community relations, rather than evangelistic outreach (1 Cor 10–11). References to the church growing as a building or body deal with intra-community maturity, and the agents of growth are always God or Paul (1 Cor 3:9–15; Eph 2:19–22; 4:16). Finally, Bowers says Philippians 1 commends *individuals* for preaching the gospel, but does not consider evangelistic outreach in relation to a congregation.[83]

As an evangelical missionary in Africa, Bowers cannot be accused of being "anti-missions." In fact, he offers his scholarship as a possible theological justification for *para-church* missions.[84] It must be noted that Bowers is correct to raise the question of whether Paul made any clear statements to show that he expected anything beyond a passive or supportive missionary role for his congregations. Bowers attempts to construct his understanding of Paul's missionary expectations on a thorough study of the Pauline writings – following the framework of a modern biblical theological approach which respects the individual voices of the New Testament authors. One cannot criticize Bowers' return to the text, though we will later question some of his conclusions and his neglect of other data.

David Bosch

Leading ecumenical missiologist David Bosch (1929–92) may also be cited as holding a view similar to Bowers. Bosch agrees with many traditionalists that Paul planted churches strategically, putting them in places from which the gospel would easily spread.[85] Nevertheless, Bosch sees the primary missionary action of these churches as centripetal. "Being" is more important than "doing" for the early church. Bosch writes, "[The church's] primary mission in the world is to *be* this new creation."[86] Citing 1 Thessalonians 1:8; 2 Corinthians 3:2; and Romans 1:8; 16:19, Bosch argues, "These comments probably do not suggest that the Thessalonian, Corinthian, and Roman churches are actively involved in direct missionary outreach, but rather that they are 'missionary by their very nature,' through their unity, mutual love, exemplary conduct, and radiant joy."[87] Elsewhere, Bosch writes,

> Paul's whole argument is that the attractive lifestyle of the small Christian communities gives credibility to the missionary outreach in which he and his fellow-workers are involved. The primary responsibility of 'ordinary' Christians

---

83 Ibid., 92–101, 104.
84 Ibid., 111.
85 Bosch, *Transforming Mission*, 130–31.
86 Ibid., 168. Bosch seems to think of the church's "being" as moral behavior, while Paul speaks of the church's being in decidedly more ontological and supernatural categories.
87 Ibid.

is not to go out and preach, but to support the mission project through their appealing conduct and by making 'outsiders' feel welcome in their midst.[88]

John P. Dickson

In *Mission-Commitment in Ancient Judaism and in the Pauline Communities* (2003), Dickson presents the reader with a revised copy of his Macquarie University dissertation.[89] As the title suggests, Dickson attempts to highlight similarities between Second Temple Judaism's commitment to convert Gentiles and Paul's expectation of his congregations' "mission-commitment." Dickson is in the minority in seeing a clear motif of explicit missionary interest in Second Temple Judaism,[90] but he attempts to show how this commitment went far beyond verbal proclamation.[91] In fact, such missions-commitment was more usually expressed through ethical apologetic or the self-conscious modeling of the true worship of God. Dickson argues that this pre-Christian Jewish communal missionary ethos informed Paul's expectations of his own communities.[92]

Dickson argues that Paul expected local *evangelists*, not local congregations, to continue proclaiming the gospel.[93] Dickson also contends that Paul reserved the gospel word group (εὐαγγελ-ιονίζομαι) for authorized eschatological heralds of the gospel under the influence of passages in Isaiah such as 40:9, 52:7, and 61:1. Thus, while the local Christian communities primarily functioned in supportive, attractive or apologetic roles, Paul only spoke of authorized heralds like himself, apostolic coworkers or evangelists as explicit

---

88 Ibid., 138.
89 Dickson's dissertation was entitled, "Promoting the Gospel: 'Mission-Commitment' in the Churches of Paul Against its Jewish Background" (Ph.D. diss., Macquarie University, 2001).
90 Rainer Riesner aptly summarizes recent scholarship on the missionary dimension of Second Temple Judaism: ". . . our evidence does not allow us to speak of a pre-Christian Jewish mission in the sense of intended activity. Even after the discussions of the last ten years there is 'no single item of conclusive evidence' for Jewish 'missionary activity among the Gentiles'" ("A Pre-Christian Jewish Mission?," in *The Mission of the Early Church to Jews and Gentiles*, WUNT 127, ed. Jostein Ådna and Hans Kvalbein [Tübingen: Mohr Siebeck 2000], 249). Riesner is quoting from L. H. Feldman, *Jew and Gentile in the Ancient World: Attitudes and Interactions from Alexander to Justinian* (Princeton: Princeton University Press, 1993), 293. Likewise, L. J. Lietaert Peerbolte concludes, "The phenomenon of proselytizing mission cannot be traced back to either Jewish or pagan cults in the pre-Christian era" (*Paul the Missionary*, 257).
91 Dickson, *Mission-Commitment*, 84–85.
92 Ibid., 313.
93 Ibid., 151.

gospel proclaimers.[94] Dickson writes, "Contrary to the conclusions of D. van Swigchem, P. T. O'Brien, J. P. Ware, and R. L. Plummer, the proclamation of the gospel never appears as even a minor duty of Paul's converts."[95]

Without going into great detail, we can summarize that Dickson sees debated texts (e.g., 1 Thess 1:8, Phil 1:14; 2:15–17; Eph 6:15) as not referring to congregational evangelism. Dickson writes, "Nowhere [in Paul's letters] are believers portrayed as responsible for or engaged in the task of preaching the gospel."[96] In later chapters, I will be looking at these debated passages in more detail.

Besides offering alternative interpretations of debated texts, it is important to note three significant weaknesses of Dickson's study. First, Dickson fails to adequately summarize and interact with scholars who have previously written on this subject. In fact, his superficial summary of several scholars' works creates "straw men" in relation to his own observations and gives a false impression of his study's originality.[97] Second, Dickson falsely dichotomizes the role of the congregation and the role of the evangelists. Certainly, in Paul's understanding, persons called "evangelists" are (at least usually) part of local communities and thus to speak of an evangelist's role in proclamation is to speak of the activity of one member of the congregation.[98] Third, it is not at all clear that Paul reserved the gospel word group to refer to the proclamation of authorized heralds. Indeed, in Ephesians 6:15, as will be argued more extensively in a future chapter, it seems that Paul draws from the εὐαγγελ- word group to describe the necessity of ordinary believers to be prepared for gospel proclamation.

Stephen Chambers

In a 2004 dissertation at St. Michael's College (Canada), Stephen Chambers

---

94 Ibid., 311–12.

95 Ibid., 311.

96 Ibid., 131.

97 For example, on page 312, note Dickson's dismissal of Paul Bowers's work. In fact, Bowers's published thoughts on this subject differ little from Dickson's. Also, in gross oversimplification on page 10, Dickson writes, "The works of Ollrog, Bowers, O'Brien, Ware and Van Swigchem focus *almost exclusively* [my emphasis] on proclamation as the indicator of mission-commitment and, in so doing, miss the significance of a great part of the evidence, both Jewish and Pauline." The brief discussion of Swigchem below will show that Dickson's summary is clearly not fair. Furthermore, on page 4, note 9, Dickson writes, "Essentially, Plummer's argument [i.e., the main thesis of his dissertation] is that Paul's injunctions to imitate him include the obligation to reflect his missionary proclamation." Dickson, in fact, wrongly summarizes the main thesis of my dissertation, as the reader of my revised dissertation (i.e., this book) can testify.

98 See Eph. 4:11; 2 Tim. 4:5; cf. Acts 21:8.

asks what evangelistic behavior Paul expects from his converts in 1 Corinthians.[99] Chambers says that he focuses solely on this letter because it has a "greater volume of relevant material" than other Pauline letters.[100] He concludes that Paul "was concerned to maintain the integrity of his churches' purity: their separation from the non-Christian world, not their engagement with it."[101] According to Chambers, "It was more in spite of, than because of, Paul's own intention, that the communities he founded eventually became larger and more numerous."[102] In this view, Paul's brief, representative preaching throughout the Roman Empire completely fulfilled the apostle's sense of obligation to his missionary commission.[103] In a later chapter, we will be examining in more detail some of the passages in 1 Corinthians which, I will argue, support a more active missionary role for this Pauline congregation.

APOSTLE-CHURCH MISSION CONTINUITY

Taking a careful examination of the Pauline writings are also those scholars who see more direct continuity between Paul's missionary labors and what he expected of his churches, while at the same time recognizing the superficiality of most traditional approaches.

Douwe van Swigchem

Dutchman Douwe van Swigchem provides possibly the most significant treatment of Paul's missionary expectations by a modern scholar. Swigchem not only recognizes the evidential problem facing adherents of the traditional view, but provides an extensive study of the Pauline and Petrine epistles in defense of apostolic-congregational missionary continuity. In his doctoral dissertation, *Het missionair karakter van de Christelijke gemeente volgens de brieven van Paulus en Petrus* (1955), Swigchem argues that in spite of the few direct textual commands to evangelize in the epistles, we should view the church as *missionary in essence*.[104] Undeniably, the apostles play a special role

---

99   Stephen Lionel Chambers, "Paul, His Converts, and Mission in 1 Corinthians" (Ph.D. diss., St. Michael's College [Canada], 2004). Chambers' supervisor was Terence L. Donaldson, with whom he shows considerable agreement in his conclusions. Cf. Donaldson, "The Absence in Paul's Letters of Any Injunction to Evangelize," 1–14.

100 Chambers, 48.

101 Ibid., ii.

102 Ibid., iii.

103 Ibid., 334–36. Chambers writes, ". . . Paul neither foresaw nor required his converts' missionary activity but genuinely considered their churches, as small and scattered as they were, to be an adequate representative harvest of the Gentiles" (ibid., 336).

104 The author's summary of his book, pp. 256–66, has been translated into English by M. H. Woudstra.

in the early Christian mission, but it is not a role that excludes the broader church's evangelistic obligation. Furthermore, it should not be forgotten that the apostles themselves are part of the church (Eph 4:11; Col 1:24–25).[105] Swigchem's 276-page monograph makes a significant contribution to our discussion and will be summarized in the following paragraphs.

The early Pauline and Petrine churches demonstrate their sense of missionary obligation in numerous ways, says Swigchem. First, the churches express interest in receiving news about the apostles' missionary work, and they assist the apostles by their prayers, financial support, and concern for the newly established congregations.[106] The churches also provide evangelistic co-workers for the apostles, and they rejoice at the news of the frontier missionary work.[107] Second, churches clearly distinguish themselves from outsiders who have not received God's mercy (Rom 8:1; Gal 4:8–9; 1 Thess 1:8–9; 5:9; 2 Thess 1:5–8). Outsiders are not viewed as enemies, but as potential believers. Members of the Christian congregation have received a divine pardon, while non-believers remain under God's judgment. As recipients of a salvation of which the outsiders are unaware, the church is under compulsion to evangelize (1 Thess 4:5; 2 Thess 1:8–10; 1 Pet 2:11).[108] Third, the apostles repeatedly present the church's ethical behavior as a light to draw outsiders to the gospel.[109] Fourth, the apostles expect the churches to imitate their missionizing activity (1 Cor 4:16; 9:19–23; 11:1; Phil 3:17; 1 Thess 1:6).[110] Fifth, the apostles command the churches to follow Christ's example, which includes the proclamation of the gospel in the midst of opposition (Rom 15:3; 1 Cor 11:1; Eph 5:2; Phil 2:5–11; Col 3:13; 1 Thess 1:6; 1 Pet 3:13–19).[111] Sixth, Swigchem claims that he can identify direct injunctions to missionary activity in the Pauline and Petrine epistles (Eph 6:15; Phil 1:27; Col 4:5–6; 1 Pet 3:15; 4:16).[112] Seventh, the churches are praised for their missionary activity, from which one can deduce that the apostles had no need to enjoin an activity which was already in progress (Rom 1:8; Phil 1:5, 14; 1 Thess 1:8).[113] Eighth, both Luke and Paul employ λόγος τοῦ κυρίου, εὐαγγέλιον, and closely related expressions to refer to the gospel-preaching of ordinary church members (Acts

---

105 Swigchem, *Het missionair karakter*, 15–23.
106 Rom 15:18–32; 1 Cor 16:9; 2 Cor 2:12; Eph 6:21–22; Phil 1:12; 4:10; Col 4:2–4, 7–9; 1 Thess 5:25; 2 Tim 1:15; 4:10.
107 Swigchem, *Het missionair karakter,* 23–39. See 1 Cor 16:15–18; 2 Cor 8:16–19; Gal 1:23–24; Phil 2:22; Col 4:9; 2 Thess 1:4.
108 Swigchem, *Het missionair karakter,* 40–77.
109 Ibid., 78–108. See Rom 12:17–21; 13:1–8; 1 Cor 11:5–16; 2 Cor 3:1–3; Phil 2:15; Col 4:4–6; 1 Thess 4:12; Titus 2:5, 8, 10; 3:1–2; 1 Pet 2:9–12.
110 Swigchem, *Het missionair karakter,* 109–17.
111 Ibid., 117–23.
112 Ibid., 123–30.
113 Ibid., 130–41.

8:4; 13:49; 19:10,20; Rom 10:15; 1 Thess 1:8; 2 Thess 3:1).[114]

In the latter half of his book, Swigchem discusses various missionary roles within the church and the church's motivation for mission. While the church is active in both word and deed, its "actions are subservient to the Word, by underscoring it or by preparing its coming."[115] The manner in which church members witness will vary based on their station in life and gifting, yet all are called to testify. Even the meetings of the church are intended to have a secondary evangelistic function (1 Cor 14:23–25; Eph 5:14; 6:23; 1 Tim 2:1–3; 1 Pet 5:14).[116]

Swigchem finds three overarching motives for the church's mission. First, the church is motivated by mercy – the mercy which has been experienced through Christ and overflows to those still under condemnation.[117] Second, the church is motivated by the dominion of Jesus and the glory of God. The church must obey Jesus' command to "make disciples of all nations" (Matt 28:19) and extend his kingdom reign for God's glory.[118] Third, the church is motivated by an eschatological vision. Mission work prepares for the ultimate consummation of the kingdom and the realization of God's promises.[119] These three motives can be stated Christocentrically as "Christ's mercy, His dominion, and the fulfillment which He is to bring."[120]

Among the works we will survey, Swigchem offers perhaps the most detailed study of Paul's missionary expectations of his churches.[121] It should be noted that at the end of his careful study, Swigchem arrives at a similar conclusion to that of Roland Allen, with whom he shows considerable familiarity.[122] Like Allen, Swigchem thinks there is plenteous evidence for the early church's evangelistic zeal. Going beyond Allen, Swigchem claims one of the primary aims of the apostles' ethical injunctions is to make sure that the

---

114 Ibid., 141–63.

115 Ibid., 261.

116 Ibid., 189–98.

117 Ibid., 221–27.

118 Ibid., 227–32.

119 Ibid., 233–38.

120 Ibid., 238–40, 265.

121 Bowers notes that he has heard of Swigchem through Ridderbos, but says that he has not had access to his writings (Bowers, "Church and Mission," 107–08 n. 2). Herman Ridderbos praises Swigchem and endorses his conclusions (Herman Ridderbos, *Paul: An Outline of His Theology*, trans. John Richard de Witt [Grand Rapids: Eerdmans, 1975], 432–38). This work translates *Paulus: Ontwerp van zijn theologie.*

122 Note Swigchem's references to Allen on page 11 and in the footnotes on pages 32, 132, 208, and 220 (*Het missionair karakter*).

congregations' lifestyle will complement their verbal witness.[123]

In spite of his insightful treatment and citation of numerous Pauline texts, Swigchem shares some weaknesses with the traditional approach. Swigchem's logical proofs are reasonable, although they often lack direct scriptural support. For example, Swigchem arguably provides a sufficient number of biblical references to prove that the Pauline churches were concerned with the progress of the gospel and were indeed evangelistic – especially centripetally (i.e., attractively or passively). Yet, the evidence is lacking in regards to providing a theological undergirding for Paul's expectation of this missionary behavior – especially centrifugal (outward-directed) evangelism. In other words, in light of the few direct commands from Paul, *why* did the apostle expect his congregations to evangelize? Swigchem's work also has the methodological deficiency of uncritically mixing evidence in the Gospels, Acts, and epistles. Some of his assertions are more dubious – for example, his identification of direct commands to evangelize in the epistles. In fact, some of these verses are not generally recognized as commands to evangelize (Eph 6:15; Phil 1:27), while others would be described more accurately as representative of a centripetal (inward-drawing or passive) missionary concern (Col 4:5–6). Still, in his attention to the Pauline writings in the investigation of what Paul expected evangelistically from his churches, Swigchem was truly a pioneer in the application of biblical theological method to answer missiological questions.

Peter T. O'Brien

Peter T. O'Brien employs a significant portion of his recent book, *Gospel and Mission in the Writings of Paul*, to answer challenges to the view that Paul expected his congregations to be evangelistic in direct continuity with the apostle's own mission.[124] O'Brien acknowledges the dearth of evangelistic references in Paul's letters, and comments, "The recurring and puzzling question that has arisen out of our study of Paul and the dynamic of the gospel has been: why is so little written in the Pauline letters about the need for

---

123 Ridderbos comments, "One may even think that so little is expressly said on the missionary stance of the church because it was not so much necessary to stimulate it to activity, as that this be manifested in the right manner, i.e., not in words only, but above all in good works" (*Paul*, 434–35). Johannes Verkuyl, also following Swigchem, writes, "[The churches' missionary mandate] was a matter beyond dispute and a duty for which they needed no prodding" (J. Verkuyl, *Contemporary Missiology: An Introduction*, ed. and trans. Dale Cooper [Grand Rapids: Eerdmans, 1978], 113).

124 The same arguments are restated by O'Brien in a more recent volume co-written with Andreas J. Köstenberger, *Salvation to the Ends of the Earth*, 191–99. Steve Strauss endorses O'Brien's arguments ("Missions Theology in Romans 15:14–33," *BSac* 160 [2003]: 463–64).

Christians to evangelize?"[125] O'Brien offers two reasons for Paul's failure to enjoin evangelistic outreach more explicitly. First, "the essential place of the gospel in salvation history" inevitably leads redeemed persons to spread the message of God's saving activity.[126] Basing his arguments on Romans 1:1–17, O'Brien claims that the gospel of Jesus Christ is now the locus of God's salvation-historical intervention to bring redemption to all nations.[127] Upon being included in the dynamic march of the gospel, persons demonstrate their commitment to Christ's universal lordship by spreading his dominion in gospel proclamation.[128]

According to O'Brien, the second main reason Paul fails to command evangelistic outreach more clearly is his propensity to speak of the gospel spreading from a "divine perspective." Paul's approach does not emphasize human agency, but God's grace and sovereignty (e.g., Col 1:5–6; 1 Thess 1:5; 2 Thess 2:13; 3:1–2).[129] "Paul and others will be engaged in preaching," writes O'Brien, "but the stress is on the dynamic march of the gospel itself."[130] This point is significant, but has been noted only infrequently by previous scholars.[131]

O'Brien also claims that critics of missionary continuity overstate their case, because Paul does, in fact, speak of congregational evangelism and missionary activity more than critics are willing to accept. For example, in the passages where Paul exhorts his converts to imitate him, missionary activity is a direct implication of the text (1 Cor 4:16; 9:19–23; 10:31–11:1; Phil 3:17; 1 Thess 1:6, 7; 2 Thess 3:7–9).[132] O'Brien writes, "The apostle's earnest desire and goal of saving men and women was an essential element in the servant pattern he

---

125 O'Brien, *Gospel and Mission*, 137.

126 Ibid., 76. Similarly, Peter G. Bolt claims that after Christians have internalized the truth of the gospel, an inner compulsion will drive them to evangelize (Peter G. Bolt, "Mission and Witness," in *Witness to the Gospel: The Theology of Acts*, ed. I. Howard Marshall and David Peterson [Grand Rapids: Eerdmans 1998], 191–214).

127 O'Brien, *Gospel and Mission*, 53–77. This argument is akin to the logical arguments made by Green, Swigchem, and others.

128 Ibid., 76–77. O'Brien writes, "If we have understood that Jesus Christ is at the heart of God's redemptive plan and that the divine purposes find their fulfillment, climax, and consummation in his saving work, then we who have come under his rule as Lord must be wholly committed to the furtherance of those saving purposes in which Gentiles, along with Jews, are brought into obedience to him" (ibid., 77).

129 Ibid., 138.

130 Ibid.; Köstenberger and O'Brien, *Salvation to the Ends of the Earth*, 192–93.

131 E.g., J. Ware, "The Thessalonians as a Missionary Congregation: 1 Thessalonians 1, 5–8," *ZNW* 83 (1992): 128. We will discuss this point at length in the next chapter.

132 O'Brien, *Gospel and Mission*, 83–107; Köstenberger and O'Brien, *Salvation to the Ends of the Earth*, 194–96.

adopted ('I have made myself a slave to all, so that I might win as many as possible,' 1 Cor 9:19). Paul was committed to the good of others and he defines this in terms of saving them (10:33)."[133] O'Brien also maintains that Paul's statements in Philippians show the apostle expected his churches to evangelize actively. Both the apostle's approval of others' evangelistic preaching and his statement about the Philippians' commitment to the gospel demonstrate his anticipation of congregational missionary work (Phil 1:5, 14–18, 27, 30; 2:16).[134]

O'Brien offers his exegesis of Ephesians 6:10–20 as the capstone of his argument. Calling the passage the "Pauline Great Commission," he claims that it clearly demonstrates that Paul expected all believers in his churches to be involved in a world-wide missionary campaign. O'Brien asserts that believers having their "feet fitted with the readiness that comes from the gospel of peace" and wielding "the sword of the Spirit" are references to evangelistic readiness and proclamation (Eph 6:15, 17).[135] While believers' method of spreading the gospel will vary based on their contexts and spiritual gifts, the obligation of dissemination falls upon all.[136] Some of the debated texts and assertions that O'Brien bases upon them will be revisited in later chapters.

James Patrick Ware

One of the most significant scholarly contributions to argue for missionary continuity between the apostle Paul and his expectations of his churches is the 1996 Yale dissertation of James Patrick Ware, "'Holding Forth the Word of Life': Paul and the Mission of the Church in the Letter to the Philippians in the Context of Second Temple Judaism."[137] Ware asserts that one of Paul's main purposes in writing the letter to the Philippians is to discuss their partnership with him in mission – a partnership which entails the obligation of lay-Christians to preach the gospel to their non-believing neighbors. The entire book of Philippians should thus be read through the lens of evangelism.

Ware begins his dissertation by examining the state of evangelism in ancient Judaism, especially second temple Judaism. He concludes that while there is plenteous evidence for a passive evangelistic role of the elect community in

---

133 O'Brien, *Gospel and Mission*, 137.

134 Ibid., 114–19; Köstenberger and O'Brien, *Salvation to the Ends of the Earth*, 194.

135 O'Brien, *Gospel and Mission*, 119–31; Köstenberger and O'Brien, *Salvation to the Ends of the Earth*, 196–98.

136 O'Brien, *Gospel and Mission*, 130–31.

137 Just prior to sending this manuscript to the publisher, I discovered that James Ware's revised dissertation has just been published as: *The Mission of the Church in Paul's Letter to the Philippians in the Context of Ancient Judaism*, NovTSup 120 (Leiden: Brill, 2005). Regrettably, I am unable to interact with Ware's revision. I have agreed, however, to write a book review of Ware's new volume, which will appear in a forthcoming edition of *JETS*.

diaspora Judaism, there is little, if any, evidence for active evangelistic outreach.[138] Next, Ware turns to Philippians, where he finds Paul employing the passive evangelistic vocabulary of second temple Judaism in an active way. For example, the presentation of the community as an evangelistic light in the midst of darkness (i.e., mediating salvation to the darkened Gentile world) is common in second temple Judaism.[139] Paul goes farther, though, by commanding his congregation to "hold forth" the word of life (Phil 2:16). Ware argues that "hold forth" is in fact the correct translation of ἐπέχοντες, and that BAGD's extra-biblical citations in favor of "hold fast" are misleading.[140] We will look at these claims in more detail when we examine Philippians 2:16 in chapter three.

Outside of Philippians, Ware claims that the only other overt reference to a Pauline congregation's missionary activity is 1 Thessalonians 1:5–8.[141] Yet, even if only two of the apostle's letters contain clear references to congregational evangelism, Paul's silence in his other letters should not be taken as an indication of disinterest, says Ware. Rather, these other congregations must have needed no injunction to evangelize. Ware explains, "Such a conclusion is suggested by the missionizing fervor of the earliest Christian communities as depicted in Acts, and by passages in Paul's letters such as 1 Thessalonians 1:5–8, where Paul praises his converts for spreading the word but does not command them to do so."[142] Ware summarizes, "Paul did not regard his missionary commission as fulfilled in his own preaching activity, but understood himself as the founder of *new mediatorial communities through which his own preaching would be extended through the independent missionizing activity of his converts.*"[143]

---

138 Ware, "'Holding Forth,'" 104–64. This view of second temple Judaism is substantiated by Scot McKnight (*Light Among the Gentiles*, 30–77). The LXX translation of Isaiah 40–55 highlights the Jewish community's passive mediatorial role in bringing salvation to the Gentiles (Ware, "'Holding Forth,'" 65–103). See also *Sibylline Oracles*, 3.573–600; *Fragments* 1.25b–32a; Wis 2:12–5:13; 10:15–21; 17:2–18:4; Tob 13:11 [Sinaiticus]; Philo, *De Virtutibus* 175–86; *De Specialibus Legibus* 2.162–67; *De Vita Mosis* 1.149; *De Abrahamo* 98; Rom. 2:17–20; Justin Martyr *Dialogue with Trypho* 122 (Ware, "'Holding Forth,'" 104–59). Ware argues that rabbinic texts which assert an active centrifugal mission for Judaism cannot be securely dated prior to the rise of Christianity, and thus have likely been influenced by the Christian mission ("'Holding Forth,'" 164 n. 1). E.g., see *Sifre Deut.* 32; *Genesis Rabbah* 39:16; *'Abot de Rabbi Nathan B* 26; *b. 'Aboda Zara* 136. Ware contends that *Testament of Levi* 14:3–4 also likely reflects Christian redaction ("'Holding Forth,'" 162).

139 See the texts in the previous note.

140 Ware, "'Holding Forth,'" 299. Cf. BAGD, 285; BDAG, 362.

141 Ware, "Thessalonians," 126–31.

142 Ware, "'Holding Forth,'" 327.

143 Ibid., 328.

I. Howard Marshall

I. Howard Marshall has published a recent essay devoted exclusively to the question of Paul's expectations of his churches' missionary activity. In "Who Were the Evangelists?" (2000), Marshall shows familiarity with the current discussion and favors, for the most part, interpretations of debated texts that show Paul-church missionary continuity.[144] Marshall also independently arrives at a reading of 1 Thessalonians 1:8 that is similar to Ware's.[145] Marshall admits, however, that the theme of the congregations' missionary obligation "is present in somewhat rudimentary form in Paul."[146] He accounts for this inchoate theology of mission by agreeing with Bowers that a world-wide missionary vision was a new arrival on the scene of world religions.[147] "[The] witness of a local church in its vicinity was not yet a fully developed idea," explains Marshall.[148]

In support of the early Pauline communities' missionary activity, Marshall claims that the authors of the Gospels and Acts also expected local communities of believers to be active in mission. While persons may claim that the "Great Commission" passages apply only to the apostles, there is no way around the descriptions of church-based mission in Acts, says Marshall (e.g., Acts 8:1–4; 19:10).[149] In parallel fashion, it is undeniable that Paul knew and approved of evangelism by the congregations he founded (e.g., Phil 1:12–14; 1 Thess 1:8).[150] In conclusion, Marshall warns, "We must be careful not to draw rigid distinctions where none exist or to read the New Testament against the anachronistic background of the modern church with its carefully defined spheres of activity."[151]

Eckhard J. Schnabel

Rightly hailed as the most comprehensive work on Christian missions since Adolf Von Harnack's classic, Schnabel's massive two-volume *Early Christian Mission* (2004) is a monument of careful biblical and historical reflection.[152] As a sub-section of his study on Paul, Schnabel devotes twenty-five pages to "The

---

144 Marshall, "Who Were the Evangelists?," 251–63.

145 Ibid., 259.

146 Ibid., 263.

147 Ibid., 262; cf. Paul Bowers, "Paul and Religious Propaganda in the First Century," *NovT* 22 (1980): 316–23.

148 Marshall, "Who Were the Evangelists?," 263.

149 Ibid., 262.

150 Ibid. Marshall writes, "There is an openness in Paul's letters and elsewhere to witness by individual Christians" (ibid., 260). Cf. 1 Cor 7:16; Titus 2:10; 1 Pet 3:1.

151 Ibid., 263.

152 The original German edition was published in 2002 under the title *Urchristliche Mission* (Wuppertal: Brockhaus).

Missionary Work of the Christian Communities."[153] Schnabel rightly notes the apparent lack of explicit exhortation to congregational evangelism in Paul's letters.[154] Crediting Bowers, Schnabel applauds a New Testament theological approach that does not simply assume an evangelistic interest, but demands clear evidence in the text.[155] At the same time, Schnabel rejects several of Bowers's readings of disputed texts (e.g., 1 Thess 1:5–8; Phil 2:14–17; 1 Cor 10:31–11:1; Eph 6:10–20) and generally favors the conclusions of James Patrick Ware, Peter T. O'Brien, I. Howard Marshall, and Robert L. Plummer.[156] That is, while the evidence is not overwhelming, it is enough to convince Schnabel that ". . . Paul indeed assumed that Christians would be involved in missionary outreach at least on the local level."[157] Besides the debated explicit expectations of congregational evangelism in Paul's letters, Schnabel considers the missionary purpose of conduct in the family, conduct in worship services, conduct in pagan society, willingness to suffer, and eschatological responsibility.[158]

Unique to Schnabel's discussion is the breadth of his historical and canonical reflection. In his comprehensive treatment, Schnabel never looses site of the influence of the mission of the Twelve and the mission of Jesus upon the apostle to the Gentiles.[159] While arguing from the Great Commission or the logic of the gospel, Schnabel does not speak reductionistically as in some popular missiological overstatements, but he probes all possible lines of influence on Paul and his congregations.[160]

Schnabel also presents a helpful discussion of "The Letter to the Romans as a Missionary Document," in which he draws out the missiological implications of the purpose and theology of Paul's letter to the Romans.[161] This brief section is useful in showing how major portions of one of Paul's most significant letters bear directly upon the mission of the church.

---

153 *Early Christian Mission*, 1451–75.
154 Ibid., 1455. Schnabel writes, ". . . the studies by Bowers provide a necessary correction to the popular notion that the pivotal impetus of the early Christian mission was the work of 'normal believers' who 'gossiped the gospel' in everyday life and in the context of their normal familial and professional relationships, representing a 'total mobilization' of the early church" (ibid., 1455).
155 Ibid.
156 Ibid., 1459–65. In citing R. L. Plummer, Schnabel is, of course, not citing this current work, but my dissertation on the same topic, completed in 2001. See Robert Lewis Plummer, "The Church's Missionary Nature: The Apostle Paul and His Churches" (Ph.D. diss., Southern Baptist Theological Seminary, 2001).
157 *Early Christian Mission*, 1456.
158 Ibid., 1465–72.
159 Ibid.
160 Ibid., 1456–57.
161 Ibid., 1472–75.

John Piper

Pastor and scholar John Piper has greatly influenced the theology and practice of missions through his publications. For example, in the mid-1990s, the International Mission Board (IMB) of the Southern Baptist Convention (the largest missions-sending agency in the world) sent all of its career missionaries a copy of Piper's *Let the Nations Be Glad! The Supremacy of God in Missions*.[162] Piper does not enter into the specific debate over a Pauline theology of congregational mission. Piper does, however, attempt to provide an overarching theological basis for congregational mission. Piper draws from numerous biblical texts in his synthesizing presentation. In that sense, he could be classed with the some of the more superficial pre-1950 approaches, which paint with broad strokes. On the other hand, Piper draws from enough Pauline texts that he must be included, as least peripherally, as an example of a biblical theological approach to the question of Paul's missionary expectations.[163] Piper believes that all of the biblical record is best summarized as the story of God glorifying himself.[164] Thus, when humans remove themselves from the center of the biblical story, they gain a proper perspective on the important motif of God's self-glorification in Scripture. According to Piper, once people embrace the biblical imperative of God's self-glorification as the purpose and passion of their own life, there is a compulsion to spread this fame throughout the whole world. That is, until God is rightly glorified by all people, there remains a dissatisfaction and longing for the proper glory to be given to God.[165] Arguably, from a broad biblical and logical perspective, Piper is correct. In Paul's own writings, however, the connection of the apostle's expectations of his congregations' evangelistic activity and God's self-glorification is arguably not a clear theme. In his organizational categories, Piper seems more influenced by the Westminster Catechism than Pauline language.

G. K. Beale

Beale is also an example of a New Testament theologian whose presentation of broad themes in Scripture is helpful, but leaves one seeking a distinctly Pauline presentation unsatisfied. In *The Temple and the Church's Mission*, Beale

---

162 John Piper, *Let the Nations Be Glad! The Supremacy of God in Missions* (Grand Rapids: Baker, 1993). Hayward Armstrong, a former career missionary with the IMB, could not confirm whether the book was sent in 1994 or 1995. The Office of Overseas Operations at the IMB could not confirm the exact date that the book was sent.

163 See, for example, Piper's many references from Paul's letters on pages 20–21.

164 Ibid., 22.

165 Ibid., 40. See the similar approach in Christopher R. Little, "Mission in the Way of Paul: With Special Reference to Twenty-First Century Christian Mission" (Ph.D. diss., Fuller Theological Seminary, 2003), 59–90.

explores the theme of the temple (God's dwelling place among men) from the Garden of Eden to the New Heaven and New Earth.[166] In brief, Beale explains, "My thesis is that the Old Testament tabernacle and temples were symbolically designed to point to the cosmic eschatological reality that God's tabernacling presence, formerly limited to the holy of holies, was to be extended throughout the whole earth." If this thesis is correct, then Paul's temple imagery should be taken as implying the inevitable growth and accomplishment of God's plan to fill the earth with his glory – that is, implying global evangelization. In fact, that is how Beale interprets Pauline temple imagery (e.g., Eph 2:19–22; 2 Cor 6:16–18).[167] Because Beale references numerous Pauline texts and is obviously concerned that his arguments have adequate textual support, I have included him with post-1950 New Testament Theology approaches. Unfortunately, Beale's thesis is so canonically interwoven that it is nearly impossible to simply draw out his points on the Pauline texts and consider them apart from his broader thesis. Biblical texts that Beale cites will be considered apart from his thesis in future chapters.

Norbert Schmidt

In his thesis, "The Apostolic Band – A Paradigm for Modern Missions?" Schmidt argues that a two-structure Christian presence (i.e., church and mission society) lacks biblical support. He concludes, "All Apostolic functions that were not unique in time and kind were handed over to the churches as a whole, rather than to any individuals within or outside the local congregations."[168] Apostolic functions which did not devolve upon the church were (1) eyewitness testimony to Christ's resurrection and (2) mediation of revelation.[169] The apostles' teaching (1 Tim 3:15; 2 Tim 2:2; 2 Pet 3:2, 15), disciplining (Acts 5; 20:17–38; 1 Cor 5; 3 John; Rev 2:1–3:22), and evangelizing work, however, was continued by the churches.[170] Thus, Schmidt is arguing for clear missionary continuity between Paul and his congregations.

Unfortunately, Schmidt also provides little exegetical defense for the

---

166 G. K. Beale, *The Temple and the Church's Mission: A Biblical Theology of the Dwelling Place of God*, NSBT 17 (Leicester: Apollos; Downers Grove: InterVarsity, 2004).

167 See, for example, Beale's statements on pages 245 and 263.

168 Norbert Schmidt, "The Apostolic Band – A Paradigm for Modern Missions?" (Th.M. thesis, Trinity Evangelical Divinity School, 1985), iv. Schmidt further clarifies, "We therefore define apostolic continuity as the process by which the Church takes over certain privileges and functions of the Apostles. It does not imply that the Apostles, as the initial bearers of certain privileges and functions, had to pass away before the Church would be able to take over and exercise a number of these privileges and functions" (ibid., 76).

169 Ibid.

170 Ibid., 81–83.

church's continuity with the apostolic mission. He briefly mentions that the body and temple metaphor imply the church's continuation of the apostle's mission (1 Cor 12:28; Eph 2:20; 4:11).[171] When Schmidt introduces the section of his thesis specifically devoted to showing the continuity between the apostolic mission and the church, he writes, "This is the most important aspect of the Apostolic work with respect to the research question of this thesis, and we therefore need to take care to confirm the proposal of this chapter."[172] Surprisingly, only one page of argumentation follows this solemn pronouncement. Negatively, Schmidt asserts that no New Testament writer provides evidence of Paul's unique ministry finding any successors after his death.[173] Positively, Schmidt claims, "The Apostle [Paul] . . . instilled some of his own fervor and the missionary commission he had received into 'his' churches."[174] Schmidt sets up his study as a rigorous biblical theological investigation, but fails to adequately complete the task.

Indeed, as we noted at the outset of this chapter, no one can doubt Paul's personal missionary vision. "Woe to me if I do not proclaim the gospel," declares Paul (1 Cor 9:16). Elsewhere, he writes, "Christ did not send me to baptize, but to proclaim the gospel" (1 Cor 1:17). Preaching the gospel to non-believers is the *sine qua non* of Paul's apostleship.[175] Yet, how does Paul's apostolic missionary vision relate to the church as a whole? Are the churches simply the result of Paul's work, or are they also under a divine obligation to preach the gospel to non-believers? If it can be shown that Paul views the churches he founded as continuing his apostolic mission, then we have grounds for asserting a significant missionary role for the churches in Paul's thought.

Previous research on apostleship in Paul has given little attention to the relation between the apostle's mission and the church's mission. When the apostles' mission is taken into account, two opposite errors often appear. Either the apostles' mission is uncritically used as a pattern for the church's mission.[176] Or, the apostles' mission is severed from and contrasted with the church's mission.[177] When scholars do address Paul's understanding of

---

171 Ibid., 77. Schmidt also references John 17:20–21 and John 20:21 (ibid., 78).

172 Ibid., 83.

173 Ibid.

174 Ibid., 84. Schmidt cites Phil 1:5; 2:25; 4:10–18; 1 Thess 1:8; Rom 15:22–23.

175 Paul can also refer to his ministry to believing communities as "preaching the gospel" (Rom 1:15). In a recent article, however, John P. Dickson argues that scholars have been wrong to understand Romans 1:15 as a reference to Paul preaching to believers in Rome. He contends, "Paul's gospel language never refers to ongoing Christian instruction and only ever connotes announcements which are *news* to those who hear them" (John P. Dickson, "Gospel as News: εὐαγγελ- from Aristophanes to the Apostle Paul" *NTS* 51 [2005]: 212–30).

176 E.g., Allen, *Missionary Methods*.

177 E.g., Bowers, "Church and Mission."

apostleship, they seem most interested in investigating the conceptual background of the term "apostle" and debating whom Paul would have considered an apostle and why.[178] In addition to Schmidt's thesis, however, a few other significant studies hint at the fruitfulness of investigating further the relationship between the apostolic mission and the church's mission. C. K. Barrett, for example, divides his book, *The Signs of an Apostle*, into two parts: (1) The Apostles in the New Testament, and (2) The Apostolicity of the Church.[179] He writes,

> A church is not apostolic if it is not apostolic – that is, if it does not enter into the mission that the Lord entrusts to his people. 'Are all apostles?' Paul asked, clearly expecting the answer No; that is, all are not wandering missionaries, who go from place to place to preach and found Christian societies. All are not apostles, but it is the church as a whole that has inherited the commission, 'As the Father has sent me, so I send you' (John 20:21), and it is the church as a whole, with its infinite variety of personal gift and equipment, that fulfills the commission. The nature of the task will vary from age to age and from place to place, and the church's organization, structure, and method must change to meet changing circumstances; indeed, changing, adaptable structures might be said to be a better mark of apostolicity than an order received from remote ages and carefully preserved. Readiness and fitness for the evangelistic mission, and – as it may not be superfluous to add in these days, when 'mission' is a vogue word but all too seldom a practical programme – the actual carrying out of the evangelistic mission, are true apostolicity.[180]

Barrett's argument is logical, but where is the exegetical evidence from the New Testament – specifically, from Paul's letters? What texts can we place our finger on to show that Paul expected the churches to continue his apostolic mission? Why not argue, as some have, that Paul conceived of the Christian mission as fulfilled through an ongoing "apostolic band" functioning semi-independently of the churches?[181] The Christian mission would thus best be

---

178 E.g., Rudolf Schnackenburg, "Apostles Before and During Paul's Time," in *Apostolic History and the Gospel: Biblical and Historical Essays Presented to F. F. Bruce on His 60th Birthday*, ed. W. Ward Gasque and Ralph P. Martin, trans. Manfred Kwiran and W. Ward Gasque (Grand Rapids: Eerdmans, 1970), 287–303; Arnold Ehrhardt, *The Apostolic Succession in the First Two Centuries of the Church* (London: Lutterworth, 1953); Walter Schmithals, *The Office of Apostle in the Early Church*, trans. John E. Steely (Nashville: Abingdon, 1969).

179 C. K. Barrett, *The Signs of an Apostle: The Cato Lecture 1969* (London: Epworth, 1970). Barrett's presentation in this text seems at odds with his assertions elsewhere regarding Paul's missionary vision. See the previous discussion in this chapter.

180 Ibid., 91.

181 E.g., Ralph D. Winter, "The Two Structures of God's Redemptive Mission," *Missiology* 2 (1974): 121–39; Arthur F. Glasser, "The Apostle Paul and the

described as "para-church."[182]

George W. Peters, T. W. Manson, Hans Küng, and many others assert that the church is "apostolic" and continues the apostolic mission.[183] Indeed it is not difficult to find many scholars who espouse this thesis.[184] What is lacking, however, is a careful explication of the New Testament documents to prove this point. Moreover, little attention has been given specifically to *Paul's* view of apostolic continuity. If the apostle Paul viewed the church as continuing the apostolic mission, where does he clearly indicate that point in his extant correspondence? While promising in its suggestions, Schmidt's thesis that the churches inherit the mission of the apostles needs further textual substantiation.

Conclusion

What sort of missionary work did the apostle Paul expect from his churches? As we have seen in this chapter, scholars have approached this question in a variety of ways, and the issue continues to be debated. Within the last fifty years, there has been a more thoughtful return to the Pauline writings in an attempt to provide a cogent textually-based answer to this disputed question. Still, among recent works, rather than a consensus, we find a dichotomy. Some scholars argue that Paul's writings reflect only a passive or supportive missionary vision for his churches in distinct discontinuity with his own centrifugal evangelism. Others see evidence for greater continuity between the apostle's own outward-directed missionary labors and his evangelistic

---

Missionary Task," in *Perspectives on the World Christian Movement: A Reader*, Rev. ed., ed. Ralph D. Winter and Steven C. Hawthorne (Pasadena: William Carey Library; Carlisle: Paternoster, 1992), A125–33; Edward F. Murphy, "The Missionary Society as an Apostolic Team," *Missiology* 4 (1976): 103–18; Michael C. Griffiths, "Today's Missionary, Yesterday's Apostle," *Evangelical Missions Quarterly* 21 (1985): 154–65.

182 Bowers, "Church and Mission," 111.

183 George W. Peters, *A Biblical Theology of Missions* (Chicago: Moody, 1972), 220; T. W. Manson, *The Church's Ministry* (London: Hodder & Stoughton, 1948), 32, 51–52; Hans Küng, *The Church*, trans. Ray Ockenden and Rosaleen Ockenden (New York: Sheed and Ward, 1967), 355–56.

184 E.g., Edmund P. Clowney, "The Biblical Theology of the Church," in *The Church in the Bible and the World: An International Study*, ed. D. A. Carson. (Exeter: Paternoster; Grand Rapids: Baker, 1987), 44–45; John P. Newport, "The Purpose of the Church," in *The People of God: Essays on the Believers' Church*, ed. Paul Basden and David S. Dockery (Broadman: Nashville, 1991), 32; Robert B. Sloan, "Images of the Church in Paul," in *The People of God: Essays on the Believers' Church*, ed. Paul Basden and David S. Dockery (Broadman: Nashville, 1991), 161–64; Arnold Ehrhardt, *The Apostolic Ministry*, Scottish Journal of Theology Occasional Papers 7 (Edinburgh: Oliver and Boyd, 1958), 6.

expectations of his churches.

One of the major conclusions of our historical survey is that we cannot be content with assumptions when it comes to discussing Paul's expectations of his churches' missionary activity. We must carefully consider the entire Pauline corpus and build our conclusions on a meticulous evaluation of the evidence. As we continue in the next chapter, we will explore further the suggestion of Norbert Schmidt and others – i.e., that an exploration of the church's continuity with the apostolic mission holds promise for understanding the church's role in mission. No one doubts the evangelistic mission of the apostles, and if it can be shown that Paul expects his churches to continue this apostolic mission, we will have provided a firm foundation for the church's missionary task. We hope to demonstrate that Paul viewed the church's ministry in close continuity with the apostolic ministry. This point becomes most clear when we see that, for Paul, both the church and the apostolic mission are characterized by the presence of the same dynamic gospel – God's effective, self-diffusing word.

It will be noticed that some of the most promising elements of more recent proposals (e.g., the dynamic nature of the gospel in Peter T. O'Brien and the apostolic goal of founding mediatorial communities in James Patrick Ware) will also appear in our study. Here I hope to go further, however, by providing extensive exegetical support and an over-arching theological framework for these insights. We will see that Paul expected God's word (i.e., the gospel) to propel his congregations in evangelistic outreach. Thus, the churches were to function in direct continuity with the apostles' mission because both were determined by God's powerful word.

CHAPTER 2

The Church's Mission in the Pauline Letters:
A Theological Basis for Apostolic Continuity

The purpose of this chapter is to show that Paul's understanding of the gospel as the dynamic, effective word of God provides a theological basis for a continuity of mission between the apostles and the churches. Before we undertake that task, however, we first need to clarify Paul's understanding of two important concepts that will reappear throughout our study: "church" and "apostle."

Definitions

What, according to Paul, is the church? After answering this question, we will turn to the identity and mission of the apostles. The purpose of this brief definitional section is not to discuss these terms exhaustively, but only to lay the groundwork for the remainder of our study.

Church

If we are going to speak of the "church" (ἐκκλησία) as continuing the apostles' mission then it is imperative that we clarify what Paul meant by this term.[1] He employs the word ἐκκλησία to refer to two realities.[2] First, for

---

1   Significant studies that have addressed Paul's understanding of the church include: L. Coenen, "Church...," "ἐκκλησία," in *NIDNTT*, 1:291–307; J. Roloff, "ἐκκλησία," in *EDNT*, 1:410–15; K. L. Schmidt, "καλέω...," in *TDNT*, 3:501–36; Robert B. Sloan, "Images of the Church in Paul," 148–65; Helen Doohan, *Paul's Vision of Church*, Good News Studies 32 (Wilmington, DE: Michael Glazier, 1989); Robert J. Banks, *Paul's Idea of Community: The Early House Churches in Their Historical Setting* (Grand Rapids: Eerdmans, 1980); Klaus Berger, "Volksversammlung und Gemeinde Gottes: Zu den Anfängen der christlichen Verwendung von 'ekklesia,'" *ZTK* 73 (1976): 167–207; L. Cerfaux, *The Church in the Theology of St. Paul*, trans. Geoffrey Webb and Adrian Walker (New York: Herder and Herder, 1959); Ronald Y. K. Fung, "Some Pauline Pictures of the Church," *EvQ* 53 (1981): 89–107; Helmut Merklein, "Die Ekklesia Gottes. Der Kirchenbegriff bei Paulus und in Jerusalem," in *Studien zu Jesus und Paulus*,

Paul, the "church" is the entire community of persons redeemed by Christ – without limitations of time and space. For example, in Ephesians 5:25, Paul writes, "Christ loved the church and gave himself up for her."[3] The "church" here clearly refers to all persons who receive forgiveness through Christ's death. This reality is sometimes referred to as the "universal church."[4]

Paul also uses ἐκκλησία to refer to local manifestations of the universal church – whether believers meeting in a house or all the believers in a city. For example, Paul speaks of the "the church of the Laodiceans" (Col 4:16), "the church of God that is in Corinth" (1 Cor 1:2), "the church of the Thessalonians" (1 Thess 1:1), and "the church in [Philemon's] house" (Phlm 1:2).[5] These local congregations are not churches in distinction from the universal church, but simply manifestations of that universal reality in a localized setting.[6] It is with

---

WUNT 43 (Tübingen: Mohr, 1987), 1:296–318; Gerhard Delling, "Merkmale der Kirche nach dem Neuen Testament," *NTS* 13 (1966–67): 297–316.

2   LXX usage likely influenced the early church's choice of the Greek word ἐκκλησία as a self-designation (e.g., Deut 4:10; 9:10; 18:16; 23:2–4; 23:9; 31:30). See Coenen, "Church...," "ἐκκλησία," in *NIDNTT*, 1:292–96; K. L. Schmidt, "καλέω...," in *TDNT*, 3:527–28.

3   See also 1 Cor 12:28; Eph 1:22; 3:10, 21; 5:23–24, 27, 29, 32; Col 1:18, 24.

4   O'Brien objects to the idea of a "universal" church, and claims that the passages normally taken to refer to a universal church more accurately describe a heavenly gathering in which the earthly church "participates" (Peter T. O'Brien, "Church," in *DPL*, ed. Gerald F. Hawthorne, Ralph P. Martin, and Daniel G. Reid [Downers Grove: InterVarsity, 1993], 125–26).

5   The word ἐκκλησία occurs 62 times in Paul and 114 times in the NT. Paul most commonly uses the term to refer to a local body of believers. He also frequently employs the plural form, churches (ἐκκλησίαι), to refer to multiple congregations in a certain region (1 Cor 16:1, 19; 2 Cor 8:1; Gal 1:2, 22; cf. Rom 16:4, 16; 1 Cor 7:17; 11:16; 14:33, 34; 2 Cor 8:19, 23, 24; 11:8, 28; 12:13). For a lucid presentation of the different Pauline uses of ἐκκλησία, see Fenton John Anthony Hort, *The Christian Ecclesia: A Course of Lectures on the Early History and Early Conceptions of the Ecclesia and Four Sermons* (London: Macmillan, 1897; reprint, 1908), 107–52.

6   Donald Guthrie writes, "It is a natural progression from local groups to think of the sum total of those groups as a unified concept. Yet it would not be correct to say that the universal church was simply a conglomerate of many local communities, for each local community was in essence *the* church of God" (D. Guthrie, *New Testament Theology* [Downers Grove: InterVarsity, 1981], 743). Roloff comments, "The *ecclesia universalis* is neither a secondary union made up of individual autonomous churches, nor is the local congregation only an organizational sub-unit of the total Church. Rather, both the local assembly of Christians and the trans-local community of believers are equally legitimate forms of the ἐκκλησία created by God ("ἐκκλησία," in *EDNT* 1:411). Schmidt agrees ("καλέω...," in *TDNT* 3:506).

these localized manifestations of the universal church that we are concerned. In Paul's thinking, how did these visible communities of believers relate to the apostles' mission?

It should also be noted that the concept of a local body of believers is often present in Paul's writing where the term "church" is not used. For example, Paul addresses the church as saints (ἅγιοι), the elect (ἐκλεκτοί), and with numerous metaphorical descriptions.[7] Regardless of what Paul calls these early believers in Jesus, our concern is with how Paul understands the relationship of his apostolic mission to these localized groups of Christians.

Apostle

Now we need to specify more clearly who an "apostle" is, and what is the "apostolic mission" that is being continued. The word ἀπόστολος occurs thirty-four times in Paul's letters.[8] In half of these instances, Paul uses the term as an identifying title for himself.[9] Although in Koine Greek ἀπόστολος could mean anything from "naval expedition" to "passport," Paul uses the term with two main senses.[10]

First, Paul employs ἀπόστολος in the general sense of "messenger" or "accredited representative." In 2 Corinthians 8:23, Paul speaks of the

---

7   E.g., 1 Cor 3:9; 6:2; 2 Cor 13:12; Phil 4:22; Col 3:12; 2 Tim 2:10. For Pauline metaphors of the church, see Paul S. Minear, *Images of the Church in the New Testament* (Philadelphia: Westminster, 1960).

8   This statistic includes all of the traditional Pauline letters. Following is an exhaustive list of the occurrences of ἀπόστολος in the New Testament: Matthew (1); Mark (2); Luke (6); John (1); Acts (28); Romans (3); 1 Corinthians (10); 2 Corinthians (6); Galatians (3); Ephesians (4); Philippians (1) ; Colossians (1); 1 Thessalonians (1); 1 Timothy (2); 2 Timothy (2); Titus (1); Hebrews (1); 1 Peter (1); 2 Peter (2); Jude (1); Revelation (3) (80 occurrences total).

9   Rom 1:1; 11:13; 1 Cor 1:1; 4:9; 9:1; 9:2; 15:9; 2 Cor 1:1; Gal 1:1; Eph 1:1; Col 1:1; 1 Thess 2:7; 1 Tim 1:1; 2:7; 2 Tim 1:1; 1:11; Titus 1:1.

10 For extra-biblical occurrences of ἀπόστολος, see K. H. Rengstorf, "ἀποστέλλω...," in *TDNT,* 1:407–13. As opposed to its near synonyms (e.g., πέμπω), ἀποστέλλω and its cognates seem *to emphasize the person sending the messenger and the conveyal of his authority to the messenger* (Rengstorf, "ἀποστέλλω...," in *TDNT,* 1:398; Erich von Eicken and Helgo Lindner, "Apostle," "ἀποστέλλω," in *NIDNTT,* 1:127; G. H. R. Horsley, ed., *NewDocs,* 2:82–83. The verb ἀποστέλλω and its cognates are also used more frequently than their near synonyms in religious contexts. Rengstorf, "ἀποστέλλω," in *TDNT,* 1:399–400; Eicken and Lindner, "Apostle," "ἀποστέλλω," in *NIDNTT,* 1:127; G. H. R. Horsley, *NewDocs* 4.81 (e.g., Zech 2:12, 13; 6:15; Isa 6:6, 8; 9:7; Epictetus 3.22.23; 3.22.46; 4.8.31). Πέμπω and ἀποστέλλω, however, are sometimes used interchangeably (e.g., Luke 7:3, 10; John 5:36–38; Josephus, *Ant.* 7.191; 11.190–91; 12.181–83).

"messengers of the churches" [ἀπόστολοι ἐκκλησιῶν]. Likewise in Philippians 2:25, Paul designates Epaphroditus as an accredited representative [ἀπόστολος] of the church at Philippi. This use of ἀπόστολος to mean a single messenger has sparse testimony in extra-biblical Greek, but is found occasionally from the time of Herodotus (5th century BC) onwards.[11] Writers from the Koine period most frequently employ ἀπόστολος in maritime contexts,[12] but a few use it with the general sense of "messenger" or "envoy."[13]

Paul's second main use of ἀπόστολος could be called "technical." He uses the term to refer to a group of specially-recognized leaders in the early Christian movement. We are concerned with the mission of these leaders. More precisely, we are concerned with *Paul's understanding* of the apostles' mission – revealed primarily through Paul's understanding *of his own mission*. Admittedly, Paul saw his apostolic mission as differing somewhat from the other apostles. This difference, however, was a difference in sphere, not in authority, office, or general task (2 Cor 10:13–16; Gal 2:7–9). We are warranted, then, to speak of "*the* apostolic mission" even though much of our study will draw solely upon *Paul's* apostolic mission.

About the apostolic office and mission, the following things can be garnered from Paul's letters:

1. The apostles were eyewitnesses of Jesus' resurrection (1 Cor 9:1; 15:7–9; cf. Acts 1:2–3, 22; 4:33).

2. The apostles were specially commissioned by Jesus, according to God's will (Rom 1:1; 1 Cor 1:1; 15:7–9; 2 Cor 1:1; Gal 1:1, 12, 15–16; Eph 1:1; Col 1:1; 1 Tim 1:1; 2:7; 2 Tim 1:1, 11). Scholars debate whether or not Jesus actually named a limited group of people as authoritative eyewitnesses of his ministry and resurrection (Luke 6:13).[14]

---

11 Herodotus 1.21; cf. 5:38. The more common terms for a single messenger are ἄγγελος, κῆρυξ, πομπός, and πρεσβευτής.

12 E.g., to refer to a fleet or shipping order (W. Dittenberger, ed., *Sylloge Inscriptionum Graecarum*, 2nd ed., 3 vols. [Leipzig: Hirzelium, 1898–1901], §153b [325 BC]; Arthur S. Hunt, ed., *The Oxyrhynchus Papyri*, vol. 9 [London: Oxford University Press, 1912], §1197, line 13 [AD 211]). For several maritime examples from the papyri, see MM, s.v. "ἀπόστολος"; Ceslas Spicq, *Theological Lexicon of the New Testament*, ed. and trans. James D. Ernest (Peabody, MA: Hendrickson, 1994), 1:187–88.

13 3 Kings 14:6 [LXX]; Symm. Isa. 18:2; Brunet de Presle, ed., "Paris Papyri," in *Notices et Extraits* XVIII. ii (Paris, 1865), 411 f. [191 BC], as noted in MM, s.v. "ἀπόστολος"; Josephus uses ἀπόστολος to refer to a delegation of Jews sent to Rome (*Ant.* 17.300).

14 Some scholars think the title ἀπόστολος is a later redactional insertion (e.g., Lucien Cerfaux, "Pour l'histoire du titre *Apostolos* dans le Nouveau Testament," in

Nevertheless, for Paul, there was no question of Jesus' designation of Paul and others to this office.[15] The exact number and identity of the apostles, however, cannot be precisely determined from Paul's letters.[16]

3. The apostles' mission was to make known the good news about Jesus' salvific life, death, and resurrection (Rom 1:1; Eph 3:2–7; 1 Tim 2:7; 2 Tim 1:10–11; cf. Acts 1:21–22; 4:33). The apostles' primary task was an *evangelistic* one. This evangelistic mission, however, went beyond proclamation. We will explore these different dimensions of Paul's apostolic mission and their ecclesiastical parallels in later chapters.

4. The apostles exercised a supra-congregational teaching and disciplining role.[17] In some sense, this teaching and disciplining role was simply a logical continuation of the apostles' mission. In their evangelism, the apostles' goal was not to garner superficial adherence to the gospel, but to establish mature congregations.[18]

5. The apostles performed miracles in confirmation of the gospel (Rom 15:18–19; 2 Cor 12:12; Acts 2:43).

As we know from Paul's letters and the other New Testament writings, the early church recognized in the apostles' teaching a certain abiding and revelatory authority. Peter describes Paul's letters as "scripture" (γραφή), and Paul sets his teaching on the same level as the Lord's commands.[19] Not every word or deed of the apostles, however, was considered to have revelatory authority. The gospel itself, as revealed to the apostles, could later sit in judgment on the apostles' teaching or behavior (Gal 1:8–9; 2:11–21). Also,

---

Recueil Lucien Cerfaux: Études d'exégèse et d'histoire religeuse, BETL 71, rev. ed., vol. 3 [Leuven: Leuven University Press, 1985], 185–200). Others, however, argue that Jesus designated a limited group of his disciples as ἀπόστολοι (i.e., as the Hebrew/Aramaic equivalent of this word) (e.g., Spicq, *Theological Lexicon of the New Testament*, 1: 189 n. 13). For discussion of the possible Hebrew/Aramaic term underlying ἀπόστολος, see Rengstorf, "ἀποστέλλω...," in *TDNT*, 1:413–20; C. K. Barrett, "*Shaliah* and Apostle" in *Donum gentilicium: New Testament studies in honour of David Daube*, ed. E. Bammel, C. K. Barrett, and W. D. Davies (Oxford: Clarendon, 1978), 88–102.

15 Luke apparently shared Paul's view. See Luke's report of the apostles' prayer as they were seeking to find a replacement for Judas: "Lord, you know everyone's heart. Show us which one of these two *you have chosen*" (my emphasis, Acts 1:24).

16 It is debated whether Paul counted James, Barnabas, Junia(s), and Andronicus as apostles (Rom 16:7; 1 Cor 9:6; 15:7; Gal 1:19; cf. Acts 14:1–4).

17 E.g., 1 Cor 5:9–13; 7:25–28; 2 Cor 2:1–11; Gal 5:2–3; Phil 3:1–21; 4:2.

18 See Paul Bowers, "Fulfilling the Gospel," 185–98.

19 2 Pet 3:15–16; 1 Cor 7:10–12; 1 Thess 2:13.

while apostolic coworkers and itinerant evangelists functioned in ways similar to the apostles, it appears that Paul did not consider non-apostles to have an inherent supra-congregational authority or a revelatory role of the type he exercised.[20] Certain elements of the apostolic mission could not be continued. The church could not produce new authoritative eyewitnesses of Jesus' resurrection. Nevertheless, as we shall see, Paul considered the general apostolic missionary obligation to devolve upon each local congregation. That is, each church, as a whole (not simply individuals within it), inherited the apostles' obligation of making known the gospel.

Theological Basis of the Church's Apostolic Mission[21]

On what basis did Paul expect this replication of his apostolic mission in the life of the church? While some texts seem to indicate that Paul instructs the churches to engage in mission (e.g., Eph 6:15; Phil 2:16; Titus 2:10), and praises them for missionary activity (e.g., Phil 1:14–18; 1 Thess 1:8), it is doubtful that Paul viewed his (often incidental) comments as a compelling theological basis for the church's mission. If such were the case, one would expect Paul to provide more frequent and explicit direction. Also, while Paul regularly references his apostolic authority in instructing the church, deeper theological themes serve as the basis of such remarks. At the root of Paul's thinking is God, Christ, the Holy Spirit, the cross, redemption, and the gospel – not his own authority. What deeper theological theme, then, lies at the root of Paul's expectation that the church will be active in missionary work?

Gustav Warneck, "the father of modern missiology," attempted to found Paul's missionary vision on Jesus' Great Commission (Matt 28:18–20).[22]

---

20 Apostles could apparently exercise their authority or revelatory functions through apostolic delegates (e.g., Timothy, Mark). Nevertheless, such functions were never inherent to apostolic delegates, but only to the apostles themselves (Gal 1:1; 1 Tim 6:20; 2 Tim 1:1–2; Titus 1:5; 3:12).

21 Much of the following discussion about the theological basis for the church's mission appeared in slightly altered format in my earlier article, "A Theological Basis for the Church's Mission in Paul," *WTJ* 64 (2002): 253–71. The material reappears here with the permission of the editor of *Westminster Theological Journal*.

22 Gustav Warneck, *Missionslehre*, 2nd ed., 1:91, 183–85. Warneck attacks Ernst Troeltsch (1865–1923) and other liberal scholars who attempt to found the church's mission on moral and humanitarian concerns (G. Warneck, *Missionsmotiv und Missionsaufgabe nach der modernen religionsgeschichtlichen Schule*). William Carey, "the father of modern missions," also tried to base the church's missionary obligation on the Great Commission. The first chapter of his famous *Enquiry* is titled "An Enquiry whether the Commission given by our Lord to his Disciples be not still binding on us" (William Carey, *An Enquiry*, 7–13).

Evangelical scholars up to the present time have followed in his footsteps.[23] The assertion that Paul or the Pauline churches were motivated to missionize by the Great Commission, however, lacks convincing evidence in the Pauline epistles.[24] Paul does not often cite the Gospel traditions or appeal to their authority. Indeed, no clear allusion to the Great Commission can be found in Paul's letters.[25]

As we saw in the previous chapter, some scholars have proposed that the theological basis of the Pauline churches' mission is found in the activity of the Holy Spirit to promote evangelism. First popularized by Roland Allen's *Missionary Methods: St. Paul's or Ours?* (1912), this thesis finds support mainly in the book of Acts.[26] There can be little doubt that Luke presents the person of the Holy Spirit as a basis and guiding force for the early church's mission.[27] Michael Green observes, "Every initiative in evangelism recorded in Acts is the initiative of the Spirit of God."[28] In Paul's letters, however, we do not find such a frequent or prominent association of Spirit and mission.

Possibly the most promising theological basis for the mission of the church (in Paul's letters) can be found in the apostle's references to the gospel. A few scholars have recently noted the importance of the nature of the gospel in Paul's thought – suggesting that the dynamic nature of the gospel is key to understanding what motivated the church to engage in mission.[29] In speaking of

---

23 Harry R. Boer documents the dominance of the Great Commission in modern missionary thought in chapter one, "The Role of the Great Commission in Modern Missions," of his book (H. R. Boer, *Pentecost and Missions*, 15–27). Also see Michael Green, *Evangelism in the Early Church*, rev. ed., 277-78, 382. Laypeople and popular Christian authors are especially prone to assume that Paul and his churches were familiar with and motivated by Jesus' Great Commission.

24 See Boer, "The Great Commission and Missions in the New Testament" (*Pentecost and Missions*, 28–47).

25 A. W. Argyle, however, claims that he can demonstrate Paul's familiarity with the oral tradition of Jesus' missionary instructions to the seventy (Argyle, "St. Paul and the Mission of the Seventy," *JTS*, n.s., 1 [1950]: 63).

26 Roland Allen, *Missionary Methods*, 198–202; see also H. R. Boer, *Pentecost and Missions*; Dean S. Gilliland, *Pauline Theology*, 187–88; Don N. Howell, Jr., "Confidence in the Spirit," 203–21.

27 E.g., see Acts 1:8; 4:29–31; 6:10; 8:29, 39–40; 10:19–20, 44–47; 11:12; 13:2–4; 16:6–7; 20:22–23.

28 Green, *Evangelism in the Early Church*, rev. ed., 209.

29 Köstenberger and O'Brien, *Salvation to the Ends of the Earth*, 192–93; O'Brien, *Gospel and Mission*, 96–97, 113–14; 127–28, 138; idem, "Thanksgiving and the Gospel in Paul," *NTS* 21 (1974–75): 153–55; Ware, "Thessalonians," 128; J. Lambrecht, "A Call to Witness by All: Evangelisation in 1 Thessalonians," in *Teologie in Konteks*, ed. J. H. Roberts et al. (Johannesburg: Orion, 1991), 324–25; cf. John Howard Schütz, *Paul and the Anatomy of Apostolic Authority*, SNTSMS 26 (Cambridge: Cambridge University Press, 1975), 51–53; Morna D. Hooker, "A

the apostle's understanding of "the dynamic nature of the gospel," I mean that Paul viewed the gospel (or "the word of God") as an "effective force" which inevitably goes forth and accomplishes God's will. The same "word" that indwells apostles also indwells ordinary Christians in the church. In each case, the word cannot be contained.[30] If God's word truly dwells in an individual or community, that individual or community will inevitably be characterized by the further spreading of that word.[31] While the concept of a "dynamic word" lacks parallel in ordinary human activity, it has ample theological precedent in the Old Testament (Isa 55:10–11; Jer 23:29).

We shall now turn to some specific passages in Paul's letters to demonstrate that Paul did indeed view the gospel as a dynamic, uncontainable force. Based on Paul's comments, it is reasonable to conclude that the nature of the gospel served as a theological basis for his expectation that the church would engage in missionary activity that paralleled his own apostolic mission. After this study of Paul's theology of the church's mission, we shall briefly compare the apostle's understanding with the broader New Testament witness. Finally, after a concluding section, I will present two short excursuses on (1) Discontinuity of Missionary Activity Between the Old Testament and New Testament, and (2) The Pauline Co-Workers.

The Nature of the Gospel

While several scholars have noted the dynamic nature of the gospel in Paul's thought, no attempt has been made to discuss this nature in detail as it relates to the mission of the church.[32] In the paragraphs below, I will seek to demonstrate that (1) Paul speaks of the gospel as a dynamic power or force; (2) for Paul, this dynamic nature of the gospel is integrally related to his apostolic missionary work; and (3) in Paul's thought, the dynamic nature of the gospel is also

---

Partner in the Gospel: Paul's Understanding of His Ministry," in *Theology and Ethics in Paul and His Interpreters: Essays in Honor of Victor Paul Furnish*, ed. Eugene H. Lovering, Jr. and Jerry L. Sumney (Abingdon: Nashville, 1996), 88–89; Judith M. Gundry Volf, *Paul and Perseverance: Staying in and Falling Away* (Tübingen: Mohr; Louisville: Westminster, 1990), 247–54; Einar Molland, *Das Paulinische Euangelion: Das Wort und die Sache* (Oslo: Jacob Dybwad, 1934), 53–54.

30   Lambrecht, in reference to 1 Thess 1:6–8, writes, "The gospel is nothing but power and Spirit and full conviction. The apostles and those who receive the word are so empowered that they become as it were automatically witnesses and examples in their turn ("A Call to Witness by All," 324).

31   So O'Brien, *Gospel and Mission*, 96–97, 113–14, 127–28, 138; idem, "Thanksgiving and the Gospel in Paul," 153–55.

32   O'Brien has provided possibly the most extensive reflections on this subject to date (*Gospel and Mission*, 96–97, 113–14, 127–28, 138).

integrally related to the church's mission.

The Gospel as "Power"

Paul most frequently uses the term "gospel" (or synonymous expressions) to describe the *content* of his message or the *act of proclaiming* that message.[33] Paul can, however, also refer to the gospel as a *powerful, effective, and dynamic force.* Just as "the word of the Lord" (Hebrew, יהוה דבר) in the Old Testament inevitably accomplishes God's will,[34] so Paul's gospel is not simply a definable

---

33 Εὐαγγέλιον (or synonyms) refers primarily to the *content* of the message proclaimed in the following representative verses: Rom 10:8; 16:25; 2 Cor 2:17; 4:2, 3, 4; 9:13; 11:4; Gal 1:6; 2:2; Eph 1:13. Εὐαγγέλιον refers primarily to the *act of proclaiming* the message in the following representative verses: Rom 1:1, 9; 1 Cor 9:23; 2 Cor 2:12; 10:14; Gal 2:7; Phil 1:5; 2:22; 4:15. O'Brien remarks, "It is a well-known fact that εὐαγγέλιον within the Pauline corpus is often used as a *nomen actionis*" ("Thanksgiving and the Gospel in Paul," 153). Ulrich Becker writes, "*Euangelion*, as used by Paul, does not mean only the content of what is preached, but also the act, process and execution of the proclamation" (U. Becker, "Gospel...," "εὐαγγέλιον," in *NIDNTT*, 2:111). Danker agrees (BDAG, 402). Also see Joseph A. Fitzmyer, "The Gospel in the Theology of Paul," *Int* 33 (1979): 341. For the conceptual background of Paul's use of εὐαγγέλιον and εὐαγγελίζω, see Peter Stuhlmacher, *Das paulinische Evangelium: I. Vorgeschichte*, FRLANT 95 (Göttingen: Vandenhoeck & Ruprecht, 1968).

34 E.g., see Gen 15:1, 4; Exod 9:20–21; Num 3:16, 51; 11:23; 15:31; 24:13; 36:5; Deut 5:5; 9:5; 18:22; 34:5; Josh 8:27; Isa 55:10–11; Jer 20:7–9; 23:29. Cranfield writes, "Paul's thought of the message as being effective power (cf. 1 Cor 1.18) is to be understood in the light of such OT passages concerning the divine word as Gen 1.3, 6, etc.; Ps 147.15; Isa 40.8b; 55.10f; Jer 23.29 (cf. also Wisd. 18.14–16)" (C. E. B. Cranfield, *A Critical and Exegetical Commentary on the Epistle to the Romans*, ICC [Edinburgh: T. & T. Clark, 1975], 1:87–88). McKenzie writes, "The word of Yahweh may be called sacramental in the sense that it effects what it signifies. When Yahweh posits the word-thing, nothing can prevent its emergence" (John L. McKenzie, "The Word of God in the Old Testament," *TS* 21 [1960]: 196). Also see Oskar Grether, *Name und Wort Gottes im Alten Testament*, BZAW 64 (Giessen: Töpelmann, 1934), esp. 59–185; Becker, "Gospel...," "εὐαγγέλιον," in *NIDNTT*, 2:108–09; Frank Ritchel Ames, "דבר," in *NIDOTT*, 1:913–14; W. H. Schmidt, "דבר," in *TDOT*, 3:111–25; Anthony C. Thiselton, "The Supposed Power of Words in the Biblical Writings," *JTS* 25 (1974): 283–99; Kevin Vanhoozer, "God's Mighty Speech-Acts: The Doctrine of Scripture Today," in *A Pathway into the Holy Scripture*, ed. Philip E. Satterthwaite and David F. Wright (Grand Rapids: Eerdmans, 1994), 143–81. Elsewhere in Romans, Paul again speaks of the effective word of the Lord – this time in relation to the promise made to Abraham. In Romans 9:6, Paul writes, "It is not as though the word of God had failed. For not all Israelites truly belong to Israel." Paul is concerned to show that when God speaks,

content about what God has done or promised, but is also *the effective decree or power* of accomplishing God's will.

In Romans 1:16 Paul writes, "For I am not ashamed of the gospel; for *it is the power of God for salvation* to everyone who believes, to the Jew first and also to the Greek."[35] In this verse, "I am not ashamed of the gospel" is the main statement. Paul then provides a reason for his lack of shame in the following γάρ clause. Paul states that he is not ashamed of the gospel because it is "the power of God for salvation to everyone who believes" (δύναμις γὰρ θεοῦ ἐστιν εἰς σωτηρίαν παντὶ τῷ πιστεύοντι). Θεοῦ should be understood here as a genitive of source or possession – i.e., Paul is speaking of "power" that comes from, belongs to, or is possessed by, God.[36] The εἰς clause (εἰς σωτηρίαν) describes the result of this power. The gospel is divine power that results in, or brings about, the salvation of everyone who believes in it. Here the gospel is described not simply as the content of what Jesus has done to bring about salvation, but is actually the effective "power" which applies that salvation to believing Jews and Gentiles.

This "dynamic" quality of the gospel has been noted by numerous scholars. Robert H. Mounce, for example, comments,

> The heart of v. 16 is that the gospel is the saving power of God. Salvation is not only initiated by God but is carried through by his power. To say that the gospel is 'power' is to acknowledge the dynamic quality of the message. In the proclamation of the gospel God is actively at work in reaching out to the hearts of people. The gospel is God telling of his love to wayward people. It is not a lifeless message but a vibrant encounter for everyone who responds in faith. Much religious discourse is little more than words and ideas about religious subjects. Not so the gospel. The gospel is God at work. He lives and breathes through the declaration of his redemptive love for people. To really hear the gospel is to experience the presence of God. The late evangelist Dwight L. Moody commented that the gospel is like a lion. All the preacher has to do is to open the door of the cage and get out of the way![37]

---

what he says happens. This is true of both promises made to the patriarchs and the promise of salvation in the gospel for all whom God has chosen.

35 My translation and emphasis.

36 See Daniel B. Wallace, *Greek Grammar beyond the Basics: An Exegetical Syntax of the New Testament* (Grand Rapids: Zondervan, 1996), 81–82, 109–10.

37 Robert H. Mounce, *Romans*, NAC, vol. 27 (Nashville: Broadman, 1995), 70. Schreiner comments, "The δύναμις θεοῦ (*dynamis theou*, power of God) in the gospel signifies the effective and transforming power that accompanies the preaching of the gospel" (Thomas R. Schreiner, *Romans*, BECNT [Grand Rapids: Baker, 1998], 60). See also James D. G. Dunn, *Romans 1–8*, WBC, vol. 38A (Dallas: Word, 1988), 39.

Similarly, Joseph A. Fitzmyer writes,

> Whenever the gospel is proclaimed, God's power becomes operative and succeeds in saving. His power thus catches up human beings and through the gospel brings them to salvation . . . . As used here [in Rom 1:16], the phrase [δύναμις θεοῦ] formulates the dynamic character of God's gospel; the word may announce the death and resurrection of Jesus Christ, but the emphasis is on that word as a force or power unleashed in human history.[38]

It is important to note, however, that the gospel is an effective power only because of its association with God (δύναμις θεοῦ).[39] The gospel, as *God's* power, manifests his saving intervention on behalf of people in the death and resurrection of Jesus Christ (Rom 1:17).[40] Cranfield makes a similar observation,

> The gospel is [God's effective power to save] by virtue of its content, its subject, Jesus Christ. It is He Himself who is its effectiveness. His work was God's decisive act for men's salvation, and in the gospel, in the message of which He is

---

38 Joseph A. Fitzmyer, *Romans*, AB, vol. 33 (New York: Doubleday, 1993), 256. Elsewhere, Fitzmyer writes, "Paul views the gospel not merely as an abstract message of salvation nor as a series of propositions about Christ (e.g., "Jesus is Lord") which human beings are expected to apprehend and give assent to, but rather as a salvific force unleashed by God himself in human history through the person, ministry, passion, death, and resurrection of Jesus, bringing with it effects that human beings can appropriate by faith in him" ("The Gospel in the Theology of Paul," 343). Ulrich Becker writes, "In the very act of proclamation [the gospel's] content becomes reality, and brings about the salvation which it contains" (Becker, "Gospel...," "εὐαγγέλιον," in *NIDNTT*, 2:111).

39 In concluding his study of "the word of God" in the Old Testament, McKenzie writes, "The developments and refinements of the Israelite idea of word show a certain consistency of pattern. The basis of this consistency lies in the conception of the spoken word as a distinct reality charged with power. It has power because it emerges from a source of power which, in releasing it, must in a way release itself" (McKenzie, "Word of God in the Old Testament," 205).

40 On understanding δικαιοσύνη θεοῦ as God's saving power, see Mark A. Seifrid, *Christ, Our Righteousness: Paul's Theology of Justification*, NSBT 9 (Leicester: Apollos; Downers Grove: InterVarsity, 2000), 35–48; Otfried Hofius, "Wort Gottes und Glaube bei Paulus," in *Paulus und das antike Judentum*, WUNT 58, ed. Martin Hengel and Ulrich Heckel (Tübingen: Mohr, 1991), esp. 390; Schreiner, *Romans*, 63–76; Ernst Käsemann, "'The Righteousness of God' in Paul," in *New Testament Questions of Today*, trans. W. J. Montague (Philadelphia: Fortress, 1969), 168–82; Peter Stuhlmacher, *Gerechtigkeit Gottes bei Paulus*, FRLANT 87 (Göttingen: Vandenhoeck & Ruprecht, 1965), 78–84, 222–27; Dunn, *Romans 1–8*, 40–42.

the content, He presents Himself to men as it were clothed in the efficacy of His saving work.[41]

Another passage which demonstrates that Paul spoke of the gospel as a "power" is 1 Corinthians 1:17–25. Here, the apostle writes,

> For Christ did not send me to baptize but to proclaim the gospel, and not with eloquent wisdom, so that the cross of Christ might not be emptied of its power. For *the message about the cross* is foolishness to those who are perishing, but to us who are being saved *it is the power of God.* For it is written, "I will destroy the wisdom of the wise, and the discernment of the discerning I will thwart." Where is the one who is wise? Where is the scribe? Where is the debater of this age? Has not God made foolish the wisdom of the world? For since, in the wisdom of God, the world did not know God through wisdom, God decided, through the foolishness of our proclamation, to save those who believe. For Jews demand signs and Greeks desire wisdom, but we proclaim Christ crucified, a stumbling block to Jews and foolishness to Gentiles, *but to those who are called, both Jews and Greeks, Christ the power of God and the wisdom of God.* For God's foolishness is wiser than human wisdom, and God's weakness is stronger than human strength.[42]

The same two elements that were emphasized in our discussion of Romans 1:16 are also present in this passage. First, the gospel, or "the message about the cross" (ὁ λόγος ὁ τοῦ σταυροῦ), is called the *power* of God (δύναμις θεοῦ, v. 18).[43] Second, the power of the gospel is a *derived* power. The gospel is "power" because it comes from or belongs to God (θεοῦ, genitive of source or possession), and because it announces effectively God's act of redemption in Christ's historical death and resurrection. Paul varies his references to "the gospel" to emphasize this point. In verses 17–18, he interchanges a verbal cognate of "gospel" (εὐαγγελίζεσθαι) with "the message about the cross" (ὁ λόγος ὁ τοῦ σταυροῦ). In verse 23, Paul does not say that he proclaims "the gospel," but "Christ crucified" (Χριστὸν ἐσταυρωμένον). The *source* and *content* of Paul's gospel is what makes it "power."

We should also note a third element about this powerful gospel that is present in this 1 Corinthians text – that is, God's providential plan of

---

41   Cranfield, *Romans*, 1:89.

42   My emphasis.

43   Leon Morris comments, "[The gospel] is not simply good advice, telling us what we should do. Nor is it information about God's power. It *is* God's power" (Leon Morris, *The First Epistle of Paul to the Corinthians: An Introduction and Commentary*, rev. ed., TNTC 7 [Leicester: InterVarsity; Grand Rapids: Eerdmans, 1985], 44). Gerhard Friedrich writes, "The Gospel does not merely bear witness to salvation history; it is itself salvation history" (G. Friedrich, "εὐαγγελίζομαι...," in *TDNT*, 2:731).

predestining and saving certain persons. It is this electing activity of God that enables Paul to call the gospel "the power of God." In verse 23–24, Paul writes, "We proclaim Christ crucified, a stumbling block to Jews and foolishness to Gentiles, *but to those who are called*, both Jews and Greeks, *Christ the power of God and the wisdom of God.*"[44] The gospel (or the proclamation of "Christ crucified") does not constitute God's saving power to all people, but only to those who are "called" (τοῖς κλητοῖς).[45] As the effective power of God, the gospel accomplishes God's goal in saving all whom he calls – eliciting repentance and faith from hearts regenerated by the Holy Spirit (Rom 8:29–30; 10:14–17).[46]

Thomas Schreiner agrees that the theme of election runs throughout this passage. He writes,

> The succeeding context of 1 Cor. 1 clarifies that the power of the gospel lies in its effective work in calling believers to salvation (1 Cor. 1:23–24, 26–29). The preaching of the Word does not merely make salvation possible but effects salvation in those who are called. The inseparable connection between the power of God and election is also revealed in 1 Thess 1:4–5. Paul knows that the Thessalonians are elect (v. 4) "because" (ὅτι, *hoti*) his gospel οὐκ ἐγενήθη εἰς ὑμᾶς ἐν λόγῳ μόνον ἀλλὰ καὶ ἐν δυνάμει . . . cf. also 1 Cor. 2:4–5.[47]

We should also note that this element of God's effectual calling lies in the background of the Romans passage previously discussed (see Rom 1:1–7).

To summarize, from our brief consideration of Romans 1:16 and 1 Corinthians 1:17–25, we can conclude that Paul spoke of the gospel as an effective power. The gospel is "power" because of its source (God), its content (Christ's salvific death and resurrection), and its role in God's plan to save all persons whom he has predestined. God's calling is *effectual* and is made *actual* in the preaching and hearing of the gospel. This dynamic nature of the gospel is

---

44 My emphasis.

45 L. Coenen writes, "Paul understands calling as the process by which God calls those, whom he has already elected and appointed, out of their bondage to this world, so that he may justify and sanctify them (Rom 8:29f.), and bring them into his service. This means that the call is part of God's work of reconciliation and peace (1 Cor 7:15)" (L. Coenen, "Call," "καλέω," in *NIDNTT*, 1:275). K. L. Schmidt writes, "If God or Christ calls a man, this calling or naming is a *verbum efficax* (K. L. Schmidt, "καλέω...," in *TDNT*, 3:489). Note meaning number 4 of καλέω in BDAG, "choose for receipt of a special benefit or experience" (BDAG, 503). Cf. Jost Eckert, "καλέω...," in *EDNT*, 2:242–43.

46 G. Strecker writes, "Εὐαγγέλιον is a spirit-empowered word which also produces pneumatic deeds; for it manifests the election of the person [1 Thess 1:4], which was made at the beginning, as a call to salvation [1 Thess 2:12]" (Georg Strecker, "εὐαγγέλιον," in *EDNT*, 2:72).

47 Schreiner, *Romans*, 60.

in continuity with Old Testament references to "the word of the Lord."

The Dynamic Gospel and Paul's Apostolic Mission

We will now briefly overview several Pauline texts where the apostle makes a more explicit link between the gospel as "power" and his missionary work. Minimal contextual information on verses will be provided. Our goal is simply to show that Paul spoke of the gospel as a power in relation to his missionary work.

In 1 Corinthians 14:36, Paul asks the Corinthian believers, "Did the word of God go out [ἐξῆλθεν] from you? Or are you the only ones it has reached [κατήντησεν]?"[48] With this sarcastic question, Paul intends to remind the Corinthians that they were not the starting point of the gospel, nor its only destination.[49] Because the gospel did not originate with the Corinthians and they were not its only adherents, the disorderly Corinthian worship services should not be viewed as normative, but as aberrant. For the purposes of our study, it is important to note that in his incidental remark of 1 Corinthians 14:36, Paul portrays the "word of God" (i.e., the gospel) in the active role of "going out" [ἐξῆλθεν] and "arriving" [κατήντησεν]. These verbs are frequently used in Acts to describe persons on a journey.[50] In this rhetorical question to the Corinthian Christian community, Paul almost personifies the gospel as a traveling missionary. Not the activity of gospel heralds, but the activity of the gospel itself, is emphasized.

Paul makes a similar reference to the gospel in 1 Thessalonians 1:5, where he writes, "Our gospel came . . ." (τὸ εὐαγγέλιον ἡμῶν . . . ἐγενήθη). Though Paul could have written, "we came with the gospel" (cf. 2 Cor 10:14),[51] he chooses to depict the gospel as the agent arriving in Thessalonica to accomplish God's will of saving persons. Also, it is noteworthy that Paul says the gospel did not come in word only (ἐν λόγῳ μόνον), but also in *power* (ἀλλὰ καὶ ἐν δυνάμει) and in the Holy Spirit (καὶ ἐν πνεύματι ἁγίῳ).

Likewise, in 1 Corinthians 9:12, Paul describes the gospel in its triumphal

---

48 My translation. Obviously, the gospel did not "go out" (i.e., originate) from Corinth, for Paul was the one who founded the congregation there (1 Cor 2:1–5; 3:5–10; Acts 18:1–18). Likewise, the Corinthians should not think they are the only ones whom the gospel has reached.

49 Archibald Robertson and Alfred Plummer, *A Critical and Exegetical Commentary on the First Epistle of St Paul to the Corinthians*, 2nd ed., ICC (Edinburgh: T. & T. Clark, 1914), 326; cf. Richard B. Hays, *First Corinthians*, Interpretation (Louisville: John Knox, 1997), 244.

50 See the uses of ἐξέρχομαι in Acts 1:21; 7:3, 4, 7; 10:23; 11:25; also see the uses of καταντάω in Acts 16:1; 18:19, 24; 20:15; 21:7; 25:13.

51 O'Brien notes this point. He adds, "Gospel is ... regarded as a living force, almost personalized" ("Thanksgiving and the Gospel in Paul," 153).

march across the ancient Roman empire. He does not speak of himself as conveying the gospel to others; his concern is that he not *stand in the way* of God's word. In reference to his ministry with Barnabas, Paul writes, "We endure anything rather than put an obstacle in the way of the gospel of Christ" (ἀλλὰ πάντα στέγομεν, ἵνα μή τινα ἐγκοπὴν δῶμεν τῷ εὐαγγελίῳ τοῦ Χριστοῦ). The gospel is depicted as the active agent bringing salvation. Paul's role is simply to stay out of its way.[52]

In like manner, in 2 Timothy 2:8–9, Paul writes, "Remember Jesus Christ, raised from the dead, a descendant of David – that is my gospel, for which I suffer hardship, even to the point of being chained like a criminal. But the word of God is not chained [ὁ λόγος τοῦ θεοῦ οὐ δέδεται]." Here we see the gospel described as both "content" (Jesus Christ raised from the dead) and "power" (the unchained word). While Paul can be put in prison and his ministry curtailed or stopped, no such thing is true for "the word of God" (i.e., the gospel). God's word is effective and will continue to bring salvation to all whom he has predestined.

This inevitable growth and certain salvific work of God's word can be conveyed by an agricultural metaphor, as in Colossians 1:5–7. There, Paul addresses the Colossian believers as follows: "You have heard of this hope before in the word of the truth, the gospel that has come to you. Just as it is bearing fruit and growing in the whole world, so it has been bearing fruit among yourselves from the day you heard it and truly comprehended the grace of God." The gospel not only "comes" (παρόντος) to the Colossians, it "grows" (αὐξανόμενον)[53] and "bears fruit" (καρποφορούμενον). These agricultural metaphors speak to the inherent certainty of growth which is present in the gospel because it is God's effective word.[54] The gospel is not only "bearing fruit" and "growing" among the Colossians, but "in the whole world" (ἐν παντὶ τῷ κόσμῳ). This growth and fruit-bearing can be nothing other than the gospel's advance as persons believe in the gospel and then mature in the faith.[55]

---

52 Hooker is wrong, however, to see the gospel as personified in 1 Cor 9:23 ("A Partner in the Gospel," 88–89). Other scholars who claim that Paul presents himself as a co-laborer of the personified gospel in 1 Cor 9:23 include the following: O'Brien, *Gospel and Mission*, 96–97; Gundry Volf, *Paul and Perseverance*, 247–54; Molland, *Das Paulinische Euangelion*, 53–54.

53 Cf. 1 Cor 3:7; Acts 6:7; 12:24; 19:20.

54 Cf. 1 Cor 9:11–12; Rom 1:16; 1 Cor 1:17–25.

55 Concerning the "fruit-bearing" and "growth" of the Colossian Christian community (Col 1:10), O'Brien writes, "'Fruit-bearing' is to be understood as a crop of good deeds (cf. Phil 1:11), while the growth of the gospel points to the increasing number of converts" (*Gospel and Mission*, 113). So Eduard Lohse, *Colossians and Philemon*, trans. William R. Poehlmann and Robert J. Karris, ed. Helmut Koester, Hermeneia (Philadelphia: Fortress, 1971), 19–20; Martin Dibelius, *An die Kolosser,*

In all of the passages discussed above, the gospel is described as the active agent of salvation. Paul, however, can also speak of himself as the agent and the gospel as the "dynamic means" by which his ministry is accomplished. In 1 Corinthians 4:15, Paul writes, "In Christ Jesus, through the gospel, I gave birth to you" (διὰ τοῦ εὐαγγελίου ἐγὼ ὑμᾶς ἐγέννησα).[56] Here the gospel is the means of bringing about the spiritual birth of Paul's converts. One gets the sense that Paul's various metaphorical references to the gospel are attempts to describe the dynamic nature of an entity which, in some sense, remains beyond human definition.

Another term which Paul uses to describe his relationship with the dynamic gospel is the verb πληρόω. There are three passages where Paul employs πληρόω (or πληροφορέω), and we will now briefly discuss the significance of these verses. In Romans 15:18–19, Paul writes,

> For I will not venture to speak of anything except what Christ has accomplished through me to win obedience from the Gentiles, by word and deed, by the power of signs and wonders, by the power of the Spirit of God, so that from Jerusalem and as far around as Illyricum I have fulfilled the gospel [NRSV: fully proclaimed the good news] of Christ.[57]

Scholars have debated what Paul means when he says that he has "fulfilled the gospel" [πεπληρωκέναι τὸ εὐαγγέλιον]. The two main interpretations of this phrase are (1) Paul is saying that he has essentially completed all the expected evangelism in the named territories; Jesus' imminent return allows only for a rushed, representative preaching of the gospel.[58] (2) Paul is saying that he has fulfilled his apostolic obligation to pioneer new evangelistic work in the named territories.[59] This second option seems to have the most contextual support, as Paul highlights his apostolic desire to preach in virgin territories (Rom 15:20), while not disallowing the continued spreading of the gospel which he elsewhere approves and enjoins (Phil 1:14; 2:16).

Although most scholars rightly favor this last option, they frequently miss a Pauline emphasis in the text by deviating from the verb/noun distinction in the original Greek construction. In Romans 15:19, Paul uses a verbal form of "fulfill" with the noun "gospel" as the object. Although the noun can have

---

Epheser, an Philemon, ed. Heinrich Greeven, 3rd rev. ed., HNT 12 (Tübingen: Mohr, 1953), 6.

56 My translation.

57 My translation.

58 E.g., Renan, *Saint Paul*, 492–93; Wrede, *Paul*, 47–48; C. K. Barrett, "New Testament Eschatology," 228; Althaus, *Der Brief an die Römer*, 147; Johannes Munck, *Paul and the Salvation of Mankind*, 48, 51–55, 276–78.

59 E.g., Harnack, *Mission and Expansion*, 1:73–74; Bornkamm, *Paul*, 54; Dahl, *Das Volk Gottes*, 241; Schreiner, *Romans*, 768–70; Cranfield, *Romans*, 2:762, 766.

connotations of "preaching" the gospel, this meaning of εὐαγγέλιον is not clear in Romans 15:19 (contra NRSV's translation). Paul's use of similar expressions in Colossians 1:25 [πληρῶσαι τὸν λόγον τοῦ θεοῦ] and 2 Timothy 4:17 [τὸ κήρυγμα πληροφορηθῇ] indicate that a verbal form of πληρόω followed by a nominal form of "gospel" (εὐαγγέλιον, λόγον, κήρυγμα) is a stylized expression for the apostle. This point is significant when we remember that the gospel is the powerful word of God, according to Paul.

What does Paul mean, then, when he speaks of "fulfilling" [πληρόω] the gospel? The Greek verb πληρόω can mean fulfill, make full, complete, or accomplish.[60] In references to prophecy or God's word, πληρόω denotes the bringing about of what God has ordained to happen.[61] The gospel, as "God's word," is fulfilled when it progresses savingly through the lost world (Rom 15:19–20). Paul "fulfills" this message when he becomes its servant (διάκονος τοῦ εὐαγγελίου) by conveying it to others.[62] God is the author of the message, and regardless of Paul's participation, the word of God will "be fulfilled." Paul, however, delights to be used in this process (Phil 1:12–18). For the purposes of our study, it is significant that in three separate places Paul speak of his ministry as "fulfilling the gospel" (or "word," or "message"). This construction reminds us that the gospel, for Paul, was God's dynamic word – a powerful entity in continuity with Old Testament prophetic references to "the word of the Lord."

The Dynamic Gospel and the Church's Mission

Paul also speaks of the gospel as a dynamic force that is active in the churches. For example, in 1 Thessalonians 2:13–16, Paul writes,

> We also constantly give thanks to God for this, that *when you received the word of God that you heard from us, you accepted it not as a human word but as what it*

---

60 See BDAG, 827–29. The semantic range of πληρόω is illustrated by the following sections in Louw and Nida: §13.106; §30.29; §33.144; §35.33; §59.33; §59.37; §68.26. I disagree with Louw and Nida's classification in §33.199.

61 See Matt 1:22; 2:15, 17, 23; 4:14; 8:17; 12:17; 13:35; Mark 14:49; Luke 1:20; 4:21; Acts 1:16; 3:18; James 2:23. Also see Reinier Schippers, "Fullness," "πληρόω," in *NIDNTT*, 1:736–38. Concerning the fulfillment of "the word of Yahweh" in the Old Testament, McKenzie writes, "Frequently the word of Yahweh is said 'to be fulfilled' (as in 1 Kgs 2:27, the word which predicted the downfall of the priestly house of Eli) or 'to be established' (as in Jer 29:10, the promise of restoration from exile). In these phrases is described the coming into existence of the thing signified by the word, the 'fullness' of the reality of word-thing" (McKenzie, "Word of God in the Old Testament," 196).

62 See Eph 3:6–7; Col 1:23.

really is, God's word, which is at work in you believers. For you, brothers and
sisters, became imitators of the churches of God in Christ Jesus that are in Judea,
for you suffered the same things from your own compatriots as they did from the
Jews, who killed both the Lord Jesus and the prophets, and drove us out; they
displease God and oppose everyone by hindering us from speaking to the Gentiles
so that they may be saved. Thus they have constantly been filling up the measure
of their sins; but God's wrath has overtaken them at last.[63]

According to 1 and 2 Thessalonians, both Paul and the church in
Thessalonica have faced and are facing persecution. Paul and his co-workers
face opposition to their gospel proclamation (1 Thess 2:1–2). The
Thessalonians encounter hostility for similar reasons, as demonstrated by the
text above. In this passage, Paul says that the church in Thessalonica has
undergone the same sort of persecution that the churches in Judea endured from
"the Jews." Paul then expands on the belligerence of "the Jews" toward the
Judean churches by mentioning several of their hostile acts – killing Jesus,
murdering the prophets, driving out Paul and his co-workers, and hindering
Paul and his co-workers from proclaiming the gospel to the Gentiles. This list
of attacks demonstrates that Jewish anger was consistently directed against
adherence to and proclamation of Jesus. As "imitators" (μιμηταί) of the
churches in Judea, the church in Thessalonica apparently also faced opposition
for their adherence to and/or proclamation of faith in Jesus. Asserting that the
suffering itself was the activity being imitated begs the question. As Jo-Ann
Brant rightly observes, "The equation of 'imitation' with suffering affliction
ignores the fact that the Thessalonians were engaged in some activity that
incurred the opposition of others."[64]

For the purposes of our study in this chapter, it is important to note that the
Thessalonians' imitative missionary behavior of proclaiming and suffering are
produced by "God's word" which is "at work" in the Thessalonian believers
(λόγον θεοῦ, ὃς καὶ ἐνεργεῖται ἐν ὑμῖν τοῖς πιστεύουσιν) (1 Thess
2:13). Not Paul's human instruction – but the divine message that he conveyed
– is the source of life which determines the Thessalonians' present missionary
position.

Similarly, in 2 Thessalonians 3:1, Paul writes, "Finally, brothers and sisters,
pray for us, so that the word of the Lord may spread rapidly ["run," τρέχη] and
be glorified everywhere, just as it is among you [καθὼς καὶ πρὸς ὑμᾶς]."
Here again, Paul is not the agent of mission; *the word itself* is "running." Not
only through Paul's ministry, but also through the Thessalonians, this word is
running its inevitable God-ordained course.

In 1 Thessalonians 1:8, Paul describes "the word of the Lord" as "ringing"
or "sounding forth" (ἐξήχηται) from the Thessalonian congregation. Here

---

63   My emphasis.
64   Jo-Ann A. Brant, "The Place of *mimēsis* in Paul's Thought," *SR* 22 (1993): 292.

again, the gospel seems to take on a life of its own. The church is not described explicitly as announcing or proclaiming the gospel, but is depicted as the launching point for the powerful word's *self-diffusion*.[65]

Because there is some debate over what this passage means, it is necessary for us to examine it in more detail. 1 Thessalonians 1:6–8 reads,

> And you became imitators of us and of the Lord, for in spite of persecution you received the word with joy inspired by the Holy Spirit, so that you became an example to all the believers in Macedonia and in Achaia. For the word of the Lord has sounded forth [ἐξήχηται] from you not only in Macedonia and Achaia, but in every place your faith in God has become known [ἐξελήλυθεν, "gone forth"], so that we have no need to speak about it.

Some scholars have claimed that "the word of the Lord sounding forth" (1:8) does not refer to the gospel proclamation of the Thessalonian church. Paul Bowers, for example, argues that 1 Thessalonians 1:9 gives us the *non-evangelistic* content of the "word of the Lord" (1:8) which rang forth from the Thessalonians.[66] This "word of the Lord," says Bowers, was the news of the Thessalonians' conversion that served to encourage existing Christian congregations.[67] Yet, both the majestic connotations of the verb ἐξηχέω and Paul's other uses of λόγος in the Thessalonian correspondence favor understanding ἀφ' ὑμῶν γὰρ ἐξήχηται ὁ λόγος τοῦ κυρίου (1:8) as the Thessalonians' evangelistic proclamation.[68] Indeed, in 2 Thessalonians 3:1, where Paul requests prayer "that *the word of the Lord* may spread rapidly and be glorified everywhere (my emphasis)," no one doubts that "the word of the Lord" means the Christian gospel.

Further confirmation for reading 1 Thessalonians 1:8 as evangelistic is possibly found in 1:3, where Paul has already described the Thessalonians'

65　Scholars who agree that 1 Thess 1:6–8 describes the evangelistic activity of the Thessalonians include Ware, "Thessalonians," 126–31; Schütz, *Paul and the Anatomy of Apostolic Authority*, 227–28; David M. Stanley, "'Become Imitators of Me': The Pauline Conception of Apostolic Tradition," *Bib* 40 (1959): 866–67; Swigchem, *Het missionair karakter*, 131–32; J. Lambrecht, "A Call to Witness by All," 324–25; Andrew D. Clarke, "'Be Imitators of Me': Paul's Model of Leadership," *TynBul* 49 (1998): 336–38; Marshall, "Who Were the Evangelists?," 259.

66　Bowers, "Church and Mission," 98.

67　Ibid.

68　See BDAG, 349–50; 1 Thess 1:6; 2:13; 2 Thess 3:1. See Ware, "Thessalonians," 127 n. 8; see also Bartholomäus Henneken, *Verkündigung und Prophetie im Ersten Thessalonicherbrief: Ein Beitrag zur Theologie des Wortes Gottes*, SBS 29 (Stuttgart: Katholisches Bibelwerk, 1969), 62–64. Henneken writes in reference to verse 8, "Es ist hier an eine aktive Verkündigung durch die Thessalonicher zu denken" (63).

activity with some of his favorite terms for evangelistic work, i.e., κόπος (or κοπιάω) and ἔργον (or cognates).[69] The evangelistic labors of the Thessalonians, which are *only alluded to* in verse 3, are made more explicit in verse 8 (i.e., the word sounding forth).

If we are correct in reading the text as outline above, the explanatory γάρ clause in verse 8 (ἀφ' ὑμῶν γὰρ ἐξήχηται ὁ λόγος τοῦ κυρίου) is best understood as an explanation of how the Thessalonians became a τύπος for other believers (v. 7). The Thessalonian Christians were an example to others by virtue of their being a launching point for the gospel. The replication of the apostolic mission was complete in them.[70] As the "word of the Lord" had progressed effectively through the apostle Paul, now it was advancing through the Thessalonian church (1 Thess 1:8; 2:13–14; 2 Thess 3:1).

Several scholars have noted this evangelistic reference to the dynamic word of the Lord in 1 Thessalonians 1:8. James Patrick Ware, for example, comments on the text: "The word is pictured as an active force, radiating out from the Thessalonians by its own power."[71] Along the same lines, Lambrecht writes, "God's initiative is irresistible; the Lord's word is a dynamic, out-reaching and contagious power: 'It will not return to me empty without accomplishing my purpose and succeeding in the task for which I sent it' (Is 55:11)."[72]

If, in agreement with Ware and Lambrecht, we have correctly interpreted 1 Thessalonians 1:8, how then are we to understand verses 9–10? Unlike Bowers, we should not understand these verses as the non-evangelistic content of "the word of the Lord." Let us now look more closely at this debated text:

> For the people of those regions report about us what kind of welcome we had among you, and how you turned to God from idols, to serve a living and true God, and to wait for his Son from heaven, whom he raised from the dead – Jesus, who rescues us from the wrath that is coming. (1 Thess 1:9–10)

Bowers is undoubtedly correct to consider this passage as belonging to the same discourse unit as verses 1–8.[73] Yet, a proper interpretation of verses 9–10

---

69   See Ware, "Thessalonians," 127–28 n. 9. Cf. 1 Thess 3:2; 3:5; Rom 16:3, 21; 1 Cor 3:8–9, 13–15; 9:1; 15:10; 16:10; 2 Cor 10:15; Gal 4:11; Phil 1:22; 2:16; 2:30.

70   As the apostolic example fades into the background, the example of the churches themselves and their leaders comes to the foreground (e.g., 1 Cor 1:2; 11:16; 14:33; 2 Cor 8–9; Phil 3:17; Thess 1:6; 2:14–16; 2 Thess 3:7–9; 1 Pet. 5:3). This process did not take long, as Paul and the other apostles rarely lingered with their new churches (see Acts).

71   Ware, "Thessalonians," 128.

72   Lambrecht, "A Call to Witness by All," 325.

73   The entirety of chapter 1 (vv. 1–10) serves as a coherent unit – the Pauline introduction and thanksgiving. Chapter 1, verse 10 is followed by a clear shift to the

does not demand that "the word of the Lord sounding forth" in verse 8 be reduced to the report of the Thessalonians' conversion circulating among believers. Indeed, it seems that in verse 9, Paul touches on a second point, related to his prior discussion in verse 8. As the gospel was progressing effectively through the Thessalonian Christians, large numbers of people had become aware of their conversion. Likely, not only the Thessalonians' evangelistic proclamation (1:8), but their public break from idolatry (1:9) had resulted in their religious conversion becoming widely noticed. As the news of the Thessalonians' conversion spread through both non-believers and believers, Christians in Macedonia and Achaia took up the news and reported it to Paul (1:9–10). The fact that other Christian believers had heard of and were talking about the Thessalonians' dramatic conversion does not deny the Thessalonians' evangelistic proclamation. Rather, such reports further confirm that the Thessalonians were effectively making known their Christian presence.

Paul describes a similar dynamism of the gospel in relation to the church in Colossae. In Colossians 3:16–17, Paul says that the gospel is an entity which "dwells in" (ἐνοικέω) the believers. He writes,

Let the word of Christ[74] dwell in [ἐνοικείτω] you richly; teach and admonish one another in all wisdom; and with gratitude in your hearts sing psalms, hymns, and spiritual songs to God. And whatever you do, in word or deed, do everything in the name of the Lord Jesus, giving thanks to God the Father through him.

The gospel's "dwelling in" the Colossians will be manifested by their "teaching" (διδάσκοντες) and "admonishing" (νουθετοῦντες) one another in the pattern of the apostle himself (as will be examined further in chapter four).[75] As the gospel "takes up residence" in believers, they will be competent to teach and encourage each other (cf. 2 Tim 1:5).

In 1 Corinthians 15:1–2, Paul speaks of the gospel as a "sphere" in which believers "stand." He writes,

Now I would remind you, brothers and sisters, of the good news that I proclaimed to you, which you in turn received, in which also you stand [ἐν ᾧ καὶ ἑστήκατε], through which also you are being saved, if you hold firmly to the message that I proclaimed to you – unless you have come to believe in vain.

---

body of the letter in chapter 2, verse 1 (Αὐτοὶ γὰρ οἴδατε ἀδελφοί, τὴν εἴσοδον ἡμῶν τὴν πρὸς ὑμᾶς ὅτι οὐ κενὴ γέγονεν).

74 Ὁ λόγος τοῦ Χριστοῦ is generally understood as a reference to the gospel (T. K. Abbott, *A Critical and Exegetical Commentary on the Epistles to the Ephesians and to the Colossians*, ICC [Edinburgh: T. & T. Clark, 1897], 290).

75 Διδάσκοντες and νουθετοῦντες should be understood as instrumental participles with an imperative force.

To speak of the gospel metaphorically as a place in which one "stands" illustrates again that there is more to Paul's understanding of "the gospel" than content and the act of proclaiming that content. The gospel is a sphere in which the power of salvation is operative. The church is now within that sphere, and because of the gospel's dynamic quality, the church is "caught up" in the gospel and becomes an agent of its continuing advance.

Paul's description of his converts as "first fruits" (ἀπαρχή) also demonstrates the dynamic nature of the gospel in relation to the church's continued missionary advance. According to the Old Testament, "first fruits" were the initial offering of the year's agricultural produce to God.[76] These "first fruits" represented the whole of the harvest which was yet to come.[77] "First fruits" retains this sense of "an initial part representing the guaranteed whole" in its various New Testament occurrences.[78] In Paul's thinking, the initial convert[s] whom he calls "first fruits" represent the beginning of God's harvest, of which the rest is guaranteed by the certain fruit-bearing quality of the word of God. For example, in Romans 16:5, Paul writes, "Greet my beloved Epaenetus, who was the [first fruits] in Asia for Christ." Also, in 1 Corinthians 16:15, Paul says, "Now, brothers and sisters, you know that members of the household of Stephanas were the [first fruits] in Achaia, and they have devoted themselves to the service of the saints." Because of the nature of the gospel that Paul has passed on to his initial converts, he knows that the harvest will continue. The "unchained word" will continue its triumphant and powerful advance – effecting salvation for all whom the Lord has called (Rom 8:29–30; 1 Cor 1:24; 2 Tim 2:9). Although Paul often chooses not to stress the human agents through whom God's word progresses, it is noteworthy that for Paul such progression inevitably entails the proclamation and hearing of the gospel (Rom 10:14–15).

Paul's Theology of Mission within the Broader New Testament Understanding of the Church's Mission

If we are correct in describing Paul's theology of the church's mission as based primarily on the dynamic nature of the gospel, we must then ask how this emphasis fits within the broader New Testament theology of mission. Because Acts is one of the main texts upon which missiologists base their missionary reflections, it is appropriate that we briefly compare Luke's theology of the church's mission in Acts with the Pauline theology of the church's mission

---

76   E.g., Exod. 23:16, 19; 34:22, 26; Lev. 2:12, 14; 23:10, 17, 20; Num. 18:13; 28:26; Deut. 18:4; 26:10–11. See Richard O. Rigsby, "First Fruits," in *ABD*, 2:796–97.
77   See Hans-Georg Link and Colin Brown, "Sacrifice, First Fruits...," "ἀπαρχή," in *NIDNTT*, 3:415–17.
78   See Rom 8:22–23; 11:16; 1 Cor 15:20, 23; Rev 14:4. Cf. BDAG, 98.

outlined above. As we noted at the beginning of this chapter, in Acts, Luke presents the person of the Holy Spirit as the primary basis and guiding force of the early church's mission. Paul, on the other hand, does not give the Spirit such a prominent place in his missionary reflections. The apostle's references to the Holy Spirit, however, are easily harmonized with Luke's missionary presentation. According to Paul, the Spirit reveals the gospel to believers (Gal 3:3; 1 Cor 2:9–13), is received by believing the message (Gal 3:2; 4:6–7; Eph 1:13–14; 2:15–22), "builds up" the church (i.e., both numerically and by increasing maturity) through the supernatural gifts he provides (1 Cor 12–14), enables verbal confession of allegiance to Jesus (1 Cor 12:3), and directs believers' conduct (Rom 8:4). In spite of such references to the Spirit, Paul's letters lack the explicit connection between Spirit and mission that Luke frequently provides.[79]

While giving prominence to the Spirit's role in mission, Luke also refers to the "word of God" (i.e., the gospel) as a dynamic, effective power. Commentators on Acts have long noted the important "summary" sections which punctuate the book with the missionary statement, "the word of God grew" (ὁ λόγος τοῦ θεοῦ ηὔξανεν).[80] This understanding of the gospel as a dynamic missionary force parallels Paul's missionary theology.

Consequently, we can see that Paul and Luke do not so much differ on their missionary theology, as they emphasize different complementary elements of the same vision. Paul emphasizes the effective *message* communicated by the Holy Spirit. Luke, on the other hand, emphasizes the *person* of the Holy Spirit who makes the gospel effective in its hearers. Neither Paul nor Luke, however, completely neglects the missionary element that his counterpart emphasizes.[81] Indeed, Paul and Luke are discussing the same reality – simply from two

---

79   E.g., Acts 1:8; 4:29–31; 6:10; 8:29, 39–40; 10:19–20, 44–47; 11:12; 13:2–4; 16:6–7; 20:22–23.

80   See Acts 6:7; 12:24; 19:20; cf. Acts 2:41; 4:4, 29, 31; 6:2, 4; 8:4, 14, 25; 10:36, 37, 44; 11:1, 19; 13:5, 7, 44, 46, 48, 49; 14:3, 25; 15:7, 35, 36; 16:6, 32; 17:11, 13; 18:11; 19:10; 20:32. Also see Jerome Kodell, "'The Word of God Grew': The Ecclesial Tendency of Λόγος in Acts 1,7; 12,24; 19,20," *Bib* 55 (1974): 505–19; Brian S. Rosner, "The Progress of the Word," in *Witness to the Gospel: The Theology of Acts*, ed. I. Howard Marshall and David Peterson (Grand Rapids: Eerdmans 1998), 215–33; Ernst Haenchen, *Die Apostelgeschichte*, 15th ed., MeyerK 3 (Göttingen: Vandenhoeck & Ruprecht, 1968), 217, 330, 502.

81   The dynamic power of the word is possibly only slightly less prominent than the Spirit in Luke's missionary thought. For example, see the verses cited in the previous footnote. Michael Green comments, "The man who, more than anyone in the early Church, has given us his assessment of the factors in evangelism is St. Luke. And for him the two main ones are the very factors which humans do not provide, namely the Spirit of God and the Word of God" (*Evangelism in the Early Church*, rev. ed., 209).

different angles. Ultimately both Luke and Paul are God-centered because, for them, it is either God's *presence* or God's effective *word* which is the primary basis of the church's mission. It is not surprising, then, that Paul and Luke are often reticent to speak of human agency in the spread of the gospel and prefer to stress the activity of God.[82]

Another important element that must be set alongside Paul's theology of the church's mission is the Great Commission (Matt 28:18–20; Luke 24:46–49; John 20:21; Acts 1:8; cf. Mark 16:15). How does the theological basis of the church's mission that we outlined in this chapter harmonize with missiologists' frequent reliance upon the Great Commission? Arguably, the Great Commission is none other than Christ's verbal command sanctioning in human activity what is present in the self-diffusing word. Thus, scholars who have attempted to found the Pauline churches' mission upon the Great Commission have not been entirely wrong. A clear command to evangelize is part of the churches' heritage, and Paul likely was familiar with the Great Commission (at least in the form of oral tradition). If so, we would expect him to have passed on this command to the churches (Acts 20:27). Yet, Paul also knew that divine requirements could never be met by those who walk according to the flesh, but only by those who walk according to the Spirit (Rom 8:4). Believers who have the indwelling Spirit of Christ, then, manifest the life and righteousness which God *gives* and *requires* of his children (Rom 8:11, 14–17). Thus, scholars are correct to say that the church inherits the Great Commission from the apostles – as long as they understand that two other sides of this reality (i.e., Spirit and word) must be present to have a complete understanding of the church's missionary motivation.[83] It would seem, then, that missiologists (who have frequently emphasized Jesus' explicit command to missionize and the role of the Spirit in promoting mission) should now include a third element in discussing the church's missionary motivation – the role of the dynamic word of God. This multi-faceted dimension of the church's missionary motivation is illustrated by the diagram on the following page.

---

82   E.g., Rom 9:24, 1 Cor 1:27–30; 3:5–9; 2 Cor 1:21–22; 1 Thess 5:23–25; Acts 6:7; 12:24; 19:20.

83   George W. Peters remarks, "[The church] inherits the Great Commission from the apostles of Christ and becomes responsible for its realization. Too long has pietistic individualism dominated the mind and scene of Protestantism in relation to the Great Commission while the church was left asleep" (*A Biblical Theology of Missions*, 220–21).

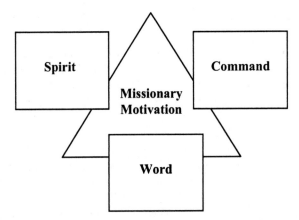

Fig. 1. The church's missionary motivation as Spirit, Command, and Word.

Conclusion

The main purpose of this chapter is to demonstrate that Paul speaks of the gospel as a dynamic entity that propelled both him (as an apostle) and the churches (as gospel-created and gospel-empowered entities) into the further spread of God's word. We have also seen that the Pauline emphasis on "word" harmonizes well with broader New Testament themes of "Spirit" and "command" as a theological basis for the church's mission.

If Paul did indeed expect missionary activity from the churches on the basis of the dynamic gospel, then we would also expect some confirmation of this expectation in the apostle's explicit commands. Rudolf Bultmann long ago rightly observed that the essential pattern of Pauline paranesis is: "Become what you already are!"[84] Though Paul expected the self-diffusive gospel to produce spontaneously missionary churches, it would be odd if certain occasions never prompted the apostle to provide some hortatory material in confirmation of his theological pre-conviction. As we turn to the next chapter, the main question we will ask is: are there explicit imperatives in Paul's letters that confirm that the apostle expected the gospel to progress through the churches?

---

84 Rudolf Bultmann, *Theology of the New Testament*, trans. Kendrick Grobel (New York: Charles Scribner's Sons, 1951), 1:332. Cf. Käsemann, who speaks of Pauline ethics as living under the lordship of Christ, whom God has graciously established over us (Ernst Käsemann, *Commentary on Romans*, trans. and ed. Geoffrey W. Bromiley [Grand Rapids: Eerdmans, 1980], 179).

Excursus: Discontinuity of Missionary Activity Between the Old Testament and New Testament

The theological study presented above is also an aid in understanding the discontinuity between the elect community's mission in the Old Testament (i.e., Israel's mission) and the elect community's mission in the New Testament (i.e., the church's mission). Although many popular missiological studies have claimed that the missionary witness of God's people in both the Old and New Testaments is an active, centrifugal outreach,[85] most scholars are in agreement that the missionary witness of God's people in the Old Testament is overwhelmingly passive.[86] Also, a fair number of critical scholars agree with the main tenor of my study – i.e., that Paul expected the church to have an active missionary role.[87] If God's people in the Old Testament are passive witnesses and God's people in the New Testament are active witnesses, what accounts for this discontinuity?

The nature of God's word (i.e., the gospel) and the presence of the Holy Spirit are the key to this puzzle. While God's word and Spirit came to specific members of the elect community in the Old Testament (e.g., 1 Sam 10:10; Hos 1:1; Ezek 2:2), a broader outpouring of the Spirit and word awaited eschatological fulfillment (Joel 2:28–32). The early church recognized in their experiences the fulfillment of prophetic texts which predicted a general outpouring of the Spirit and the self-diffusing word (Acts 2:16–21; 1 Cor 12:13). No longer did the Spirit and word come only to specific individuals for a limited duration. With the inauguration of the eschaton in Christ's death and resurrection, the Spirit and word came to stay (Acts 1:8). Because God's Spirit is a missionary spirit (i.e., revealing himself to humans and enabling their God-glorifying response) and God's word is dynamic and effective, the abiding presence of Spirit and word with the elect community guarantees its active missionary role.

---

85   E.g., Walter C. Kaiser, Jr., *Mission in the Old Testament: Israel as a Light to the Nations* (Grand Rapids: Baker, 2000), 9.

86   Jeremias writes, "[According to the Old Testament] the Gentiles will not be evangelized where they dwell, but will be summoned to the holy Mount by the divine epiphany" (J. Jeremias, *Jesus' Promise to the Nations,* trans. S. H. Hooke, SBT 24 [London: SCM, 1958], 60); also see Köstenberger and O'Brien, *Salvation to the Ends of the Earth,* 34–36; J. Blauw, *The Missionary Nature of the Church: A Survey of the Biblical Theology of Mission* (London: Lutterworth, 1962), 34–35, 40–41; Eckhard J. Schnabel, "Israel, the People of God, and the Nations" (paper presented in the Biblical Theology Group at the annual meeting of the Evangelical Theological Society, Nashville, TN, November 2000), 2; cf. Scot McKnight, *A Light among the Gentiles,* 11–29, 115–17.

87   See chapter one.

Excursus: Pauline Co-workers

Because my thesis deals with the relationship of apostle, church, and mission, a detailed discussion of the Pauline co-workers is beyond the scope of this work. A few short comments, however, are in order. The New Testament records nearly one hundred persons who worked alongside the apostle Paul.[88] The most important question for our thesis is: if Paul viewed the church as continuing the apostolic mission, who were these co-workers and what was their relationship to his mission?

Although the New Testament evidence is not as explicit on Paul's co-workers as we might like, it seems best to classify these persons into two main categories – those who functioned under the auspices of the apostles and those who functioned under the auspices of the churches. Under the "apostle rubric" are such persons as Timothy or Titus (2 Tim 1:2; Titus 1:4). They derived their authority from the apostle who commissioned them for a particular task.[89] Because this authority is solely a *derived* authority, after the last apostle died, we would not expect any new apostolic delegates of this kind.

Under the second rubric, that of the "churches' mission," we find persons recruited from within the local congregations to accompany or aid the apostles on their journeys (1 Cor 16:15–18; 2 Cor 8:18–19). These persons manifest the churches' concern and support of the apostolic mission.[90] A prime example of such workers are the delegates from the churches who accompany Paul with the collection for the saints in Jerusalem (2 Cor 8:23–24; 9:1–5). These people are both extensions of the churches and actual participants in the apostles' mission. Because of the apostolic element inherent in these delegates' mission, their ministry is also limited in duration by the life span of the apostles.

Finally, under the rubric of the "churches' mission" we also find persons who seem to function semi-independently of the apostles. Apollos, for example, preached in various cities (Acts 18:24–28; 1 Cor 3:5), but was apparently not connected with any apostle and was not bound by Paul's requests (1 Cor 1:12; 3:4–6, 22; 16:12). Apollos and other itinerant ministers of this kind have been taken by some scholars as evidence that there was a class of full-time missionaries that functioned independently of both the apostles and the churches. It seems better, however, to include these individuals under the rubric of the churches' mission. We have evidence in the New Testament that the churches sometimes sent out their gifted teachers, evangelists, and prophets to minister to other congregations and to begin new churches (Rom 16:1). It

---

88   E. Earle Ellis, "Coworkers, Paul and His" in *DPL*, ed. Gerald F. Hawthorne, Ralph P. Martin, and Daniel G. Reid (Downers Grove: InterVarsity, 1993), 183.

89   See William D. Mounce, *Pastoral Epistles*, WBC, vol. 46 (Nashville: Thomas Nelson, 2000), 187.

90   My view on the co-workers *from the local communities* is similar to Ollrog's understanding of this point (Ollrog, *Paulus und seine Mitarbeiter*).

appears that the churches would often send letters of commendation to authenticate such workers, while apostles themselves needed no such identifier (2 Cor 3:1–3). Furthermore, in confirmation of our thesis, Luke describes Apollos as traveling with such a letter (i.e., functioning in a role subsidiary to a local church [Acts 18:27]). Thus, it appears that we should not read too much into Paul's silence on Apollos' subsidiary relationship to a local church (e.g., 1 Cor 1:12; 3:4–9).

In conclusion, I would argue that any person's work in the advance of the gospel must be subsumed under either the category of "apostle" or "church." Paul's letters do not contain sufficient theological reflection to provide a basis for the ongoing mission of an "apostolic band." I admit, however, that the New Testament documents are not as explicit as one might like in discussing the Pauline co-workers.

CHAPTER 3

Paul's Instructions to Evangelize

Paul is not prone to offer commands that are unrelated to the particular situations that occasioned his letters. In fact, it is striking how ethically "incomplete" any one of his letters is in isolation from the broader Pauline corpus and New Testament witness. Only two of Paul's letters, for example, provide *detailed* instructions on the moral qualifications of church leaders (1 Tim 3:1–13; Titus 1:5–9). Along similar lines, Paul's epistles to the Galatians and Philippians offer no particular instructions on family relations, while 1 Corinthians is the only one of Paul's letters to mention the Lord's supper (1 Cor 10:21; 11:17–34). Indeed, even Paul's magisterial letter to the Romans fails to discuss in detail numerous topics we might expect from a more "general" letter (e.g., eschatology, Christology, church order).[1]

Given Paul's occasional approach to ethical instruction, we should be careful not to draw conclusions based on the frequency of his instructions regarding certain matters. Yet, if the apostle understood the church as having an active missionary role (as we maintained in the previous chapter), we would expect some evidence of this understanding in the form of Paul's explicit instructions to evangelize. The purpose of this chapter is to examine specific texts that could be classified as Pauline imperatives for the church to engage in mission. Due to the space limitations of this work, not all relevant texts can be examined.

Although it is reasonably clear from our study in the last chapter that Paul expected the dynamic gospel to continue to go forth from the churches, one might argue that this "going forth" need not entail active proclamation. While I have argued in chapter two that such an active role for the church is certainly implied in Paul's theology of the gospel, it is made more explicit in his commands. As we will see, Paul instructs the churches to declare the gospel, as well as to witness to it passively through their behavior. In the churches' active and passive witness (both of which Paul commands and expects), the gospel continues to run its triumphant course in the world. We will begin by looking at Paul's commands to witness actively and then turn to his commands for passive witness. It should be noted that this modern distinction between "active" and

---

1   W. G. Kümmel, *Introduction to the New Testament*, trans. Howard Clark Kee, rev. ed. (Nashville: Abingdon, 1975), 312.

"passive" witness would likely have seemed artificial to Paul; the apostle's own understanding of Christian witness was more holistic – involving, in one seamless fabric, the Christian's gospel-determined existence, behavior, and proclamation.

Pauline Commands to Witness Actively

In this section we will look at specific instructions in three of Paul's letters that indicate that the apostle expected the churches to proclaim the gospel actively, i.e. by taking the initiative to declare it to others and not simply through their behavior or in answering inquiries. The letters we will look at are: Philippians, Ephesians, and 1 Corinthians. The imperatives in 1 Corinthians entail both an active and passive dimension, which serves well as a transition to the next section of this chapter, "Pauline Commands to Witness Passively."

Paul's Instructions to the Philippians to Proclaim the Gospel

In Paul's letter to the Philippians, he speaks both of the Christians in his current setting (i.e., the city where he is writing this letter) and those in Philippi as proclaiming the gospel.[2] Though these references to the churches' proclamation have been questioned, a brief examination will confirm their validity.

After his opening prayer and thanksgiving in the epistle to the Philippians, Paul begins the body of the letter by presenting the bold evangelistic witness of the Christians in his current context as an example for his addressees. In Philippians 1:12–18, he writes,

> I want you to know, brothers [NRSV: beloved], that what has happened to me has actually helped to spread the gospel, so that it has become known throughout the whole imperial guard and to everyone else that my imprisonment is for Christ; and most of the brothers [NRSV: brothers and sisters], having been made

---

2   I hold to a Roman provenance of Philippians, but an Ephesian or Caesarean setting would not alter the conclusions of this study. For an overview of the different options, see Kümmel, *Introduction to the New Testament*, 324–32. For the Ephesian hypothesis, see Clayton R. Bowen, "Are Paul's Prison Letters from Ephesus?," *AJT* 24 (1920): 112–35, 277–87; Adolf Deissmann, "Zur ephesinischen Gefangenschaft des Apostels Paulus," in *Anatolian Studies Presented to Sir William Mitchell Ramsay*, ed. W. H. Buckler and W. M. Calder (Manchester: University of Manchester Press, 1923), 121–27. For the Caesarean hypothesis, see Lewis Johnson, "The Pauline Letters from Caesarea," *ExpTim* 68 (1956–57): 24–26. For a Corinthian provenance, see S. Dockx, "Lieu et date de l'épître aux Philippiens," *RB* 80 (1973): 230–46. And, for a recent defense of the Roman origin of the letter, see Peter T. O'Brien, *The Epistle to the Philippians: A Commentary on the Greek Text*, NIGTC (Grand Rapids: Eerdmans, 1991), 19–26.

confident in the Lord by my imprisonment, dare to speak the word with greater boldness and without fear.

Some proclaim Christ from envy and rivalry, but others from goodwill. These proclaim Christ out of love, knowing that I have been put here for the defense of the gospel; the others proclaim Christ out of selfish ambition, not sincerely but intending to increase my suffering in my imprisonment. What does it matter? Just this, that Christ is proclaimed in every way, whether out of false motives or true; and in that I rejoice.[3]

It would seem that this text presents irrefutable evidence that the church in the city from which Paul writes was proclaiming the gospel in the same way that Paul did. Yet, W. P. Bowers claims that to understand this text properly, one must distinguish between *individuals* whom God calls to missionize and the general congregational obligation, which is to evangelize only centripetally (passively).[4]

Bowers' distinction, however, does not appear to be supported by a careful analysis of the text. Paul gives no indication that the persons preaching in his current setting belong to a special class of missionary professionals. On the contrary, Paul's use of ἀδελφοί – the standard term to refer to ordinary members of the Christian community – militates against this thesis (Phil 1:14).[5] Moreover, Paul not only states that the brothers have been emboldened to preach, but that *most of the brothers* (τοὺς πλείονας τῶν ἀδελφῶν) have been so encouraged. These ordinary laypersons are described as "speaking the word of God" (λαλεῖν τὸν λόγον) or "preaching Christ" (κηρύσσειν τὸν χριστόν, καταγγέλλειν τὸν χριστόν) or engaging in activity "for the advance of the gospel" (εἰς προκοπὴν τοῦ εὐαγγελίου). This is the same terminology Paul uses to describe his own missionary proclamation.[6]

What, then, is Paul's purpose in describing the Christians in his current setting as active proclaimers of the gospel? To answer this question, we must first look back to 1:5, where Paul introduces the idea of the Philippians' partnership in the gospel's advance (τῇ κοινωνίᾳ ὑμῶν εἰς τὸ εὐαγγέλιον). Although the reference to "partnership" in 1:5 highlights the Philippians' financial contribution to Paul's ministry (4:15), it is sufficiently

---

3   I have altered the gender-neutral language of the NRSV to bring out the parallel in the original text: ἀδελφοί . . . ἀδελφῶν (vv. 12, 14).

4   Bowers, "Church and Mission," 104.

5   Paul has just referred to the Philippian congregation with the same term, ἀδελφοί (Phil 1:12), which should be understood as a reference to both men and women in the congregation. Both sexes in his current context were proclaiming the gospel boldly (v. 14).

6   E.g., Rom 10:8–15; 1 Cor 1:23; 2:1; 9:14; 15:12; 2 Cor 1:19; 4:5; 11:4; Col 1:28; 4:3–4; 1 Thess 2:2; cf. Rom 1:8.

broad to include a variety of activity for the progress of the gospel.[7] Thus, after introducing the idea of his addressees' partnership in the gospel's advance (1:5), Paul then provides the paranetic example of believers in his current context (vv. 12–18).[8]

While Paul introduces the Philippian church's partnership in the gospel in 1:5 and offers the evangelistic example of ordinary Christians in 1:12–18, it is not until 2:16 that Paul explicitly instructs the Philippian congregation to "hold forth the word of life" (λόγον ζωῆς ἐπέχοντες). That is, Paul tells the Philippian congregation to proclaim the gospel to non-Christian persons in hopes that they too will accept the life-giving message. Some scholars claim that ἐπέχοντες should be translated "hold fast," and thus they understand the passage as referring to the Philippians perseverance and faithfulness – but not their offering of the gospel to the non-believing world.[9] James Patrick Ware,

---

7   Because the word εὐαγγέλιον in Philippians 1:5 does not serve as the object of κηρύσσω or a similar verb, it should be understood as referring to "promoting" or "proclaiming" the gospel (cf. Rom 1:1, 9; 1 Cor 9:23; 2 Cor 2:12; 10:14; Gal 2:7; Phil 2:22; 4:15). Κοινωνία followed by εἰς and the accusative denotes *active* participation (Rom 15:26; 2 Cor 9:13) (O'Brien, *Epistle to the Philippians*, 62). Lightfoot remarks, "Here [in Phil 1:5], as the context shows, [κοινωνία] denotes cooperation in the widest sense, [the Philippians'] participation with the Apostle whether in sympathy or in suffering or in active labour or in any other way. At the same time their almsgiving was a signal instance of this cooperation, and seems to have been foremost in the Apostle's mind" (J. B. Lightfoot, *Saint Paul's Epistle to the Philippians* [London: Macmillan, 1913; reprint, Grand Rapids: Zondervan, 1953], 83). A similar view is adopted by Hawthorne, O'Brien, and Gnilka (Gerald F. Hawthorne, *Philippians*, WBC, vol. 43 [Waco, TX: Word, 1983], 19; O'Brien, *Epistle to the Philippians*, 61–63; Joachim Gnilka, *Der Philipperbrief*, 2nd ed., HTKNT 10.3 [Freiburg: Herder, 1976], 44–45). Heinrich Seesemann, however, understands the contested phrase (τῇ κοινωνίᾳ ὑμῶν εἰς τὸ εὐαγγέλιον) passively, in reference to the Philippians' adherence to the gospel (H. Seesemann, *Der Begriff* KOINΩNIA *im Neuen Testament,* Beihefte zur Zeitschrift für die neutestamentliche Wissenschaft und die Kunde der älteren Kirche 14 [Giessen: Töpelmann, 1933], 73–83; cf. Friedrich Hauck, "κοινός...," in *TDNT*, 3:805). The "dynamic" quality of the noun εὐαγγέλιον throughout Paul's letter to the Philippians, however, seems to undercut Seesemann's interpretation (1:7, 12, 16, 27; 2:22; 4:3, 15) (O'Brien, *Epistle to the Philippians*, 62).

8   Paul's personal delight in the gospel's advance also compelled him to discuss the subject (Phil 1:18).

9   Translations and scholars that favor understanding ἐπέχοντες as "holding fast" (or similar expressions) include the following: RSV; NRSV; NASB; Vern Sheridan Poythress, "'Hold Fast' versus 'Hold Out' in Philippians 2:16," *WTJ* 63 (2002): 45–53; Erich Haupt, "Der Brief an die Philipper," in *Die Gefangenschaftsbriefe*, 7th ed., MeyerK, vol. 9 (Göttingen: Vandenhoeck & Ruprecht, 1902), 98–99; J. Hugh Michael, *The Epistle of Paul to the Philippians*, MNTC (New York: Harper, 1927),

however, has convincingly shown that "hold forth" is in fact the correct translation of this word.[10] Evaluating the current discussion over ἐπέχοντες, Ware writes, "The debate has become arbitrary and ossified, as the vast majority of modern interpreters are entirely dependent on dictionary entries for their knowledge of the term, and no original research on the word as used by ancient authors has been offered in over a century."[11] Ware then provides an extensive study of the extra-biblical literature and concludes, "It can be stated categorically that the verb ἐπέχω does not bear the sense *hold fast* in any ancient passage, and the etymology and usage of the word . . . preclude such a meaning"[12] For example, in Dio Chrysostom's *Twelfth, or Olympic, Discourse* (12.31) and in Philostratus *Imagines* (1.2.2), ἐπέχω clearly means to hold forth

---

107–08; Martin Dibelius, *An die Thessalonicher I II, An die Philipper*, 3rd rev. ed., HNT 11 (Tübingen: Mohr, 1937), 82; Otto Glombitza, "Mit Furcht und Zittern: Zum Verständnis von Philip. II 12," *NovT* 3 (1959): 105; Edvin Larsson, *Christus als Vorbild: Eine Untersuchung zu den paulinischen Tauf- und Eikontexten*, Acta Seminarii Neotestamentici Upsaliensis XXIII–1962 (Uppsala: Almquist & Wiksells, 1962), 270–71; Otto Merk, *Handeln aus Glaben: Die Motivierungen der paulinischen Ethik*, Marburger Theologische Studien 5 (Marburg: Elwert, 1968), 185; Ralph P. Martin, *Philippians*, NCB (Grand Rapids: Eerdmans; London: Marshall, Morgan & Scott, 1976; reprint, 1989), 106 (page citations are to the reprint edition); Gnilka, *Der Philipperbrief*, 153; Hawthorne, *Philippians*, 103–04; Wolfgang Schenk, *Die Philipperbriefe des Paulus* (Stuttgart: Kohlhammer, 1984), 223; O'Brien, *Epistle to the Philippians*, 297; Moisés Silva, *Philippians*, BECNT (Grand Rapids: Baker, 1992), 146. Scholars and translations that favor understanding ἐπέχοντες as "holding forth" include the following: NIV; NEB; JB; KJV; John Eadie, *A Commentary on the Greek Text of the Epistle of Paul to the Philippians* (London: Richard Griffin, 1859), 142–44; Lightfoot, *Saint Paul's Epistle to the Philippians*, 118; F. W. Beare, *A Commentary on the Epistle to the Philippians*, HNTC (New York: Harper and Brothers, 1959), 92–93; Ernst Lohmeyer, *Der Brief an die Philipper*, 14th ed., MeyerK, vol. 9.1 (Göttingen: Vandenhoeck & Ruprecht, 1974), 109–10; I-Jin Loh and Eugene A. Nida, *A Handbook on Paul's Letter to the Philippians*, UBS Handbook Series (New York: United Bible Societies, 1977), 71; F. F. Bruce, *Philippians*, GNC (San Francisco: Harper & Row, 1983), 60–61.

10   BDAG's extra-biblical citations in favor of "hold fast" are misleading. For example, ἐπέχω in *T. Joseph* 15.3 and Josephus *B.J.* 1.230 does not mean "hold fast," but to check or stop oneself. Similarly, in Plutarch, *Otho* 17.3 and Diodorus Siculus 12.27.3, ἐπέχω is used in its common intransitive sense "with regard to rumors, commotions or moods which *spread* or *come over* peoples, cities or crowds" (Ware, "Holding Forth," 299). Cf. BDAG, 362. The four other New Testament occurrences of ἐπέχω are intransitive, and thus provide little assistance in understanding Philippians 2:16 (Luke 14:7; Acts 3:5; 19:22; 1 Tim 4:16).

11   Ware, "Holding Forth," 290–91.

12   Ibid., 299–300.

or offer something to some person or thing.[13] Likewise, in Philippians 2:16, λόγον ζωῆς ἐπέχοντες ("holding forth the word of life") is an offering of the gospel to those who do not presently adhere to it – a proclamation of the gospel by the Philippian church.

This understanding is further confirmed by the broader context of our contested word. The surrounding verses read,

> Do all things without murmuring and arguing, so that you may be blameless and innocent, children of God without blemish in the midst of a crooked and perverse generation, in which you shine like stars in the world, holding forth the word of life, so that I can boast on the day of Christ that I did not run or labor in vain. (Phil 2:14–16)[14]

It should first be noted that we are dealing with hortatory material here. The governing finite verb of this long sentence is the *command* to do (ποιεῖτε) all things without murmuring or arguing. The purpose of this "doing" is so that the Philippian Christians will be godly (ἵνα γένησθε ἄμεμπτοι κτλ.). As holy children of God, the Philippians are to bring light to "a crooked and perverse generation," just as the heavenly luminaries enlighten the universe (v. 15).[15] This image of the people of God as luminous entities often appears in second temple Jewish literature as an expression of the community's attractive force.[16] In Philippians 2:14–16, however, Paul employs the image with an active, evangelistic meaning – a point he makes clear by the following circumstantial participle. The church at Philippi is described as extending the gospel to those outside their community (λόγον ζωῆς ἐπέχοντες). The participle ἐπέχοντες probably acts epexegetically, expressing the manner in which the Philippian Christians are to "shine" (φαίνεσθε). While the participle ἐπέχοντες is not actually an imperative, the governing finite verb ποιεῖτε imparts an imperatival sense to all of 2:14–16a. In 2:16b, Paul says that the church should do all the things mentioned in 2:14–16a "*so that* [he] can boast on the day of Christ that [he] did not run or labor in vain" (my translation and emphasis). The fact that this boast remains contingent on the Philippians'

---

13   For further examples, see Ware's detailed discussion of ἐπέχω (Ware, "Holding Forth," 289–303).

14   My translation.

15   Cf. Matt 5:16; Luke 16:8; John 12:36; Rom 13:11–14; Eph 5:8–16; 1 Thess 5:4–5.

16   Isa 42:6 [LXX]; 49:6 [LXX]; Rom 2:17–20; Tob 13:11–13 [Sinaiticus]; Wis 18:4; Philo, *De Virtutibus* 179; *Testament of Levi* 14.3–4; Justin Martyr *Dialogue with Trypho* 122; *Sibylline Oracles, Fragments* 1.25–35. See Ware, "Holding Forth," 104–62. When the Qumran documents refer to community members as "sons of light," evangelistic relationships with outsiders do not seem to be in view (e.g., 1QS 1:9; 2:16; 1 QM 13:5, 16). The "sons of light" are, however, depicted as having a declaratory role – albeit, one directed at their existing community (1 QM 13:8–10).

continued obedience to Paul's instructions in 2:14–16a demonstrates that the participle ἐπέχοντες has an imperatival sense.[17] Thus, we find in Philippians 2:16 explicit instructions from Paul for the church to evangelize.

The question arises – given the infrequency of Paul's explicit references to the church's proclaiming task – can we pinpoint a reason the apostle might instruct his converts so forthrightly in this letter? It appears that the opposition and persecution, which the Philippian believers were facing, threatened to diminish the church's verbal witness (Phil 1:27–30; 4:5; cf. Wis 2:19). Thus, Paul thought it necessary to remind them to speak the gospel fearlessly (Phil 1:14, 19–20, 28–30; 2:16; 4:5).[18] One should not conclude, however, that opposition always intimidated the early Christians – as illustrated by Paul's comment that believers in his current context have been further emboldened by the threat of persecution (Phil 1:14; cf. 1 Thess 1:1–8).

Paul's Instructions to the Ephesians to Proclaim the Gospel

Paul's letter to the Ephesians also demonstrates the apostle's expectation that the churches would be active in proclaiming the gospel.[19] The text we are mainly concerned with is Ephesians 6:15, but we must first understand how this verse fits within the context of the letter.

Paul's epistle to the Ephesians can be divided into two broad sections. Chapters 1–3 serves as an extended thanksgiving with heavy doctrinal content, followed in chapters 4–6 by paranesis dealing with numerous topics of timely significance to Paul's addressees – church unity, spiritual gifts, living according to the "new self," practical injunctions about the old and new life, speech, sexual morality, living as children of the light, wise and spirit-filled living, household relationships, and standing firm in spiritual battle and in constant prayer.[20] It is in the final exhortative section of his letter (Eph 6:10–20) that Paul employs military imagery to instruct the Ephesian Christians to live victoriously in the cosmic struggle against evil. The only way to be victorious in spiritual battle, says Paul, is to put on the armor that God has provided – the armor of truth, righteousness, faith, salvation, etc.

The element of this armor with which we are mainly concerned is found in

---

17 It would be wrong, however, to call ἐπέχοντες an imperatival participle. See Wallace, *Greek Grammar beyond the Basics*, 650–52; MHT, 3:343; H. G. Meecham, "The Use of the Participle for the Imperative in the New Testament," *ExpTim* 58 (1946–47): 207–08; C. K. Barrett, "The Imperatival Participle," *ExpTim* 59 (1947–48): 165–66.

18 Ware makes this observation (Ware, "Holding Forth," 302–03).

19 For a missions study of the whole letter, see Edwin D. Roels, *God's Mission: The Epistle to the Ephesians in Mission Perspective* (Grand Rapids: Eerdmans, 1962).

20 My wording in this sentence is dependent on the outline by Andrew T. Lincoln, *Ephesians*, WBC, vol. 42 (Dallas: Word, 1990), xliii.

Ephesians 6:15. Here, Paul describes accoutrements which relate to the Christian soldier's feet: καὶ ὑποδησάμενοι τοὺς πόδας ἐν ἑτοιμασίᾳ τοῦ εὐαγγελίου τῆς εἰρήνης. The translation of one Greek word in this verse is debated (ἑτοιμασίᾳ), so we must first provide a correct English rendering of the text before we determine if this verse asserts an evangelistic role for the church(es) in Ephesus.[21]

So, what does the term ἑτοιμασία mean? The word is predominantly used to mean "readiness," "preparedness," or "preparation."[22] Contrary to some claims, ἑτοιμασία never means "firm footing" or "steadfastness" in the LXX or New Testament.[23] Yet the word can be used to describe the foundation of a building (Ezra 2:68; Zech 5:11), base of an altar or throne (Ezra 3:3; Ps 89:14 [LXX 88:15]) or a governmental position (Dan 11:7, 20, 21 [Theodotion]). In all these instances, however, the *preparedness* of the position or foundation is still determinative.[24]

Lacking any overriding contextual reasons to the contrary, ἑτοιμασία in Ephesian 6:15 should be translated in continuity with its meaning elsewhere in the New Testament and Septuagint – i.e., as "readiness" or "preparedness."

21　Scholars who read Ephesians 6:15 as evangelistic include the following: Leon Morris, *Expository Reflections on the Letter to the Ephesians* (Grand Rapids: Baker, 1994), 206; Clinton E. Arnold, *Power and Magic: The Concept of Power in Ephesians* (Cambridge: Cambridge University Press, 1989; Grand Rapids: Baker, 1992), 111; idem, *Powers of Darkness: Principalities and Powers in Paul's Letters* (Downers Grove: InterVarsity, 1992), 157; Swigchem, *Het missionair karakter*, 128; J. Blauw, *The Missionary Nature of the Church*, 102; Otto Weber, "Kirchenmission? Eine Mission in gegliederter Vielfalt," *EMZ* 17 (1960): 136; Heinrich Schlier, *Der Brief an die Epheser: Ein Kommentar* (Dusseldorf: Patmos, 1957), 296; Joachim Gnilka, *Der Epheserbrief*, Theologischer Kommentar zum Neuen Testament 10.2 (Freiburg: Herder, 1971), 311–12; Josef Ernst, *Die Briefe an die Philipper, an Philemon, an die Kolosser, an die Epheser* (Regensburg: Friedrich Pustet, 1974), 400; A. Oepke, "ὅπλον...," in *TDNT*, 5:312. Scholars who do not see Ephesians 6:15 as referring to the proclamation of the gospel include the following: Heinrich August Wilhelm Meyer, "Critical and Exegetical Hand-Book to the Epistle to the Ephesians," in *Meyer's Commentary on the New Testament: Galatians and Ephesians*, rev. and ed. William P. Dickson, trans. Maurice J. Evans (New York: Funk & Wagnalls, 1884), 543–45; Lincoln, *Ephesians*, 448–49; T. K. Abbott, *A Critical and Exegetical Commentary on the Epistles to the Ephesians and to the Colossians*, 185; William Hendriksen, *New Testament Commentary: Exposition of Ephesians* (Grand Rapids: Baker, 1967), 277; and Edwin D. Roels, *God's Mission*, 218–19.

22　See Pss 10:17 (LXX 9:38); 65:9 (LXX 64:10); Nah 2:3 (LXX 2:4); Wis 13:12; *Ep. Arist.* 182; cf. Josephus *Ant.* 10.1.2 [ἑτοιμός].

23　Lincoln agrees (*Ephesians*, 449). Contra Amalric F. Buscarlet, "The 'Preparation' of the Gospel of Peace," *ExpTim* 9 (1897–98), 38–40.

24　Meyer, "Ephesians," 544.

What, then, does it mean to have one's feet fitted with the "readiness of the gospel of peace"? What is one ready or prepared to do? How does the gospel relate to this readiness?

Paul's language in Ephesians 6:15 appears to allude to Isaiah 52:7, "How beautiful upon the mountains are the feet of the messenger who announces peace, who brings good news, who announces salvation, who says to Zion, 'Your God reigns.'" Paul obviously saw this text as descriptive of the evangelistic task, for he employs it elsewhere in a clear reference to the apostolic preaching of the gospel (Rom 10:15).[25] In the Old Testament passage that Paul quotes (Isa 52:7), the prophet Isaiah speaks of a future day when Israel (Judah) will return from Babylonian captivity to settle peacefully again in her homeland (Isa 52:1–12).[26] Israel's present oppressors will then be the ones suffering under the Lord's wrath (Isa 51:22–23). In the midst of this vision of joyful restoration, the prophet Isaiah commends a paradigmatic messenger who proclaims "peace," "good news," and "salvation" to Jerusalem; this messenger is described as having "beautiful feet." That is, the messenger's approaching feet are a synecdoche, representing both the herald and his joyful announcement of salvation.

Another Old Testament passage that Paul might be alluding to in Ephesians 6:15 is Nahum 1:15–2:3 (LXX 2:1–2:4). This text has virtually been ignored in discussions of Eph 6:15 – an especially odd oversight since the passage both announces the "feet" of one bringing good news and employs the term ἑτοιμασία in connection with military imagery. Similar to the Isaianic passage, the text in Nahum celebrates the announcement of God's deliverance of Israel from the hands of enemy oppressors (in this case, the Assyrians).[27]

While the passages in both Isaiah and Nahum discuss the salvation of Israel, the Isaianic text in particular points forward to a greater deliverance. Isaiah speaks of God as accomplishing salvation for *all nations* (Isa 52:10) through his suffering servant (Isa 52:13–53:12), which will result in God's supernatural provision of descendents for the "barren woman" Israel (Isa 54:1).

Beyond Isaiah's references to a coming messianic deliverer, there are other reasons that the apostle might see these passages in both Nahum and Isaiah as

---

25 Rom 10:15 reads, "And how are they to proclaim [the Lord] unless they are sent? As it is written, 'How beautiful are the feet of those who bring good news!'" Paul understands "the messenger" (singular) in Isa 52:7 as paradigmatic and thus shifts to the plural, i.e., *"those* who bring good news."

26 A. S. Herbert writes, "[Isa 52:7–12] is a hymn which celebrates the LORD's triumphant return to Zion leading his people from captivity into a new freedom. Jerusalem is to be liberated; the exiles will bring back the sacred vessels in readiness for the restoration of the temple worship" (A. S. Herbert, *The Book of the Prophet Isaiah: Chapters 40–66*, CBC [Cambridge: Cambridge University Press, 1975], 106).

27 See Nah 1:8, 14; 2:1–2; 3:18.

descriptive of preaching the gospel. Both texts present God as the victor over enemy powers. God is the one who has brought peace and blessing, which must be joyfully proclaimed. Yet, one may rightly ask, why does Paul choose to touch on this subject at this point in his letter? Perhaps, as Paul discusses God's defeat of cosmic enemy powers (Eph 1:3, 20–23; 6:12–13; cf. 2:14–17), his mind turns to Old Testament texts that speak of God's mighty deliverance and the subsequent proclamation of that salvation. The combination of these Old Testament texts with Paul's current concerns may help explain what influenced Paul to speak so explicitly at this point about the church's readiness to proclaim the gospel.

Whatever the source of Paul's reflections, it appears that the NRSV offers a correct translation of Ephesians 6:15 as, "As shoes for your feet put on whatever will make you ready to proclaim the gospel of peace." This imperative to evangelize is further confirmed by two other elements in the immediate context. First, Paul's reference in Ephesians 6:17 to Christians wielding the sword of the Spirit ("which is the word of God") also has possible evangelistic connotations. The weapon described here, the μάχαιρα, was a short, sharp sword used in close-range offensive combat.[28] This image of the "word of God" as an offensive weapon ties in with Paul's frequent references to the "word of God" as a dynamic force, which inevitably advances.[29] For a Christian to wield the "sword of the Spirit" appears to mean that a Christian would so adhere to and announce the gospel that the "word of God" would advance in its victorious course.[30] In reference to Ephesians 6:17, Clinton Arnold remarks, "The Word of God and the work of the Spirit are the means by which the people of God step out in defiance of Satan and rob his domain."[31]

A second indication that the church's evangelistic proclamation is in view in Ephesians 6:15 and 6:17 is Paul's request in verses 18–20 that the Ephesians pray for his fearless proclamation of the gospel. In the two other instances where Paul requests prayer for his evangelistic mission, the apostle also mentions a missionary role for the congregation he addresses (Col 4:2–4, 5–6; cf. 2 Thess 2:16–17; 3:1–2). Paul seems unwilling to request prayer for his gospel preaching without also noting the missionary work of his churches. Thus, it appears that in Ephesians, as in Philippians, Paul instructs the church to be an active witness.

---

28 As distinguished from the ῥομφαία, or long sword (Lincoln, *Ephesians*, 451).

29 E.g., 1 Cor 9:12; 14:36; Col 1:25; 1 Thess 1:6–8; 2:13; 2 Thess 3:1. See chapter two.

30 Lincoln reads Ephesians 6:17 similarly, as asserting that "the gospel conquers the alienating hostile powers and brings about God's saving purposes" (Lincoln, *Ephesians*, 451).

31 Arnold, *Powers of Darkness*, 157.

Paul's Instructions to the Corinthians to Evangelize[32]

In numerous places, Paul exhorts the recipients of his letters to imitate him, or the concept of imitation is present.[33] Such calls to imitate a leader or teacher were not unusual in the ancient world, and just as the modern English injunction "imitate me" is inherently ambiguous, only the context of an ancient command clarifies what sort of imitation is expected.[34] That is, when Paul or another ancient leader told his or her followers, "μιμηταί μου γίνεσθε," the context of this statement clarified the extent and purpose of the desired imitation.[35] Specifically with Paul, we are concerned with what aspects of his life he expects his converts to imitate. Does the imitative behavior Paul desires

---

32   The following discussion of imitation language appears in slightly altered format in my 2001 article in *Journal of the Evangelical Theological Society*. It reappears here with permission of the editor of *JETS*. A more recent study that both agrees with and cites my *JETS* article is Andrew Cowan's "The Glory of God, Evangelism, and the Imitation of Paul," *Stulos Theological Journal* 12 (2004): 57-67.

33   All Pauline uses of μιμέομαι or (συμ-) μιμητής: 1 Cor 4:16; 11:1; Phil 3:17; 1 Thess 1:6; 2:14; 2 Thess 3:7, 9; Eph 5:1. Outside of Paul, the only other New Testament occurrences of μιμέομαι (or cognates) are found in Hebrews 6:12; 13:7; and 3 John 11. For the Pauline *concept* of imitation, see, e.g., 1 Cor 7:6–7; 10:31–11:1; Gal 4:12–20; Phil 4:9; 1 Tim 1:15–17; 2 Tim 1:13; 2:2; 3:10; Acts 20:35. It is commonly noted that Paul does not mention imitation of himself in letters to churches which he did not found (e.g., in Romans or Colossians).

34   Of course, the semantic ranges of μιμέομαι and μιμητής do not overlap exactly with their modern English counterparts, e.g., note the Greek philosophical and artistic usage of μιμέομαι (W. Michaelis, "μιμέομαι...," in *TDNT*, 4:659–63); Brant unconvincingly tries to impose this specialized philosophical meaning of μιμέομαι on Paul's usage (Brant, "The Place of *mimēsis* in Paul's Thought," 285–300). It should be noted that the English word "imitation" does perhaps more commonly carry negative connotations of "mimicry" than its Greek counterpart (see E. Larsson, "μιμέομαι...," *EDNT*, 2:428–30; Louw and Nida §41.44; §41.45; Willis Peter De Boer, *The Imitation of Paul: An Exegetical Study* [Kampen: Kok, 1962], 211).

35   Though few ancient speakers or writers prescribe imitation of themselves, there seems to be no conceptual difference between Paul's injunctions and others' frequent appeals to imitate a third party (e.g., *T. Benj.* 3.1; 4.1; Seneca *Epistulae Morales* 6.5–6; 7.6–9; 11.8–10; Dio Chrysostom *Discourse* 55.4–5; for first-person appeals, see 2 Macc 6:27–28; 4 Macc 9:23; cf. Josephus *Ant.* 1.109). So Ernest Best (*Paul and His Converts* [Edinburgh: T. & T. Clark, 1988], 68–70); contra Adele Reinhartz ("On the Meaning of the Pauline Exhortation: '*mimētai mou ginesthe* – Become Imitators of Me,'" *SR* 16 [1987]: 395–96). Paul can be so bold because of his confidence in the gospel to shape the communities he founded, his apostolic authority, and his ultimate dependence upon Christ (1 Cor 11:1; Phil 1:5–6; 1 Thess 1:4–8). Cf. Abraham J. Malherbe, *Paul and the Thessalonians: The Philosophic Tradition of Pastoral Care* (Philadelphia: Fortress, 1987), 58.

from his congregations include an emulation of his missionary concern and activity?

Pauline imitation texts have received limited attention in recent years.[36] Even less regard has been given to possible evangelistic meanings in Paul's references to imitation. Although numerous scholars have briefly noted an evangelistic dimension to the Pauline imitation texts,[37] the topic has only recently been the subject of more extensive debate. On the one side, W. P.

---

36   Significant monographs which address the subject include: Elizabeth A. Castelli, *Imitating Paul: A Discourse of Power*, LCBI (Louisville: Westminster/John Knox, 1991); Best, *Paul and His Converts*, esp. 59–72; Benjamin Fiore, *The Function of Personal Example in the Socratic and Pastoral Epistles*, AnBib 105 (Rome: Biblical Institute, 1986); Mark Edward Hopper, "The Pauline Concept of Imitation," (Ph.D. diss., Southern Baptist Theological Seminary, 1983); John Howard Schütz, *Paul and the Anatomy of Apostolic Authority*, SNTSMS 26 (Cambridge: Cambridge University Press, 1975), esp. 226–32; Pedro Gutiérrez, *La Paternité spirituelle selon Saint Paul*, Ebib (Paris: J. Gabalda, 1968), esp. 178–88; Hans Dieter Betz, *Nachfolge und Nachahmung Jesu Christi im Neuen Testament*, BHT 37 (Tübingen: Mohr, 1967); Donald Manly Williams, "The Imitation of Christ in Paul with Special Reference to Paul as Teacher" (Ph.D. diss., Columbia University, 1967); Ceslas Spicq, *Théologie Morale du Nouveau Testament*, Ebib, 2 vols. (Paris: J. Gabalda, 1965), esp. 2:720–30; De Boer, *Imitation of Paul*; Anselm Schulz, *Nachfolgen und Nachahmen: Studien über das Verhältnis der neutestamentlichen Jüngerschaft zur urchristlichen Vorbildethik*, SANT 6 (Munich: Kösel, 1962), esp. 308–31; E. J. Tinsley, *The Imitation of God in Christ: An Essay on the Biblical Basis of Christian Spirituality* (London: SCM, 1960), 138–40.

37   Especially with 1 Cor 11:1 and 1 Thess 1:6–8. For example, see Betz, *Nachfolge und Nachahmung*, 143–44; Andrew D. Clarke, "'Be Imitators of Me': Paul's Model of Leadership," *TynBul* 49 (1998): 337–38; Hans Conzelmann, *1 Corinthians*, Hermeneia (Philadelphia: Fortress, 1975), 92 [1 Cor 4:16]; Schütz, *Paul and the Anatomy of Apostolic Authority*, 227–29; Gordon D. Fee, *The First Epistle to the Corinthians*, NICNT (Grand Rapids: Eerdmans, 1987), 489–90; Reinhartz, "Pauline Exhortation," 398–99; Malherbe, *Paul and the Thessalonians*, 54; Jerome Murphy-O'Connor, "Freedom or the Ghetto (*I Cor.*, VIII, 1–13; X, 23–XI, 1)," *RB* 85 (1978): 573; De Boer, *Imitation of Paul*, 158, 207; Stanley, "'Become Imitators of Me,'" 874; Williams, "Imitation of Christ in Paul," 241–42; 351–55; Brant, "The Place of *mimēsis* in Paul's Thought," 289–92; Linda L. Belleville, "'Imitate Me, Just as I Imitate Christ': Discipleship in the Corinthian Correspondence," in *Patterns of Discipleship in the New Testament*, MNTS, ed. Richard N. Longenecker (Grand Rapids: Eerdmans, 1996), 126; Derek Newton, *Deity and Diet: The Dilemma of Sacrificial Food at Corinth*, JSNTSup 169 (Sheffield: Sheffield Academic Press, 1998), 380–81; Tinsley, *Imitation of God in Christ*, 138; Edwin Judge, "The Teacher as Moral Exemplar in Paul and in the Inscriptions of Ephesus," in *In the Fullness of Time: Biblical Studies in Honour of Archbishop Donald Robinson*, ed. David Peterson and John Pryor (Homebush West, NSW [Australia]: Lancer, 1992), 196.

Bowers claims that Paul's commands to imitate him have been wrongly interpreted to support an active missionary role for the church.[38] On the other side, Peter T. O'Brien offers the Pauline imitation texts as a theological foundation for the church's missionary obligation.[39] In an attempt to help settle this debate, we will now examine Paul's commands to imitate him and related passages in 1 Corinthians (imitation commands: 1 Cor 4:16; 11:1; related passages: 7:12–16; 14:23–25). Our objective is to discover, according to Paul's explicit indications, whether his commands to imitate him in 1 Corinthians include an evangelistic component.

FIRST CORINTHIANS 4:16

Of Paul's two commands to imitate him in 1 Corinthians, the first appears in chapter 4, verse 16. Let us now look at this passage in context. 1 Corinthians 4:14–17 reads,

> I am not writing this to make you ashamed, but to admonish you as my beloved children. For though you might have ten thousand guardians in Christ, you do not have many fathers.[40] Indeed, in Christ Jesus I became your father through the gospel. I appeal to you, then, be imitators of me. For this reason I sent you Timothy, who is my beloved and faithful child in the Lord, to remind you of my ways in Christ Jesus, as I teach them everywhere in every church.

This short passage is so general in tone that it is difficult to delimit further

---

38 I.e., Paul conceived only of a passive mission of attraction for his churches (Bowers, "Church and Mission," 92–95). The following scholars reject or ignore an evangelistic intent in one or more of the imitation texts: Stephen Chambers, "Paul, His Converts, and Mission in 1 Corinthians," 147-55; Victor Paul Furnish, *Theology and Ethics in Paul* (Nashville: Abingdon, 1968), 218–23; Castelli, *Imitating Paul,* 89–117; Stephen E. Fowl, "Imitation of Paul/of Christ," in *DPL*, ed. Gerald F. Hawthorne and Ralph P. Martin (Downers Grove: InterVarsity, 1993), 428–31; D. A. Carson, "Pauline Inconsistency: Reflections on I Corinthians 9.19–23 and Galatians 2.11–14," *Churchman* 100 (1986): 16 (concerning 1 Cor 11:1).

39 O'Brien, *Gospel and Mission,* 83–107; Also note Odo Haas's discussion of "Die Person des Paulus als Missionsmittel." (*Paulus der Missionar: Ziel, Grundsätze und Methoden der Missionstätigkeit des Apostels Paulus nach seinen eigenen Aussagen* [Münsterschwarzach: Vier-Türme, 1971], 69–79). Cf. Swigchem, *Het missionair karakter,* 109–17.

40 Paul's understanding of himself as his converts' spiritual father provides a basis for his appeals to imitation. See 2 Cor 6:13; 12:14; Gal 4:19; Phil 2:22; 1 Thess 2:7, 11; 1 Tim 1:2, 18; 2 Tim 1:2; 2:1; Titus 1:4; Phlm 10; cf. John 5:19; 8:39, 44; *b. Sanh.* 19b. Also see Gutiérrez, *La Paternité spirituelle selon Saint Paul,* 179–81; Best, *Paul and His Converts,* 29–58; Fiore, *Function of Personal Example,* 175; Williams, "Imitation of Christ in Paul," 165; Castelli, *Imitating Paul,* 100–01.

what sort of imitative behavior is expected.[41] The broader context, however, does give some indication. Paul has just finished chiding the Corinthians for their undue adulation of certain leaders, celebration of worldly wisdom, and triumphalism (1:10–4:13).[42] In contrast to the Corinthians, the apostles are threatened, viewed as fools, mocked as weak, persecuted, and even considered "the rubbish of the world" (4:8–13).[43] It is this correct embodiment of Christian leadership and existence, as typified in the apostles' acceptance of worldly disapproval and suffering, that Paul hopes his converts will imitate. Humility and the way of the cross are diametrically opposed to the triumphalism of the Corinthians.[44] Paul thus aptly terms his "gospel lifestyle" as his "ways in Christ

---

41   Referring to the passage, Boykin Sanders remarks, "Paul offers almost no guidance that would enable us to ascertain specifically what aspects of his life are to be imitated. The lack of specificity on Paul's part has vexed many interpreters of 1 Cor 4:16" (B. Sanders, "Imitating Paul: 1 Cor 4:16," *HTR* 74 [1981]: 353). Castelli, drawing on Foucault, argues that Paul's vagueness is intentional and furthers his exercise of power to enforce sameness (*Imitating Paul*, 110). In response, see Anthony C. Thiselton's excursus on "Mimesis and Alleged Paternal Authoritarianism (4:15–16)" in *The First Epistle to the Corinthians: A Commentary on the Greek Text*, NIGTC (Grand Rapids: Eerdmans; Carlisle: Paternoster, 2000), 371–73. See L. Belleville for a concise presentation of the views held by major commentators as to what Paul meant by "be imitators of me" in 1 Cor 4:16 (Belleville, "'Imitate Me, Just as I Imitate Christ,'" 122–23).

42   First Corinthians 1:10–4:21 is best understood as a single unit, with 4:14–21 as the concluding paragraph. This understanding of 1 Corinthians' structure is widely accepted. E.g., see Conzelmann, *1 Corinthians*, 30; C. K. Barrett, *A Commentary on the First Epistle to the Corinthians* (New York: Harper & Row, 1968), 28; Fee, *First Corinthians*, 183; Raymond F. Collins, *First Corinthians*, SP, vol. 7 (Collegeville, MN: Liturgical Press, 1999), 195. Note the framing brackets: Παρακαλῶ δὲ ὑμᾶς (1:10) . . . παρακαλῶ οὖν ὑμᾶς (4:16).

43   Possibly we should view the ταῦτα of 4:14 (i.e., the "things" Paul is writing with which he does not wish to shame the Corinthians) as referring to the entire discussion of Paul's and Apollos' servant ministry which begins at 3:5. Boykin Sanders reads the text this way and bases his interpretation largely on the parallel ταῦτα of 1 Cor 4:6 and 4:14 ("Imitating Paul," 353–54). In the end, according to Sanders, Paul is exhorting the Corinthians to have a selfless communal concern which excludes divisiveness (ibid., 361–63).

44   W. D. Spencer advocates a similar reading. He writes, "What has [Paul] just told us are 'his ways'? They are the list of sufferings. Paul's suffering is both the content and the methodology of his teaching. By suffering he seeks to remove all obstacles in his hearers' process of learning. Though entitled to material benefits (1 Cor 9:11), he forgoes them if necessary to promote God's reign and undergoes hunger instead (9:12b; 6:3). Indeed, suffering can be substitutionary, taking the place of his learners or providing the payment of the civil price for bringing them the gospel (Eph 3:1, 13; Col 1:24; 2 Tim 2:10). It can be a tool for encouragement, helping the learners to speak more boldly on their own (Phil 1:12–14). It encourages prayer

Jesus," since the Lord who suffered and died on behalf of humanity is in some sense pictured in them (1 Cor 1:23–24; 2:2).[45]

It is noteworthy that the persecutions which the apostles endure result from speaking openly "the foolishness of the cross" (1:18; 4:8–13). For Paul, opposition and suffering are almost always related to his proclamation of the gospel.[46] If the Corinthians are to imitate Paul by enduring suffering, mocking, and persecution, it is not "suffering for suffering's sake." For the Corinthians, as for the apostles, their open adherence to and proclamation of the "foolishness of the cross" will result in the world's disapproval and opposition.[47]

In Paul's absence, Timothy, by his exemplary life and verbal explanation, is to set before the Corinthians the apostle's ways in Christ that correspond which his teaching (4:17).[48] The primary example that Timothy is bringing to the Corinthians is the same one that his "father in the gospel" models – holding *to* and holding *out* the gospel amidst opposition.[49]

FIRST CORINTHIANS 11:1

Paul's other imitation command occurs in chapter 11, verse 1. The injunction to imitation appears at the close of Paul's response to the Corinthians' division

---

participation in Paul's ministry (2 Cor 1:11)" (William David Spencer, "The Power in Paul's Teaching [1 Cor 4:9–20]," *JETS* 32 [1989]: 57).

45 B. Sanders, "Imitating Paul," 356.

46 Note 1 Cor 16:8–9, "But I will stay in Ephesus until Pentecost, for a wide door for effective work has opened to me, and there are many adversaries." Also see Acts 9:15–16; 20:23–24; Rom 8:36; 1 Cor 15:30–32; 2 Cor 1:8–9; 2:14–3:3; 4:7–12; 6:4–10; 11:23–33; Phil 1:14–18; Col 4:3; 1 Thess 3:2–4; 2 Tim 1:8; 2:3; 3:10–12; 4:5. See chapter four for a more detailed study of the relationship between suffering and evangelism in Paul's thought.

47 Compare Paul's descriptions of the Thessalonians, who imitate him, the Lord, and the churches in Judea by their suffering in proclaiming the gospel (1 Thess 1:6–8; 2:14–16; 2 Thess 1:4–10). Brant rightly observes, "The equation of 'imitation' with suffering affliction ignores the fact that the Thessalonians were engaged in some activity that incurred the opposition of others" ("The Place of *mimēsis* in Paul's Thought," 292).

48 Gutiérrez detects an allusion to a common Hebrew idiom here (חלך בדרך) (e.g., see Judg 2:17; 1 Sam 8:3–5; Prov 2:13; 3:23) (Gutiérrez, *La Paternité spirituelle selon Saint Paul*, 181 n. 4). De Boer notes, "The Old Testament used the term *way* or *ways* to designate the religious affiliation and commitment which the course and events of one's life expressed" (*Imitation of Paul*, 148).

49 "If Timothy comes, see that he has nothing to fear among you, for *he is doing the work of the Lord just as I am*" (emphasis added) (1 Cor 16:10; cf. 1 Cor 15:58). In regard to 1 Corinthians 4:16, Conzelmann notes, "The summons cannot be separated from Paul's missionary work" (*1 Corinthians*, 92).

over eating εἰδωλόθυτον, "idol meat" (chs. 8–10).[50] Certain "strong"[51] members of the community are eating meat sacrificed to idols (8:1–9) and attending "non-religious" banquets that gather in pagan temples (8:10–11).[52] "Weak" members of the community, however, view such activities as having spiritual significance and are themselves being incited to partake in such meals. From the weak members' viewpoint, when they "give in" and partake of questionable food, they engage in idolatrous syncretism. Thus, the weak are being led to sin against their own consciences by participating in what they consider idolatry, and if they persist, will be "destroyed" [ἀπόλλυται] (8:11–13). While Paul agrees with the strong Corinthians' assessment of meat sacrificed to idols in theory (i.e., it has no ultimate spiritual significance), he argues that the principle of self-denial for the good of the other takes priority. Paul avers, "Therefore, if food causes my brother to fall, I will never eat meat, so that I may not cause my brother to fall" (8:13, my translation).[53] Just as Paul gives up his right to receive financial support or take along a believing wife so that no stumbling block will be put in the way of his evangelistic ministry (9:1–27), the strong Corinthians should give up their right to eat meat sacrificed to

---

50   First Corinthians 8:1–11:1 should be read as a unity. See the arguments of John C. Brunt, "Love, Freedom, and Moral Responsibility: The Contribution of I Cor. 8–10 to an Understanding of Paul's Ethical Thinking," in *Society of Biblical Literature 1981 Seminar Papers*, ed. Kent Harold Richards (Chico, CA: Scholars Press, 1981), 19–20; Fee, *First Corinthians*, 487. Contra Johannes Weiss, *Der erste Korintherbrief*, 9th ed., MeyerK 5 (Göttingen: Vandenhoeck & Ruprecht, 1910), XL–XLIII; Walter Schmithals, *Die Gnosis in Korinth: Eine Untersuchung zu den Korintherbriefen*, 3rd ed. (Göttingen: Vandenhoeck & Ruprecht, 1969), 89; Jean Héring, *The First Epistle of Saint Paul to the Corinthians*, trans. A. W. Heathcote and P. J. Allcock (London: Epworth, 1962), xii–xiv.

51   Though Paul does not use the term "strong" in 1 Corinthians, we will adopt this designation for the believers who favored eating idol meat (cf. Rom 15:1).

52   Wedding and funeral banquets, as well as other social meetings, were commonly held within the precincts of a temple. See Peter D. Gooch, *Dangerous Food: 1 Corinthians 8–10 in Its Context*, Studies in Christianity and Judaism 5 (Waterloo, Ontario: Wilfrid Laurier University Press, 1993), 1–46; Wendell Lee Willis, *Idol Meat in Corinth: The Pauline Argument in 1 Corinthians 8 and 10* (Chico, CA: Scholars Press, 1985), 63 n. 234; Ramsay MacMullen, *Paganism in the Roman Empire* (New Haven: Yale University Press, 1981), 36–42; Franz Poland, *Geschichte des griechischen Vereinswesens* (Leipzig: B. G. Teubner, 1909), 503–13. Gordon Fee thinks the issue throughout 1 Corinthians 8:1–10:22 is "the eating of sacrificial food at the cultic meals in the pagan temples," but such a reading does not seem to account for Paul's accommodating attitude in chapter 8 (Fee, *First Corinthians*, 359–60).

53   The term "brothers" for Paul obviously includes both male and female members of the congregation, and for ease of expression, we will use the term in this way as well.

idols, if that action proves spiritually harmful to their weak brothers.

In chapter 10, Paul shifts from discussing the principle of self-denial to denouncing idolatry as unfaithfulness. Paul cites examples from the Old Testament as to how God deals with the unfaithful. Indeed, the Lord's destruction of the Israelites, even after he had rescued them from Egypt, stands as a warning against presumption and unfaithfulness (10:1–13). An example of similar presumption in Paul's own day would be partaking in an idolatrous religious ceremony (10:14–22).[54] Even in cases where idolatry is not involved (e.g., meat from the market, or "non-religious" banquets in a pagan temple), if another's conscience is in danger, one should refrain from eating (10:23–30).[55]

Paul clues the reader that he is concluding this discussion on debated eating practices with his use of the inferential οὖν and a general summarizing tone (εἴτε οὖν ἐσθίετε εἴτε πίνετε εἴτε τι ποιεῖτε) (10:31). It is here that Paul instructs his converts to imitate him, and as we noted above, only the context of this command will clarify the kind of imitation expected. Keeping in mind the broader context outlined above, let us now look particularly at 1 Corinthians 10:31–11:1. The text reads,

> So, whether you eat or drink, or whatever you do, do everything for the glory of God. Give no offense to Jews or to Greeks or to the church of God, just as I try to please everyone in everything I do, not seeking my own advantage, but that of many, so that they may be saved. Be imitators of me, as I am of Christ.

In this concluding paragraph to the lengthy discussion on idol meat, Paul emphasizes the salvific intentions of his accommodating behavior (something he has already highlighted in 9:19–23). The σύμφορον (good, advantage, benefit) which Paul seeks for all persons is none other than their salvation (ἵνα σωθῶσιν). The question, then, is whether Paul expects the Corinthians to exercise this same concern for others' salvation. Or, is the apostle's self-denial simply an analogy for the Corinthian Christians' behavior towards one another?

Paul answers this question for us by signifying that the strong brothers' accommodation also has salvific intentions. Paul says that if the weak brothers

---

54 See Conzelmann, *1 Corinthians*, 177; John C. Brunt, "Rejected, Ignored, or Misunderstood? The Fate of Paul's Approach to the Problem of Food Offered to Idols in Early Christianity," *NTS* 31 (1985): 114.

55 Note the argument's structure: (A) idol meat issue, (B) apostolic paradigm and Old Testament example, (A¹) idol meat issue. Hopper claims that Paul employs epideictic discourse in 1 Corinthians, whereby he introduces an issue, digresses, and then returns to the main issue (Hopper, "The Pauline Concept of Imitation," 128). This ABA pattern of argumentation has been noted by others (e.g., Fee, *First Corinthians*, 16; John J. Collins, "Chiasmus, the 'ABA' Pattern, and the Text of Paul," in *Studiorum Paulinorum Congressus Internationalis Catholicus 1961*, 2 vols., AnBib 17–18 [Rome: Biblical Institute, 1963], 2:575–83).

persist in sinning against their own conscience, they will be destroyed (ἀπόλλυται γὰρ ὁ ἀσθενῶν) (8:11).[56] Paul's other uses of ἀπόλλυμι make clear that this destruction refers to the weak brothers' ultimate state.[57] The strong brothers' self-denial is meant to prevent the weak brothers from sinning against their conscience in idolatry, for no idolater will inherit the kingdom of God (6:9–11). But does the strong brothers' salvific concern extend beyond those presently identified with the Christian community?[58]

Several factors would seem to indicate that it does. First, the salutation of 1 Corinthians shows that Paul understands the teaching of this letter as applying beyond the concerns that occasioned it. The letter is not addressed simply to the Corinthians, but also to "all those who in every place call on the name of our Lord Jesus Christ."[59] Undoubtedly, Paul's first epistle to the Corinthians is a

---

56　Paul's reference to a person as an ἀδελφός can pertain to the person's outward relationship to the Christian community rather than his or her spiritual state (e.g., 1 Cor 1:11; 5:11; Rom 14:15, 21; cf. Matt 18:15–17; Acts 20:30; 1 John 5:16). Also, Paul's remark that the brother is one δι' ὃν Χριστὸς ἀπέθανεν (1 Cor 8:11) does not indicate that Paul views that person as definitively saved. Cf. Rom 14:15; 2 Peter 2:1, "But false prophets also arose among the people, just as there will be false teachers among you, who will secretly bring in destructive opinions. *They will even deny the Master who bought them – bringing swift destruction on themselves*" (emphasis added).

57　E.g., see 1 Cor 1:18, 19; Rom 2:12; 14:15; 2 Cor 2:15; 4:3; 2 Thess 2:10.

58　Thiselton includes "self-sacrifice for the sake of Christ and the salvation of others" within the imitation that Paul enjoins (*The First Epistle to the Corinthians*, 796).

59　First Corinthians 1:2; cf. 1 Cor 4:17; 7:17; 11:16; 14:33. Weiss's proposal that this universal address is a later interpolation has no manuscript support (Weiss, *Der erste Korintherbrief*, 4). Grammatically, the phrase cannot be understood as referring to κλητοῖς ἁγίοις (J. B. Lightfoot, *Notes on Epistles of St Paul from Unpublished Commentaries* [London: Macmillan, 1895], 145; contra Georg Heinrici, *Kritisch Exegetisches Handbuch über den ersten Brief an die Korinther*, 6th ed., Meyers Kommentar über das Neue Testament [Göttingen: Vandenhoeck & Ruprecht, 1881], 13; Frederic Louis Godet, *Commentary on First Corinthians* [Edinburgh: T. & T. Clark, 1889; reprint, Grand Rapids: Kregel, 1977], 45; Robertson and Plummer, *First Corinthians*, 3; cf. 2 Cor 1:1; Phil 1:1). Furthermore, the words ἐν παντὶ τόπῳ are too general to be restricted to believers in the province of Achaia (contra Charles Hodge, *An Exposition of the First Epistle to the Corinthians* [New York: Robert Carter & Brothers, 1857; reprint, Grand Rapids: Baker, 1980], 5; Francis Baudraz, *Les Épîtres aux Corinthiens: Commentaire* [Geneva: Labor et Fides, 1965], 20; cf. 2 Cor 1:1). It appears Paul wrote with a consciousness that his letters, though occasional, would circulate (Col 4:16; 2 Pet 3:15–16); other attempts to explain 1 Corinthians 1:2 are not convincing. For example, see Manuel Guerra, who argues that πάντες οἱ ἐπικαλούμενοι τὸ ὄνομα τοῦ κυρίου are leaders of the Christian community at Corinth ("Los 'epikaloúmenoi' de 1 Cor 1,2, directores y sacerdotes de la comunidad cristiana en

profoundly occasional letter; specific issues at Corinth prompted Paul to write this letter and the Corinthians are the primary addressees. Yet, if Paul writes with the broader church also in view, he surely intends the underlying principles of his specific advice to extend beyond the issues addressed. Second, in 1 Corinthians 10:31, Paul signifies that his concluding remarks on the food issue have implications beyond the Corinthians' current situation. He writes, "So, whether you eat or drink, or *whatever you do, do everything for the glory of God* (emphasis added) (10:31)."[60] Third, after broadening the scope of his conclusion with this introductory remark, Paul follows in 10:32 with a command that explicitly extends beyond the Christian community. The apostle writes, "Give no offense to Jews or to Greeks or to the church of God." Thus, Paul instructs the Corinthians to consider the repercussions of their actions not only for persons identified with the church, but also for those outside the church – both non-believing Jews and Greeks.[61] Christians are to be blameless or inoffensive in their relationship to such outsiders (ἀπρόσκοποι . . . γίνεσθε).[62] Such behavior should not be misunderstood as avoiding offense at any cost for the sake of politeness or civil peace.[63] A Christian is to avoid offense in *adiaphora* for the sake of the gospel and its progress.[64] This point is clarified by Paul's elaboration of what it means for Christians to be blameless in relation to others. He explains that their behavior should be parallel to his own; he adds, "just as (καθώς) I try to please (ἀρέσκω)[65] everyone in

---

Corinto," *Scripta Theologica* 17 [1985]: 11–72) or Ulrich Wickert, who claims that Paul presents the universal church as somehow joining in the writing of this epistle ("Einheit und Eintracht der Kirche im Präskript des ersten Korintherbriefes," *ZNW* 50 [1959]: 73–82).

60 Also, see Paul's earlier statement in 10:23–24, "'All things are lawful,' but not all things are beneficial. 'All things are lawful,' but not all things build up (οἰκοδομεῖ). Do not seek your own advantage, but that of the other (τοῦ ἑτέρου)." Bowers acknowledges that the term "other" here is so general that it must be understood as including unbelievers (such as the non-Christian dinner host of 10:27) (Bowers, "Church and Mission," 94 n. 1). "Building up" for Paul means both the maturation and multiplication of the church, as we will see in our discussion of 1 Corinthians 14:23–25.

61 Cf. Col 4:5–6; 1 Thess 4:11–12.

62 Cf. Acts 24:16; Phil 1:10.

63 We do not find here an early form of *christliche Bürgerlichkeit* (Dibelius).

64 Robertson and Plummer comment, "An ill-advised exhibition of Christian freedom might shock Jews and an ill-advised rigour about matters indifferent might excite the derision of Greeks, and thus those who might have been won over would be alienated" (*First Corinthians*, 224).

65 A conative present (BDF §319). Here, ἀρέσκω does not mean "to please" in the sense of "doing or believing what others dictate" (Gal 1:10; cf. Matt 14:6; Mark 6:22), but connotes "serving in the interests of others" (P. Richardson and P. W.

everything I do, not seeking my own advantage, but that of many, so that they may be saved" (1 Cor 10:33). This explicit parallel between Paul's salvifically-oriented activity and the "blamelessness" of his addressees implies that the term ἀπρόσκοποι connotes an active missionary role for the congregation.[66] The Corinthian Christians must not only regulate their behavior to avoid offense; they must actively work for the "building up" of the church – i.e., both the maturation and multiplication of the church (10:23; 14:3; 14:24–25).[67]

In the final sentence of this concluding paragraph on the idol meat issue, Paul injects the imperative, "Be imitators of me, as I am of Christ" (11:1).[68] Standing alone, this command is ambiguous, but the preceding verses make clear that we should understand it as a restatement of Paul's exhortation to evangelistically-motivated service to others. The appeal to imitate Paul flows as a natural reiteration of the previous discussion, but the concluding reference to Christ is somewhat more enigmatic. Given the immediate context (i.e., the preceding verse), Paul seems to be saying that Christ was a model for him in that Christ did not seek his own advantage, but that of others – for their salvation. This understanding of Christ as selflessly giving himself for others' salvation corresponds with Paul's presentation of Christ in his other letters as well as the gospel traditions.[69]

Gooch, "Accommodation Ethics," *TynBul* 29 [1978]: 113). See MM, s.v. "ἀρέσκω."

66 Murphy-O'Connor writes, "Paul has dedicated himself to 'seeking the advantage of many in order that they may be saved' (x, 33). It is not enough that the Corinthians avoid creating stumbling-blocks, they must positively empower the conversion of Jews and Gentiles and the continuing growth of their fellow Christians" ("Freedom or the Ghetto," 573). Richardson and Gooch comment, "[Let us address] a question about the effectiveness of accommodating one's behaviour for the good of others. Where their 'good' means not just their feeling comfortable but instead their ultimate salvation, accommodation has to be accompanied by additional procedures whereby the others are moved away from their present way of life and brought into the freedom of the gospel. Otherwise accommodation will only be the confirmation of their way of life ('If you're living like us our life must be acceptable')" (Richardson and Gooch, "Accommodation Ethics," 115).

67 See chapter four for a more detailed discussion of "building up."

68 For a brief survey of major commentators' views on this verse, see Belleville, "'Imitate Me, Just as I Imitate Christ,'" 122–25.

69 E.g., Rom 15:1–7; 2 Cor 8:9; Eph 5:1–2; Phil 2:5–11; Mark 8:31–35; 10:45; Luke 19:10. See Peter T. O'Brien, "The Gospel and Godly Models in Philippians," in *Worship, Theology and Ministry in the Early Church: Essays in Honor of Ralph P. Martin*, JSNTSup 87, ed. Michael J. Wilkins and Terence Paige (Sheffield: Sheffield Academic Press, 1992), 273–84; L. W. Hurtado, "Jesus as Lordly Example in Philippians 2:5–11," in *From Jesus to Paul: Studies in Honour of Francis Wright Beare*, ed. Peter Richardson and John C. Hurd (Waterloo, Ontario: Wilfrid Laurier University Press, 1984), 113–26. Also see Richardson's

Paul's mention of his (and Christ's) salvifically-oriented service to others, along with the triple reference to the "Jews, Greeks, and church of God" in 10:32 points us back to a passage which closely parallels our current one. In chapter 9:12, 19–23, Paul discusses the same three groups with evangelistic intentions.[70] A closer look at this passage will help us understand the accommodating behavior Paul commands the Corinthians to imitate in 1 Corinthians 11:1. In chapter 9, Paul writes,

> Nevertheless, we [Paul and Barnabas] have not made use of this right [to material benefit], but we endure anything rather than put an obstacle in the way of the gospel of Christ . . . . For though I am free with respect to all, I have made myself a slave to all, so that I might win more of them. To the Jews I became as a Jew, in order that I might win Jews. To those under the law I became as one under the law (though I myself am not under the law) so that I might win those under the law. To those outside the law I became as one outside the law (though I am not free from God's law but am under Christ's law) so that I might win those outside the law. To the weak I became weak, so that I might win the weak. I have become all things to all people, that I might by all means save some. I do it all for the sake of the gospel, so that I may share in its blessings (1 Cor 9:12, 19–23).[71]

Here we get a clearer picture of what Paul means by his attempts to "please" all people (1 Cor 10:33). The apostle adjusts his behavior in morally and doctrinally inconsequential areas so as not to put an unnecessary barrier between a non-believer (or person of questionable faith) and the gospel. In the

---

presentation of Jesus' pattern of accommodation in the Synoptic Gospels (Richardson and Gooch, "Accommodation Ethics," 131–40).

70   In chapter 9, Paul calls these groups "the Jews" or "those under the law" (Jewish non-believers), "those outside the law" (Greek non-believers), and "the weak" (persons in the church with inadequate or hesitating faith). Paul uses the term "win" loosely – applying it to both non-believers and "the weak." One should not understand "the weak" as an outright non-Christian category, as does Karl Heim, *Die Gemeinde des Auferstandenen: Tübinger Vorlesungen über den 1. Korintherbrief*, ed. Friso Melzer (Munich: Neubau, 1949), 120. Cf. Rom 5:6.

71   For the rabbinic background of 'win' as a missionary term, see David Daube, *The New Testament and Rabbinic Judaism* (London: Athlone, 1956), 352–61. Daube thinks that Paul is following his rabbinic heritage in his missionary accommodation, but Carson convincingly argues that some fundamental differences remain (Daube, 336–46; Carson, "Pauline Inconsistency," 9–10). Carson also demonstrates that Paul's account of his confrontation with Peter in Antioch (Gal 2) can be reconciled with his principle of accommodation (1 Cor 9) (Carson, 6–45). Carson is responding mainly to Peter Richardson, "Pauline Inconsistency: I Corinthians 9:19–23 and Galatians 2:11–14," *NTS* 26 (1979–80): 347–62. Also see Richardson and Gooch, "Accommodation Ethics," 89–142; cf. Günther Bornkamm, "The Missionary Stance of Paul in I Corinthians 9 and in Acts," in *Studies in Luke-Acts*, ed. Leander E. Keck and J. Louis Martyn (Nashville: Abingdon, 1966), 194–207.

church's relationship with the same groups (Jews, Greeks, the weak), it is also to exercise the principle of self-denial in striving for the other's salvation (10:32–11:1).

Particularly striking in 1 Corinthians 9:19–23 is Paul's repetition of the phrase "in order that I might win/save" (vv. 19, 20 [2x], 21, 22 [2x]). There can be no doubt of the apostle's evangelistic purpose. It is noteworthy that Paul here presents himself as subject of the verbs σῴζω and κερδαίνω. This grammatical construction implies the active role that Paul has (under God) in bringing about the salvation of his converts. Likewise, in 1 Corinthians 7:16 (which we will examine below), Paul refers to members of the Corinthian congregation as subjects of the verb σῴζω in an evangelistic context. Both Paul and his converts take an active role in bringing about the salvation of non-believers.

We should also note that 1 Corinthians chapter 9 further elucidates Paul's imitation command by clarifying the relationship between the apostle's exemplary evangelistic self-denial and the nature of the gospel. In 9:12, Paul describes the gospel as a dynamic force that he does not want to hinder through his insistence upon apostolic rights. The gospel is in some sense depicted as an independent power that inevitably accomplishes God's will; one may hinder or further its advance, but its ultimate effectiveness is guaranteed.[72] Ascertaining this dynamic nature of the gospel is important for understanding why Paul expects his converts to reproduce his self-sacrificial behavior for the salvation of others (10:31–11:1). Once the gospel becomes effective in its hearers, they too are included in its dynamic advance. They are either fellow partners with Paul or stumbling blocks; there is no middle ground.[73] Each person, according to his or her situation and giftedness, is a co-partner in the work of the gospel. Ultimately, it is the nature of the gospel that provides the theological basis for Paul's expectations of his churches' evangelistic activity in imitation of his own (see chapter two).

---

72 See Rom 1:16, Phil 1:12; Col 1:5–6; 1 Thess 1:5–8; 2:13–14; 2 Thess 3:1; 2 Tim 2:9. Also see Schütz, *Paul and the Anatomy of Apostolic Authority*, 51–52; Gundry Volf, *Paul and Perseverance*, 251; O'Brien, *Gospel and Mission*, 138. The Old Testament background of the effective "word of the Lord" has certainly influenced Paul's thinking (e.g., Isa 55:11). John Howard Schütz comments, "What does Paul understand by a 'gospel' which could be 'hindered'? He cannot be speaking about hindering the *content* of the gospel. Nor can he mean that he will refrain from damaging his own *delivery* of it. To grasp the metaphors here we must imagine the gospel as a force or agency able to accomplish something, having a purpose toward which it proceeds. Paul will do nothing to thwart that thrust of the gospel toward its own goal. The renunciation of his apostolic 'right' seems to him a small price to pay to assure this" (*Paul and the Anatomy of Apostolic Authority*, 52).

73 Matt 12:30, "Whoever is not with me is against me, and whoever does not gather with me scatters."

FIRST CORINTHIANS 7:12–16

Looking beyond the imitation texts and their immediate contexts, we find that 1 Corinthians offers corroborating evidence that Paul expected his converts to imitate him through missionary activity. For example, in chapter 7:12–16, Paul makes another call for soteriologically-motivated self-denial. The apostle exhorts a believing spouse to live at peace with a non-believing spouse. The ultimate goal of this irenic behavior is not temporal harmony, but eschatological salvation. Paul writes, "Wife, for all you know, you might save your husband. Husband for all you know, you might save your wife" (1 Cor 7:16).[74] In this conjugal relationship, as in other relationships, the evangelistic

---

74 Another translation/interpretation of this verse is "How do you know, wife, if you will save your husband? Or, how do you know, husband, if you will save your wife? [So, don't try to force the non-believing spouse to stay if he or she desires to leave. You have no guarantee that you will bring about his or her salvation, and such intransigence on your part will only bring about strife, but God has called us to peace.]" Regardless of whether one favors the "optimistic" or "pessimistic" translation, the significance of the verse remains the same for our study: Paul assumes that the Corinthian Christians desire the salvation of non-believers. In favor of the optimistic translation are the Greek fathers (Josef Blinzler, "Die 'Heiligkeit' der Kinder in der alten Kirche: Zur Auslegung von 1 Kor 7,14," in *Aus der Welt und Umwelt des Neuen Testaments,* Stuttgarter biblische Beiträge [Stuttgart: Katholisches Bibelwerk, 1969], 171 n. 46); Joachim Jeremias, "Die missionarische Aufgabe in der Mischehe (I Cor 716)," in *Neutestamentliche Studien für Rudolf Bultmann zu seinem siebzigsten Geburtstag,* ed. Walther Eltester, 2nd ed., BZNW 21 (Berlin: Töpelmann, 1957), 255–60; C. Burchard, "Εἰ nach einem Ausdrück des Wissens oder Nichtwissens Joh 925, Act 192, I Cor 116, 716," *ZNW* 52 (1961): 73–82; John Calvin, *The First Epistle of Paul The Apostle to the Corinthians.* trans. John W. Fraser (Edinburgh: Oliver and Boyd; Grand Rapids: Eerdmans, 1960), 150; Lightfoot, *Notes on Epistles of St Paul,* 227; Collins, *First Corinthians,* 267, 272; Barrett, *First Corinthians,* 167; Fee, *First Corinthians,* 305; Richard A. Horsley, *1 Corinthians,* Abingdon New Testament Commentaries (Nashville: Abingdon, 1998), 99–100; F. F. Bruce, *1 and 2 Corinthians,* NCB (London: Oliphants, 1971), 70; Wolfgang Schrage, *Der erste Brief an die Korinther,* 4 vols., EKKNT 7 (Zurich: Benziger, 1991–2001), 2:112; cf. 1 Peter 3:1. In favor of the pessimistic translation are Sakae Kubo, "I Corinthians VII. 16: Optimistic or Pessimistic?," *NTS* 24 (1978): 539–44; Robertson and Plummer, *First Corinthians,* 144; Héring, *First Corinthians,* 53; Conzelmann, *1 Corinthians,* 124; Baudraz, *Les Epîtres aux Corinthiens,* 62; Godet, *First Corinthians,* 350–51; Heinrici, *an die Korinther,* 184–85; Morris, *First Epistle of Paul to the Corinthians,* 108. Orr and Walther suggest that σῴζω in 1 Cor 7:16 could refer to the "healing" of the marriage (William F. Orr and James Arthur Walther, *1 Corinthians,* AB, vol. 32 [Garden City, NY: Doubleday, 1976], 214). Thiselton argues that neither an optimistic nor pessimistic interpretation suffices. A correct translation, Thiselton says, should emphasize the limits of a Christian's knowledge, the sovereignty of

concern of believers is assumed. Paul does not write, "[Believing] wife, you must desire, pray, and actively work for your husband's salvation." Such active concern is assumed. Paul mentions the possibility of an *already* desired outcome (i.e., the salvation of a non-believing spouse) to encourage the Christian towards peaceful and self-sacrificial behavior.

While including the attractive behavior of the spouse, Paul's instructions in 7:12–16 cannot be relegated to simply the "passive" category of missionary activity. As we noted above, Paul depicts the believing husband and wife as subjects of the verb σῴζω, implying their active role. Furthermore, from Paul's comments elsewhere, it is clear that he thinks non-believers must accept certain propositional truths before they can be considered saved (15:3–11).[75] How would the non-believing spouse discover these truths unless his or her partner articulates them? It is artificial and illogical to assume that Paul envisions a situation where the believing spouse would never take the initiative to discuss the gospel. Such silence would be culpable, given the non-believer's desperate situation (1:18).

FIRST CORINTHIANS 14:23–25

First Corinthians 14:23–25 also reveals Paul's assumption that the Corinthians are concerned for non-believers' salvation. The text reads,

> If, therefore, the whole church comes together and all speak in tongues, and outsiders or unbelievers enter, will they not say that you are out of your mind? But if all prophesy, an unbeliever or outsider who enters is reproved by all and called to account by all. After the secrets of the unbeliever's heart are disclosed, that person will bow down before God and worship him, declaring, "God is really among you."

In this passage, Paul presupposes the Corinthians' desire for non-Christians to be convicted of sin and turn to the Lord in faith.[76] To accomplish this desire,

---

God, and the need to trust him in uncertain situations (*The First Epistle to the Corinthians*, 539–40).

75 J. Christiaan Beker writes, "In 1 Corinthians 15 we have a striking example that the coherence of the gospel for Paul is not simply an experiential reality of the heart or a 'Word beyond all words' that permits a translation into a multitude of worldviews" (J. Christiaan Beker, *The Triumph of God: The Essence of Paul's Thought*, trans. Loren T. Stuckenbruck [Minneapolis: Fortress, 1990], 76).

76 All commentators are agreed that non-believers are at least included in Paul's phrase ἰδιῶται ἢ ἄπιστοι (14:23). Schrage argues that ἰδιῶται and ἄπιστοι should *not* be understood as referring to two distinct classes of people (*Der erste Brief an die Korinther*, 3:411). Barrett favors understanding this phrase as descriptive of one group, i.e., "unbelieving outsiders" (Barrett, *First Corinthians*, 324–25). See Walter Rebell, "Gemeinde als Missionsfaktor im Urchristentum: I Kor 14,24f. als Schlüsselsituation," *TZ* 44 (1988): 117–34.

Paul explains, communication within the church meeting should be intelligible to a visiting non-believer.[77]

Because the paradigmatic non-believer whom Paul mentions is motivated to his believing declaration mainly through "listening in" to the Christian worship service, one may be inclined to label this Christian witness as "passive."[78] Yet, how did the non-believer come to be in the church meeting unless he or she had been invited by others? If we restrict ourselves to a passive understanding of the congregation's witness, we would have to say that the congregation sang so loudly and beautifully that some non-believers were attracted to the meeting – but no one invited them.

Paul's assumption that the Corinthians are concerned for non-believers' salvation (1 Cor 7:12–16; 14:23–25) is undergirded by the apostle's theological reflection elsewhere in the letter. Non-believers are classed with "the world," which is under God's condemnation (1:21; 11:32). Non-believers are "wrongdoers" (ἄδικοι) who will not inherit the kingdom of God (6:9). They are in need of God's cleansing, sanctification, and justification (6:11). Believers, on the other hand, have been cleansed, forgiven, are victorious over death, and will inherit God's kingdom (1:2; 6:11; 15:3, 50–58). Motivated by love (13:1–13), believers must desire and work for the salvation of those who do not share in their blessed estate.

Circumstantial evidence also seems to indicate that the Corinthians imitated Paul in his missionary concern. Priscilla and Aquila, who had resided in Corinth during Paul's initial evangelistic tour (Acts 18:1–3) are leaders of a congregation in Ephesus at the time of his writing (1 Cor 16:8, 19; Acts 18:18–26). Similarly, it appears that the former synagogue ruler from Corinth, Sosthenes, is now co-laboring in the mission field along with Paul (1 Cor 1:1; Acts 18:17).[79] Certainly, Paul did not expect the missionary concern of the Christians in Corinth to be expressed in bland uniformity. Some persons would primarily seek the salvation of non-believers in their own home (1 Cor 7:16), others would primarily testify to non-believing neighbors (1 Cor 10:31–11:1; 14:24–25), and others would even travel with the apostle or start churches in

---

77 Craig Blomberg writes, "Verses 21–25 remind us that Christian worship must at least periodically relate directly to the unbeliever. This in turn presupposes that non-Christians will regularly be present at Christian worship, most commonly no doubt because Christian friends have invited them" (*1 Corinthians*, NIV Application Commentary [Grand Rapids: Zondervan, 1994], 274).

78 David Garland notes, "[The Christian worship service] should expose [nonbelievers] to the divine presence so that they confess, 'I ought not to live as I do but must change and allow God to effect that change'" (*1 Corinthians*, BECNT [Grand Rapids: Baker, 2003], 653–54).

79 Kümmel suggests this possibility (*Introduction to the New Testament*, 279).

new cities (1 Cor 16:19; 1 Cor 1:1; cf. Acts 18:17–26).[80] While the obligation of gospel dissemination falls upon the church as a whole, an individual believer's giftedness and life situation determine the manifestation of that obligation.

The Church's Active Witness: Concluding Thoughts

There can be no doubt that Paul instructs and approves of his churches actively proclaiming the gospel. In Philippians, Ephesians, and 1 Corinthians, we have examined texts in which Paul commands the churches to declare the gospel, to be prepared to do so, or to imitate him in the way that he strives for the salvation of non-Christians. Also, in Philippians, we saw that Paul approvingly mentions that ordinary Christians in his current setting have been emboldened to preach the gospel because of his example.

Although we find some unmistakable references to the congregations' proclaiming activity, it is surprising that we do not find more – especially given Paul's frequent self-references to preaching the gospel.[81] This paucity of overt references to the churches' gospel proclamation can be accounted for in several ways: (1) As we noted at the outset of the chapter, Paul's letters address specific occasions, and one cannot determine the relative importance of topics by how frequently or extensively Paul treats them. (2) Paul often speaks of the gospel spreading from a divine perspective, which serves to de-emphasize the importance of human agency.[82] (3) It is likely that many of the churches that Paul addresses were already active in making known the gospel, so his main concern is not that they *begin* proclaiming the gospel, but that they *confirm* their witness through a faithful lifestyle. We will touch on this point in more detail in the following sections of this book – not least, in the immediately following section about the church's "passive" witness.

Pauline Commands to Witness Passively

Having examined Paul's imperatives to active ecclesiastical witness, we now turn to discuss Paul's understanding of the church's passive witness. Paul and his co-workers carefully regulated their lives to avoid giving any offense to potential converts. Paul expected churches to do the same. We have already

---

80 Paul undoubtedly expected apostles and some other persons to be involved in full-time ministry, as distinguished from the majority of the church (1 Cor 9:14; 12:28).

81 See, e.g., Rom 1:1, 9, 15; 15:16, 19, 20; 1 Cor 1:17; 9:16; 15:1; 2 Cor 2:12; 10:16; 11:7; Gal 1:8, 11; 2:2; Eph 6:19; Phil 1:7; 1 Thess 1:5; 2:2, 4, 9; 2 Tim 1:11; 2:8; 4:17.

82 E.g., Col 1:5–6; 1 Thess 1:5–8; 2:13; 2 Thess 3:1. See O'Brien, *Gospel and Mission*, 138; Schütz, *Paul and the Anatomy of Apostolic Authority*, 52–53.

noted this concern for behavioral witness in the Corinthian imitation texts. Paul's instructions concerning the gospel-determined regulation of one's behavior, however, can be found in many other places. We will now turn to a few representative texts.

First, we need to establish that Paul himself was concerned that his behavior authenticate the gospel. A text which demonstrates this point is 2 Corinthians 6:3–7, where Paul writes,

> We are putting no obstacle in anyone's way, so that no fault may be found with our ministry, but as servants of God we have commended ourselves in every way: through great endurance, in afflictions, hardships, calamities, beatings, imprisonments, riots, labors, sleepless nights, hunger; by purity, knowledge, patience, kindness, holiness of spirit, genuine love, truthful speech, and the power of God.

Though this text also speaks of suffering as a part of Paul's missionary task, I want to highlight that Paul and his co-workers testify to the truth of the gospel through their "purity, knowledge, patience, kindness, holiness of spirit, genuine love, [and] truthful speech" (2 Cor 6:6–7). Paul's conduct is an essential part of his gospel proclamation. As Peter T. O'Brien notes, "[Paul's] behaviour and personal example could not finally be distinguished from the message he preached: his life authenticated the gospel."[83]

Another text which shows Paul's concern that his way of life confirm his proclamation of the gospel is 1 Thessalonians 2:5–12,

> As you know and as God is our witness, we never came with words of flattery or with a pretext for greed; nor did we seek praise from mortals, whether from you or from others, though we might have made demands as apostles of Christ. But we were gentle among you, like a nurse tenderly caring for her own children. So deeply do we care for you that we are determined to share with you not only the gospel of God but also our own selves, because you have become very dear to us.
>
> You remember our labor and toil, brothers and sisters; we worked night and day, so that we might not burden any of you while we proclaimed to you the gospel of God. You are witnesses, and God also, how pure, upright, and blameless our conduct was toward you believers. As you know, we dealt with each one of you like a father with his children, urging and encouraging you and pleading that you lead a life worthy of God, who calls you into his own kingdom and glory.

We see here in 1 Thessalonians, as in the passage previously noted from 2 Corinthians, that Paul wants his behavior to verify, rather than contradict, the gospel. Because the gospel is the truth about God, the herald of that gospel must reflect the truthfulness and goodness of God's character. Thus, it is essential that Paul, and whoever else proclaims the gospel, be "pure, upright,

---

83   O'Brien, *Gospel and Mission*, 89.

and blameless" in all of his or her conduct (1 Thess 2:10).

Not only Paul, but also the churches are to authenticate the gospel to outsiders through their behavior. Paul instructs the churches to live ethically in various passages, and in many cases an unstated evangelistic concern likely provides a partial basis for Paul's instructions. In this study, however, our interest is only in those texts where Paul explicitly mentions a concern for the evangelistic effect of Christians' behavior on outsiders. We will now seek to demonstrate that Paul expected the churches' lifestyle to authenticate the gospel to potential converts in the same way that his own conduct did.

Possibly the densest concentration of Pauline texts which have the opinion of outsiders in view is found in the Pastoral epistles.[84] Traditionally, these passages have been taken to represent a later, "settled" form of Christianity, which is attempting to co-exist peacefully with the surrounding environment.[85] This "Christian good citizenship" (*christliche Bürgerlichkeit*) understanding of these passages in the Pastorals, however, fails to take into account the evangelistic intent of the congregation's behavior. Because of space limitations, we will limit ourselves to the careful study of one text, Titus 2:1–10, which presents a strong case for our thesis.[86]

---

84   E.g., 1 Tim 2:1–4; 3:7; 2 Tim 2:24–25; 4:5; Titus 1:9; 2:1–10; 3:1–2. See also Eph 5:6–16; 1 Thess 4:11–12; 2 Thess 3:7–9; cf. 1 Pet 2:9–12; 3:1. While the majority of critical scholars claim non-Pauline authorship for the Pastoral Epistles, I accept the letters as authentically Pauline. This view is shared by a sizeable minority of scholars, including the following: Mounce, *Pastoral Epistles*, xlvi–cxxxvi; Luke Timothy Johnson, *Letters to Paul's Delegates: 1 Timothy, 2 Timothy, Titus*, The New Testament in Context (Valley Forge, PA: Trinity Press International, 1996), 1–33; E. E. Ellis, "Pastoral Letters," in *DPL*, ed. Gerald F. Hawthorne, Ralph P. Martin and Daniel G. Reid (Downers Grove: InterVarsity, 1993), 659–61; D. A. Carson, Douglas J. Moo, and Leon Morris, *An Introduction to the New Testament* (Grand Rapids: Zondervan, 1992), 359–71; Donald Guthrie, *The Pastoral Epistles*, 2nd ed., TNTC 14 (Leicester: InterVarsity; Grand Rapids: Eerdmans, 1990), 17–62.

85   Martin Dibelius and Hans Conzelmann, *The Pastoral Epistles*, trans. Philip Buttolph and Adela Yarbro, Hermeneia (Philadelphia: Fortress, 1972).

86   Scholars who recognize a missionary goal in the paranesis of Titus 2:1–10 include the following: Walter Lock, *A Critical and Exegetical Commentary on the Pastoral Epistles (I & II Timothy and Titus)*, ICC (Edinburgh: T. & T. Clark, 1924), 137, 142–43; C. K. Barrett, *The Pastoral Epistles* (Oxford: Clarendon, 1963), 133–34; Peter Lippert, *Leben als Zeugnis: Die werbende Kraft christlicher Lebensführung nach dem Kirchenverständnis neutestamentlicher Briefe,* SBM 4 (Stuttgart: Katholisches Bibelwerk, 1968), 50–54; J. N. D. Kelly, *The Pastoral Epistles: I & II Timothy, Titus*, BNTC (London: Adam & Charles Black, 1963; reprint, 1976), 243 (page citations are to reprint edition); Jerome D. Quinn, *The Letter to Titus: A New Translation with Notes and Commentary and An Introduction to Titus, I and II Timothy, The Pastoral Epistles*, AB, vol. 35 (New York: Doubleday, 1990), 149; L. T. Johnson, *Letters to Paul's Delegates*, 235; Donald Guthrie, *Pastoral Epistles*,

We will begin at the end of Titus 2:1–10 and work our way backwards.[87] The last two verses of the section, vv. 9–10, are often cited as one of the clearest "missions texts" in the Pastorals. Here, Paul writes,

δούλους ἰδίοις δεσπόταις ὑποτάσσεσθαι ἐν πᾶσιν, εὐαρέστους εἶναι, μὴ ἀντιλέγοντας, μὴ νοσφιζομένους, ἀλλὰ πᾶσαν πίστιν ἐνδεικνυμένους ἀγαθήν, ἵνα τὴν διδασκαλίαν τὴν τοῦ σωτῆρος ἡμῶν θεοῦ κοσμῶσιν ἐν πᾶσιν.

The most important question for our thesis is this: how should we translate the verb κοσμῶσιν? Does κοσμῶσιν have an evangelistic sense, as it is often given in translations (i.e., "to make attractive")? Or, does it simply mean "to honor"? That is, do slaves behave in a certain way so as to make Christian teaching attractive to their masters? Or, do slaves behave in a certain way so as to honor the faith they profess by acting in accordance with it?

The semantic range of the verb κοσμέω could support either reading. H. Balz (*EDNT*) favors the second option, translating κοσμέω as "give honor to."[88] Indeed, references can be found from the sixth century B.C. to the third century A.D. which employ κοσμέω in the sense of "to honor."[89] If the verb

---

209; Gordon D. Fee, *1 and 2 Timothy, Titus*, rev. ed., NIBC (Peabody, MA: Hendrickson, 1988), 191, 194; George W. Knight III, *The Pastoral Epistles: A Commentary on the Greek Text*, NIGTC (Grand Rapids: Eerdmans; Carlisle: Paternoster, 1992), 316–18; Hayne P. Griffin, Jr., "Titus," in *1, 2 Timothy, Titus*, by Thomas D. Lea and Hayne P. Griffin, Jr., NAC, vol. 34 (Nashville: Broadman, 1992), 308–09; Alan Padgett, "The Pauline Rationale for Submission: Biblical Feminism and the *hina* Clauses of Titus 2:1–10," *EvQ* 59 (1987): 52; Mounce, *Pastoral Epistles*, 416; John Stott, *Guard the Truth: The Message of 1 Timothy & Titus*, The Bible Speaks Today Series (Downers Grove: InterVarsity, 1996), 189, 191–92; Robert J. Karris, *The Pastoral Epistles*, New Testament Message 17 (Wilmington, DE: Michael Glazier, 1979), 116; Philip H. Towner, *1–2 Timothy & Titus*, IVPNTCS (Downers Grove: InterVarsity, 1994), 234–35; idem, *The Goal of Our Instruction: The Structure of Theology and Ethics in the Pastoral Epistles*, JSNTSup 34 (Sheffield: JSOT, 1989), 192–99; I. Howard Marshall, *A Critical and Exegetical Commentary on the Pastoral Epistles*, ICC (Edinburgh: T. & T. Clark, 1999), 250, 256.

87 Paul's instructions to the Christian community (Titus 2:1–10) are presented as the antithesis of his attack on the false teachers (Titus 1:10–16) (Marshall, *Pastoral Epistles*, 237). See Alfons Weiser, "Titus 2 als Gemeindeparänese," in *Neues Testament und Ethik*, ed. Helmut Merklein (Freiburg: Herder, 1989), 405–06.

88 H. Balz, "κοσμέω," in *EDNT*, 2:309; cf. BDAG, 560.

89 E.g., Πατρίδα κοσμήσω, λιπαρὴν πόλιν (Theognis 947, sixth cent. B.C., LCL 258 [1931]: 340); . . . οἵτινες ἐξουσίαν διδόασιν ταῖς γυναιξὶν ταῖς τῶν τριῶν τέκνων δικαίῳ κεκοσμημένα[ι]ς ἑαυτῶν κυριεύειν καὶ χωρ[ὶς] κυρίου χρηματίζειν ἐν αἷς ποιοῦν[τ]αι οἰκονομίαις ("[Laws

has this sense in Titus 2:10, the debated text should be translated "that they may honor the teaching of God our Savior in every way." It is noteworthy that while a prominent reference work favors translating κοσμέω with the sense of "honor," no major Bible translations follow it.[90]

Κοσμέω appears ten times in the New Testament and twenty-two times in the LXX.[91] It can refer to the adorning, preparing, or honoring of a table, temple, person, house, lamp, tomb, etc.[92] The overwhelming use of κοσμέω in the NT and LXX conveys the sense of adorning in an attractive fashion. Such adornment is done with the implied or expressed intent of drawing the attention or admiration of others. In the one other instance of κοσμέω in the Pastorals (1 Tim 2:9), κοσμέω is used to instruct women not to adorn themselves with fine clothes or jewelry, but with good deeds. In this context, κοσμέω carries connotations of decorating for the purpose of being viewed with pleasure or attraction by others – likely the same sense it carries in Titus. If we are correct in reading κοσμέω in this way, Paul is saying that a slave's righteous conduct will make the Christian message more appealing to outsiders (cf. 1 Tim 6:1).[93] Paul's description of the Christian message as "the teaching of God our *Savior*" (my emphasis) further emphasizes that the slaves are to adorn the gospel with a salvific intent.[94]

---

have been made] . . . which enable women who are honoured with the right of three children to be independent and act without a guardian in all business which they transact") (Bernard P. Grenfell and Arthur S. Hunt, eds., *The Oxyrhynchus Papyri*, vol. 12 [London: Oxford University Press, 1916], 1467, ll. 2–8 [English translation, p. 197]).

90   But, see Dibelius and Conzelmann, *Pastoral Epistles*, 139.

91   I.e., in Alfred Rahlf's edition of the LXX. In Hatch and Redpath's concordance to the Septuagint, twenty-eight occurrences of κοσμέω are listed. The six variants not listed in Rahlf's occur in Eccl 1:15; Ezek 16:58; 23:40; Jdt 10:3; Sir 25:1; 48:11.

92   See Matt 12:44; 23:29; 25:7; Luke 11:25; 21:5; 1 Tim 2:9; Titus 2:10; 1 Pet 3:5; Rev 21:2; 21:19; 2 Chr 3:6; Esth 1:6; Eccl 7:13; Jer 4:30; Ezek 16:11, 13; 23:41; Mic 6:9; Jdt 12:15; Ep Jer 1:10; 2 Macc 9:16; 3 Macc 3:5; 5:45; 6:1; Sir 16:27; 29:26; 38:28; 42:21; 45:12; 47:10; 50:9; 50:14.

93   A similar text is found in 3 Macc 3:5, "but since they adorned their style of life with the good deeds of upright people (τῇ δὲ τῶν δικαίων εὐπραξίᾳ κοσμοῦντες τὴν συναναστροφήν), they were established in good repute with everyone." Cf. 3 Macc 6:1.

94   Paul's frequent description of God as "Savior" in the Pastorals is unique to these letters and is indicative of Paul's underlying evangelistic concerns (1 Tim 1:1; 2:3; 4:10; Titus 1:3; 2:10, 13; 3:4). Stephen Charles Mott argues, "Behind the usage of σωτήρ, χάρις, χρηστότης and φιλανθρωπία in describing conversion from evil in Tit. ii 10–14 and iii 3–7 is the Judaism represented by Philo, especially, and also the Wisdom of Solomon and Fourth Maccabees" (S. C. Mott, "Greek Ethics

The broader context of Titus 2:10 also argues in favor of a missiological reading. In the following verse, Titus 2:11, we find an overt evangelistic intent introduced by a causal γάρ: Ἐπεφάνη γὰρ ἡ χάρις τοῦ θεοῦ σωτήριος πᾶσιν ἀνθρώποις. Slaves should behave well so as to make the Christian gospel attractive to their masters, *because* the grace of God has appeared savingly for all kinds of people – i.e., both slaves and masters.[95] It is likely that this causal γάρ clause not only has the injunction to slaves in view, but all of the instructions in Titus 2.[96] The whole *Haustafel* is permeated with a consciousness of outsiders' observation.[97]

Another reason for understanding κοσμέω with connotations of attraction to outsiders is the instructions to Titus (and implicitly to all young men) which immediately precede the teaching to slaves.[98] Outsiders are explicitly put in view. Titus is told to model good works and sobriety for the young men ἵνα ὁ ἐξ ἐναντίας ἐντραπῇ μηδὲν ἔχων λέγειν περὶ ἡμῶν φαῦλον (Titus

and Christian Conversion: The Philonic Background of Titus II 10–14 and III 3–7," *NovT* 20 [1978]: 47).

95   I am reading πᾶσιν ἀνθρώποις as referring to "all people without distinction," rather than "all people without exception" (Titus 2:11). I translate πᾶσιν ἀνθρώποις as 'all kinds of people' to bring out this sense. The preceding paranesis directed to different groups of people, with even more groups of outsiders in view, supports such a reading.

96   So Charles J. Ellicott, *The Pastoral Epistles of St. Paul: With a Critical and Grammatical Commentary, and a Revised Translation*, 3rd ed. (London: Longman, Green, Longman, Roberts & Green, 1864), 198.

97   Cf. Eph 5:21–6:9; Col 3:18–4:1; 1 Pet 2:18–3:7. Scholars debate whether Titus 2:1–10 should be included in the *Haustafel* (household code) genre. Dibelius, Conzelmann, and Barrett recognize a modified representation of a *Haustafel* (Dibelius and Conzelmann, *Pastoral Epistles*, 139; Barrett, *Pastoral Epistles*, 134). Lillie notes that the passage lacks references to family relationships and reciprocal duties, as one would expect in a *Haustafel* (William Lillie, "The Pauline House-tables," *ExpTim* 86 [1974–75]: 180). Fee thinks Titus 2:1–10 has only a superficial similarity to a *Haustafel* (Fee, *1 and 2 Timothy, Titus*, 184). See I. Howard Marshall's excursus on "Household codes and station codes" (*Pastoral Epistles*, 231–36; see also Hermann von Lips, "Die Haustafel als 'Topos' im Rahmen der urchristlichen Paränese: Beobachtungen anhand des 1. Petrusbriefes und des Titusbriefes," *NTS* 40 (1994): 261–80.

98   Cf. 1 Tim 5:1–2. Paul's instructions to Titus are correctly read as extending to all young men (for whom Titus is the model). So Towner, *Goal of Our Instruction*, 194–95; Lippert, *Leben als Zeugnis*, 51–52; Fee, *1 and 2 Timothy, Titus*, 190; Dibelius and Conzelmann, *Pastoral Epistles*, 141; Marshall, *Pastoral Epistles*, 251; Joachim Jeremias, *Die Briefe an Timotheus und Titus*, 7th ed., NTD 9 (Göttingen: Vandenhoeck & Ruprecht, 1954), 62–63; Norbert Brox, *Die Pastoralbriefe*, 4th ed., RNT 7 (Regensburg: Pustet, 1969), 294–96. Contra Mounce, *Pastoral Epistles*, 413.

2:8). This ἵνα clause, while directing attention outside the church, admittedly has no overt evangelistic focus. The singular "opponent" (ὁ ἐξ ἐναντίας) should likely be understood as a generic reference to any adversary (whether inside or outside the church) whom Titus and the church in Crete are facing. Also, the "us" (ἡμῶν) about whom the opponent[s] have nothing bad to say would seem to extend most naturally to the entire church, including Titus and Paul. Paul says that Titus' (and implicitly all the young men's) behavior and speech should produce "shame" in their opponents. This "shame" should probably be understood not simply as public embarrassment, but the remorse of genuine repentance which accompanies saving faith (cf. 1 Tim 1:20; 2 Thess 3:14–15; Matt 5:14–16; 1 Pet 2:12; 3:16).[99] Admittedly, if we were to view this verse out of context, it might be read as concerned with quieting criticism for political or other non-evangelistic reasons.[100] Nevertheless, this entire *Haustafel* should be read as a unit. Apart from the question of whether Titus 2:1–10 is an authentic 'house code,' the author's systematic form of address argues against indiscriminately fracturing it.[101] The connecting γάρ at the end of the section should not be limited to one of the groups addressed, but refers back to all of this paranetic section. Each different class of believers should behave according to Paul's instruction so outsiders will be attracted to the gospel, which now manifests the grace of God savingly to all kinds of people.

A closer look at the *Haustafel* reveals a four-part progression from less-overt to more-overt statements of evangelistic intent. We have just discussed the latter two of these four steps. In the first step (the instructions to older men), no mention of outsiders is made. In the second step (the paranesis to older women and younger women), Paul says that women are supposed to act respectably ἵνα μὴ ὁ λόγος τοῦ θεοῦ βλασφημῆται (Titus 2:5).[102] This verse states the object of the blasphemy, the "word of God" (cf. 2 Tim 2:9) or gospel, but it does not state the agent of the blasphemy. In Titus 2:5, as in a similar passages dealing with blasphemy or slander, we must use the broader context to

---

99 So Marshall, *Pastoral Epistles*, 256; Gottfried Holtz, *Die Pastoralbriefe*, THKNT 13 (Berlin: Evangelische Verlagsanstalt, 1965), 222; cf. Howard C. Kee, "The Linguistic Background of 'Shame' in the New Testament," in *On Language, Culture, and Religion: In Honor of Eugene A. Nida*, ed. Matthew Black and William A. Smalley (The Hague: Mouton, 1974), 133–47.

100 That is, in line with the *christliche Bürgerlichkeit* interpretation. Another unlikely interpretation of Titus 2:8 is that Paul is employing a hypothetical opponent as an "objective" measurement of the community's obedience – similar to his approach in 1 Timothy 3:7.

101 πρεσβύτας (2:2), πρεσβύτιδας (2:3), νέας (2:4), νεωτέρους (2:6), δούλους (2:9).

102 Knight asserts, "The concluding words, 'that God's word may not be dishonored,' may be more closely connected with the immediately preceding clause but should be regarded as referring to all that precedes" (Knight, *Pastoral Epistles*, 309).

determine *by whom* the word of the Lord is blasphemed when a Christian engages in forbidden behavior. Are the agents of the potential blasphemy members of the Christian community? In such a case, Paul would be saying that Christian wives should submit to their husbands so that the wives, *as Christians*, would not be guilty of slandering the teaching they profess.

An argument in favor of this reading can be found in 1 Timothy 1:19–20 where, Paul hands the heretics over to Satan to be taught not to blaspheme (ἵνα παιδευθῶσιν μὴ βλασφημεῖν). It is clear from this passage that persons within the Christian community can be guilty of blaspheming God. Blasphemy is equated with rejecting faith and a good conscience (1:19). So, in 1 Timothy 1:19–20, the agents of the blasphemy are those who have rejected the faith, while the object of the blasphemy is God. Neither the agent nor the object of the blasphemy is stated directly, but both are clearly inferred.[103]

While it is grammatically possible in Titus 2:5 to understand the Christian women as the agents of blasphemy, this reading is unlikely. Paul's choice of the "word of God" as the object of the blasphemy points towards calumny directed at the Christian message, rather than God himself, as one might expect in the case of blasphemy from a member of the community.[104] Furthermore, a concern that *outsiders* not slander God (or his word) because of the unholy behavior of his people is a motif in the Old Testament.[105] It would not be unusual to find Paul employing this theme. The main evidence, however, that argues for slander originating outside the community is the two following "steps" in our *Haustafel* evangelistic staircase. Paul's instruction to the next group (τοὺς νεωτέρους, Titus 2:6), is qualified by the purpose clause, ἵνα ὁ ἐξ ἐναντίας ἐντραπῇ μηδὲν ἔχων λέγειν περὶ ἡμῶν φαῦλον (Titus 2:8). And finally, the fourth step, as we have already seen, speaks of slaves adorning the gospel (i.e. making it attractive) through their righteous conduct.

The *Haustafel* staircase can be summarized by the following progression. (1)

---

103 First Timothy 1:19–20 is similar to 1 Corinthians 5:5, where an unnamed immoral man is handed over "to Satan for the destruction of the flesh, so that his spirit may be saved in the day of the Lord."

104 Knight comments, "For a wife to fail to be submissive to her husband or to be unloving or impure, etc., would allow non-Christians to say that Christianity makes people worse rather than better and therefore that its message is not only useless but bad" (Knight, *Pastoral Epistles*, 309). Luther interprets the verse similarly. Regarding its application, he writes, "God wants to use your life to convert other nations, that the kingdom of Christ may be expanded . . . . God Himself gives everything freely. But He demands that we not give offense to others who are to be converted and that we not alienate them from our doctrine" (Martin Luther, "Lectures on Titus," in *Luther's Works*, vol. 29, trans. and ed. Jaroslav Pelikan [St. Louis: Concordia, 1968], 57).

105 E.g., Isa 52:5; Ezek 36:20–36; cf. Rom 2:24; 1 Tim 6:1; Jas 2:7; 2 Pet 2:2; *2 Clem.* 13:2

Older men are to act righteously [no reason stated]. (2) Older women and younger women are to behave respectably, so that the gospel will not be reviled [by outsiders].[106] (3) Young men [especially Titus] are to live prudently, so that outsiders will not have anything bad to say about Christians. (4) Slaves are to act righteously, so that outsiders will find the gospel attractive. Appropriately at the end of this stair-step instruction to various classes of people, we find the causal γάρ statement, "for the grace of God has appeared savingly for all kinds of people." This progression can be illustrated by the following diagram.

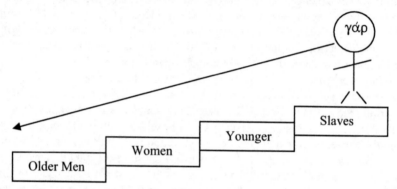

Fig. 2. The relationship of the γάρ clause in Titus 2:11 to the preceding context.

The evangelistic intent of Titus chapter two becomes clear when read as a whole unit, rather than unconnected segments.[107] All the various segments of the Christian community are to live praiseworthy lives – not simply for the sake of obeying God, but also because their behavior will commend or detract from

---

106 Yet, the women's gender-specific behavior is not simply pragmatic, as is made clear by the theological brackets of our passage (Titus 1:1; 2:11–15) and Paul's comments elsewhere (Eph 5:22–24; Col 3:18; 1 Tim 2:11–15; cf. 1 Pet 3:1–8). See John Piper and Wayne Grudem, eds., *Recovering Biblical Manhood and Womanhood: A Response to Evangelical Feminism* (Wheaton: Crossway, 1991), esp. 140–208; George W. Knight III, *The New Testament Teaching on the Role Relationship of Men and Women* (Grand Rapids: Baker, 1977); contra Padgett, "Pauline Rationale for Submission," 39–52.

107 It would be a mistake, however, to assume that the ethical behavior enjoined in the Pastorals is only presented as the means of accomplishing an evangelistic goal. Are women to avoid drunkenness and slander only as the means of promulgating the gospel (Titus 2:3)? Clearly an ontological principle is also in view, as is made clear by Paul's opening sentence in chapter 2: "But as for you, [Titus,] teach what is consistent with sound doctrine." Cf. Titus 2:11–15. See Mounce, *Pastoral Epistles*, 418–19; Clara Burini, "τῇ ὑγιαινούσῃ διδασκαλίᾳ: Una norma di vita cristiana in *Tito* 2,1," *Vetera Christianorum* 18 (1981): 275–85.

the gospel.[108] We started this section by citing texts which show that an essential part of Paul's apostolic vision was living in such a way that his conduct authenticated the gospel. In studying Titus 2:1–10, we have discovered that Paul also expected the churches' behavior to advance the proclamation of the gospel.[109] Paul commanded the church to witness "passively."

Conclusion

In this chapter, we have examined several passages in Paul's letters where he instructs the church to evangelize. As we explained at the outset, we have employed the somewhat artificial distinction between (1) Paul's commands to be an "active" witness, and (2) Paul's commands to be a "passive" witness. Our study confirms that Paul expected the church to play both an active and passive role in missions. Such active and passive elements are occasionally inextricably interwoven in Paul's thought (esp. in 1 Corinthians), and our active/passive dichotomy would likely have seemed strange to him.

In the next chapter, we will examine further evidence that Paul thought of the churches as engaged in the same multi-orbed missionary activity that he was. Indeed, if the gospel served to propel the churches in the same apostolic mission in which Paul was engaged, we would also expect Paul to mention, at least incidentally, other activities of the churches that paralleled his apostolic mission.

---

108 See Knight, "Excursus: Motivations for Appropriate Conduct: 2:1–10," in *Pastoral Epistles*, 316–18.

109 See also 1 Cor 10:31–11:1; Eph 5:6–16; 1 Thess 4:12; 2 Thess 3:7–9; 1 Tim 3:7; 6:1; cf. Acts 2:43–47; 1 Pet 2:9–12; 3:1–2.

Incidental Evidence that Paul Expected the Churches to Spread the Gospel in the Apostolic Pattern

Looking beyond Paul's explicit imperatives to evangelize, the apostle often makes incidental remarks showing that he expected the gospel to propel the church in missionary activity that paralleled his own apostolic mission. In this chapter, we will begin by looking at three other facets of the apostolic mission that Paul describes as replicated in the life of the church. They are: (1) miracles in confirmation of the gospel (2) praying for missions and the church, and (3) teaching and "building up" the church.

The latter half of this chapter is reserved for a more in-depth study of the role of suffering in Paul's mission and the mission of the church. The frequency of Paul's references to suffering warrant this extended treatment. We will find that Paul's remarks on suffering provide significant evidence in confirmation of our thesis and form an appropriate *inclusio* to our opening study on the dynamic nature of gospel.

Miracles, Prayer and Teaching in Paul and in the Church

If Paul believed that the gospel created a missionary church in continuity with the apostolic mission (see chapter two), then we would expect Paul to depict, at least incidentally, the church as engaged in various missionary activities which parallel his own. That is, not only would Paul give explicit imperatives that sanctioned the church's verbal witness; he would also mention the church as doing other "apostolic missionary activities." The first of these incidental parallels we will look at is the presence and role of miracles in the ministry of the apostles and the life of the church.

Divine Confirmation of the Gospel through Miracles

We will argue below that churches continue the apostolic mission by confirming the gospel with signs, wonders, and miracles.[1] There can be no

---

1   Paul and his churches assumed the reality of miracles, so that issue will not be
     addressed here. For a rebuttal of naturalistic objections to the miraculous, see

doubt that Paul describes his own gospel ministry as characterized by such miraculous manifestations.[2] In Romans 15:18–19, he writes,

> For I will not venture to speak of anything except what Christ has accomplished through me to win obedience from the Gentiles, by word and deed, by the power of signs and wonders, by the power of the Spirit of God, so that from Jerusalem and as far as Illyricum I have fulfilled the good news of Christ.[3]

These "signs and wonders," in continuity with the Old Testament pattern, demonstrate God's saving intervention on behalf of his people.[4] In 2

Norman L. Geisler, *Miracles and Modern Thought* (Grand Rapids: Zondervan; Dallas: Probe Ministries International, 1982).

2   G. H. Twelftree writes, "Paul's testimony is that miracles occurred wherever he proclaimed the good news and that they remained essential in the life of the church" (G. H. Twelftree, "Signs, Wonders, and Miracles," in *DPL*, ed. Gerald F. Hawthorne, Ralph P. Martin, and Daniel G. Reid [Downers Grove: InterVarsity, 1993], 875). Cf. Jacob Jervell, "Der schwache Charismatiker," in *Rechtfertigung: Festschrift für Ernst Käsemann zum 70. Gerburtstag*, ed. J. Friedrich, W. Pöhlmann, and P. Stuhlmacher (Tübingen: Mohr; Göttingen: Vandenhoeck & Ruprecht, 1976), 185–98. For a succinct discussion of the words σημεῖον, τέρας, and δύναμις, see Twelftree's article (875–77). For more detailed studies, see Karl Heinrich Rengstorf, "σημεῖον...," *TDNT* 7:200–69; idem, "τέρας," *TDNT* 8:113–26; Walter Grundmann, "δύναμαι...," *TDNT* 2:284–317; S. Vernon McCasland, "Signs and Wonders," *JBL* 76 (1957): 149–52.

3   This translation is a minor alteration of the NRSV. For missiological reflections on this passage, see O'Brien, *Gospel and Mission*, 34–36. Cf. 2 Cor 4:7; 6:7; Eph 3:7; Col 1:29.

4   See Exod 3:20; 7:3, 9; 8:23; 10:1–2; 11:9–10; 15:11; Num 14:22; Deut 4:34; 6:22; 7:19; 11:3; 26:8; 29:3; 34:11; Josh 3:5; 24:17; Neh 9:10; Pss 78:43; 105:27; 135:9; Jer 32:20–21; Dan 4:2–3; 6:27; Acts 7:36; cf. Philo *De Vita Mosis* 1.210; Josephus *Ant.* 2.12.3–2.13.1 (O'Brien, *Gospel and Mission*, 35; Twelftree, "Signs, Wonders, and Miracles," 875; D. A. Carson, "The Purpose of Signs and Wonders in the New Testament," in *Power Religion: The Selling Out of the Evangelical Church?*, ed. Michael Scott Horton [Chicago: Moody, 1992], 91–94). See Jean-Louis Ska's discussion of "Les plaies d'Égypte, 'signes et prodiges' accomplis par un prophète," in Jean-Louis Ska, "La sortie d' Égypte (Ex 7–14) dans le récit sacerdotal (P^g) et la tradition prophétique," *Bib* 60 (1979): 192–98. Also, see Lampe's helpful reflections on the Old Testament background for miracles in the New Testament (G. W. H. Lampe, "Miracles in the Acts of the Apostles," in *Miracles: Cambridge Studies in their Philosophy and History*, ed. C. F. D. Moule [London: A. R. Mowbray, 1965], 163–78). Cf. Fritz Stolz, "Zeichen und Wunder: Die prophetische Legitimation und ihre Geschichte," *ZTK* 69 (1972): 125–44; John Woodhouse, "Signs and Wonders in the Bible," in *Signs & Wonders and Evangelicals: A Response to the Teaching of John Wimber*, ed. Robert Doyle (Homebush West, NSW [Australia]: Lancer, 1987), 17–35.

Corinthians 12:12, Paul again notes the supernatural phenomena that mark his ministry: "The signs of a true apostle were performed among you with utmost patience, signs and wonders and mighty works."[5] Similarly, in 1 Corinthians 2:4–5, Paul writes, "My speech and my proclamation were not with plausible words of wisdom, but with a demonstration of the Spirit and of power, so that your faith might rest not on human wisdom but on the power of God" (cf. 1 Thess 1:5). Interestingly, in 2 Thessalonians 2:9, Paul says that Satan also employs miracles (albeit counterfeit) to attract followers.[6] It seems that one of the main purposes of miracles (whether true or false) is to confirm one's message in the hopes of gaining adherents.[7]

The question, then, is whether, non-apostles – specifically persons in the churches that Paul addresses – also produced miracles in confirmation of the gospel. Two texts seem to indicate that they did. In Galatians 3:5, Paul asks the Galatian believers, "Does God supply you with the Spirit and work miracles (ἐνεργῶν δυνάμεις) among you by your doing the works of the law, or by your believing what you heard?" Admittedly, this text does not say that outsiders were aware of the miracles in the Galatian church. Another Pauline text, 1 Corinthians 12:9–30, however, implicitly points beyond the congregation. In 1 Cor 12:9–30, Paul speaks of persons in the church as having the gifts of performing miracles (ἐνεργήματα δυνάμεως, δυνάμεις, 12:10, 28–29) and healings (χαρίσματα ἰαμάτων, 12:9, 28, 30).[8] When Paul says all gifts (including miracles) should be used for "building up" (οἰκοδομή) the church, this "building up" includes both the incorporation of new believers (note the "unbelievers" of 1 Cor 14:24) as well as the maturing

---

5   It seems that Paul thought all authentic apostles performed miracles, though miracles in themselves did not qualify one for the apostolic office. See my discussion of the term "apostle" in chapter two. Also see Jacob Jervell, "The Signs of an Apostle: Paul's Miracles," trans. Roy A. Harrisville, in *The Unknown Paul: Essays on Luke-Acts and Early Christian History* (Minneapolis: Augsburg, 1984), 77–95; Ernst Käsemann, "Die Legitimität des Apostels: Eine Untersuchung zu II Korinther 10–13," *ZNW* 41 (1942): 33–71. Käsemann wrongly sees miracles as of little importance to Paul.

6   Cf. Exod 7:8–8:18; Deut 13:1–5; Matt 24:24; Mark 13:22; Rev 13:13–14; Josephus *Ant.* 20.8.6.

7   Concerning Paul's miracles in Acts, Susan Marie Praeder concludes, "Paul's activity as a miracle worker is everywhere linked to his activities and experiences as a missionary to the Jews and the Gentiles of the Mediterranean world" (S. M. Praeder, "Miracle Worker and Missionary: Paul in the Acts of the Apostles," in *Society of Biblical Literature 1983 Seminar Papers*, ed. Kent Harold Richards [Chico, CA: Scholars Press, 1983], 128).

8   Cf. Jas 5:13–16.

of present ones (14:23–26).[9] Non-believers will be attracted and converted through the miracles performed by gifted members of the Corinthian church. Indeed, if one of the main purposes of the apostles' miracles is to confirm the gospel message, it would be surprising if miracles performed by non-apostles did not serve a similar function.

The evangelistic purpose of miracles in early Christianity, while mentioned in Paul's letters, is made more explicit in the narratives of Acts.[10] Here we find a definite pattern: miracles serve the dual intention of benefiting the Christian/convert and attracting the notice of outsiders.[11] For example, in Acts 3:1–4:22, Peter and John heal a crippled man with the result that many persons heed their subsequent evangelistic preaching (4:4). While some miracles are not understood properly or are not received well by all witnesses (5:11–13; 14:8–20), they inevitably attract some converts (5:14; 14:21–22). The close relationship between evangelistic preaching and confirming miracles is further shown by the early church's prayer in Acts 4:29–30. The prayer, as recorded in Acts, reads, "Lord, . . . grant to your servants to speak your word with all boldness, while you stretch out your hand to heal, and signs and wonders are

---

9   We have touched on the evangelistic meaning of "building up" in chapter three, and will deal with it in more detail below.

10   In Acts, we also receive a secondary report of the miracles which Paul performed during his apostolic ministry (13:4–12; 14:3, 8–18; 15:12; 16:16–18; 19:11–12; 20:7–12; 28:1–9). Jervell notes, "Of the eleven miracle narratives related in Acts, seven have to do with Paul" ("Signs of an Apostle," 80). Also see T. W. Crafer, *The Healing Miracles in the Book of Acts: A Practical and Devotional Study* (London: Society for Promoting Christian Knowledge, [1939]); John A. Hardon, "The Miracle Narratives in the Acts of the Apostles," *CBQ* 16 (1954): 303–18; John Fenton, "The Order of the Miracles performed by Peter and Paul in Acts," *ExpTim* 77 (1965–66): 381–83; Frans Neirynck, "The Miracle Stories in the Acts of the Apostles: An Introduction," in *Les Actes des Apôtres: Traditions, rédaction, théologie*, BETL 48, ed. J. Kremer (Gembloux: Ducolot; Leuven: Leuven University Press, 1979), 169–213. Neirynck also lists two relevant dissertations, to which I have not had access: M. H. Miller, "The Character of Miracles in Luke-Acts" (Th.D. diss., Graduate Theol. Union [Berkeley, CA], 1971; S. H. Kanda, "The Form and Function of the Petrine and Pauline Miracle Stories in the Acts of the Apostles (Ph.D. diss., Claremont Graduate School, 1973) (Neirynck, "Miracle Stories in the Acts of the Apostles," 170 n. 2). Bruno Bauer and those who follow him wrongly contrast the picture of Paul as a miracle worker in Acts with the apostle's supposed "non-miraculous" self-portrait in his letters (Bruno Bauer, *Die Apostelgeschichte: Eine Ausgleichung des Paulinismus und des Judenthums innerhalb der christlichen Kirche* [Berlin: Gustav Hempel, 1850], 7–25).

11   See Acts 1:8; 2:19, 22, 43; 3:1–4:22; 5:12; 6:8; 8:6, 13; 13:4–12; 14:3, 8–18; 15:12; 16:16–18; 19:11–12; 20:7–12; 28:1–9.

performed through the name of your holy servant Jesus."[12] The answer to this prayer, recorded in the following verse, shows that the "servants" prayed for here included all the church. Luke writes, "When they had prayed, the place in which they were gathered together was shaken; and *they were all filled with the Holy Spirit and spoke the word of God with boldness* (my emphasis)."

As the prayer above intimates, apostles are not the only ones performing miracles in the book of Acts. Non-apostles perform miracles as well, and the evangelistic purpose of such wonders is made more explicit than in Paul's letters. For example, during Philip's missionary tour of Samaria, his miracles serve to attract and convince his listeners (8:5–14). Similarly, Stephen's proclamation of the gospel is accompanied by miracles (6:7–10). As the gospel makes its way outwards from the original recipients (i.e., the apostles), God also empowers non-apostles to confirm the gospel through signs, wonders, and miracles (cf. Acts 1:8; Heb 2:4). Thus, the apostolic function of confirming the gospel through miracles is replicated in the life of the churches.[13] While this ecclesiastical pattern is unmistakably present in Acts, it is implicitly present in Paul's letters, as we saw above (1 Cor 12:9–10, 28–30; 14:23–26). Both the apostles and the churches perform miracles in confirmation of the gospel.

Praying for Missions and the Church

It is unlikely that Paul bifurcated his prayers into "missions-related" and "church-related" categories. As D. A. Carson has cogently argued, Paul's prayer life, like his ministry, was woven from the seamless fabric of his God-centered vision.[14] Yet, for the purposes of this study, we will classify Paul's

---

12   According to Luke, Peter saw this same evangelistic purpose in Jesus' miracles. Note Peter's speech on the day of Pentecost: "You that are Israelites, listen to what I have to say: Jesus of Nazareth, a man attested to you by God with deeds of power, wonders, and signs that God did through him among you, as you yourselves know . . ." (Acts 2:22; cf. Acts 10:36–39). Jesus, at least in some settings, viewed his own miracles in this same way (Matt 11:20–24).

13   The question of the modern church's relationship to this New Testament pattern is a complex one. See D. A. Carson, "Purpose of Signs and Wonders," 89–118; James M. Boice, "A Better Way: The Power of the Word and Spirit," in *Power Religion*, 119–36; Robert Doyle, ed., *Signs & Wonders and Evangelicals: A Response to the Teaching of John Wimber* (Homebush West, NSW [Australia]: Lancer, 1987).

14   Carson writes, "Paul sees mission in holistic, even cosmic terms. The glory of God, the reign of Christ, the declaration of the mystery of the gospel, the conversion of men and women, the growth and edification of the church, the defeat of the cosmic powers, the pursuit of holiness, the passion for godly fellowship and unity in the church, the unification of Jews and Gentiles, doing good to all but especially to fellow-believers – these are all woven into a seamless garment. All the elements are held together by a vision in which God is at the centre and Jesus Christ effects the

references to prayer – with the realization that the apostle's actual understanding of prayer, like his approach to ministry in general, was more holistic.

Even from a cursory reading of Paul's letters, it quickly becomes clear that he frequently prayed for the churches to which he wrote.[15] In these prayers, Paul most commonly *intercedes* for the spiritual health and well-being of the congregations – for their experience of peace, grace and mercy, their unity, their increasing spiritual insight, their knowledge of God's will, or their manifestation of good works, love, and spiritual health.[16] Paul also routinely *thanks* God in prayer for the congregations' exhibition of faith, love, or obedience.[17]

This preponderance of intra-community concerns in Paul's prayers are rightly explained by Carson,

> The church was multiplying so quickly that the apostles could not always keep up: the church in Antioch was not founded by an apostle, and neither was the church in Rome or the church in Colosse. In this sort of environment the intertwining of ministry and prayer was so wholesome and inescapable that our piecemeal approach would seem atomistic, even bizarre. Moreover, at the practical level this sort of environment meant that the most urgent problems faced by church leaders were often the problems *inside the multiplying fledgling churches*. Small wonder, then, that a large proportion of Paul's recorded prayers are devoted to the spiritual maturation of believers.[18]

---

changes for his glory and his people's good" (D. A. Carson, "Paul's Mission and Prayer," in *The Gospel to the Nations: Perspectives on Paul's Mission*, ed. Peter Bolt and Mark Thompson [Downers Grove: InterVarsity, 2000], 182).

15 See these significant studies which discuss Paul's prayers: Roland Gebauer, *Das Gebet bei Paulus: Forschungsgeschichtliche und exegetische Studien* (Giessen: Brunner, 1989); Krister Stendahl, "Paul at Prayer," *Int* 34 (1980): 240–49; Peter T. O'Brien, *Introductory Thanksgivings in the Letters of Paul*, NovTSup 49 (Leiden: Brill, 1977); Gordon P. Wiles, *Paul's Intercessory Prayers: The Significance of the Intercessory Prayer Passages in the Letters of St. Paul*, SNTSMS 24 (London: Cambridge University Press, 1974); David M. Stanley, *Boasting in the Lord: The Phenomenon of Prayer in Saint Paul* (New York: Paulist, 1973); Jerome D. Quinn, "Apostolic Ministry and Apostolic Prayer," *CBQ* 33 (1971): 479–91.

16 E.g., Rom 15:5–6, 13, 33; 16:20; Gal 6:16, 18; Eph 1:16–19; 1 Thess 3:9–13; 5:23–24; 2 Thess 1:11; 2:16–17; 3:5, 16; 2 Tim 1:16, 18; 4:16. According to Robert Morgenthaler's *Statistik des neutestamentlichen Wortschatzes*, Paul uses sixteen different words for prayer a total of 105 times in his 13 letters (as cited by W. B. Hunter, "Prayer," in *DPL*, ed. Gerald F. Hawthorne, Ralph P. Martin, and Daniel G. Reid [Downers Grove: InterVarsity, 1993], 729).

17 E.g., Rom 1:8–10; Phil 1:3–10; Col 1:3; 1 Thess 1:2–8; 2 Tim 1:3; Phlm 4–6.

18 Carson, "Paul's Mission and Prayer," 183.

Also we should note that Paul considered the maturing of the churches as simply an extension of his evangelistic work. Paul's apostolic consciousness did not stop at gaining converts, but an essential part of his missionary vision was the maturing of Christians.[19]

We can, however, distinguish in Paul's prayers explicit evangelistic concerns (i.e., matters related to the initial proclamation and reception of the gospel), and as that is the focus of our study, we will now turn to these salvifically-oriented prayers. Paul's missions-related prayers can be divided into several categories: (1) Prayers of thanksgiving for the congregations' missionary activity (Phil 1:3–5; 1 Thess 1:2–8; cf. Rom 1:8).[20] (2) Prayers for the salvation of certain persons (Rom 10:1).[21] (3) Prayers that have the churches' relationship with outsiders in view (1 Thess 3:12; cf. Rom 15:7–13).[22]

Because there are no copies of the churches' letters to Paul, we do not have direct access to their prayers. For our thesis, however, the most important question is this: how did Paul expect the churches to pray? And, can we demonstrate a continuity between Paul's apostolic task of praying for the

---

19 Bowers, "Fulfilling the Gospel," 185–98. David M. Stanley writes, "In reality, [the Pauline thanksgiving] is an account for his addressees of the prayer of petition as well as of gratitude Paul made for them before writing. Thus it attests Paul's conviction that his own intercession was in fact a significant part of his apostolic responsibility" (Stanley, "Imitation in Paul's Letters: Its Significance for His Relationship to Jesus and to His Own Christian Foundations," in *From Jesus to Paul: Studies in Honour of Francis Wright Beare*, ed. Peter Richardson and John C. Hurd [Waterloo, Ontario: Wilfrid Laurier University Press, 1984], 133).

20 The missionary references in Phil 1:3–5 and 1 Thess 1:2–8 have been explicated above.

21 Admittedly, in Romans 10:1, Paul prays only for the salvation of the rebellious Jewish race as a whole. Yet, it is reasonable to assume that Paul reveals here a principle of spiritual intercession that he applies to lost Gentiles as well. D. A. Carson, on the other hand, sees Romans 10:1 as not having implications beyond the recalcitrant Jewish nation. Carson writes, "Although there are . . . occasional exhortations to pray for Paul in the context of his apostolic ministry, and although almost all the prayers are in one fashion or another gospel-related, on first reflection it is surprising that there is little intercession for the lost, little evidence of systematic praying for the conversion of men and women, few examples of what we might call mission praying – that is, praying specifically for the outreach of the gospel, not least in cross-cultural contexts . . . . The closest approximation to that sort of intensity [in prayer] for the lost [in Paul's letters] is in Paul's agonized supplication for his fellow-Jews – and here, of course, there are special themes operating" (Carson, "Paul's Mission and Prayer," 176).

22 In 1 Thess 3:12, Paul writes, "And may the Lord make you increase and abound in love for one another *and for all* [καὶ εἰς πάντας], just as we abound in love for you [my emphasis]."

churches and the churches' independent responsibility to pray for others?

We do indeed find continuity between Paul's prayers and the apostle's report of the churches' prayers. Most frequently, as would be expected by the occasional nature of Paul's letters, Paul requests prayers for his own ministry. Yet, Paul also expects the churches to pray more generally for the advance of the gospel and to intercede for other churches. Thus, at least in these two areas, we find the churches replicating Paul's understanding of his apostolic prayer task. That is, the churches pray for their evangelistic relationship with outsiders and pray for other churches.

Of primary importance for our thesis is the fact that Paul asks the church to pray for their evangelistic relationship with outsiders. For example, in 1 Timothy 2:1–4, Paul writes,

> First of all, then, I urge that supplications, prayers, intercessions, and thanksgivings be made for everyone, for kings and all who are in high positions, so that we may lead a quiet and peaceable life in all godliness and dignity. This is right and is acceptable in the sight of God our Savior, who desires everyone to be saved and to come to the knowledge of the truth.

In this passage, Paul enjoins the church to pray "for everyone" (without distinction) (2:1). Paul then highlights praying for one significant class of persons – kings and rulers (2:2). The immediate reason given for this intercession is the resulting "quiet and peaceable" existence that will be made available to the Christian community to live in "all godliness and dignity" (2:2). The following statement, however, points beyond a quiet and godly life as an end in itself. Paul adds, "This is right and is acceptable in the sight of God our Savior, who desires everyone to be saved and to come to the knowledge of the truth" (2:3–4). The emphasis on salvation in the passage is made clear not only by Paul's use of the title "Savior" for God, but also the descriptive phrase that God "desires everyone to be saved and to come to the knowledge of the truth."[23] There is an unmistakable evangelistic dimension to the civil peace for

---

23 Mounce understands the passage as countering the heretics who were trying to limit salvation (and thus also prayers for salvation) to a select group (Mounce, *Pastoral Epistles*, 77). Barrett takes a similar view (*The Pastoral Epistles*, 50–51). Philip Towner writes, "That soteriology forms the centerpoint of the passage (vv. 1–7) is evident, first, from the description of God as 'Savior' (v. 3) and from the reference to God's salvific will (v. 4). Verses 3–4 explain the instructions to pray for all men (for their salvation), and then receive substantiation from the formulated piece that follows in vv. 5–6 (*gar*, v. 5; see below, Chapter 9). Then, as we have seen, within the traditional material *mesitēs* and *anthrōpos* are saturated with soteriological significance. Finally, the thought of salvation is implicit in v. 7, where it is explained that the redemptive Christ-event (as summarized in vv. 5–6) forms the content of Paul's proclamation" (Towner, *Goal of Our Instruction*, 82).

which Paul enjoins prayer.[24] Indeed, it is not hard to imagine certain political or societal situations which would allow for a wider promulgation of the gospel; that is, in fact, what Paul seems to envision.[25]

About 1 Timothy 2:1–4, Philip Towner comments,

> It may seem strange that the author would think of the church's relation to the state when the central theme is salvation, but apparently the connection was a common one, for a mission impulse is also evident in Rom 13.1ff. and 1 Pet 2.13ff. Moreover, providing a peaceful and orderly society was the state's domain, so prayer for it was calculated to ensure that the best possible conditions for spreading the gospel were obtained: the *ēremon kai hēsychion bion*.[26]

Paul's concern for the church's relationship to outsiders was only one aspect of his life as an intercessor. The apostle labored in prayer for many areas of the churches' community life, and expected the congregations to replicate this intercessory ministry for each other. We find this point made in several of Paul's incidental references. For example, in 2 Corinthians 9:14, Paul approvingly describes the Judean Christians as longing for and praying for the Gentile believers.[27] Also in Ephesians 6:18, Paul commands the recipients of his letter to pray for all the saints (περὶ πάντων τῶν ἁγίων). This general designation extends beyond Christians at Ephesus (Eph 1:1), as Paul clarifies by designating himself more particularly as one of these "saints" to be prayed for (Eph 6:19).

Another way in which the churches involve themselves in mission is by praying for Paul's mission and travels (as frequently requested by the apostle). In this way the churches to which Paul writes are able to partner with him in the

---

24 Towner writes, "But for what reason are all men to be prayed for? Nothing less than for their salvation. Not only does the designation *ho sōtēr hēmōn theos* (v. 3) point to this, but it is also the bold announcement of v. 4 that the will of God with respect to all men is their salvation. The tradition inserted at this point (vv. 5–6) describes the instrument by which God's salvific will is accomplished – the self-offering of Christ *hyper pantōn*. Verses 3–6 are wholly taken up with salvation . . . . Moreover, since v. 4 is given in substantiation of the command of vv. 1–2 . . . , it follows that the prayer, at least 'for all men,' has salvation as its goal" (Towner, *Goal of Our Instruction*, 202).

25 This desire for peaceful civil conditions would initially seem to contradict Paul's understanding of suffering as ordained by God for the good of Christians and advancement of the gospel. Yet, Paul holds this paradox together under the sovereignty of God. Note my more extensive comments about this biblical tension in the section on suffering below.

26 Towner, *Goal of Our Instruction*, 203.

27 Second Corinthians 9:14, "[The Judean Christians] long for you [the Corinthian Christians] and pray for you because of the surpassing grace of God that he has given you."

task of world evangelization. The churches are to pray for the success of Paul's endeavors, his safety or deliverance, his travel plans, his bold and clear proclamation of the gospel, and an open door for the gospel.[28] Interestingly, when Paul requests prayer for his proclamation of the gospel, in the immediate context there is always a statement about the church's evangelistic relationship to outsiders (e.g., Eph 6:15, 19–20; Col 4:2–4, 5–6; cf. 2 Thess 2:16–17; 3:1–2). Paul seems unwilling to request prayer for his gospel preaching without also mentioning the missionary work of his churches. It should also be noted that while we can suppose that Paul would have expected his churches to pray for other itinerant missionaries or prophets, the unique relationship between an apostle and the churches is in some sense unrepeatable.

Although Paul asks the churches to pray for his evangelistic endeavors (Eph 6:19–20; Col 4:2–4; 2 Thess 3:1–2), it is striking that he never speaks of praying for his own missionary success.[29] Is it possible that Paul's silence indicates that he did not pray for his own missionary campaigns? Did he conceive of such prayer as only coming from others? This unlikely suggestion is built on the same logical basis as the argument made by W. P. Bowers regarding the passive missionary role of Paul's churches.[30] An "argument from silence" is inherently dangerous and only as convincing as the circumstantial evidence and logic that underlie it. When Paul requests others to pray for his missionary work, he almost certainly reveals matters about which he prays as well. It just so happens that Paul's letters, due to their occasional nature, do not record his own prayers for the success of his evangelistic preaching.

In summary, Paul prayed for the churches' relationship with outsiders, for the churches' internal spiritual health, and (in all likelihood) for his own mission. Paul expected the churches to also pray for these same things. The apostolic ministry of prayer is replicated in the churches.[31]

---

28 See Rom 15:30–33; 2 Cor 1:8–11; Eph 6:19–20; Phil 1:19; Col 4:2–4; 1 Thess 5:25; 2 Thess 3:1–2; Phlm 22.

29 Rom 10:1 is a general prayer for the salvation of the Jews and not a prayer for Paul's effective proclamation to them. Also, in Rom 15:30–33, Paul asks the Roman Christians "to join" [συναγωνίσασθαι] with him in praying for the acceptance of his collection in Jerusalem and his safe travel to Rome (in order to visit the established Roman congregation). Paul's gospel ministry to non-believers is not mentioned.

30 The only difference is that in the case of the church's missionary proclamation, Paul's letters do contain some incontrovertible evidence that the churches were indeed proclaiming the gospel – with the apostle's instruction and approval. See chapter three.

31 For a more popular study of prayer in missions, see John Piper, *Let the Nations be Glad!*, 41–70.

Teaching and Building up the Church

In his article, "Fulfilling the Gospel: The Scope of the Pauline Mission," W. P. Bowers has convincingly shown that Paul's missionary vision entailed not only the founding of churches, but the maturing of those young congregations.[32] Thus, it is wrong to say (as some scholars have), that Paul was satisfied in founding only superficial "beachheads" for the gospel.[33] Paul's continued relationship with the churches (in which he taught and admonished them), was in some sense an extension of his initial evangelistic ministry. Due to this intertwining of teaching and initial evangelism in Paul's ministry, it is appropriate in this missiological study to ask if Paul spoke of the churches as performing didactic functions parallel to his own.

Paul does indeed speak of the church as teaching in the same way that he has.[34] For example, in Romans 15:14, Paul writes to the church in Rome, "I myself feel confident about you, my brothers and sisters, that you yourselves are full of goodness, filled with all knowledge, and able to instruct one another." The Greek word here translated "to instruct" (νουθετέω) is the same word used elsewhere by Paul to describe his apostolic ministry of teaching and admonishment (1 Cor 4:14; Col 1:28).

Both congregational leaders and ordinary believers now have an obligation to carry on instruction/admonition in the apostolic pattern. For example, in 1 Thessalonians 5:12, the leaders of the church are described as those who admonish the congregation (νουθετοῦντας ὑμᾶς). Also, in 2 Thessalonians 3:15, all believers are exhorted to admonish (νουθετεῖτε) community members who do not obey Paul's teaching. Finally, in Colossians 3:16, Paul writes, "Let the word of Christ dwell in you richly; teach and admonish one another (νουθετοῦντες ἑαυτούς) in all wisdom."

In the last verse quoted above, Paul also instructs the members of the church community to teach (διδάσκοντες) one another. The verb διδάσκω is used elsewhere by Paul to describe his (or his co-workers) pedagogical relationship with the churches (e.g., 1 Cor 4:17; Col 1:28; 2 Thess 2:15). Both ordinary believers and recognized leaders are to "teach" one another, though the didactic ministries will obviously differ (cf. Col 3:16; 1 Tim 2:12; 2 Tim 2:2).

Paul also describes his ministry to the church as "building up" (οἰκοδομέω) the church. This "building" language will now be examined in more detail. Our aim is to understand in what way Paul expects this construction ministry to be replicated by the church.

Paul speaks of himself as a building expert (ἀρχιτέκτων) appointed by

---

32 Bowers, "Fulfilling the Gospel," 185–98.

33 E.g., Renan, *Saint Paul*, 492–93; Wrede, *Paul*, 47–48; C. K. Barrett, "New Testament Eschatology," 228; Althaus, *Der Brief an die Römer,* 147.

34 Though the churches, of course, do not exercise this teaching function over multiple congregations.

God to lay the foundation of the churches – which is none other than Jesus Christ (1 Cor 3:9–11). Paul and other apostles had the unrepeatable function in the history of the church of announcing (initially) the gospel as God's authoritative revelation. This fact is conveyed by numerous of Paul's remarks: (1) The apostles are appointed "first" in the body – both chronologically and conceptually, in that they originally promulgated and safeguarded the authoritative proclamation of the gospel (1 Cor 12:27–28). (2) Paul calls the apostles (and prophets) the "foundation" of the church, with Jesus Christ as the chief cornerstone, and other believers as building blocks (Eph 2:19–22). (3) Paul is concerned about apostolic spheres of influence and does not want to build on "someone else's foundation," but wants to lay foundations (i.e., start churches) in unreached territories (Rom 15:20–21; 2 Cor 10:13–16). (4) Every aspect of Paul's and his co-workers' ministry is for the building up of the church (2 Cor 12:19). (5) The authority for such building up comes from the Lord himself (2 Cor 13:10). Paul nowhere says the churches play a foundational role of the same type that he and the other apostles do. As we noted in chapter two, some elements of the apostolic ministry could not be reproduced by the church. The church is, however, not only spoken of as the object of Paul's or God's construction, but also as a builder.[35]

In Ephesians 4:11–16, Paul describes apostles, prophets, evangelists, and 'pastors and teachers' as all sharing the task of equipping the saints, so that they (the saints) will engage in the ministry (διακονία) for the "building up the body of Christ" (Eph 4:12).[36] While there is debate over whether Paul is here describing all believers as active in building up the body or only recognized leaders, the most likely interpretation is that *all Christians* are active in building up the body.[37] Indeed, Paul's variation in prepositions (πρός. . .εἰς. . .εἰς. . .)

---

35 Note Otto Michel's discussion of οἰκοδομεῖν in Paul's thought as a "Specific Apostolic Activity" and as a "Spiritual Task of the Community" (Otto Michel, "οἶκος...," in *TDNT*, 5:140–42).

36 Roels points out that the term διακονία is not reserved for "office-bearers of the church" (e.g., Acts 6:1; 11:29; 1 Cor 12:5; 16:15; 2 Cor 9:12; Rev 2:19) (Edwin D. Roels, *God's Mission*, 193–94).

37 So Roels, *God's Mission*, 192–95; F. F. Bruce, *The Epistles to the Colossians, to Philemon, and to the Ephesians*, NICNT (Grand Rapids: Eerdmans, 1984), 349; G. B. Caird, *Paul's Letters from Prison (Ephesians, Philippians, Colossians, Philemon) in the Revised Standard Version* (London: Oxford University Press, 1976), 76; Robert G. Bratcher and Eugene A. Nida, *A Translator's Handbook on Paul's Letter to the Ephesians* (New York: United Bible Societies, 1982), 102; Brooke Foss Westcott, *Saint Paul's Epistle to the Ephesians* (London: Macmillan, 1906; reprint, Grand Rapids: Baker, 1979), 62–63; J. Armitage Robinson, *St. Paul's Epistle to the Ephesians: A Revised Text and Translation with Exposition and Notes*, 2nd ed. (London: Macmillan, 1904), 98–99; Ernst Käsemann, "Epheser 4, 11–16," in *Exegetische Versuche und Besinnungen*, vol. 1 (Göttingen:

supports the contention that the πρός clause (πρὸς τὸν καταρτισμὸν τῶν ἁγίων) describes the work of the enumerated leaders, while the εἰς clauses (εἰς ἔργον διακονίας, εἰς οἰκοδομὴν τοῦ σώματος τοῦ χριστοῦ) describe the work of the saints. This interpretation is further supported by the immediate context. For example, in verse 7, there is already an emphasis on "each" individual Christian. And, in verses 15–16, Paul speaks of each member of the body of Christ as involved in "building up": "But speaking the truth in love, we must grow up in every way into him who is the head, into Christ, from whom the whole body, joined and knit together by every ligament with which it is equipped, as each part is working properly, promotes the body's growth in building itself up in love."

The building process described in Ephesians 4:11–16 seems to deal exclusively (or mainly) with the spiritual growth of persons already aligned with the gospel. Some scholars, however, have attempted to read the "building up" here as including the addition of new members to the community.[38]

In other texts, Paul also speaks of all Christians as "building up" the church. That is, the same local congregation is both the "building" under construction (1 Cor 3:9), and the "builders" who continue that construction (1 Cor 14:1–26). Christians "build up" the church by edifying and instructing one another, as well as adding to their numbers (1 Cor 14:1–26).

This point is especially seen in 1 Corinthians 14:23–25, which reads,

> If, therefore, the whole church comes together and all speak in tongues, and outsiders or unbelievers enter, will they not say that you are out of your mind? But if all prophesy, an unbeliever or outsider who enters is reproved by all and called to account by all. After the secrets of the unbeliever's heart are disclosed, that person will bow down before God and worship him, declaring, "God is really among you."

Vandenhoeck & Ruprecht, 1960), 288–92; Gnilka, *Der Epheserbrief*, 213; Markus Barth, *Ephesians*, AB, vol. 34A (Garden City, NY: Doubleday, 1974), 439–40, 478–81; C. Leslie Mitton, *Ephesians*, NCB (London: Oliphants, 1976), 151; Walter Lock, *The Epistle to the Ephesians* (London: Methuen, 1929), 49; Franz Mußner, *Der Brief an die Epheser*, Ökumenischer Taschenbuch-kommentar zum Neuen Testament 10 (Gütersloh: Gerd Mohn, 1982), 127.

38 Caird comments on Ephesians 4:12, "The *building up* of *the body of Christ* is not achieved by pastoral concentration on the interior life of the church, but by training every member for his part in the church's mission to the world" (Caird, *Paul's Letters from Prison*, 76). See also Senior and Stuhlmueller, *Biblical Foundations for Mission*, 204–07; Regina Pacis Meyer, *Kirche und Mission im Epheserbrief*, SBS 86 (Stuttgart: Katholisches Bibelwerk, 1977), 72–77; Edmund Schlink, "Christ and the Church," *SJT* 10 (1957): 6–7; cf. E. Schweizer, "Die Kirche als Leib Christi in den paulinischen Antilegomena," *TLZ* 86 (1961): 241–56; idem, "The Church as the Missionary Body of Christ," *NTS* 8 (1961–62): 1–11; contra Hahn, *Mission in the New Testament*, 147 n. 1.

We briefly discussed this passage in chapter three, where we noted that in this text Paul presupposes the Corinthians' desire for non-Christians to be convicted of sin and turn to the Lord in faith.[39] To accomplish this assumed desire, communication within the church meeting should be intelligible to a visiting non-believer, explains Paul. Tongues may "build up" (οἰκοδομέω) individual Christians, but prophecy "builds up" the church (14:4, 5, 12, 17, 26). Paul's description of non-believers coming to faith through prophecy is the primary example he gives of how intelligible speech "builds up" the body. Thus, "building up" the church apparently includes not only the edification of current believers, but the addition of new members (14:23–25; 8:1; 10:23–24, 31–33).

In reference to the verb οἰκοδομέω (and its cognates) in 1 Corinthians 14, Otto Michel aptly remarks, "The term edification [οἰκοδομή] comprises two aspects, on the one side inner strengthening in might and knowledge, and on the other outer winning and convincing."[40] Paul and Apollos are no longer the only ones building the Corinthian church (3:9–17); they serve as an example of the proper attitude the now numerous builders should have among themselves (4:6). As believers admonish one another and mix among outsiders, the church is "built up" through both maturation and multiplication (1 Cor 5:9–10; 10:23–24; 14:26; Rom 15:1–3, 7–13; cf. Jer 12:16).

Indeed, when Jesus says, "I will build my church" (οἰκοδομήσω μου τὴν ἐκκλησίαν), none doubt that these words indicate the inclusion of new disciples, as well as the maturing of current ones (Matt 16:18). One should not be surprised to find this same concept in Paul. On "upbuilding" in Paul's letters, Ridderbos rightly states,

> In accordance with the redemptive-historical character of the church this upbuilding must be seen first of all as the continuing work of God with his people (Rom. 14:19, 20), whose temple and dwelling place it is. This continuing and consummating work consists both in the bringing in of those who till now have been without (cf. Rom. 15:20ff.) and in the inner strengthening and perfecting of all who in Christ now belong to it (1 Cor. 14:3; 1 Thess. 5:11, *et al.*).[41]

While we can make a strong case that the addition of new members to the church is part of the "building up" in 1 Corinthians 14:26, other "building" texts where initial evangelism is not so explicitly mentioned may also include this sense (e.g., Rom 14:19; 15:2; 1 Cor 14:3, 5, 12; Eph 4:11–16; 4:29).

---

39 All commentators are agreed that non-believers are at least included in Paul's phrase "ἰδιῶται ἢ ἄπιστοι" (14:23). Barrett favors understanding this phrase as descriptive of one group, i.e., "unbelieving outsiders" (Barrett, *First Corinthians*, 324–25). See Walter Rebell, "Gemeinde als Missionsfaktor im Urchristentum: I Kor 14,24f. als Schlüsselsituation," *TZ* 44 (1988): 117–34.

40 Michel, "οἶκος...," in *TDNT*, 5:142.

41 Ridderbos, *Paul*, 432.

Although Paul clearly differentiates between saved and unsaved persons, he sometimes speaks in a uniform fashion to the needs of both groups. Both need to be "built up." One group needs to be added initially to the building, while the other needs some finer stone-work. Paul can even describe the ministry he wishes to administer to an existing congregation as "preaching the gospel" (Rom 1:15).[42] This fact reminds us that even after being incorporated into the church, believers are always in need of that same grace and life-giving gospel which first delivered them from the domain of darkness.

To summarize this section, we can say that Paul taught, admonished, and "built up" the church. All of these activities were part of his expansive missionary vision. Likewise, in continuity with the apostolic mission, Paul expected the congregations to teach, admonish, and "build up" one another.

Suffering in Paul and in the Church

Just as the apostles' miracles, prayers, and ministry of teaching/"building up" found their parallel in the churches, so the apostolic pattern of suffering was reproduced in the churches. Due to Paul's frequent references to suffering and the important role suffering has in confirming my thesis, I have bracketed our discussion of it to the section below.

I will begin by briefly noting Paul's references to suffering in his own mission and the life of the church. I will then proceed to explore the reasons for Christian suffering. According to Paul, why is it that early Christians – both apostles and ordinary believers – suffer? We will see that Paul's understanding of Christian identity and the offensiveness of the gospel are important for answering this question. A brief study of the early Christians' social context will also help clarify this matter. Finally, we will discuss two Pauline texts (2 Cor 4:7–15; Col 1:24–25) and two Pauline letters (Philippians, Thessalonians) to see what additional insights they give us into Paul's understanding of suffering.

Christian Identity: Why the Apostles and Church Suffered

Paul could not conceive of his apostolic mission apart from suffering.[43] This

---

42 Contra Dickson, "Gospel as News," 212.

43 Pobee comments, "Persecutions and sufferings were a *sine qua non* of Paul's apostolic ministry" (John S. Pobee, *Persecution and Martyrdom in the Theology of Paul*, JSNTSup 6 [Sheffield: JSOT Press, 1985], 106). Hafemann agrees: "The questions of the inevitability and purpose of suffering in the life of Christians in general, and in the life of Paul as an apostle in particular, are recurring themes of great significance throughout Paul's letters" (S. J. Hafemann, "Suffering" in *DPL*, ed. Gerald F. Hawthorne, Ralph P. Martin, and Daniel G. Reid [Downers Grove:

fact is made clear by numerous passages in the Pauline epistles.[44] Likewise, in the book of Acts, Luke confirms that Paul saw suffering as inherent to his apostolic ministry (Acts 9:15–16; 20:23).[45] In parallel fashion, Paul repeatedly describes the churches as undergoing suffering and signifies that he sees such ongoing persecution as a normal feature of Christian existence (Rom 8:16–17; Gal 6:12; Phil 1:29–30; 1 Thess 2:14–16; 3:3–4; 2 Tim 1:8; 2:3; 3:12).[46]

What was it about the apostles and churches that made them the target of outsiders' unwavering opposition? To answer this question, we must delve into Paul's thinking on two related topics: Christian identity and the offensiveness of the gospel. First, we will look at Christian identity – i.e., characteristics of Christian existence shared by both apostles and ordinary believers. Second, we will see how, in Paul's thinking, such common elements of Christian existence

---

InterVarsity, 1993], 919). Furnish writes, "Paul regards suffering not just as an occasional experience of apostles but as the essential and continuing characteristic of apostolic service" (Victor Paul Furnish, *II Corinthians*, AB, vol. 32A [Garden City, NY: Doubleday, 1984], 283). See also Scott J. Hafemann, *Suffering and the Spirit: An Exegetical Study of II Cor. 2:14–3:3 within the Context of the Corinthian Correspondence,* WUNT 2.19 (Tübingen: Mohr, 1986).

44 See 1 Cor 4:9–13; 15:30–32; 16:8–9; 2 Cor 1:3–10; 2:14–17; 4:7–12; 6:4–10; 11:22–28; Gal 6:17; Phil 1:14, 27–30; 3:10; Col 1:24–25; 4:3; 2 Tim 1:8, 11–12; 2:8–11; 3:10–15.

45 Describing the pattern of suffering in Acts, Paul House writes, "Suffering normally follows ministry. Then quite often suffering provides the opportunity for more ministry. Through trouble the gospel spreads from Jerusalem to Samaria (8:4–24) and finally to Rome (20:17–28:31). Paul and his coworkers seem to know when to move to other places through the opposition they arouse (cf. 13:48–52; 14:5–6; 14:19–20; 16:25–40; 17:10; 17:13–15; etc.). Indeed, it is a rare thing for the first apostles or for Paul to have assurance of safety (e.g. 9:31; 12:1–19; 18:9–11; 19:1–20)" (Paul R. House, "Suffering and the Purpose of Acts," *JETS* 33 [1990]: 320–21). Later, House writes, "Clearly suffering is a major force in the gospel's expansion. It is a rare thing for the Way to spread without it. Various summaries in the text point to this conclusion (8:4; 9:16; 14:22; 20:22–24; 21:13; etc.), as does the flow of the book's last nine chapters. Certainly the gospel moves, but never without pain" (ibid., 326). See also Brian Rapske, "Opposition to the Plan of God and Persecution," in *Witness to the Gospel: The Theology of Acts,* ed. I. Howard Marshall and David Peterson (Grand Rapids: Eerdmans 1998), 235–56.

46 Luke confirms that Paul viewed suffering as inherent to normal Christian existence (Acts 14:22). Also note Jesus' comment to his disciples in John 15:20, "Remember the word that I said to you, 'Servants are not greater than their master.' If they persecuted me, they will persecute you." Cf. Matt 5:10–12; 10:25; Mark 8:34–35; 13:9; Luke 21:12–19; John 12:25; Heb 13:12–14; Jas 1:2–4; 1 Pet 2:20–23; 3:8–9; 4:1, 12–19. Pobee comments, "Paul interprets the persecutions that were met by the various congregations in consequence of embracing the Christian message as a *sine qua non* of being in Christ" (Pobee, *Persecution and Martyrdom,* 107).

proved offensive to non-Christians.

In discussing Christian identity, we must first refer back to the insights we gained about the gospel in chapter two. There, we saw that Paul viewed the dynamic gospel as indwelling both apostles and churches. In Paul's thinking, it was impossible to have a church or apostle apart from the gospel. The genuine presence of the gospel was the determiner of Christian identity (Gal 1:6–9).

This gospel, which birthed and directed Christians (1 Cor 4:15), was nothing other than the salvific message about Jesus Christ and the assurance (to believers) of his indwelling presence (Rom 8:31–39; 1 Cor 1:23). It is for this reason that Paul can often speak interchangeably about the preaching of "God's word" or the preaching of "Christ."[47] Paul can even describe his apostolic mission as carrying around in his own body "the death of Jesus" (2 Cor 4:10).

Paul not only viewed his apostolic existence, but the Christian life generally, as inextricably identified with Christ. Christians are "buried with [Christ] by baptism," and raised with him to walk in newness of life (Rom 6:4). In the celebration of the Lord's supper, believers "proclaim the Lord's death until he comes" (1 Cor 11:26). In Romans 10:9–10, Paul says that to be a Christian, one must identify oneself with Jesus Christ – both externally and internally. He writes, "If you *confess with your lips* that Jesus Christ is Lord and *believe in your heart* that God raised him from the dead, you will be saved" (my emphasis). In Colossians 1:18, Paul describes Christians metaphorically as the "body of Christ," with Jesus Christ as the head (cf. Eph 1:22–23). In Eph 2:19–22, Paul says that believers are stones in a building, of which Jesus Christ is the cornerstone. In surveying Paul's various references to Christian identity it becomes clear that to be a Christian – to have received the life-giving message of the gospel – is to be inextricably associated with the person of Jesus Christ. Thus, for Paul, the whole of Christian identity might be summarized as determined by two overlapping qualities – the acceptance of and abiding presence of God's word, and the lordship of and abiding presence of God's son.

The relationship of suffering and Christian identity becomes clear when we understand that Paul's two main identifiers of Christian existence – gospel and Christ – were offensive to the non-Christian world. This point becomes especially significant when we note that Paul expected the gospel to spread spontaneously from its adherents (see chapter two). An offensive message spreading spontaneously from the people who hold to it will inevitably result in opposition and suffering. Given this situation, Paul consistently presents Christians – apostles included – with two options: (1) being ashamed of the gospel, and thus denying the faith (Gal 1:6–9; 6:12), or (2) allowing the gospel to run its dynamic course through their lives and thus suffering for it (2 Tim 1:8; 3:12; cf. Luke 9:23–27). Although a Christian's suffering may not entail

---

47   E.g., Rom 10:8–15; 1 Cor 1:23; 2:1; 9:14; 15:12; 2 Cor 1:19; 4:5; 11:4; Phil 1:12–18; Col 1:28; 4:3–4; 1 Thess 2:2.

persecution for the sake of the gospel (e.g., dangers from "rivers" and "bandits" [2 Cor 11:26; cf. 1 Cor 7:28; 2 Cor 12:7; Gal 4:13]),[48] in Paul's mind, it usually does.

What about the gospel is offensive? According to Paul, the gospel heralds God's judgment of human wickedness and false righteousness (Rom 1:16–32; Phil 3:7–9; 1 Thess 1:9; 2 Thess 2:11–12), and in defiance of that message, non-believers will attack the bearers of it (1 Cor 1:18–25; 1 Thess 1:6; 2 Thess 1:4–8; cf. Act 7:51–60; 1 Pet 4:1–5). The "world" which is opposed to God and his word (1 Cor 1:20–21; 2 Cor 3:14) will oppose the announcers of that word as well (John 15:18–19; 17:14, 16; Acts 9:4–5; 1 John 3:13; 4:4–6). Behind non-Christians' rejection of (and antagonism towards) God's messengers is not faultless ignorance or misunderstanding, but a morally culpable rejection of God's truth (Rom 1–3; 2 Thess 1–2). Furthermore, behind these human opponents stand demonic forces who oppose God and his Christ (2 Cor 4:4; Eph 6:10–18; 1 Thess 2:18; 2 Thess 2:1–12).

The offensiveness of the gospel becomes especially clear when we consider the central subject of the gospel – Christ crucified. Paul views his gospel ministry (and, by extension, the description applies to the mission of the churches) as the parading of Christ crucified before the eyes of fallen humanity (Gal 3:1). This picture of the crucified Christ serves as a constant reminder that a horrific death was needed to rectify humanity's desperate state. The crucifixion declares both the awesome love of God and the miserable "failing grade" that even the best of fallen human behavior deserves (i.e., the punishment Christ received was the just penalty for even the finest of human religiosity) (Phil 3:3–10). Such an assessment does not sit well with those who prefer a more favorable evaluation of their spiritual condition, and so such persons attack those through whom the gospel of Christ progresses (Phil 3:2–3; Gal 6:12–15).

Because the identity of both the apostles and ordinary believers is determined by the presence of an offensive gospel and identification with a rejected Messiah (Gal 3:10–14), true Christians must, by their very nature, face hostility. It is due to this fact – the fundamental Christological grounding of Christian suffering – that Paul frequently refers to his or other believers' suffering in direct relation to Christ's suffering (e.g., Rom 8:17; 2 Cor 1:5; 2:14–15; 4:10; Gal 6:12; Phil 3:10; Col 1:24–25). Also, we should note that

---

48 See Winter's discussion of the "dangers of travel" in the first-century Roman empire (Bruce W. Winter, "Dangers and Difficulties for the Pauline Missions," in *The Gospel to the Nations: Perspectives on Paul's Mission*, ed. Peter Bolt and Mark Thompson [Downers Grove: InterVarsity, 2000], 286–88). See also Lionel Casson, *Travel in the Ancient World* (n.p.: George Allen & Unwin, 1974; Baltimore: Johns Hopkins University Press, 1994); Raymond Chevallier, *Roman Roads* (Berkeley: University of California Press, 1976).

Paul's view that suffering is inevitable for all Christians demonstrates the apostle's expectation that the word of God and presence of Christ would advance to the non-believing world through all Christians (Rom 8:16–17; 2 Tim 3:12).

A similar understanding of the certainty of Christian suffering and its relation to Christian identity can be found elsewhere in the New Testament. In Acts 9:4, for example, Luke reports that Jesus asked the pre-Christian Paul, "Saul, Saul, why do you persecute me?" Paul, of course, was not actually persecuting Jesus, but the early Christians who were his "body" – who were united with him in baptism, confession, and the Lord's supper. These early Christians were so identified with their Lord that Jesus could refer to Paul's persecution of *them* as a persecution of *him*.

Likewise, in the Synoptic tradition, Jesus promises that his followers will face persecution and suffering (Matt 5:10–12; Luke 21:16). The reason for this persecution and suffering is the world's hatred of *Jesus* (Matt 10:25; 24:9; Mark 13:9–13; Luke 21:17). Indeed, it is outsiders' animosity toward the *Lord himself* that elicits their attacks on Christians. The opponents of Jesus hated him because of his teachings and claims, which must have been embodied and promulgated by Jesus' followers if they faced the same opposition as him. Thus, we find in the Synoptic tradition a significant parallel to Paul's understanding of the relationship of Christian identity and suffering.

First Peter also witnesses to the connection between Christian identity and suffering. Believers are there described as "sharing Christ's sufferings" (4:13), "reviled for the name of Christ" (4:14), and suffering "as . . . Christian[s] . . . [i.e.] because [they] bear this name" (4:16). Peter notes that if Christians are persecuted for their faith, they should rejoice because their suffering confirms that the Spirit of God truly rests on them (4:14). The Christians' opponents are preeminently defined by their rejection of the gospel (and by extension, its bearers). That is, the opponents are those who "do not obey the gospel of God" (4:17).

In the book of Revelation, John also presents suffering as bound up with a Christian's identification with Jesus. In Revelation 1:9, John introduces himself to the churches as "I, John, your brother who share with you in Jesus the *persecution* and the *kingdom* and the *patient endurance* . . ." (my emphasis). The three nouns italicized in the previous sentence are introduced by a single article in Greek – implying that there is a close relationship between them.[49] John seems to assert that one cannot experience the kingdom without the accompanying persecution and requisite patient endurance. This holistic picture of Christian experience is pre-eminently defined by a Christological qualifier – that is, the totality of this experience is "in Jesus." The following seven letters to the churches in Asia Minor also make clear that identification with Jesus

---

49   See Granville Sharp's canon (ἐν τῇ θλίψει καὶ βασιλείᾳ καὶ ὑπομονῇ).

invariably results in persecution.[50]

We have seen both in Paul's letters and the broader New Testament witness that the world is incited to persecute Christians because of their offensive gospel and rejected Christ. Yet, if everyone but Christians hates the gospel, it would seem that the Christian faith would cease to spread. The miracle, however, is that God can change the hearts of his enemies. In this process, God uses the apostles and churches as agents to proclaim his word, but ultimately God himself removes the veil from unbelieving hearts (2 Cor 3:13–16). So, although the gospel brings life to persons living in animosity towards it, it does this only in so far as God, in his mercy, deigns to awaken hearts to his offer of grace (Rom 9:16–18). We should note this last point so that in our emphasis on the offensiveness of the gospel to the non-Christian world, we do not forget that Paul and others expected some persons to respond positively to the life-giving message of the gospel (1 Cor 9:22; Eph 3:1–13).

The Social and Historical Context of Christian Suffering

If we were to interview a first-century opponent of early Christianity, and we were to ask him why he was persecuting Christians, he would likely differ from Paul's "theological evaluation" of the situation. That is, the opponent would not respond, "I hate the truth of what God has to say about my idolatrous life and human-based righteousness." Such spiritual realities (while ultimately true, according to Paul) played themselves out in the practicalities of daily life – in the familial, social, and political arenas.[51] Bruce Winter, for example, cites the following reasons for outsiders' opposition to early Christianity: the fact that Christians gathered for weekly meetings (which was against Roman law),[52] that Christians did not participate in common cultic ceremonies,[53] and that their

---

50 E.g., Rev 2:2–3, 9–10, 13, 19; 3:8–9.

51 Adeney discusses the various religious, political, economic, and social motives behind the persecution of Christians – both in New Testament times and throughout church history (David H. Adeney, "The Church and Persecution," in *The Church in the Bible and the World: An International Study*, ed. D. A. Carson [Exeter: Paternoster; Grand Rapids: Baker, 1987], 275–302).

52 See Pliny *Epistularum* 10.96; Winter, "Dangers and Difficulties," 289–90; O. F. Robinson, *The Criminal Law of Ancient Rome* (Baltimore: Johns Hopkins University Press, 1995), 80.

53 See *Mart. Pol.* 8.2; Dio Cassius 51.20.6–8; Winter, "Dangers and Difficulties," 292–93; Duncan Fishwick, *The Imperial Cult in the Latin West*, vol. 2.1, *Studies in the Ruler Cult of the Western Provinces of the Roman Empire* (Leiden: Brill, 1991), esp. 475–590; A. N. Sherwin-White, *The Roman Citizenship*, 2nd ed. (Oxford: Clarendon, 1973), 402–08; Stephen Mitchell, "The Imperial Cult," in *Anatolia: Land, Men, and Gods in Asia Minor*, vol. 1, *The Celts in Anatolia and the Impact of Roman Rule* (Oxford: Clarendon, 1993), 100–17.

leader was crucified (an offensive idea to Romans and Jews).[54] Besides these real differences from the surrounding pagan culture, Christians also faced rumors inspired by the hatred, jealousy, and fear of their opponents (Rom 3:8). As is clear from post-New Testament writings, outsiders falsely accused Christians of being cannibals, atheists, and incestuous fornicators.[55]

Both the broader New Testament witness and early extra-biblical materials confirm the historicity of early Christian suffering. As noted above, the Synoptics, 1 Peter, and Revelation speak of Christians suffering because of their identification with Jesus. First Peter, in particular, is important in this regard because it speaks of Christians being "reviled" or "blasphemed" for their failure to partake in immoral activities they once enjoyed as non-Christians (1 Pet 4:4, 14). Indeed, as a result of social conditions in the first century, Christians quickly differentiated themselves from their pagan surroundings (e.g., 1 Cor 8:1–11:1; 1 Thess 1:9–10).[56] By the Christians' withdrawal from sinful activities and their prominent new allegiance to Christ, they invited attack.

A variety of evidence in the New Testament and early Christian history indicates not only that early Christians suffered, but that the gospel was advancing through the ministry of ordinary believers. The book of Acts alone is a treasury of the entire church's active and constant witness.[57] Also, it would appear that the church at Rome was founded by ordinary Christians, as Paul fails to mention any apostle or co-worker who founded it (cf. Col 1:7). Early extra-biblical documents also confirm an active evangelistic role for the entire church, as well as the persecution that the church endured from outsiders.[58]

---

54 See 1 Cor 1:18; Gal 3:13; Winter, "Dangers and Difficulties," 292.

55 *Mart. Pol.* 9.2; Athenagoras *Supplicatio pro Christianis* 3 (F. A. March, ed., *Athenagoras,* Douglass Series of Christian Greek and Latin Writers 4 [New York: Harper & Brothers, 1876], 12); Eusebius *Historia Ecclesiastica* 5.1.14; cf. Tacitus *Annals* 13.32; 15.44; Suetonius *Claudius* 25.4; *Nero* 16.

56 See, e.g., Gooch, *Dangerous Food*, 1–46; Willis, *Idol Meat in Corinth:*, 63 n. 234; MacMullen, *Paganism in the Roman Empire*, 36–42; Poland, *Geschichte des griechischen Vereinswesens*, 503–13. Possibly the most analogous situation in our modern context is the close-quarters and predominantly pagan environment of many universities. Christian students immediately stand out in such contexts – which may partially account for the great effectiveness of collegiate Christian movements.

57 Luke consistently reports a vibrant witness by all persons in the church (e.g., Acts 4:23–31; 6:7; 8:1–4; 11:19–21; 12:24; 13:49; 15:35; 16:5; 19:10, 18–20).

58 E.g., Pliny *Epistularum* 10.96; Irenaeus *Adversus haereses* 1.10.2; Tertullian *Apologeticus* 1.7; Origen *Contra Celsum* 3.55; Eusebius *Historia Ecclesiastica* 4.7.1; Athenagoras *Supplicatio pro Christianis* 1; Tacitus *Annals* 13.32; 15.44; Suetonius *Claudius* 25.4; *Nero* 16; *Mart. Pol.* For additional evidence of early

From a sociological and historical perspective, we have an interest in knowing exactly what sorts of suffering the church endured from the hands of their oppressors. It is striking, then, that Paul does not offer specific examples of what this persecution entailed. Likely, such descriptions were superfluous for persons undergoing active opposition. On this point, Ernest Best remarks, "Paul does not describe [early Christians'] sufferings, but other parts of the New Testament supply glimpses of what they may have been: riots (Acts 17:5–9; 19:28–41), false accusations in court (I Peter 4:15–16), imprisonment (Heb. 13:3), homes and businesses broken up (Heb. 10:32–34)."[59]

Regardless of what daily activities incited opposition and what tangible forms this opposition took, it is important to note that Paul consistently assumes that non-believing outsiders are aware of Christians' religious allegiance and that is the main reason that Christians are suffering persecution. The first century context apparently did not allow for the kind of private faith that is often found among modern Western Christians. This fact helps explain why Paul infrequently gives explicit instruction in his letters regarding the churches' missionary work. There was apparently little need to do so since many Christians were effectively making their presence known. In such a setting, the modern dichotomy between "active" and "passive" witness seems to break down.

Yet, how – one may rightly press the question – did the non-believers learn of their Christian neighbors' faith? As noted above, Paul assumes this fact rather than explicitly stating it. One must suppose that ordinary Christians were actively announcing their faith, as Paul occasionally mentions (1 Thess 1:8; Phil 1:12–18; 2:16; Eph 6:15) and as confirmed by other biblical and extra-biblical sources (see above). Also, the Christians' radically changed behavior attracted attention because of its implicit rejection of others' religious views and the dominant cultural and societal structures (1 Thess 1:9–10).

Patterns of Christian Suffering in the Pauline Letters

We will now take a brief look at two Pauline passages and two Pauline letters to see if they exhibit the pattern of suffering we have summarized above. Furthermore, we will seek any additional insights on Paul's understanding of Christian suffering which might be present in the texts.

SECOND CORINTHIANS 4:7–15

This passage deals primarily with Paul's reflections on his apostolic sufferings.

Christian evangelism and the concomitant persecution, see Harnack, *Mission and Expansion*, 2:1–32.

59 Ernest Best, *Second Corinthians*, Interpretation (Atlanta: John Knox, 1987), 10.

The text reads:

> But we have this treasure in clay jars, so that it may be made clear that this extraordinary power belongs to God and does not come from us. We are afflicted in every way, but not crushed; perplexed, but not driven to despair; persecuted, but not forsaken; struck down, but not destroyed; always carrying in the body the death of Jesus, so that the life of Jesus may also be made visible in our bodies. For while we live, we are always being given up to death for Jesus' sake, so that the life of Jesus may be made visible in our mortal flesh. So death is at work in us, but life in you.
>
> But just as we have the same spirit of faith that is in accordance with scripture – "I believed, and so I spoke" – we also believe, and so we speak, because we know that the one who raised the Lord Jesus will raise us also with Jesus, and will bring us with you into his presence. Yes, everything is for your sake, so that grace, as it extends to more and more people, may increase thanksgiving, to the glory of God (2 Cor 4:7–15).[60]

By his use of "we" in this passage, Paul distinguishes himself from the

---

60 Some scholars claim that when Paul lists his "catalogues of sufferings" or *Peristasenkataloge* (Rom 8:35; 1 Cor 4:10–13; 2 Cor 4:8–9; 6:4–10; 11:23–29; 12:10; Phil 4:12), he is following a conventional Hellenistic form used to legitimize a sage or leader (e.g., Plutarch *Moralia* 326D–333C; 361E–362A; 1057D–E; Epictetus *Discourses* 2.19.12–28; 4.7.13–26; Seneca *Epistulae Morales* 85.26–27). So Rudolf Bultmann, *Der Stil der paulinischen Predigt und die kynisch-stoische Diatribe*, FRLANT 13 (Göttingen: Vandenhoeck & Ruprecht, 1910; reprint, 1984), esp. 15–19; John T. Fitzgerald, *Cracks in an Earthen Vessel: An Examination of the Catalogues of Hardships in the Corinthian Correspondence*, SBLDS 99 (Atlanta: Scholars Press, 1988), 203–07. Other scholars have proposed Jewish apocalypticism or a mixture of Greek and Jewish elements as the background for Paul's lists of sufferings (e.g., Wolfgang Schrage, "Leid, Kreuz und Eschaton: Die Peristasenkataloge als Merkmale paulinischer theologia crucis und Eschatologie," *EvT* 34 [1974]: 141–75; Robert Hodgson, "Paul the Apostle and First Century Tribulation Lists," *ZNW* 74 [1983]: 59–80; Pobee, *Persecution and Martyrdom*, 13–46; Susan R. Garrett, "The God of This World and the Affliction of Paul: 2 Cor 4:1–12," in *Greeks, Romans, and Christians: Essays in Honor of Abraham J. Malherbe*, ed. David L. Balch, Everett Ferguson, and Wayne A. Meeks [Minneapolis: Fortress, 1990], 99–117). More likely, the Old Testament stories of God's suffering prophets, God's "suffering servant," and the gospel traditions provide the background for Paul's reflections (Karl Theodor Kleinknecht, *Der leidende Gerechtfertigte: Die alttestamentlich-jüdische Tradition vom "leidenden Gerechten" und ihre Rezeption bei Paulus*, WUNT 2.13 [Tübingen: Mohr, 1984]; cf. Niels Willert, "The Catalogues of Hardships in the Pauline Correspondence: Background and Function," in *The New Testament and Hellenistic Judaism*, ed. Peder Borgen and Søren Giversen [Aarhus, Denmark: Aarhus University Press, 1995], 217–43).

Corinthians whom he is addressing. This "we" also possibly includes the other apostles generally or at least Paul's apostolic co-workers (e.g., Timothy and Titus). The "we" text on which we are focusing, 2 Corinthians 4:7–15, occurs in the midst of Paul's defense against various criticisms. Some detractors are apparently claiming that Paul is insincere (2:17), that he is trying to commend himself (3:1), that he is incompetent (3:5), that he is not clear in his teaching (4:3), and that his hardships invalidate his claim to be God's approved messenger (1:3–11; 4:7–15; 6:4).[61] After reminding the Corinthians of the glorious God-revealing gospel that he preaches (4:6), Paul gives a theological *apologia* for his suffering. The apostle explains that the reason that the gospel (i.e., the "treasure") is found in such a beat-up old pot (i.e., in Paul) is that his weakness and suffering serve to magnify the truth and power of the message.[62] The apostles' trials and hardship show that they cannot be the source of the powerful message they preach.

Also, from this passage, we discover that Paul thinks suffering not only accompanies the apostles' proclamation of the gospel, but *is* a proclamation of the gospel. This fact is made clear by Paul's metaphorical descriptions of his afflictions as "carrying in [his own] body the death of Jesus" (4:10). Paul views his sufferings as picturing, in some sense, Jesus' death. When the apostle suffers in his proclamation of the gospel before potential converts, he puts on a "Passion play" in his own body. The *conveyer* of the message pictures the *content* of the message.[63] As a result of this vivid portrayal, through Paul's experience of "death" by repeated suffering, he delivers "the life of Jesus"[64] (i.e., salvation) to his addressees (vv. 10–12).

Margaret E. Thrall takes a similar view of 2 Corinthians 4:7–15, commenting,

> The apostolate is the earthly manifestation of the gospel, and apostolic suffering plays a part in this: it is the epiphany in somatic form of the Christ who was crucified. The repeated φανερωθῇ of vv. 10b, 11b would support this

---

61 Of course, it is possible that Paul's reflections are given more generally and not in response to criticisms, though the tone of 2 Corinthians argues against this (e.g., 2:1–11).

62 Hafemann writes, "The power of the gospel is so great and its glory so profound that it must be carried in a 'pot,' lest people put their trust in Paul himself" (Scott Hafemann, "'Because of Weakness' [Galatians 4:13]: The Role of Suffering in the Mission of Paul," in *The Gospel to the Nations: Perspectives on Paul's Mission*, ed. Peter Bolt and Mark Thompson [Downers Grove: InterVarsity, 2000], 137).

63 Paul possibly makes a similar reference to his suffering as a picture of Christ's death in Gal 3:1; cf. Gal 4:13; 5:11; 6:17.

64 Genitive of source.

interpretation, as would the general context, which is concerned with the presentation of the gospel (4.2–5, 13).[65]

Likewise, Victor Paul Furnish notes about this text, "The apostle's sufferings . . . are the manifestation of [Christ's] suffering and death and thus a proclamation of the gospel."[66]

COLOSSIANS 1:24–25

Paul develops ideas similar to those in the text above in Colossians 1:24–25, where he writes,

> I am now rejoicing in my sufferings for your sake, and in my flesh I am completing what is lacking in Christ's afflictions for the sake of his body, that is, the church. I became its servant according to God's commission that was given to me for you, to make the word of God fully known.[67]

This passage presents us with a puzzling phrase. If Christ's death is sufficient to pay for the sins of the world (Rom 3:23–24; 5:17; Gal 1:4), how could anything be "lacking" in those afflictions, and in what way could Paul "in [his] flesh," by his sufferings, supply what is lacking (τὰ ὑστερήματα)?

Several interpretations have been offered for this passage. For example, some scholars contend that Paul here has in mind certain "Messianic woes" that must be fulfilled before the eschaton.[68] It should be remembered, however, that the apostle is writing to a Gentile congregation that he has apparently never

---

65 Margaret E. Thrall, *A Critical and Exegetical Commentary on the Second Epistle to the Corinthians*, vol. 1, *Introduction and Commentary on II Corinthians I–VII*, ICC (Edinburgh: T. & T. Clark, 1994), 334.

66 Furnish, *II Corinthians*, 284. Similar interpretations are espoused by Best, *Second Corinthians*, 43; J. Lambrecht, "The Nekrōsis of Jesus: Ministry and Suffering in 2 Cor 4, 7–15," in *L'Apôtre Paul: Personnalité, Style et Conception du Ministère*, ed. A. Vanhoye, BETL 73 (Leuven: Leuven University Press, 1986), 140–41; Paul Barnett, *The Second Epistle to the Corinthians*, NICNT (Grand Rapids: Eerdmans, 1997), 227–38; Scott J. Hafemann, *2 Corinthians*, NIV Application Commentary (Grand Rapids: Zondervan, 2000), 184–86; cf. 1 Cor 2:1–5; 2 Cor 2:14; 12:9–10.

67 For a history of interpretation of this debated passage, see Jacob Kremer, *Was an den Leiden Christi noch mangelt: Eine interpretationsgeschichtliche und exegetische Untersuchung zu Kol. 1,24b.*, BBB 12 (Bonn: Hanstein, 1956), 5–154; John Reumann, "Colossians 1:24 ('What is Lacking in the Afflictions of Christ'): History of Exegesis and Ecumenical Advance," *CurTM* 17 (1990): 454–61.

68 E.g., Peter T. O'Brien, *Colossians, Philemon*, WBC, vol. 44 (Waco, TX: Word, 1982), 78–81. Also see Hanna Stettler, "An Interpretation of Colossians 1:24 in the Framework of Paul's Mission Theology" in *The Mission of the Early Church to Jews and Gentiles*, WUNT 127, ed. Jostein Ådna and Hans Kvalbein (Tübingen: Mohr Siebeck, 2000), 185–208.

visited or written to in the past (Col 1:3–8). Although it is possible that Paul is here assuming the congregation's background knowledge of apocalyptic Judaism, such an assumption is speculative. Furthermore, it is noteworthy that in Paul's frequent references to suffering and hardship he never explicitly speaks of "Messianic woes," as some Jewish sources arguably do.[69]

A second interpretation of Colossians 1:24–25 that has been offered is that Paul is speaking here of a "mystical" or "realistic" participation in Christ's actual sufferings.[70] This interpretation, however, is unlikely. While Paul does speak of a believer's participation in Christ's death, that event is grasped by faith and remains "extrinsic" or "alien" to the Christian (Gal 2:20).

A third way that scholars have understood Colossians 1:24–25 is that the "lack" in verse 24 means that the persons to whom Paul proclaims the gospel lack both a knowledge and an immediate visual portrayal of Christ's suffering and death (cf. the discussion of 2 Cor 4:7–15 above).[71] When Paul suffers in his proclamation of the gospel, his addressees not only learn of Christ's sacrifice, but are allowed to see a copy (albeit imperfect) of Christ's suffering on their behalf. Scholars who hold to this view claim that Paul's sufferings have no atoning significance and should not be understood as manifesting the *actual* sufferings of Christ.[72] Yet, according to this interpretation of Colossians 1:24, Paul's sufferings do put in the immediate vision of potential converts a persuasive portrayal of suffering in the pattern of the one who died to atone for

---

69 E.g., *1 Enoch* 47:1–4; 99:4; *2 Apoc. Bar.* 30:1–2; 48:30–37; 70:2; *Sib. Or.* 2.154–74; see Str–B 4.977–86; cf. Dan 12:1; Zeph 1:14–15; Matt 24:8; Mark 13:5–8; Luke 21:5–11.

70 E.g., C. Merrill Proudfoot, "Imitation or Realistic Participation: A Study of Paul's Concept of 'Suffering With Christ," *Int* 17 (1963): 140–60.

71 Hafemann writes, "Paul completes what is 'lacking' in Christ's afflictions on behalf of the church in the sense that his ministry *extends* the knowledge and reality of the cross of Christ and the power of the Spirit to the Gentile world (Col 1:23; cf. Eph 3:13)" (Hafemann, "Suffering," 920). Cf. W. F. Flemington, "On the Interpretation of Colossians 1:24," in *Suffering and Martyrdom in the New Testament: Studies Presented to G. M. Styler by the Cambridge New Testament Seminar*, ed. William Horbury and Brian McNeil (Cambridge: Cambridge University Press, 1981), 84–90.

72 Contra Erhardt Güttgemanns' understanding of 2 Corinthians 4:7–12 (E. Güttgemanns, *Der leidende Apostel und sein Herr: Studien zur paulinischen Christologie*, FRLANT 90 [Göttingen: Vandenhoeck & Ruprecht, 1966], 94–126). Cf. Gerhard Saß, *Apostelamt und Kirche: Eine theologisch-exegetische Untersuchung des paulinischen Apostelbegriffs* (Munich: Kaiser, 1939), 88–92; Hans Windisch, *Paulus und Christus: Eine biblisch-religionsgeschichtlicher Vergleich*, UNT 24 (Leipzig: Heinrich, 1934), 236–52. For the sufficiency of Christ's atoning death, see Rom 3:21–26; 6:9–10; 8:3; 1 Cor 1:18–31; 2 Cor 5:16–21; Gal 1:4; Col 2:13–14.

them.[73]

This explanation seems reasonable (especially noting the apparent parallel passage in 2 Cor 4:7–15) until one notices that Paul does not say that his sufferings supply what is lacking in the unevangelized world. No, his sufferings supply what is lacking among the Colossian Christians – an existing church that Paul has never visited (Col 1:4, 9, 24).

How then, does Paul make up for what is lacking in Christ's afflictions in the Colossian church? He says that he does so by becoming a "servant of the church" according to God's commission – to make the word of God fully known (Col 1:25). Paul proceeds to speak of his special apostolic task of unveiling the gospel in unevangelized areas (Col 1:26–29).[74] It is this pioneer missionizing activity that results in Paul's suffering on behalf of the church.

In order to understand Paul's point in Colossians 1:24–25, we must return to the point we made at the beginning of our discussion on suffering – that the fundamental grounding of Christian suffering is Christological. That is, because *all* Christians bear Christ's presence and word, they face opposition from "the world," which hates God and his Christ. As we saw in chapter two, where Christ's word – the gospel – is truly present, it will spread in accordance with its dynamic nature. As the gospel spreads through the church, it will encounter the hostility of the surrounding non-Christian world. This is so because the gospel announces the futility of human religions and human righteousness (Phil 3:7–9), thus arousing the anger of their adherents (Acts 9:4–5). In Colossians 1:24–25, Paul says that he is stepping ahead of the church in uncharted territory to make an initial unveiling of the gospel. In so doing, he bears the brunt of the world's antagonism towards God and his word. As a servant of the church, he steps before her to take the first blow of the falling sword. Paul can say that such Christ-based suffering is "lacking" in regards to the church because it is the inevitable outworking of the church's gospel-based existence. Because the word will inevitably go forth, and the world hates that word, active persecution is also inevitable. Paul willingly and joyfully steps before the church to suffer a

---

73 John Piper writes, "Christ's afflictions are not lacking in their atoning sufficiency. They are lacking in that they are not known and felt by people who were not at the cross. Paul dedicates himself not only to carry the message of those sufferings to the nations, but also to suffer with Christ and for Christ in such a way that what people see are 'Christ's sufferings.' In this way he follows the pattern of Christ by laying down his life for the life of the church" (Piper, *Let the Nations be Glad!*, 94). See Hafemann, "'Because of Weakness,'" 131–46.

74 Paul reserves his comments about the revealing of the mystery of the gospel to refer to the initial apostolic promulgation of the gospel (e.g., Rom 16:25–26; 1 Cor 2:1, 7; Eph 3:8–9; 6:19; Col 4:3–4). While Paul speaks of the churches as having the mystery of the gospel revealed to them (1 Cor 2:1, 7; Eph 1:9–10; 3:8–9; 6:19; Col 1:25–27), and of their safeguarding of that mystery (1 Tim 3:8–9), language about the churches themselves revealing the mystery is noticeably absent.

more public and extreme persecution.[75]

PHILIPPIANS

We will now briefly examine Paul's letter to the Philippians to see how the apostle describes the pattern of suffering in the community he addresses. Paul tells the Philippians, "[God] has graciously granted you the privilege not only of believing in Christ, but of suffering for him as well – since you are having the same struggle that you saw I had and now hear that I still have" (Phil 1:29–30).[76] Here we note that (1) suffering is ordained by God,[77] (2) suffering is as much a part of the Christian experience as the divine gift of faith, and (3) the church's suffering is explicitly parallel to the "same struggle" that Paul has. In Philippians 1, Paul defines his "struggle" as the persecution and imprisonment he has faced for his proclamation of the gospel (Phil 1:12–13).

Paul assumes that the non-believers surrounding the Philippian Christians are aware of their faith, offended by it, and that is why they face persecution. There are no "secret Christians" in Philippi. As noted in the "social context" section above, the means whereby a Christian's neighbors discovered his or her new-found allegiance is somewhat speculative, but we do know that Paul consistently assumes this to be the case. This fact is probably one of the most significant reasons that we do not find more explicit injunctions to evangelism in Paul's letters. The early churches did not need to *begin* making their faith known so much as they needed to *continue* to adhere to their confession and to confirm it through their holy behavior.[78]

We should also note that in the Philippian correspondence, Paul reports that his personal suffering has resulted in two auspicious outcomes. (1) More people have heard of the gospel through Paul's suffering, which has brought widespread attention to his message (Phil 1:12–13),[79] and (2) most of the

---

75 David Garrison's comment about modern pioneer missionaries is instructive: "A list of missionaries who have been engaged in Church Planting Movements reads like a catalog of calamity. Many have suffered illness, derision and shame" (D. Garrison, *Church Planting Movements* [Richmond, VA: International Mission Board of the Southern Baptist Convention, 1999], 40).

76 For a recent study of suffering in Philippians, see L. Gregory Bloomquist, *The Function of Suffering in Philippians*, JSNTSup 78 (Sheffield: Sheffield Academic Press, 1993). See also Barnabas Mary Ahern, "The Fellowship of His Sufferings (Phil 3,10): A Study of St. Paul's Doctrine of Christian Suffering," *CBQ* 22 (1960): 1–32.

77 See also 2 Cor 1:9; 2:14; 4:11; 2 Tim 1:11–12.

78 So Swigchem, *Het missionair karakter*, 260.

79 Indeed, there is no more persuasive means of promoting a cause than putting one's life on the line. Piper comments, "We measure the worth of a hidden treasure by what we will gladly sell to buy it . . . . Loss and suffering, joyfully accepted for the kingdom of God, show the supremacy of God's worth more clearly in the world

believers in the letter's city of origin[80] have been emboldened by Paul's example to declare the gospel fearlessly (Phil 1:14).[81]

FIRST AND SECOND THESSALONIANS

Paul's letters to the Thessalonian church demonstrate an understanding of persecution similar to the one we find in Philippians. Paul and his co-workers are facing opposition to their gospel proclamation (1 Thess 2:1–2). The Thessalonians encounter hostility for similar reasons, as demonstrated by 1 Thessalonians 2:14–16, where Paul writes,

> For you, brothers and sisters, became imitators of the churches of God in Christ Jesus that are in Judea, for you suffered the same things from your own compatriots as they did from the Jews, who killed both the Lord Jesus and the prophets, and drove us out; they displease God and oppose everyone by hindering us from speaking to the Gentiles so they may be saved.

It is interesting that the Thessalonians are here described as "imitators" of churches that they have never seen. What makes them imitators is their faithful adherence to the same gospel and Lord – which results in parallel opposition from the non-believing world.[82] Paul emphasizes this point earlier in the same letter, where he says the Thessalonians have imitated both him and the Lord by suffering for their faithful adherence to the gospel and their "sounding forth" of that word (1 Thess 1:6–8).

Turning back to 1 Thessalonians 2:14–16, we note that Paul's description of the persecution of the Judean churches clarifies that this persecution was "Christ-based." The list of attacks demonstrates that the anger of "the Jews"

---

than all worship and prayer" (Piper, *Let the Nations be Glad!*, 71). Piper recounts several modern stories which demonstrate that a preacher who suffers in his or her proclamation of the gospel often gains a surprising number of converts (ibid., 71–112). For more modern-day examples and reflections on suffering in mission, see David J. Bosch, "The Vulnerability of Mission," *Zeitschrift für Missionswissenschaft und Religionswissenschaft* 76 (1992): 201–16.

80 See chapter 3, n. 2.

81 Bloomquist notes, "The earliest patristic references to the suffering passages of Philippians speak of two goals of martyrdom, namely, (1) to bring about the perfection of the martyr, and (2) to witness to those who observe the martyr" (Bloomquist, *Function of Suffering in Philippians*, 18). E.g., see Ign. *Rom.* 2.2; 6; 9.2; Ign. *Eph.* 3:1; 21:2.

82 Malherbe writes, "The explicative *gar* ("for") connects the Thessalonians' reception of the word with their suffering for it. That the word was active in them resulted in their suffering at the hands of their countrymen. Paul had instructed them that suffering would be inevitable (3:3–4), so the connection he makes here could not have been unexpected" (Abraham J. Malherbe, *The Letters to the Thessalonians*, AB, vol. 32B (New York: Doubleday, 2000), 167.

was consistently directed against adherence to and proclamation of Jesus. These opponents are described as killing Jesus, murdering the prophets, driving out Paul and his co-workers, and hindering Paul and his co-workers from proclaiming the gospel to the Gentiles. Asserting that the suffering itself was the activity being imitated begs the question. As Jo-Ann Brant rightly observes, "The equation of 'imitation' with suffering affliction ignores the fact that the Thessalonians were engaged in some activity that incurred the opposition of others."[83]

This opposition endured by the Thessalonians, however, was not a surprise. Paul reminds the church in 1 Thessalonians 3:3–4, "Indeed, you yourselves know that [persecution] is what we are destined for. In fact, when we were with you, we told you beforehand that we were to suffer persecution; so it turned out, as you know."

The Thessalonian Christians did not elicit such persistent persecution by secret adherence to a new religion. Apparently, just as in the Philippian community, a dimension of their Christian faith was publicly known and offensive to non-believers. When persons in Thessalonica believed the gospel, they did not suddenly develop a personal habit that made people want to hurt them; they suffered because people knew they had aligned themselves with a new religion that was offensive to the surrounding culture. The offensive word of God and rejected Messiah was made audible and visible through the Thessalonian church.

Other passages in Paul's letters to the Thessalonian Christians confirm that the surrounding pagans were aware of the Thessalonians' faith and actively opposed them. When Paul describes the adversaries of the Thessalonians, the chief characteristic he highlights is their non-acceptance of the gospel. For example, in 2 Thessalonians 1:8, Paul describes them as "those who do not know God" and "those who do not obey the gospel of our Lord Jesus." In 2 Thessalonians 2:10, Paul says that the church's opponents have "refused to love the truth and so be saved," and in verse 12, the apostle adds that they "have not believed the truth but took pleasure in unrighteousness." In rejecting the Thessalonian church's offer of life, the surrounding pagan culture did not respond in apathy, but repulsion and a God-hating pagan revelry. The gospel, believed and proclaimed by the Thessalonians, was offensive. Indeed, the suffering of Christians in Thessalonica showed that their opponents were not simply set against a new religious group, but against *God and his word*. Thus, God's ultimate condemnation of these opponents is righteous and a cause for celebrating divine victory over his enemies (2 Thess 1:4–10; cf. Phil 1:28).

In summarizing the Pauline passages examined above, we should note that Paul describes both the apostles and the churches as undergoing God-ordained suffering. For the purposes of our study, this suffering is important because it

---

83   Brant, "The Place of *mimēsis* in Paul's Thought," 292.

reveals that the offensive, self-diffusive gospel was effectively progressing through the early Christians. As non-believers became aware of Christians' adherence to and proclamation of the gospel, they opposed the church. Also, our study on suffering has demonstrated the continuity between the apostles' ministry and the church's ministry. The apostles suffer in their mission; the church experiences similar suffering.

While Paul speaks of his personal sufferings as a means whereby Christ's atoning death is made visible to his converts (2 Cor 2:14–17; 4:8–12), he never speaks explicitly of the church's suffering in this way.[84] Nevertheless, Paul does speak of the church's suffering as directly paralleling his own apostolic missionary suffering (2 Cor 1:6–7; Phil 1:29–30; 1 Thess 2:13–16).[85] It is likely that Paul would agree that the church's suffering also had this missiological function.[86] That is, the church's suffering was not only evidence that its members were making known the gospel, but also a means of making it known.[87] If this is indeed Paul's view, it is in continuity with the gospel traditions which present persecution as an opportunity for Christians to testify to the gospel before non-believers (Mark 13:9; Luke 9:23–27; 12:4–12; 21:12–13).[88]

It should be noted that Paul never says that Christians should actively seek suffering. Christians are, however, to welcome persecution if the alternative is being ashamed of the gospel (2 Tim 1:8). In his remarks on suffering, Paul again presents us with a classic "theological tension." Although the suffering of Christians is ordained by God in a general sense (Phil 1:29), particular instances of suffering are something that Paul and others can legitimately seek and pray to avoid (Acts 22:25–29; 2 Cor 1:8–11; Phil 1:19; 1 Tim 2:1–4; cf.

---

84   Paul does speak of the Thessalonians' suffering as "evidence of the righteous judgment of God" (2 Thess 1:5). By this statement, Paul apparently means that because the Thessalonians' opponents are ruthlessly persecuting them, it is clear to all that God is righteous in bringing destruction on those opponents (1:5–9).

85   Paul viewed the suffering of apostle and church as parallel because of their similar relationship to two entities – the word of God and the world (1 Thess 2:13; 2 Thess 3:1).

86   So Lambrecht, "The Nekrōsis of Jesus," 143; contra Walter Schmithals, *The Office of Apostle in the Early Church*, trans. John E. Steely (Nashville: Abingdon, 1969), 48.

87   Sloan writes, "Thus, what the church endures by way of suffering in this present evil age is both an evangelistic witness [2 Cor 4:15] and a witness to the world of the coming, righteous judgment of God (2 Thess. 1:4–10)" (Robert B. Sloan, "Images of the Church in Paul," 164).

88   O'Toole claims that Luke presents Paul's ministry in Acts as a fulfillment of Christ's predictions that believers would testify in their sufferings for the gospel. See especially Acts 25:1–26:32 (Robert F. O'Toole, "Luke's Notion of 'Be Imitators of Me as I am of Christ,' in Acts 25–26," *BTB* 8 [1978]: 155–61).

Matt 10:23; 24:9, 15–22). The deciding factors as to whether one should embrace suffering or avoid it are (1) God's will (Phil 1:29–30), (2) the effect on others' salvation or sanctification (Phil 1:23–25; Col 1:24–25; 2 Tim 2:8–11), and (3) the glorification of God (2 Cor 4:15). Analogous to Jesus' death on the cross, the suffering of Christians brings about good (i.e., their sanctification and others' salvation) while not excusing or condoning the unjust treatment they receive (Rom 5:3–5; 8:18–19; 2 Thess 1:5–11; cf. Jas 1:2–4; Acts 2:23; 3:18–19; 4:10, 27–28; 5:28).[89]

Conclusion

Because both the mission of the apostles and the life of the church are defined by the presence of the dynamic gospel, there is an unmistakable parallel between Paul's description of his own gospel ministry and that of his churches. When all elements of this parallelism (not just overt references to "proclamation") are taken into account, it seems reasonable to conclude that Paul thought of all but the non-repeatable functions of his apostleship as devolving upon the churches. The cumulative witness of the short studies in this chapter, along with the evidence of the previous chapters, give us grounds for concluding that Paul viewed the church as continuing his apostolic mission (minus non-repeatable functions).[90] We would expect nothing less than such missionary activity from an entity defined by the same self-diffusing gospel as its apostolic founder.

The social ramifications of the gospel's progress become especially evident in Paul's remarks on suffering. Because Christian identity is fundamentally determined by the self-diffusive, offensive gospel and the rejected Christ, all believers can expect to face the same opposition that their Lord did. It is through this suffering, however, that God has chosen to magnify the glory of his word and demonstrate the nature of its object, i.e., the crucified Christ (2 Cor 4:7–15; 6:3–10; 11:23–12:10).

In the end, the consistent pattern of suffering that we find in the early church (which parallels the suffering of the apostles) is a powerful argument for the church's missionary nature. The unwavering hostility of the outside world

---

89 For a number of recent, biblical studies on suffering, see *The Southern Baptist Journal of Theology* 4, no. 2 (Summer 2000). Also, several of Hafemann's previous studies on suffering are nicely synthesized in Scott Hafemann, "The Role of Suffering in the Mission of Paul," in *The Mission of the Early Church to Jews and Gentiles*, WUNT 127, ed. Jostein Ådna and Hans Kvalbein (Tübingen: Mohr Siebeck, 2000), 165–84.

90 Thus, Norbert Schmidt is correct to conclude, "On the pages of the New Testament we do not find an explicit theology of mission, but the implicit commission initially given to the Apostles can be found in many forms with respect to the Church" (Schmidt, "The Apostolic Band – A Paradigm for Modern Missions?," 77).

towards early Christians demonstrates that the dynamic (and offensive) gospel was progressing effectively through its adherents.

CHAPTER 5

Conclusions and Implications

Conclusions

What did Paul expect the church to do in regard to missionary work? This is the question I have sought to answer in this book. Chapter one began our study by investigating previous scholarship on the topic. We found that prior to the 1950s, the majority of scholars assumed or argued that Paul expected the churches to engage actively in mission, though there was a minority of scholars who argued for apostle-church mission discontinuity. Whether advocating continuity or discontinuity, scholars in this early period generally shared a commonality of superficiality. With the application of a more rigorous biblical theological method to our missionary question in the 1950s and beyond, we continued to find a similar division among scholars. Some, in agreement with the majority of scholars in the earlier period but with more textual support, conclude that Paul envisioned an active outward-directed missionary role for the early Christian congregations. Others think Paul only imagined his churches partnering with him and attracting converts in a passive pattern.

We concluded chapter one by suggesting that the hypothesis of apostolic continuity (i.e., that Paul expected the church to continue his apostolic mission) provided a promising avenue for further research. At this juncture, I also proposed that Paul expected both the apostles and the broader church to be propelled to evangelize on the same basis – the dynamic and effective word of God. That is, Paul viewed the gospel (or "the word of God") as an "effective force" which inevitably went forth and accomplished God's will – in this case, the further spreading of the salvific message of Jesus Christ.

In chapter two, I began by clarifying what Paul means by the terms "church" and "apostle." Next, I sought to show that Paul speaks of "the gospel" not only as the *content* of his message or the *act* of proclaiming it, but as the dynamic, effective word of the Lord (Rom 1:16; 1 Cor 1:18). Such an understanding of God's word has ample precedent in the Old Testament (Isa 55:10–11; Jer 20:7–9; 23:29). Of great significance to our study is the fact that the apostle spoke of this dynamic word as integrally related to his own missionary labors (Rom 15:18–19; 1 Cor 4:15; 9:12; 14:36; Col 1:5–7, 25; 1 Thess 1:5; 2 Tim 2:8–9; 4:17), as well as the life of the church (Rom 16:5; 1 Cor 15:1–2; 16:15; Col 3:16–17; 1 Thess 1:8; 2:13–16; 2 Thess 3:1).

While scholars have traditionally proposed the Great Commission or the

Holy Spirit as the basis of Paul's ecclesiastical missionary expectations, we have found these two bases lacking textual support in the Pauline epistles. Paul's description of the gospel as a dynamic power, however, seems to provide a theological basis for his expectation that the church would engage in mission. The gospel, as God's word, is "power" which inevitably progresses through the persons and communities included in its advance. As the gospel comes to dwell in the churches, Paul is confident that the word will push the boundaries of the communities to include new people. Ultimately, Paul's confidence in the gospel to create churches which continue the apostolic mission is a confidence in the gospel's author and subject – God the Father and the Lord Jesus Christ.

In chapter two, we also saw how the Pauline understanding of the dynamic word holds promise for understanding the apparent discontinuity between the passive witness of the Old Testament elect community and the active witness of the New Testament elect community. God's "word" and "Spirit," which came to only specific persons intermittently in the Old Testament (1 Sam 10:10; Hos 1:1; Ezek 2:2), came to abide in all believers without distinction in the New Testament era (Joel 2:28–32; Acts 2:16–21; 1 Cor 12:13). This abiding gospel then propels believers outwards in mission. Such an understanding of the gospel as a basis for the church's mission does not contradict Luke's emphasis on Spirit in Acts (Acts 1:8; 4:29–31; 6:10; 8:29, 39–40; 10:19–20, 44–47; 11:12; 13:2–4; 16:6–7; 20:22–23) or Christ's command in the Gospels (Matt 28:18–20; Luke 24:47; John 20:21; cf. Acts 1:8; Mark 16:15), but serves to fill out the rich and varied biblical witness to the church's evangelistic concern. The heuristic diagram I introduced in chapter two illustrates this concept:

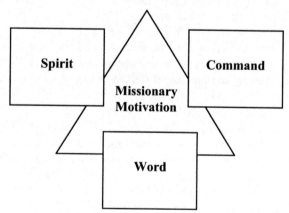

Fig. 3. The church's missionary motivation as Spirit, Command, and Word.

In chapter three, I sought to show that Paul's theological basis for the church's missionary role is also exhibited in his imperatives to witness. Because Paul's paranesis is consistently occasional, we should not judge the general importance of an issue to him by that issue's presence, frequency, or absence in his letters. Yet, if Paul did expect the churches to proclaim the gospel, we might expect at least a few situations that Paul faced to have elicited more explicit instructions on mission. Indeed, we do find imperatives for the church to evangelize in Philippians 2:16 (cf. 1:12–18), Ephesians 6:15–17, and in Paul's commands to imitate him in 1 Corinthians (4:16; 11:1; cf. 7:12–16; 14:23–25). Paul also clearly desired the church to be a "passive" witness (e.g., Col 4:6; 1 Thess 4:12; 1 Tim 6:1; Titus 2:1–10; cf. Acts 2:43–47; 1 Pet 2:9–12; 3:1–2).

In chapter four, we examined further evidence that Paul expected the gospel to propel the church outwards in an evangelistic role in continuity with the apostles. We started by looking at three incidental parallels between the apostles' and the church's mission. Paul presents both apostles and ordinary Christians as confirming the truthfulness of the gospel through miracles (Rom 15:18–19; 1 Cor 2:4; 12:9–10, 28–30; 2 Cor 12:12; Gal 3:5; cf. Acts 2:43; 3:1–4:22; 4:29–30; 6:7–10; 8:5–14). Also, both apostles and churches pray for missions and the church (Rom 1:8; 10:1; 15:13; 2 Cor 9:14; Eph 6:18–20; Phil 1:3–5; Col 4:2–4; 1 Thess 1:2–8; 3:12; 2 Thess 3:1–2; 1 Tim 2:1–4). And, finally, Paul describes both apostles and ordinary believers as "teaching," "admonishing," and "building up" the church (Rom 15:14; 1 Cor 3:9; 4:14, 17; 10:23–24, 31–33; 14:1–26; 2 Cor 12:19; 13:10; Eph 4:11–16; Col 1:28; 3:16; 1 Thess 5:12; 2 Thess 2:15; 3:15). This last parallel reminds us that Paul's expansive missionary vision did not stop at establishing superficial beachheads for the gospel. The Apostle to the Gentiles sought to establish mature congregations in Christ; he expected the churches to aim at this same goal.

The latter half of chapter four was reserved for the discussion of an especially significant parallel between the apostles' and the churches' mission. Paul frequently describes both the apostles and the churches as undergoing God-ordained suffering (Rom 8:16–17; 1 Cor 4:9–13; 15:30–32; 16:8–9; 2 Cor 1:3–10; 2:14–17; Gal 6:12, 17; Phil 1:14, 27–30; Col 1:24–25; 1 Thess 2:14–16; 3:3–4; 2 Tim 1:8; 2:3; 3:12). This suffering is important because both the apostles and ordinary believers must have shared a common characteristic that incited it. It is significant that this shared aspect of Christian existence was both (1) known to the non-Christian outsiders and (2) offensive to those outsiders. We argued that the offensive characteristic that invariably made itself known through both apostles and ordinary Christians was the presence of the dynamic gospel and the rejected Christ. Also, we noted that suffering was not only the evidence that the early Christians were effectively making their faith known, but actually was a means of making it known (2 Cor 2:14–17; 4:8–12).

This study has been preparatory in many regards. Due to the number of topics discussed and the large amount of Pauline texts cited, I have been unable to provide more than a modicum of contextual information. More detailed studies of selected texts or certain missionary activities are needed.

Also, the space limitations of our study allowed for only a limited biblical synthesis. Various elements of biblical theology that we touched on demand further attention. For example, a definitive scholarly work on the relation of the missionary role of the elect community in the Old and New Testaments is yet to be written. Also, further attention is needed to synthesize the diverse theologies of mission in the New Testament.

Implications

After answering the question, "What did Paul expect the church to do in regard to missionary activity?" the next question for any thoughtful biblical scholar should be, "So, what should the church do today?"

If we understand the New Testament documents as presenting us with the normative pattern for the church, then the modern church must be a missionary church. The church must not only take on the mantle of the apostolic mission in a general or abstract way; she must carry out the apostolic mission in concrete tasks. Just like the ancient churches that Paul addressed, modern churches should be active in proclaiming the gospel, suffering for the gospel, authenticating the gospel by their behavior, confirming the gospel through miracles, building-up the church, and praying for missions and the church.

Unlike some recent missiologists who have proposed that the apostolic mission is inherited by a para-church "apostolic band," Paul understands missions as an ecclesiastical task.[1] The apostolic mission devolves upon each church *as a whole* – not upon any particular member or group. Each individual member within the church, then, will manifest missionary activity according to his or her particular gifting and life situation. All but the unrepeatable aspects of the apostles' mission (e.g., eyewitness testimony and initial promulgation of authoritative revelation) devolve upon the church *as a whole*.

A missionary theology which places the missionary task in the hands of a few church leaders or with a para-church body lacks support from the Pauline letters. Modern para-church missions can be an attempt to solve the problem of the church's anemic missionary vision by removing the missionary task from the church.[2] Missions, rather, should be returned to the church. The most effective way to do this is to teach and preach the gospel accurately. Because the gospel is self-diffusive, when it truly dwells in a congregation, that congregation will experience "spontaneous expansion," empowered by God's

---

1   For proponents of the "apostolic band" paradigm, see chapter 1, n. 181.

2   These statements should not be taken as a condemnation of para-church organizations, but as a recognition that healthy para-church ministry is best understood as cooperative efforts of *churches* or *members* of churches. It is God's plan that "*through the church* the wisdom of God in its rich variety might now be made known to the rulers and authorities in the heavenly places" (Eph 3:10, my emphasis).

word and presence. Human distortions of the gospel or human attempts to control the dynamic nature of the gospel result in a weakened, non-missionary church.

When I began this study, I originally thought of titling it "The Missionary Obligation of the Pauline Churches." As I progressed in my study and reflection, though, I determined that that title would present a distortion of the biblical evidence. While Paul does speak of the missionary task entrusted to him as an *obligation*, it is more comprehensively described as a natural overflow of the dynamic gospel's presence in his life. The church also, because it is created and characterized by that same gospel, must be an active missionary community.

Bibliography

Books

Abbott, T. K. *A Critical and Exegetical Commentary on the Epistles to the Ephesians and to the Colossians*. International Critical Commentary. Edinburgh: T. & T. Clark, 1897.

Allen, Roland. *Missionary Methods, St. Paul's or Ours? A Study of the Church in the Four Provinces*. London: Robert Scott, 1912.

— *The Spontaneous Expansion of the Church and the Causes which Hinder It*. 3rd ed. London: World Dominion, 1956.

Althaus, Paul. *Der Brief an die Römer*. 10th ed. Das Neue Testament Deutsch 6. Göttingen: Vandenhoeck & Ruprecht, 1966.

Amberson, Talmadge R., ed. *The Birth of Churches: The Biblical Basis for Church Planting*. Nashville: Broadman, 1979.

Anderson, Ray S., ed. *Theological Foundations for Ministry: Selected Readings for a Theology of the Church in Ministry*. Edinburgh: T. & T. Clark, 1979.

Arnold, Clinton E. *Power and Magic: The Concept of Power in Ephesians*. 2nd ed. Cambridge: Cambridge University Press, 1989; Grand Rapids: Baker, 1992.

— *Powers of Darkness: Principalities and Powers in Paul's Letters*. Downers Grove: InterVarsity, 1992.

Asting, Ragnar. *Die Verkündigung des Wortes im Urchristentum dargestellt an den Begriffen "Wort Gottes," "Evangelium" und "Zeugnis."* Stuttgart: W. Kohlhammer, 1939.

Baird, William. *Paul's Message and Mission*. New York: Abingdon, 1960.

Banks, Robert J. *Paul's Idea of Community: The Early House Churches in their Historical Setting*. Grand Rapids: Eerdmans, 1980.

Bardy, Gustave. *La Conversion au Christianisme durant les Premiers Siècles*. Paris: Aubier, 1949.

Barnett, Paul. *The Second Epistle to the Corinthians*. New International Commentary on the New Testament. Grand Rapids: Eerdmans, 1997.

Barrett, C. K. *A Commentary on the Epistle to the Romans*. 2nd ed. Black's New Testament Commentaries. London: Black, 1991.

— *A Commentary on the First Epistle to the Corinthians*. New York: Harper & Row, 1968.

— *The Pastoral Epistles*. Oxford: Clarendon, 1963.

— *The Signs of an Apostle: The Cato Lecture 1969*. London: Epworth, 1970.

Barth, Markus. *Ephesians*. 2 vols. Anchor Bible, vols. 34, 34A. Garden City, NY: Doubleday, 1974.

Bauckham, Richard. *Bible and Mission: Christian Witness in a Postmodern World*. Grand Rapids: Baker; Carlisle: Paternoster, 2003.

Baudraz, Francis. *Les Epîtres aux Corinthiens: Commentaire*. Geneva: Labor et Fides, 1965.

Bauer, Bruno. *Die Apostelgeschichte: Eine Ausgleichung des Paulinismus und des*

Judenthums innerhalb der christlichen Kirche. Berlin: Gustav Hempel, 1850.

Baur, Ferdinand Christian. *Historisch-kritische Untersuchungen zum Neuen Testament.* Ausgewählte Werke in Einzelausgaben 1. Stuttgart: Friedrich Frommann, 1963.

Beale, G. K. *The Temple and the Church's Mission: A Biblical Theology of the Dwelling Place of God.* New Studies in Biblical Theology 17. Leicester: Apollos; Downers Grove: InterVarsity, 2004.

Beare, F. W. *A Commentary on the Epistle to the Philippians.* Harper's New Testament Commentaries. New York: Harper, 1959.

Beker, J. Christiaan. *The Triumph of God: The Essence of Paul's Thought.* Translated by Loren T. Stuckenbruck. Minneapolis: Fortress, 1990.

Best, Ernest. *The Letter of Paul to the Romans.* The Cambridge Bible Commentary. Cambridge: University Press, 1967.

— *One Body in Christ: A Study in the Relationship of the Church to Christ in the Epistles of the Apostle Paul.* London: S.P.C.K., 1955.

— *Paul and His Converts.* Edinburgh: T. & T. Clark, 1988.

— *Second Corinthians.* Interpretation. Atlanta: John Knox, 1987.

Betz, Hans Dieter. *Nachfolge und Nachahmung Jesu Christi im Neuen Testament.* Beiträge zur Historischen Theologie 37. Tübingen: Mohr, 1967.

Blauw, Johannes. *The Missionary Nature of the Church: A Survey of the Biblical Theology of Mission.* London: Lutterworth, 1962.

Bloesch, Donald G. *The Evangelical Renaissance.* Grand Rapids: Eerdmans, 1973.

Blomberg, Craig. *1 Corinthians.* NIV Application Commentary. Grand Rapids: Zondervan, 1994.

Bloomquist, L. Gregory. *The Function of Suffering in Philippians.* Journal for the Study of the New Testament Supplement Series 78. Sheffield: Sheffield Academic Press, 1993.

Boer, Harry R. *Pentecost and Missions.* Grand Rapids: Eerdmans; London: Lutterworth, 1961.

Bormann, Lukas, Kelly Del Tredici, and Angela Standhartinger, eds. *Religious Propaganda and Missionary Competition in the New Testament World.* Leiden: Brill, 1994.

Bornkamm, Günther. *Paul.* Translated by D. M. G. Stalker. Minneapolis: Fortress, 1995.

Bosch, David J. *Transforming Mission: Paradigm Shifts in Theology of Mission.* American Society of Missiology Series 16. Maryknoll, NY: Orbis, 1991.

— *Witness to the World: The Christian Mission in Theological Perspective.* Atlanta: John Knox, 1980.

Branick, Vincent P. *The House Church in the Writings of Paul.* Zacchaeus Studies. Wilmington, DE: Michael Glazier, 1989.

Bratcher, Robert G., and Eugene A. Nida. *A Translator's Handbook on Paul's Letter to the Ephesians.* New York: United Bible Societies, 1982.

Brown, Dale W. *Understanding Pietism.* Rev. ed. Nappanee, IN: Evangel, 1996.

Brox, Norbert. *Die Pastoralbriefe.* 4th ed. Regensburger Neues Testament 7. Regensburg: Pustet, 1969.

Bruce, F. F. *The Epistles to the Colossians, to Philemon, and to the Ephesians.* New International Commentary on the New Testament. Grand Rapids: Eerdmans, 1984.

— *1 and 2 Corinthians.* New Century Bible. London: Oliphants, 1971.

— *Paul: Apostle of the Heart Set Free.* Grand Rapids: Eerdmans, 1977.

— *Philippians.* Good News Commentary. San Francisco: Harper & Row, 1983.

Bultmann, Rudolf. *Der Stil der paulinischen Predigt und die kynisch-stoische Diatribe.* Forschungen zur Religion und Literatur des Alten und Neuen Testaments 13. Göttingen: Vandenhoeck & Ruprecht, 1910. Reprint, 1984.

— *Theology of the New Testament.* 2 vols. Translated by Kendrick Grobel. New York: Charles Scribner's Sons, 1951, 1955.

Burton, Ernest De Witt. *A Critical and Exegetical Commentary on the Epistle to the Galatians.* International Critical Commentary. Edinburgh: T. & T. Clark, 1921.

Caird, G. B. *The Apostolic Age.* London: Gerald Duckworth, 1955.

— *Paul's Letters from Prison (Ephesians, Philippians, Colossians, Philemon) in the Revised Standard Version.* London: Oxford University Press, 1976.

Calvin, John. *Commentarius in epistolas catholicas.* In vol. 55 of *Ioannis Calvini Opera quae supersunt omnia,* ed. Wilhelm Baum, Eduard Cunitz, and Eduard Reuss, 201-500. Corpus Reformatorum, vol. 83. Brunswick, NJ: C. A. Schwetschke and Son, 1896. Reprint, Johnston Reprint Corp., 1964.

— *The First Epistle of Paul The Apostle to the Corinthians.* Translated by John W. Fraser. Edinburgh: Oliver and Boyd; Grand Rapids: Eerdmans, 1960.

Carey, William. *An Enquiry into the Obligations of Christians to Use Means for the Conversion of the Heathens in which the Religious State of the Different Nations of the World, the Success of Former Undertakings, and the Practicability of Further Undertakings, Are Considered.* Leicester: Ann Ireland, 1792. Facsimile, London: Carey Kingsgate, 1961.

Carson, D. A., ed. *The Church in the Bible and the World: An International Study.* Grand Rapids: Baker, 1987.

Carver, William Owen. *The Glory of God in the Christian Calling: A Study of the Ephesian Epistle.* Nashville: Broadman, 1949.

Casson, Lionel. *Travel in the Ancient World.* N.p.: George Allen & Unwin, 1974; Baltimore: Johns Hopkins University Press, 1994.

Castelli, Elizabeth A. *Imitating Paul: A Discourse of Power.* Literary Currents in Biblical Interpretation. Louisville: Westminster/John Knox, 1991.

Cerfaux, L. *The Church in the Theology of St. Paul.* Translated by Geoffrey Webb and Adrian Walker. New York: Herder and Herder, 1959.

Chae, Daniel Jong-Sang. *Paul as Apostle to the Gentiles: His Apostolic Self-Awareness and its Influence on the Soteriological Argument in Romans.* Paternoster Biblical and Theological Monographs. Carlisle: Paternoster, 1997.

Chevallier, Raymond. *Roman Roads.* Berkeley: University of California Press, 1976.

Cicero *De amicitia.* Translated by William Armistead Falconer, under the title, *Laelius On Friendship.* In Loeb Classical Library 154. Cambridge, MA: Harvard University Press; London: William Heinemann, 1923.

Clarke, Andrew D., and Bruce W. Winter, eds. *One God, One Lord: Christianity in a World of Religious Pluralism.* 2nd ed. Grand Rapids: Baker, 1993.

Clarke, Robert. *The Uniqueness of the Church.* Ilfracombe: Arthur H. Stockwell, 1970.

Collins, Raymond F. *First Corinthians.* Sacra Pagina Series, vol. 7. Collegeville, MN: Liturgical, 1999.

Conzelmann, H. *1 Corinthians.* Hermeneia. Philadelphia: Fortress, 1975.

Costas, Orlando E. *The Church and its Mission: A Shattering Critique from the Third World.* Wheaton: Tyndale, 1974.

Crafer, T. W. *The Healing Miracles in the Book of Acts: A Practical and Devotional Study.* London: Society for Promoting Christian Knowledge, [1939].

Cranfield, C. E. B. *A Critical and Exegetical Commentary on the Epistle to the Romans.* 2 vols. International Critical Commentary. Edinburgh: T. & T. Clark, 1975, 1979.

Dahl, Nils Alstrup. *Studies in Paul: Theology for the Early Christian Mission.* Assisted by Paul Donahue. Minneapolis: Augsburg, 1977.

— *Das Volk Gottes: Eine Untersuchung zum Kirchenbewusstsein des Urchristentums.* Darmstadt: Wissenschaftliche Buchgesellschaft, 1963.

Daube, David. *The New Testament and Rabbinic Judaism.* London: Athlone, 1956.

De Boer, Willis Peter. *The Imitation of Paul: An Exegetical Study.* Kampen: Kok, 1962.

Deissmann, Adolf. *Light From the Ancient East: The New Testament Illustrated by Recently Discovered Texts of the Graeco-Roman World.* Rev. ed. Translated by Lionel R. M. Strachan. New York: George H. Doran, 1927.

— *Paul: A Study in Social and Religious History.* Translated by W. E. Wilson. New York: George H. Doran Company, 1926.

Dibelius, Martin. *An die Kolosser, Epheser, an Philemon.* 3rd rev. ed. Handbuch zum Neuen Testament 12, ed. Heinrich Greeven. Tübingen: Mohr, 1953.

— *An die Thessalonicher I II, An die Philipper.* 3rd Revised ed. Handbuch zum Neuen Testament 11. Tübingen: Mohr, 1937.

Dibelius, Martin, and Hans Conzelmann. *The Pastoral Epistles.* Translated by Philip Buttolph and Adela Yarbro. Hermeneia. Philadelphia: Fortress, 1972.

Dickson, John P. *Mission-Commitment in Ancient Judaism and in the Pauline Communities.* Wissenschaftliche Untersuchungen zum Neuen Testament 2.159. Tübingen: Mohr Siebeck, 2003.

Dittenberger, W., ed. *Sylloge Inscriptionum Graecarum.* 2nd ed. 3 vols. Leipzig: Hirzelium, 1898-1901.

Dodd, C. H. *The Apostolic Preaching and Its Developments.* London: Hodder & Stoughton, 1936. Reprint, Grand Rapids: Baker, 1980.

Dollar, Harold E. *A Biblical-Missiological Exploration of the Cross-Cultural Dimensions in Luke-Acts.* San Francisco: Mellen Research University Press, 1993.

Doohan, Helen. *Paul's Vision of Church.* Good News Studies 32. Wilmington, DE: Michael Glazier, 1989.

Doyle, Robert, ed. *Signs & Wonders and Evangelicals: A Response to the Teaching of John Wimber.* Homebush West, NSW [Australia]: Lancer, 1987.

Driver, John. *Images of the Church in Mission.* Scottdale, PA: Herald, 1997.

Dunn, James D. G. *Romans 1-8.* Word Biblical Commentary, vol. 38A. Dallas: Word, 1988.

Eadie, John. *A Commentary on the Greek Text of the Epistle of Paul to the Philippians.* London: Richard Griffin, 1859.

Ehrhardt, Arnold. *The Apostolic Ministry.* Scottish Journal of Theology Occasional Papers 7. Edinburgh: Oliver and Boyd, 1958.

— *The Apostolic Succession in the First Two Centuries of the Church.* London: Lutterworth, 1953.

Ellicott, Charles J. *The Pastoral Epistles of St. Paul: With a Critical and Grammatical Commentary, and a Revised Translation.* 3rd ed. London: Longman, Green, Longman, Roberts & Green, 1864.

Erickson, Millard J. *Christian Theology.* 2nd ed. Grand Rapids: Baker, 1998.

Ernst, Josef. *Die Briefe an die Philipper, an Philemon, an die Kolosser, an die Epheser.* Regensburg: Friedrich Pustet, 1974.

Fee, Gordon D. *1 and 2 Timothy, Titus.* New International Biblical Commentary. Rev.

ed. Peabody, MA: Hendrickson, 1988.

— *The First Epistle to the Corinthians.* New International Commentary on the New Testament. Grand Rapids: Eerdmans, 1987.

Feldman, L. H. *Jew and Gentile in the Ancient World: Attitudes and Interactions from Alexander to Justinian.* Princeton: Princeton University Press, 1993.

Ferguson, Everett. *The Church of Christ: A Biblical Ecclesiology for Today.* Grand Rapids: Eerdmans, 1996.

Fiore, Benjamin. *The Function of Personal Example in the Socratic and Pastoral Epistles.* Analecta Biblica 105. Rome: Biblical Institute, 1986.

Fishwick, Duncan. *The Imperial Cult in the Latin West.* Vol. 2.1, *Studies in the Ruler Cult of the Western Provinces of the Roman Empire.* Leiden: Brill, 1991.

Fitzgerald, John T. *Cracks in an Earthen Vessel: An Examination of the Catalogues of Hardships in the Corinthian Correspondence.* SBL Dissertation Series 99. Atlanta: Scholars Press, 1988.

Fitzmyer, Joseph A. *Romans.* Anchor Bible, vol. 33. New York: Doubleday, 1993.

Friedländer, Ludwig. *Roman Life and Manners Under the Early Empire.* Translated by Leonard A. Magnus, J. H. Freese, and A. B. Gough. 7th ed. 4 vols. London: George Routledge & Sons; New York: E. P. Dutton, [1908]-13.

Furnish, Victor Paul. *II Corinthians.* Anchor Bible, vol. 32A. Garden City, NY: Doubleday, 1984.

— *Theology and Ethics in Paul.* Nashville: Abingdon, 1968.

Garland, David E. *1 Corinthians.* Baker Exegetical Commentary on the New Testament. Grand Rapids: Baker, 2003.

Garrison, David. *Church Planting Movements.* Richmond, VA: International Mission Board of the Southern Baptist Convention, 1999.

Gebauer, Roland. *Das Gebet bei Paulus: Forschungsgeschichtliche und exegetische Studien.* Giessen: Brunner, 1989.

Geisler, Norman L. *Miracles and Modern Thought.* Grand Rapids: Zondervan; Dallas: Probe Ministries International, 1982.

Gensichen, Hans-Werner. *Glaube für die Welt: Theologische Aspekte der Mission.* Gütersloh: Gerd Mohn, 1971.

Gilliland, Dean S. *Pauline Theology and Mission Practice.* Grand Rapids: Baker, 1983.

Gnilka, Joachim. *Der Epheserbrief.* Herders Theologischer Kommentar zum Neuen Testament 10.2. Freiburg: Herder, 1971.

— *Der Philipperbrief.* 2nd ed. Herders Theologischer Kommentar zum Neuen Testament 10.3. Freiburg: Herder, 1976.

Godet, Frederic Louis. *Commentary on First Corinthians.* Edinburgh: T. & T. Clark, 1889. Reprint, Grand Rapids: Kregel, 1977.

— *Commentary on St. Paul's First Epistle to the Corinthians.* Vol. 2. Translated by A. Cusin. Clark's Foreign Theological Library—New Series 30. Edinburgh: T. & T. Clark, 1887.

Gooch, Peter D. *Dangerous Food: 1 Corinthians 8-10 in Its Context.* Studies in Christianity and Judaism 5. Waterloo, Ontario: Wilfrid Laurier University Press, 1993.

Goodman, Martin. *Mission and Conversion: Proselytizing in the Religious History of the Roman Empire.* Oxford: Clarendon, 1994.

Gordon, A. J. *The Holy Spirit in Missions: Six Lectures.* New York: Fleming H. Revell, 1893.

Grassi, Joseph A. *A World to Win: The Missionary Methods of Paul the Apostle.* Maryknoll, NY: Maryknoll, 1965.

Green, Michael. *Evangelism in the Early Church.* London: Hodder and Stoughton; Grand Rapids: Eerdmans, 1970.

— *Evangelism in the Early Church.* Rev. ed. Grand Rapids: Eerdmans, 2004.

Grenfell Bernard P., and Arthur S. Hunt, eds. *The Oxyrhynchus Papyri.* Vol. 12. London: Oxford University Press, 1916.

Grether, Oskar. *Name und Wort Gottes im Alten Testament.* Beihefte zur Zeitschrift für die altestamentliche Wissenschaft 64. Giessen: Töpelmann, 1934.

Grudem, Wayne. *Systematic Theology: An Introduction to Biblical Doctrine.* Leicester: InterVarsity; Grand Rapids: Zondervan, 1994.

Gundry Volf, Judith M. *Paul and Perseverance: Staying in and Falling Away.* Tübingen: Mohr; Louisville: Westminster, 1990.

Guthrie, Donald. *New Testament Theology.* Downers Grove: InterVarsity, 1981.

— *The Pastoral Epistles.* 2nd ed. Tyndale New Testament Commentaries 14. Leicester: InterVarsity; Grand Rapids: Eerdmans, 1990.

Gutiérrez, Pedro. *La Paternité spirituelle selon Saint Paul.* Études Bibliques. Paris: J. Gabalda, 1968.

Güttgemanns, Erhardt. *Der leidende Apostel und sein Herr: Studien zur paulinischen Christologie.* Forschungen zur Religion und Literatur des Alten und Neuen Testaments 90. Göttingen: Vandenhoeck & Ruprecht, 1966.

Haas, Odo. *Paulus der Missionar: Ziel, Grundsätze und Methoden der Missionstätigkeit des Apostels Paulus nach seinen eigenen Aussagen.* Münsterschwarzach: Vier-Türme, 1971.

Haenchen, Ernst. *Die Apostelgeschichte.* 15th ed. H. A. W. Meyer, Kritisch-exegetischer Kommentar über das Neue Testament 3. Göttingen: Vandenhoeck & Ruprecht, 1968.

Hafemann, Scott J. *2 Corinthians.* NIV Application Commentary. Grand Rapids: Zondervan, 2000.

— *Suffering and Ministry in the Spirit: Paul's Defense of His Ministry in II Corinthians 2:14-3:3.* Grand Rapids: Eerdmans, 1990.

— *Suffering and the Spirit: An Exegetical Study of II Cor. 2:14-3:3 within the Context of the Corinthian Correspondence.* Wissenschaftliche Untersuchungen zum Neuen Testament 2.19. Tübingen: Mohr, 1986.

Hahn, Ferdinand. *Mission in the New Testament.* Translated by Frank Clarke. Studies in Biblical Theology 47. London: SCM, 1965.

Hainz, Josef. *Ekklesia.* Regensburg: Friedrich Pustet, 1972.

Harnack, Adolf von. *The Mission and Expansion of Christianity in the First Three Centuries.* Edited and translated by James Moffatt. 2nd ed. 2 vols. London: Williams and Norgate; New York: G. P. Putnam's Sons, 1908.

Hawthorne, Gerald F. *Philippians.* Word Biblical Commentary, vol. 43. Waco, TX: Word, 1983.

Hays, Richard B. *First Corinthians.* Interpretation. Louisville: John Knox, 1997.

Heim, Karl. *Die Gemeinde des Auferstandenen: Tübinger Vorlesungen über den 1. Korintherbrief.* Edited by Friso Melzer. Munich: Neubau, 1949.

Heinrici, Georg. *Kritisch Exegetisches Handbuch über den ersten Brief an die Korinther.* 6th ed., Meyers Kommentar über das Neue Testament. Göttingen: Vandenhoeck & Ruprecht, 1881.

Hendriksen, William. *New Testament Commentary: Exposition of Ephesians.* Grand

Rapids: Baker, 1967.

Hengel, Martin. *Acts and the History of Earliest Christianity*. Translated by John Bowden. Philadelphia: Fortress, 1979.

— *Between Jesus and Paul: Studies in the Earliest History of Christianity*. Translated by John Bowden. London: SCM, 1983.

Henneken, Bartholomäus. *Verkündigung und Prophetie im Ersten Thessalonicherbrief: Ein Beitrag zur Theologie des Wortes Gottes*. Stuttgarter Bibelstudien 29. Stuttgart: Katholisches Bibelwerk, 1969.

Herbert, A. S. *The Book of the Prophet Isaiah: Chapters 40-66*. Cambridge Bible Commentary. Cambridge: Cambridge University Press, 1975.

Héring, Jean. *The First Epistle of Saint Paul to the Corinthians*. Translated by A. W. Heathcote and P. J. Allcock. London: Epworth, 1962.

Hinson, E. Glenn. *The Early Church: Origins to the Dawn of the Middle Ages*. Nashville: Abingdon, 1996.

— *The Evangelization of the Roman Empire: Identity and Adaptability*. Macon, GA: Mercer University Press, 1981.

Hodge, Charles. *An Exposition of the First Epistle to the Corinthians*. New York: Robert Carter & Brothers, 1857. Reprint, Grand Rapids: Baker, 1980.

Holtz, Gottfried. *Die Pastoralbriefe*. Theologischer Handkommentar zum Neuen Testament 13. Berlin: Evangelische Verlagsanstalt, 1965.

Horsley, G. H. R., ed. *New Documents Illustrating Early Christianity: A Review of the Greek Inscriptions and Papyri Published in 1977*. Vol. 2. Macquarie University: The Ancient Documents Research Centre, 1982.

— *New Documents Illustrating Early Christianity: A Review of the Greek Inscriptions and Papyri Published in 1979*. Vol. 4. Macquarie University: The Ancient Documents Research Centre, 1987.

Horsley, Richard A. *1 Corinthians*. Abingdon New Testament Commenataries. Nashville: Abingdon, 1998.

Hort, Fenton John Anthony. *The Christian Ecclesia: A Course of Lectures on the Early History and Early Conceptions of the Ecclesia and Four Sermons*. London: Macmillan, 1897. Reprint, 1908.

Hultgren, Arland J. *Paul's Gospel and Mission: The Outlook from His Letter to the Romans*. Philadelphia: Fortress, 1985.

Hunt, Arthur S., ed. *The Oxyrhynchus Papyri*. Vol. 9. London: Oxford University Press, 1912.

Jeremias, Joachim. *Die Briefe an Timotheus und Titus*. 7th ed. Das Neue Testament Deutsch 9. Göttingen: Vandenhoeck & Ruprecht, 1954.

— *Jesus' Promise to the Nations*. Translated by S. H. Hooke. Studies in Biblical Theology 24. London: SCM, 1958.

Johnson, Luke Timothy. *Letters to Paul's Delegates: 1 Timothy, 2 Timothy, Titus*. The New Testament in Context. Valley Forge, PA: Trinity Press International, 1996.

Johnston, George. *The Doctrine of the Church in the New Testament*. Cambridge: University Press, 1943.

Kähler, Martin, and Johannes Warneck. *D. Gustav Warneck 1834-1910: Blätter der Erinnerung*. Berlin: Martin Warneck, 1911.

Kaiser, Walter C., Jr. *Mission in the Old Testament: Israel as a Light to the Nations*. Grand Rapids: Baker, 2000.

Karris, Robert J. *The Pastoral Epistles*. New Testament Message 17. Wilmington, DE:

Michael Glazier, 1979.

Kasdorf, Hans. *Gustav Warnecks Missiologisches Erbe: Eine biographisch-historische Untersuchung*. Giessen: Brunnen, 1990.

Käsemann, Ernst. *An die Römer*. 2nd rev. ed. Handbuch zum Neuen Testament 8a. Tübingen: Mohr, 1974.

— *Commentary on Romans*. Translated and edited by Geoffrey W. Bromiley. Grand Rapids: Eerdmans, 1980.

Kasting, Heinrich. *Die Anfänge der urchristlichen Mission: Eine historische Untersuchung*. Beiträge zur evangelischen Theologie 55. Munich: Chr. Kaiser, 1969.

Keathley, Naymond H. *The Church's Mission to the Gentiles: Acts of the Apostles, Epistles of Paul*. Macon: Smyth & Helwys, 1999.

Kelly, J. N. D. *The Pastoral Epistles: I & II Timothy, Titus*. Black's New Testament Commentaries. London: Adam & Charles Black, 1963. Reprint, 1976.

Kertelge, Karl, ed. *Mission im Neuen Testament*. Freiburg: Herder, 1982.

Kirk, J. Andrew. *What is Mission? Theological Explorations*. London: Darton, Longman and Todd, 1999.

Kleinknecht, Karl Theodor. *Der leidende Gerechtfertigte: Die alttestamentlich-jüdische Tradition vom "leidenden Gerechten" und ihre Rezeption bei Paulus*. Wissenschaftliche Untersuchungen zum Neuen Testament 2.13. Tübingen: Mohr, 1984.

Knight, George W., III. *The New Testament Teaching on the Role Relationship of Men and Women*. Grand Rapids: Baker, 1977.

— *The Pastoral Epistles: A Commentary on the Greek Text*. New International Greek Testament Commentary. Grand Rapids: Eerdmans; Carlisle: Paternoster, 1992.

Köstenberger, Andreas J. *The Missions of Jesus and the Disciples according to the Fourth Gospel: With Implications for the Fourth Gospel's Purpose and the Mission of the Contemporary Church*. Grand Rapids: Eerdmans, 1998.

Köstenberger, Andreas J., and Peter T. O'Brien. *Salvation to the Ends of the Earth: A Biblical Theology of Mission*. New Studies in Biblical Theology 11. Leicester: Apollos; Downers Grove: InterVarsity, 2001.

Kremer, Jacob. *Was an den Leiden Christi noch mangelt: Eine interpretationsgeschichtliche und exegetische Untersuchung zu Kol. 1,24b*. Bonner biblische Beiträge 12. Bonn: Hanstein, 1956.

Kümmel, Werner Georg. *Introduction to the New Testament*. Rev. ed. Translated by Howard Clark Kee. Nashville: Abingdon, 1975.

— *The New Testament: The History of the Investigation of Its Problems*. Translated by S. McLean Gilmour and Howard Clark Kee. Nashville: Abingdon, 1972.

Küng, Hans. *The Church*. Translated by Ray Ockenden and Rosaleen Ockenden. New York: Sheed and Ward, 1967.

LaGrand, James. *The Earliest Christian Mission to "All Nations" in the Light of Matthew's Gospel*. International Studies in Formative Christianity and Judaism. Atlanta: Scholars, 1995.

Lampe, G. W. H., ed. *A Patristic Greek Lexicon*. Oxford: Clarendon, 1961.

Larkin Jr., William J., and Joel F. Williams, eds. *Mission in the New Testament: An Evangelical Approach*. American Society of Missiology Series 27. Maryknoll, NY: Orbis, 1998.

Larsson, Edvin. *Christus als Vorbild: Eine Untersuchung zu den paulinischen Tauf- und Eikontexten*. Acta Seminarii Neotestamentici Upsaliensis XXIII-1962. Uppsala:

Almquist & Wiksells, 1962.

Latourette, K. S. *The First Five Centuries.* Vol. 1, *A History of the Expansion of Christianity.* New York: Harper & Brothers, 1937.

Legrand, Lucien. *Unity and Plurality: Mission in the Bible.* Translated by Robert R. Barr. Maryknoll, NY: Orbis, 1990.

Lewis, Jonathan, ed. *World Mission: An Analysis of the World Christian Movement.* Pasadena: William Carey Library, 1987.

Liechtenhan, Rudolf. *Die urchristliche Mission: Voraussetzungen, Motive und Methoden.* Zurich: Zwingli, 1946.

Lietzmann, D. Hans. A*n die Korinther I-II.* 5th ed. Revised by W. G. Kümmel. Handbuch zum Neuen Testament 9. Tübingen: Mohr, 1969.

— *Einführung in die Textgeschichte der Paulusbriefe: An die Römer.* 5th ed. Handbuch zum Neuen Testament 8. Tübingen: Mohr, 1971.

Lightfoot, J. B. *The Epistle of St. Paul to the Galatians.* Grand Rapids: Zondervan, [1950].

— *Notes on Epistles of St Paul from Unpublished Commentaries.* London: Macmillan, 1895.

— *Saint Paul's Epistle to the Philippians.* London: Macmillan, 1913. Reprint, Grand Rapids: Zondervan, 1953.

Lincoln, Andrew T. *Ephesians.* Word Biblical Commentary, vol. 42. Dallas: Word, 1990.

Lippert, Peter. *Leben als Zeugnis: Die werbende Kraft christlicher Lebensführung nach dem Kirchenverständnis neutestamentlicher Briefe.* Stuttgarter Biblische Monographien 4. Stuttgart: Katholisches Bibelwerk, 1968.

Lock, Walter. *A Critical and Exegetical Commentary on the Pastoral Epistles (I & II Timothy and Titus).* International Critical Commentary. Edinburgh: T. & T. Clark, 1924.

— *The Epistle to the Ephesians.* London: Methuen, 1929.

Locke, John. *A Paraphrase and Notes on the Epistles of St Paul to the Galatians, 1 and 2 Corinthians, Romans, Ephesians.* Vol. 2. Edited by Arthur W. Wainwright. Oxford: Clarendon, 1987.

Loh, I-Jin, and Eugene A. Nida. *A Handbook on Paul's Letter to the Philippians.* United Bible Societies Handbook Series. New York: United Bible Societies, 1977.

Lohmeyer, Ernst. *Der Brief an die Philipper,* 14th ed. H. A. W. Meyer, Kritisch-exegetischer Kommentar über das Neue Testament, vol. 9.1. Göttingen: Vandenhoeck & Ruprecht, 1974.

Lohse, Eduard. *Colossians and Philemon.* Hermeneia. Translated by William R. Poehlmann and Robert J. Karris. Edited by Helmut Koester. Philadelphia: Fortress, 1971.

Louw, Johannes P., and Eugene A. Nida. *Greek-English Lexicon of the New Testament Based on Semantic Domains.* 2nd ed. 2 vols. New York: United Bible Societies, 1989.

MacMullen, Ramsay. *Paganism in the Roman Empire.* New Haven: Yale University Press, 1981.

Malherbe, Abraham J. *The Letters to the Thessalonians.* Anchor Bible, vol. 32B. New York: Doubleday, 2000.

— *Paul and the Thessalonians: The Philosophic Tradition of Pastoral Care.* Philadelphia: Fortress, 1987.

Manson, T. W. *The Church's Ministry.* London: Hodder & Stoughton, 1948.

March, F. A., ed. *Athenagoras*. Douglass Series of Christian Greek and Latin Writers 4. New York: Harper & Brothers, 1876.

Marshall, I. Howard. *A Critical and Exegetical Commentary on the Pastoral Epistles.* International Critical Commentary. Edinburgh: T. & T. Clark, 1999.

— *Kept by the Power of God: A Study of Perseverance and Falling Away.* London: Epworth, 1969. Reprint, Minneapolis: Bethany, 1975.

Martin, Chalmers. *Apostolic and Modern Missions.* New York: Fleming H. Revell, 1898.

Martin, Ralph P. *The Family and the Fellowship: New Testament Images of the Church.* Exeter: Paternoster. Reprint, Grand Rapids: Eerdmans, 1979.

— *Philippians.* New Century Bible. Grand Rapids: Eerdmans; London: Marshall, Morgan & Scott, 1976. Reprint, 1989.

Martin-Achard, R. *A Light to the Nations: A Study of the Old Testament Conception of Israel's Mission to the World.* Translated by John Penney Smith. Edinburgh: Oliver and Boyd, 1962.

McKnight, Scot. *A Light among the Gentiles: Jewish Missionary Activity in the Second Temple Period.* Minneapolis: Fortress, 1991.

McNeill, John T. *Modern Christian Movements.* Philadelphia: Westminster, 1954.

Merk, Otto. *Handeln aus Glaben: Die Motivierungen der paulinischen Ethik.* Marburger Theologische Studien 5. Marburg: Elwert, 1968.

Merkle, Benjamin L. *The Elder and Overseer: One Office in the Early Church.* Studies in Biblical Literature 57. New York: Peter Lang, 2003.

Meyer, Ben F. *The Early Christians: Their World Mission and Self Discovery.* Good News Studies 16. Wilmington, DE: Michael Glazier, 1986.

Meyer, Heinrich August Wilhelm. *Critical and Exegetical Hand-Book to the Epistle to the Ephesians.* In *Meyer's Commentary on the New Testament: Galatians and Ephesians.* Revised and edited by William P. Dickson. Translated by Maurice J. Evans. New York: Funk & Wagnalls, 1884.

Meyer, Regina Pacis. *Kirche und Mission im Epheserbrief.* Stuttgarter Bibelstudien 86. Stuttgart: Katholisches Bibelwerk, 1977.

Michael, J. Hugh. *The Epistle of Paul to the Philippians.* Moffatt New Testament Commentary. New York: Harper, [1927].

Michel, Otto. *Der Brief an die Römer.* 12th ed. H. A. W. Meyer, Kritisch-exegetischer Kommentar über das Neue Testament 4. Göttingen: Vandenhoeck & Ruprecht, 1963.

Minear, Paul Sevier. *Images of the Church in the New Testament.* Philadelphia: Westminster, 1960.

Mitton, C. Leslie. *Ephesians.* New Century Bible. London: Oliphants, 1976.

Molland, Einar. *Das Paulinische Euangelion: Das Wort und die Sache.* Oslo: Jacob Dybwad, 1934.

Moore, John, and Ken Neff. *A New Testament Blueprint for the Church.* Chicago: Moody, 1985.

Morris, Leon. *Expository Reflections on the Letter to the Ephesians.* Grand Rapids: Baker, 1994.

— *The First Epistle of Paul to the Corinthians: An Introduction and Commentary.* Rev. ed. Tyndale New Testament Commentaries 7. Leicester: InterVarsity; Grand Rapids: Eerdmans, 1985.

Moule, C. F. D. *An Idiom Book of New Testament Greek.* Cambridge: Cambridge University Press, 1953.

Mounce, Robert H. *Romans*. New American Commentary, vol. 27. Nashville: Broadman, 1995.

Mounce, William D. *Pastoral Epistles*. Word Biblical Commentary, vol. 46. Nashville: Thomas Nelson, 2000.

Munck, Johannes. *Paul and the Salvation of Mankind*. Translated by Frank Clarke. London: SCM, 1959.

Mußner, Franz. *Der Brief an die Epheser*. Ökumenischer Taschenbuchkommentar zum Neuen Testament 10. Gütersloh: Gerd Mohn, 1982.

Neill, Stephen. *A History of Christian Missions*. Revised by Owen Chadwick. 2nd ed. Harmondsworth, Middlesex: Penguin, 1986.

Newton, Derek. *Deity and Diet: The Dilemma of Sacrificial Food at Corinth*. Journal for the Study of the New Testament Supplement Series 169. Sheffield: Sheffield Academic Press, 1998.

Nissen, Johannes. *New Testament and Mission: Historical and Hermeneutical Perspectives*. Frankfurt am Main: Peter Lang, 1999.

O'Brien, Peter T. *Colossians, Philemon*. Word Biblical Commentary, vol. 44. Waco, TX: Word, 1982.

— *The Epistle to the Philippians: A Commentary on the Greek Text*. The New International Greek Testament Commentary. Grand Rapids: Eerdmans, 1991.

— *Gospel and Mission in the Writings of Paul: An Exegetical and Theological Analysis*. Grand Rapids: Baker; Carlisle: Paternoster, 1995.

— *Introductory Thanksgivings in the Letters of Paul*. Supplements to Novum Testamentum 49. Leiden: Brill, 1977.

— *The Letter to the Ephesians*. The Pillar New Testament Commentary. Grand Rapids: Eerdmans, 1999.

Ollrog, Wolf-Henning. *Paulus und seine Mitarbeiter: Untersuchungen zu Theorie und Praxis der paulinischen Mission*. Wissenschaftliche Monographien zum Alten und Neuen Testament 50. Neukirchen-Vluyn: Neukirchener Verlag, 1979.

Olson, C. Gordon. *What in the World is God Doing? The Essentials of Global Missions: An Introductory Guide*. Cedar Knolls, NJ: Global Gospel, 1994.

Orr, William F., and James Arthur Walther. *1 Corinthians*. Anchor Bible, vol. 32. New York: Doubleday, 1976.

Parry, R. St John. *The First Epistle of Paul the Apostle to the Corinthians*. Cambridge Greek Testament Commentaries. Cambridge: Cambridge University Press, 1916.

Peerbolte, L. J. Lietaert. *Paul the Missionary*. Contributions to Biblical Exegesis and Theology 34. Leuven: Peeters, 2003.

Peters, George W. *A Biblical Theology of Missions*. Chicago: Moody, 1972.

Pfitzner, Victor C. *Paul and the Agon Motif: Traditional Athletic Imagery in the Pauline Literature*. Supplements to Novum Testamentum 16. Leiden: Brill, 1967.

Pieper, Karl. *Paulus: Seine missionarische Persönlichkeit und Wirksamkeit*. Münster: Aschendorffschen Verlagsbuchhandlung, 1926.

Pierson, Arthur T. *The Acts of the Holy Spirit: Being an Examination of the Active Mission and Ministry of the Spirit of God, the Divine Paraclete, as Set Forth in The Acts of the Apostles*. New York: Fleming H. Revell, 1898.

— *The New Acts of the Apostles, or The Marvels of Modern Missions*. New York: Baker & Taylor, 1894.

Piper, John. *Let the Nations Be Glad! The Supremacy of God in Missions*. Grand Rapids: Baker, 1993.

Piper, John, and Wayne Grudem, eds. *Recovering Biblical Manhood and Womanhood: A Response to Evangelical Feminism.* Wheaton: Crossway, 1991.

Pobee, John S. *Persecution and Martyrdom in the Theology of Paul.* Journal for the Study of the New Testament Supplement Series 6. Sheffield: JSOT Press, 1985.

Poland, Franz *Geschichte des griechischen Vereinswesens.* Leipzig: B. G. Teubner, 1909.

Powell, Mark Allan. *God With Us: A Pastoral Theology of Matthew's Gospel.* Minneapolis: Fortress, 1995.

Quinn, Jerome D. *The Letter to Titus: A New Translation with Notes and Commentary and An Introduction to Titus, I and II Timothy, The Pastoral Epistles.* Anchor Bible, vol. 35. New York: Doubleday, 1990.

Rad, Gerhard von. *Old Testament Theology.* Vol. 2, *The Theology of Israel's Prophetic Traditions.* Translated by D. M. G. Stalker. New York: Harper & Row; Edinburgh: Oliver and Boyd, 1965.

Ramsay, W. M. *Pauline and Other Studies in Early Christian History.* New York: A. C. Armstrong and Son, 1906.

— *St. Paul the Traveller and the Roman Citizen.* London: Hodder and Stoughton; New York: G. P. Putnam's Sons, 1896.

Reinbold, Wolfgang. *Propaganda und Mission im ältesten Christentum: Eine Untersuchung zu den Modalitäten der Ausbreitung des frühen Kirche.* Forschungen zur Religion und Literatur des Alten und Neuen Testaments 188. Göttingen: Vandenhoeck & Ruprecht, 2000.

Renan, Ernest. *Saint Paul.* Paris: Michel Lévy Frères, 1869.

Ridderbos, Herman. *Paul: An Outline of His Theology.* Translated by John Richard de Witt. Grand Rapids: Eerdmans, 1975.

Riesner, Rainer. *Paul's Early Period: Chronology, Mission Strategy, and Theology.* Grand Rapids: Eerdmans, 1998.

Robertson, Archibald, and Alfred Plummer. *A Critical and Exegetical Commentary on the First Epistle of St Paul to the Corinthians.* 2nd ed. International Critical Commentary. Edinburgh: T. & T. Clark, 1914.

Robinson, J. Armitage. *St. Paul's Epistle to the Ephesians: A Revised Text and Translation with Exposition and Notes.* 2nd ed. London: Macmillan, 1904.

Robinson, O. F. *The Criminal Law of Ancient Rome.* Baltimore: Johns Hopkins University Press, 1995.

Robinson, William. *The Biblical Doctrine of the Church.* St. Louis: Bethany, 1948.

Roels, Edwin D. *God's Mission: The Epistle to the Ephesians in Mission Perspective.* Grand Rapids: Eerdmans, 1962.

Rommen, Edward, and Harold Netland, eds. *Christianity and the Religions: A Biblical Theology of World Religions.* Evangelical Missiological Society Series 2. Pasadena: William Carey Library, 1995.

Rowley, H. H. *The Missionary Message of the Old Testament.* London: Carey, 1944.

Sanders, E. P. *Paul, the Law, and the Jewish People.* Philadelphia: Fortress, 1983.

Saß, Gerhard. *Apostelamt und Kirche: Eine theologisch-exegetische Untersuchung des paulinischen Apostelbegriffs.* Munich: Kaiser, 1939.

Sauter, Gerhard. *Heilsgeschichte und Mission: Zum Verständnis der Heilsgeschichte in der Missionstheologie.* Basel: Brunnen, 1985.

Schärer, Hans. *Die Begründung der Mission in der katholischen und evangelischen Missionswissenscaft.* Theologische Studien 16. Zollikon-Zürich: Evangelischer,

1944.

Schenk, Wolfgang. *Die Philipperbriefe des Paulus.* Stuttgart: Kohlhammer, 1984.

Scheurer, Erich. *Altes Testament und Mission: Zur Begründung des Missionsauftrages.* Giessen: Brunnen, 1996.

Schlier, Heinrich. *Der Brief an die Epheser: Ein Kommentar.* Dusseldorf: Patmos, 1957.

Schlunk, D. Martin. *Paulus als Missionar.* Gütersloh: Bertelsmann, 1937.

Schmithals, Walter. *Die Gnosis in Korinth: Eine Untersuchung zu den Korintherbriefen.* 3rd ed. Göttingen: Vandenhoeck & Ruprecht, 1969.

— *The Office of Apostle in the Early Church.* Translated by John E. Steely. Nashville: Abingdon, 1969.

Schnabel, Eckhard J. *Early Christian Mission.* 2 Vols. Downers Grove: InterVarsity; Leicester: Apollos, 2004.

Schrage, Wolfgang. *Der erste Brief an die Korinther.* 4 vols. Evangelisch-Katholischer Kommentar zum Neuen Testament 7. Zurich: Benziger, 1991-2001.

Schreiner, Thomas R. *Romans.* Baker Exegetical Commentary on the New Testament. Grand Rapids: Baker, 1998.

Schulz, Anselm. *Nachfolgen und Nachahmen: Studien über das Verhältnis der neutestamentlichen Jüngerschaft zur urchristlichen Vorbildethik.* Studien zum Alten und Neuen Testament 6. Munich: Kösel, 1962.

Schütz, John Howard. *Paul and the Anatomy of Apostolic Authority.* Society for New Testament Studies Monograph Series 26. Cambridge: University Press, 1975.

Schweitzer, Albert. *The Quest of the Historical Jesus: A Critical Study of its Progress from Reimarus to Wrede.* Translated by W. Montgomery. 3rd ed. London: Adam & Charles Black, 1954.

— *Von Reimarus zu Wrede: Eine Geschichte der Leben-Jesu-Forschung.* Tübingen: Mohr, 1906.

Scott, James M. *Paul and the Nations: The Old Testament and Jewish Background of Paul's Mission to the Nations with Special Reference to the Destination of Galatians.* Wissenschaftliche Untersuchungen zum Neuen Testament 84. Tübingen: Mohr, 1995.

Seesemann, Heinrich. *Der Begriff* KOINΩNIA *im Neuen Testament.* Beihefte zur Zeitschrift für die neutestamentliche Wissenschaft und die Kunde der älteren Kirche 14. Giessen: Töpelmann, 1933.

Seifrid, Mark A. *Christ, Our Righteousness: Paul's Theology of Justification.* New Studies in Biblical Theology 9. Leicester: Apollos; Downers Grove: InterVarsity, 2000.

Senior, Donald, and Carroll Stuhlmueller. *The Biblical Foundation for Mission.* Maryknoll, NY: Orbis, 1983.

Sherwin-White, A. N. *The Roman Citizenship.* 2nd ed. Oxford: Clarendon, 1973.

Silva, Moisés. *Philippians.* Baker Exegetical Commentary on the New Testament. Grand Rapids: Baker, 1992.

Smith, David L. *All God's People: A Theology of the Church.* Wheaton: BridgePoint, 1996.

Spicq, Ceslas. *Theological Lexicon of the New Testament.* Edited and translated by James D. Ernest. Peabody, MA: Hendrickson, 1994.

— *Théologie Morale du Nouveau Testament.* Études Bibliques. 2 vols. Paris: J. Gabalda, 1965.

Stanley, David M. *Boasting in the Lord: The Phenomenon of Prayer in Saint Paul.* New

York: Paulist, 1973.

Stark, Rodney. *The Rise of Christianity: A Sociologist Reconsiders History.* Princeton: Princeton University Press, 1996.

Stott, John. *Guard the Truth: The Message of 1 Timothy & Titus.* The Bible Speaks Today Series. Downers Grove: InterVarsity, 1996.

Straub, Werner. *Die Bildersprache des Apostels Paulus.* Tübingen: Mohr, 1937.

Stuhlmacher, Peter. *Gerechtigkeit Gottes bei Paulus.* Forschungen zur Religion und Literatur des Alten und Neuen Testaments 87. Göttingen: Vandenhoeck & Ruprecht, 1965.

— *Das paulinische Evangelium: I. Vorgeschichte.* Forschungen zur Religion und Literatur des Alten und Neuen Testaments 95. Göttingen: Vandenhoeck & Ruprecht, 1968.

Swigchem, Douwe van. *Het missionair karakter van de Christelijke gemeente volgens de brieven van Paulus en Petrus.* Kampen: Kok, 1955.

Teinonen, Seppo A. *Gustav Warneckin Varhaisen Lähetysteorian Teologiset Perusteet.* Suomalaisen Teologisen Kirjallisuusseuran Julkaisuja 66. Helsinki: Savon Sanomain Kirjapaino oy, 1959.

Terry, John Mark. *Evangelism: A Concise History.* Nashville: Broadman, 1994.

Thiselton, Anthony C. *The First Epistle to the Corinthians: A Commentary on the Greek Text.* New International Greek Testament Commentary. Grand Rapids: Eerdmans; Carlisle: Paternoster, 2000.

Thrall, Margaret E. *A Critical and Exegetical Commentary on the Second Epistle to the Corinthians.* Vol. 1, *Introduction and Commentary on II Corinthians I-VII.* International Critical Commentary. Edinburgh: T. & T. Clark, 1994.

Tinsley, E. J. *The Imitation of God in Christ: An Essay on the Biblical Basis of Christian Spirituality.* London: SCM, 1960.

Towner, Philip H. *1-2 Timothy & Titus.* IVP New Testament Commentary Series. Downers Grove: InterVarsity, 1994.

— *The Goal of Our Instruction: The Structure of Theology and Ethics in the Pastoral Epistles.* Journal for the Study of the New Testament Supplement Series 34. Sheffield: JSOT, 1989.

Verkuyl, Johannes. *Contemporary Missiology: An Introduction.* Edited and translated by Dale Cooper. Grand Rapids: Eerdmans, 1978.

Visser't Hooft, W. A., and J. H. Oldham. *The Church and its Function in Society.* Chicago: Willett, Clark & Company, 1937.

Wallace, Daniel B. *Greek Grammar beyond the Basics: An Exegetical Syntax of the New Testament.* Grand Rapids: Zondervan, 1996.

Wallmann, Johannes. *Der Pietismus.* Die Kirche in ihrer Geschichte 4.O1. Göttingen: Vandenhoeck & Ruprecht, 1990.

Ware, James Patrick. *The Mission of the Church in Paul's Letter to the Philippians in the Context of Ancient Judaism.* Supplements to Novum Testamentum 120 (Leiden: Brill, 2005).

Warneck, Gustav. *Evangelische Missionslehre: Ein missionstheoretischer Versuch.* 2nd ed. 3 vols. Gotha: Friedrich Andreas Perthes, 1892-1903.

— *Missionsmotiv und Missionsaufgabe nach der modernen religionsgeschichtlichen Schule.* Berlin: Martin Warneck, 1907.

— *Outline of a History of Protestant Missions from the Reformation to the Present Time: A Contribution to Modern Church History.* Edited by George Robson.

Translated by J. P. Mitchell and Campbell M. Macleroy. New York: Fleming H. Revell, 1901.

Warneck, Johannes. *The Living Forces of the Gospel: Experiences of a Missionary in Animistic Heathendom*. Translated by Neil Buchanan. Edinburgh: Oliphant, Anderson & Ferrier, 1909.

— *Paulus im Lichte der heutigen Heidenmission*. Berlin: Martin Warneck, 1913.

Weiss, Johannes. *Der erste Korintherbrief.* 9th ed. H. A. W. Meyer, Kommentar über das Neue Testament 5. Göttingen: Vandenhoeck & Ruprecht, 1910.

Weizsäcker, Carl von. *The Apostolic Age of the Christian Church*. Translated by James Millar. 2 vols. London: Williams and Norgate; New York: G. P. Putnam's Sons, 1894-99.

Wernle, Paul. *The Beginnings of Christianity*. Edited by W. D. Morrison. Translated by G. A. Bienemann. 2 vols. Theological Translation Library, vols. 15, 17. London: Williams and Norgate; New York: G. P. Putnam's Sons, 1903-04.

— *Der Christ und die Sünde bei Paulus*. Freiburg: Mohr, 1897.

— *Paulus als Heidenmissionar*. Freiburg: Mohr, 1899.

Westcott, Brooke Foss. *Saint Paul's Epistle to the Ephesians*. London: Macmillan, 1906. Reprint, Grand Rapids: Baker, 1979.

Wette, Wilhelm Martin Leberecht de. *An Historico-Critical Introduction to the Canonical Books of the New Testament*. Translated by Frederick Frothingham. Boston: Crosby, Nichols, and Co., 1858.

Wilckens, Ulrich. *Der Brief an die Römer*. 3 vols. Evangelisch-Katholischer Kommentar zum Neuen Testament 6. Zurich: Benziger, 1978-82.

Wiles, Gordon P. *Paul's Intercessory Prayers: The Significance of the Intercessory Prayer Passages in the Letters of St. Paul*. Society for New Testament Studies Monograph Series 24. London: Cambridge University Press, 1974.

Willis, Wendell Lee. *Idol Meat in Corinth: The Pauline Argument in 1 Corinthians 8 and 10*. Chico, CA: Scholars Press, 1985.

Wilson, Stephen G. *The Gentiles and the Gentile Mission in Luke-Acts*. Society for New Testament Studies Monograph Series 23. Cambridge: University Press, 1973.

Windisch, Hans. *Paulus und Christus: Eine biblisch-religionsgeschichtlicher Vergleich*. Untersuchungen zum Neuen Testament 24. Leipzig: Heinrich, 1934.

Wrede, William. *Paul*. Translated by Edward Lummis. London: Green, 1907. Reprint, Lexington, KY: ATLA Committee on Reprinting, 1962.

Yorke, Gosnell L. O. R. *The Church as the Body of Christ in the Pauline Corpus: A Re-examination*. Lanham, MD: University Press of America, 1991.

Zerwick, Maximilian. *Biblical Greek*. Translated by Joseph Smith. Rome: Biblical Institute, 1963.

Ziesler, John. *Paul's Letter to the Romans*. TPI New Testament Commentaries. London: SCM; Philadelphia: Trinity Press International, 1989.

Articles

Adeney, David H. "The Church and Persecution." In *The Church in the Bible and the World: An International Study*, ed. D. A. Carson, 275-302. Exeter: Paternoster; Grand Rapids: Baker, 1987.

Agnew, Francis H. "The Origin of the NT Apostle-Concept: A Review of Research."

Journal of Biblical Literature 105 (1986): 75-96.

Ahern, Barnabas Mary. "The Fellowship of His Sufferings (Phil 3,10): A Study of St. Paul's Doctrine of Christian Suffering." *Catholic Biblical Quarterly* 22 (1960):1-32.

Ames, Frank Ritchel. "דבר." In *The New International Dictionary of Old Testament Theology and Exegesis*. Edited by Willem A. VanGemeren. Grand Rapids: Zondervan, 1997.

Argyle, A. W. "St. Paul and the Mission of the Seventy." *Journal of Theological Studies*, n.s., 1 (1950): 63.

Ashcroft, Morris. "Paul's Understanding of Apostleship." *Review and Expositor* 55 (1958): 400-12.

Aus, Roger D. "Paul's Travel Plans to Spain and the 'Full Number of the Gentiles' of Rom. XI 25." *Novum Testamentum* 21 (1979): 232-62.

Balz, Horst. "κοσμέω." In *Exegetical Dictionary of the New Testament*. Edited by Horst Balz and Gerhard Schneider. Grand Rapids: Eerdmans, 1991.

Bammel, Ernst. "Herkunft und Funktion der Traditionselemente in 1.Kor.15,1-11." *Theologische Zeitschrift* 11 (1955): 401-19.

Barnett, P. W. "Tentmaking." In *Dictionary of Paul and His Letters*, ed. Gerald F. Hawthorne, Ralph P. Martin, and Daniel G. Reid, 925-27. Downers Grove: InterVarsity, 1993.

Barrett, C. K. "The Imperatival Participle." *Expository Times* 59 (1947-48): 165-66.

— "New Testament Eschatology." *Scottish Journal of Theology* 6 (1953): 225-43.

— "Shaliah and Apostle." In *Donum gentilicium: New Testament studies in honour of David Daube*, ed. E. Bammel, C. K. Barrett, and W. D. Davies, 88-102. Oxford: Clarendon, 1978.

Becker, Ulrich. "Gospel...," "εὐαγγέλιον." In *The New International Dictionary of New Testament Theology*. Edited by Colin Brown. Exeter: Paternoster; Grand Rapids: Zondervan, 1986.

Belleville, Linda L. "'Imitate Me, Just as I Imitate Christ': Discipleship in the Corinthian Correspondence." In *Patterns of Discipleship in the New Testament*, McMaster New Testament Studies, ed. Richard N. Longenecker, 120-42. Grand Rapids: Eerdmans, 1996.

Berger, Klaus. "Volksversammlung und Gemeinde Gottes: Zu den Anfängen der christlichen Verwendung von 'ekklesia.'" *Zeitschrift für Theologie und Kirche* 73 (1976): 167-207.

Best, Ernest. "Paul as Model." In *Paul and His Converts*. Edinburgh: T. & T. Clark, 1988.

Blinzler, Josef. "Die 'Heiligkeit' der Kinder in der alten Kirche: Zur Auslegung von 1 Kor 7,14." In *Aus der Welt und Umwelt des Neuen Testaments*. Stuttgarter biblische Beiträge. Stuttgart: Katholisches Bibelwerk, 1969.

Bock, Darrell L. "The Use of the Old Testament in Luke-Acts: Christology and Mission." In *Society of Biblical Literature 1990 Seminar Papers*, ed. David J. Lull, 494-511. Atlanta: Scholars, 1990.

Boer, Harry R. "The Holy Spirit and Church Growth." In *Exploring Church Growth*, ed. Wilbert R. Shenk, 249-59. Grand Rapids, Eerdmans, 1983.

Boice, James M. "A Better Way: The Power of the Word and Spirit." In *Power Religion: The Selling Out of the Evangelical Church?*, ed. Michael Scott Horton, 119-36. Chicago: Moody, 1992.

Bolt, Peter G. "Mission and Witness." In *Witness to the Gospel: The Theology of Acts*, ed. I. Howard Marshall and David Peterson, 191-214. Grand Rapids: Eerdmans, 1998.

Bornkamm, Günther. "The Missionary Stance of Paul in I Corinthians 9 and in Acts." In *Studies in Luke-Acts*, ed. Leander E. Keck and J. Louis Martyn, 194-207. Nashville: Abingdon, 1966.

Bosch, David J. "Mission in Biblical Perspective." *International Review of Mission* 74 (1985): 531-38.

— "Reflections on Biblical Models of Mission." In *Toward the 21ˢᵗ Century in Christian Mission*, ed. James M. Phillips and Robert T. Coote, 175-92. Grand Rapids: Eerdmans, 1993.

— "The Structure of Mission: An Exposition of Matthew 28:16-20." In *Exploring Church Growth*, ed. Wilbert R. Shenk, 218-48. Grand Rapids, Eerdmans, 1983.

— "The Vulnerability of Mission." *Zeitschrift für Missionswissenschaft und Religionswissenschaft* 76 (1992): 201-16

Bowen, Clayton R. "Are Paul's Prison Letters from Ephesus?" *American Journal of Theology* 24 (1920): 112-35, 277-87.

Bowers, Paul. "Church and Mission in Paul." *Journal for the Study of the New Testament* 44 (1991): 89-111.

— "Fulfilling the Gospel: The Scope of the Pauline Mission." *Journal of the Evangelical Theological Society* 30 (1987): 185-98.

— "Mission." In *Dictionary of Paul and His Letters*, ed. Gerald F. Hawthorne, Ralph P. Martin, and Daniel G. Reid, 608-19. Downers Grove: InterVarsity, 1993.

— "A Note on Colossians 1:27a." In *Current Issues in Biblical and Patristic Interpretation: Studies in Honor of Merrill C. Tenney Presented by His Former Students*, ed. Gerald F. Hawthorne, 110-14. Grand Rapids: Eerdmans, 1975.

— "Paul and Religious Propaganda in the First Century." *Novum Testamentum* 22 (1980): 316-23.

Boyce, James L. "Graceful Imitation: 'Imitators of Us and the Lord' (1 Thessalonians 1:6)." In *All Things New: Essays in Honor of Roy A. Harrisville*, Word & World Supplement Series 1, ed. Arland J. Hultgren, Donald H. Juel, and Jack D. Kingsbury, 139-46. St. Paul, MN: Word & World, 1992.

Branner, John E. "Roland Allen: Pioneer in a Spirit-Centered Theology of Mission." *Missiology* 5 (1977): 175-84.

Brant, Jo-Ann A. "The Place of *mimēsis* in Paul's Thought." *Studies in Religion/ Sciences Religieuses* 22 (1993): 285-300.

Brown, Schuyler. "Apostleship in the New Testament as an Historical and Theological Problem." *New Testament Studies* 30 (1984): 474-80.

Brunt, John C. "Love, Freedom, and Moral Responsibility: The Contribution of I Cor. 8-10 to an Understanding of Paul's Ethical Thinking." In *Society of Biblical Literature 1981 Seminar Papers*, ed. Kent Harold Richards, 19-33. Chico, CA: Scholars Press, 1981.

— "Rejected, Ignored, or Misunderstood? The Fate of Paul's Approach to the Problem of Food Offered to Idols in Early Christianity." *New Testament Studies* 31 (1985): 113-24.

Bühner, Jan-Adolf. "ἀπόστολος." In *Exegetical Dictionary of the New Testament*. Edited by Horst Balz and Gerhard Schneider. Grand Rapids: Eerdmans, 1991.

Burchard, C. "Εἰ' nach einem Ausdruck des Wissens oder Nichtwissens Joh 9₂₅, Act 19₂, I Cor 1₁₆, 7₁₆." *Zeitschrift für neutestamentliche Wissenschaft* 52 (1961): 73-82.

Burini, Clara. "τῇ ὑγιαινούσῃ διδασκαλίᾳ: Una norma di vita cristiana in *Tito* 2,1." *Vetera Christianorum* 18 (1981): 275-85.

Buscarlet, Amalric F. "The 'Preparation' of the Gospel of Peace." *Expository Times* 9 (1897-98), 38-40.

Campenhausen, Hans Frhr. von. "Der urchristliche Apostelbegriff." *Studia Theologica* 1 (1947): 96-130.

Carson, D. A. "Pauline Inconsistency: Reflections on I Corinthians 9.19-23 and Galatians 2.11-14." *Churchman* 100 (1986): 6-45.

— "Paul's Mission and Prayer." In *The Gospel to the Nations: Perspectives on Paul's Mission*, ed. Peter Bolt and Mark Thompson, 175-84. Downers Grove: InterVarsity, 2000.

— "The Purpose of Signs and Wonders in the New Testament." In *Power Religion: The Selling Out of the Evangelical Church?*, ed. Michael Scott Horton, 89-118. Chicago: Moody, 1992.

Cerfaux, Lucien. "Pour l'histoire du titre *Apostolos* dans le Nouveau Testament." In *Recueil Lucien Cerfaux: Études d'exégèse et d'histoire religeuse*. Bibliotheca ephemeridum theologicarum lovaniensium 71. Rev. ed. Vol. 3. Leuven: Leuven University Press, 1985.

Clarke, Andrew D. "'Be Imitators of Me': Paul's Model of Leadership." *Tyndale Bulletin* 49 (1998): 329-60.

Clowney, Edmund P. "The Biblical Theology of the Church." In *The Church in the Bible and the World: An International Study*, ed. D. A. Carson, 13-87. Exeter: Paternoster; Grand Rapids: Baker, 1987.

Coenen, Lothar. "Call," "καλέω." In *The New International Dictionary of New Testament Theology*. Edited by Colin Brown. Exeter: Paternoster; Grand Rapids: Zondervan, 1986.

— "Church...," "ἐκκλησία." In *The New International Dictionary of New Testament Theology*. Edited by Colin Brown. Exeter: Paternoster; Grand Rapids: Zondervan, 1986.

Collins, John J. "Chiasmus, the 'ABA' Pattern, and the Text of Paul." In *Studiorum Paulinorum Congressus Internationalis Catholicus 1961*. 2 vols. Analecta biblica 17-18. Rome: Biblical Institute, 1963.

Cook, Richard B. "Paul, the Organizer." *Missiology* 9 (1981): 485-98.

Cowan, Andrew. "The Glory of God, Evangelism, and the Imitation of Paul," *Stulos Theological Journal* 12 (2004): 57-67.

Cullmann, Oscar. "Le caractère eschatologique du devoir missionaire et de la conscience apostolique de S. Paul: Étude sur le κατέχον (-ων) de 2. Thess. 2:6-7." *Revue d'Histoire et de Philosophie Religeuses* 16 (1936): 210-45.

— "Der eschatologische Charakter des Missionsauftrags und des apostolischen Selbstbewusstseins bei Paulus." In *Oscar Cullmann: Vorträge und Aufsätze, 1925-1962*, ed. Karlfried Fröhlich, 305-36. Tübingen: Mohr; Zurich: Zwingli, 1966.

— "Eschatology and Missions in the New Testament." In *The Background of the New Testament and Its Eschatology*, ed. W. D. Davies and D. Daube, 409-21. Cambridge: University Press, 1956.

Cunningham, Richard B. "Wide Open Doors and Many Adversaries." *Review and Expositor* 89 (1992): 89-98.

Daube, David. "Jewish Missionary Maxims in Paul." *Studia Theologica* 1 (1947): 158-69.

Deissmann, Adolf. "Zur ephesinischen Gefangenschaft des Apostels Paulus." In *Anatolian Studies Presented to Sir William Mitchell Ramsay*, ed. W. H. Buckler and W. M. Calder, 121-27. Manchester: University of Manchester Press, 1923.

Delling, Gerhard. "Merkmale der Kirche nach dem neuen Testament." *New Testament Studies* 13 (1966-67): 297-316.

De Ridder, Richard R. "The Old Testament Roots of Mission." In *Exploring Church Growth*, ed. Wilbert R. Shenk, 171-80. Grand Rapids, Eerdmans, 1983.

Derrett, J. Duncan M. "Paul as Master-builder." *Evangelical Quarterly* 69 (1997): 129-37.

Detwiler, David F. "Paul's Approach to the Great Commission in Acts 14:21-23." *Bibliotheca Sacra* 152 (1995): 33-41.

Dickson, John P. "Gospel as News: εὐαγγελ- from Aristophanes to the Apostle Paul." *New Testament Studies* 51 (2005): 212-30.

Dockx, S. "Lieu et date de l'épître aux Philippiens." *Revue Biblique* 80 (1973): 230-46.

Donaldson, Terence L. "The Absence in Paul's Letters of Any Injunction to Evangelize." Paper Presented at the annual meeting of the Society of Biblical Literature, Nashville, TN, November 2000.

Eckert, Jost. "καλέω...." In *Exegetical Dictionary of the New Testament*. Edited by Horst Balz and Gerhard Schneider. Grand Rapids: Eerdmans, 1991.

Eichholz, Georg. "Die ökumenische und missionarische Horizont der Kirche: Eine exegetische Studie zu Röm. 1,8-15." *Evangelische Theologie* 21 (1961): 15-27.

Eicken, Erich von, and Helgo Lindner, "Apostle," "ἀποστέλλω." In *The New International Dictionary of New Testament Theology*. Edited by Colin Brown. Exeter: Paternoster; Grand Rapids: Zondervan, 1986

Ellis, E. Earle. "Coworkers, Paul and His." In *Dictionary of Paul and His Letters*, ed. Gerald F. Hawthorne, Ralph P. Martin, and Daniel G. Reid, 183-89. Downers Grove: InterVarsity, 1993.

— "The Role of the Christian Prophet in Acts." In *Apostolic History and the Gospel: Biblical and Historical Essays Presented to F. F. Bruce on His 60th Birthday*, ed. W. Ward Gasque and Ralph P. Martin, 55-67. Grand Rapids: Eerdmans, 1970.

Everts, Janet Meyer. "Financial Support." In *Dictionary of Paul and His Letters*, ed. Gerald F. Hawthorne, Ralph P. Martin, and Daniel G. Reid, 295-300. Downers Grove: InterVarsity, 1993.

Fenton, John. "The Order of the Miracles performed by Peter and Paul in Acts." *Expository Times* 77 (1965-66): 381-83.

Fiorenza, Elisabeth Schüssler. "Miracles, Mission, and Apologetics: An Introduction." In *Aspects of Religious Propaganda in Judaism and Early Christianity*, ed. Elisabeth S. Fiorenza, 1-25. Notre Dame: University of Notre Dame Press, 1976.

Fitzmyer, Joseph A. "The Gospel in the Theology of Paul." *Interpretation* 33 (1979): 339-50.

Flemington, W. F. "On the Interpretation of Colossians 1:24." In *Suffering and Martyrdom in the New Testament: Studies Presented to G. M. Styler by the Cambridge New Testament Seminar*, ed. William Horbury and Brian McNeil, 84-90. Cambridge: Cambridge University Press, 1981.

Fowl, Stephen E. "Imitation of Paul/of Christ." In *Dictionary of Paul and His Letters*, ed. Gerald F. Hawthorne and Ralph P. Martin, 428-31. Downers Grove: InterVarsity, 1993.

Friedrich, Gerhard. "εὐαγγελίζομαι...." In *Theological Dictionary of the New*

Testament. Vol. 2. Edited by Gerhard Kittel. Translated and edited by Geoffrey W. Bromiley, 707-37. Grand Rapids: Eerdmans, 1964.

Fung, Ronald Y. K. "Some Pauline Pictures of the Church." *Evangelical Quarterly* 53 (1981): 89-107.

Garland, David E. "Evangelism in the New Testament." *Review and Expositor* 77 (1980): 461-71.

Garrett, Susan R. "The God of This World and the Affliction of Paul: 2 Cor 4:1-12." In *Greeks, Romans, and Christians: Essays in Honor of Abraham J. Malherbe,* ed. David L. Balch, Everett Ferguson, and Wayne A. Meeks, 99-117. Minneapolis: Fortress, 1990.

Gensichen, Hans-Werner. "Evangelisieren und Zivilisieren: Motive deutscher protestantischer Mission in der imperialistischen Epoche." *Zeitschrift für Missionswissenschaft und Religionswissenschaft* 67 (1983): 257-69.

Glasser, Arthur F. "The Apostle Paul and the Missionary Task." In *Perspectives on the World Christian Movement: A Reader,* Rev. ed., ed. Ralph D. Winter and Steven C. Hawthorne, A125-33. Pasadena: William Carey Library; Carlisle: Paternoster, 1992.

Glombitza, Otto. "Mit Furcht und Zittern: Zum Verständnis von Philip. II 12." *Novum Testamentum* 3 (1959): 100-06.

Greeven, Heinrich. "Die missionierende Gemeinde nach den Apostolischen Briefen." In *Sammlung und Sendung: Vom Auftrag der Kirche in der Welt,* ed. Joachim Heubach and Heinrich-Hermann Ulrich, 59-71. Berlin: Christlicher Zeitschriftenverlag, 1958.

Griffin, Hayne P., Jr. "Titus." In *1, 2 Timothy, Titus,* by Thomas D. Lea and Hayne P. Griffin, Jr. New American Commentary, vol. 34. Nashville: Broadman, 1992.

Griffiths, Michael C. "Today's Missionary, Yesterday's Apostle." *Evangelical Missions Quarterly* 21 (1985): 154-65.

Gruenler, Royce Gordon. "The Mission-Lifestyle Setting of 1 Tim 2:8-15." *Journal of the Evangelical Theological Society* 41 (1998): 215-38.

Grundmann, Walter. "δύναμαι...." In *Theological Dictionary of the New Testament.* Vol. 2. Edited by Gerhard Kittel. Translated and Edited by Geoffrey W. Bromiley, 284-317. Grand Rapids: Eerdmans, 1964.

Guerra, Manuel "Los 'epikaloúmenoi' de 1 Cor 1,2, directores y sacerdotes de la comunidad cristiana en Corinto." *Scripta Theologica* 17 (1985): 11-72.

Hafemann, Scott. "'Because of Weakness' (Galatians 4:13): The Role of Suffering in the Mission of Paul." In *The Gospel to the Nations: Perspectives on Paul's Mission,* ed. Peter Bolt and Mark Thompson, 131-46. Downers Grove: InterVarsity, 2000.

— "The Role of Suffering in the Mission of Paul." In *The Mission of the Early Church to Jews and Gentiles.* Wissenschaftliche Untersuchungen zum Neuen Testament 127, ed. Jostein Ådna and Hans Kvalbein, 165-84. Tübingen: Mohr Siebeck, 2000.

— "Suffering." In *Dictionary of Paul and His Letters,* ed. Gerald F. Hawthorne, Ralph P. Martin, and Daniel G. Reid, 919-21. Downers Grove: InterVarsity, 1993.

Hamerton-Kelly, Robert G. "A Girardian Interpretation of Paul: Rivalry, Mimesis and Victimage in the Corinthian Correspondence." *Semeia* 33 (1985): 65-81.

Hardon, John A. "The Miracle Narratives in the Acts of the Apostles." *Catholic Biblical Quarterly* 16 (1954): 303-18

Hauck, Friedrich. "κοινός...." In *Theological Dictionary of the New Testament.* Vol. 3. Edited by Gerhard Kittel. Translated and edited by Geoffrey W. Bromiley, 789-809. Grand Rapids: Eerdmans, 1965.

Haupt, Erich. "Der Brief an die Philipper." In *Die Gefangenschaftsbriefe.* 7th ed. H. A.

W. Meyer, Kritisch-exegetischer Kommentar über das Neue Testament 9. Göttingen: Vandenhoeck & Ruprecht, 1902.

Hawthorne, Gerald F. "The Imitation of Christ: Discipleship in Philippians." In *Patterns of Discipleship in the New Testament*, McMaster New Testament Studies, ed. Richard N. Longenecker, 163-79. Grand Rapids: Eerdmans, 1996.

Hengel, Martin. "Die Ursprünge der Christlichen Mission." *New Testament Studies* 18 (1971-72): 15-38.

Hock, Ronald F. "The Workshop as a Social Setting for Paul's Missionary Preaching." *Catholic Biblical Quarterly* 41 (1979): 438-50.

Hodgson, Robert. "Paul the Apostle and First Century Tribulation Lists." *Zeitschrift für die neutestamentliche Wissenschaft* 74 (1983): 59-80.

Hoekendijk, J. C. "The Church in Missionary Thinking." *International Review of Missions* 41 (1952): 324-36.

Hofius, Otfried. "Wort Gottes und Glaube bei Paulus." In *Paulus und das antike Judentum*, Wissenschaftliche Untersuchungen zum Neuen Testament 58, ed. Martin Hengel and Ulrich Heckel, 379-408. Tübingen: Mohr, 1991.

Hooker, Morna D. "A Partner in the Gospel: Paul's Understanding of His Ministry." In *Theology and Ethics in Paul and His Interpreters: Essays in Honor of Victor Paul Furnish*, ed. Eugene H. Lovering, Jr. and Jerry L. Sumney, 83-100. Abingdon: Nashville, 1996.

House, Paul R. "Suffering and the Purpose of Acts." *Journal of the Evangelical Theological Society* 33 (1990): 317-30.

Howell, Don N., Jr. "Confidence in the Spirit as the Governing Ethos of the Pauline Mission." *Trinity Journal* 17 (1996): 203-21.

Hunter, W. B. "Prayer." In *Dictionary of Paul and His Letters*, ed. Gerald F. Hawthorne, Ralph P. Martin, and Daniel G. Reid, 725-34. Downers Grove: InterVarsity, 1993.

Hurtado, L. W. "Jesus as Lordly Example in Philippians 2:5-11." In *From Jesus to Paul: Studies in Honour of Francis Wright Beare*, ed. Peter Richardson and John C. Hurd, 113-26. Waterloo, Ontario: Wilfrid Laurier University Press, 1984.

Jaffarian, E. Michael. "Paul Tipped the Balance Toward the Frontier." *Evangelical Missions Quarterly* 32 (1996): 165.

Jeremias, Joachim. "Die missionarische Aufgabe in der Mischehe (I Cor 716)." In *Neutestamentliche Studien für Rudolf Bultmann zu seinem siebzigsten Geburtstag*, ed. Walther Eltester, 2nd ed., Beihefte zur Zeitschrift für die neutestamentliche Wissenschaft 21, 255-60. Berlin: Töpelmann, 1957.

Jervell, Jacob. "Der schwache Charismatiker." In *Rechtfertigung: Festschrift für Ernst Käsemann zum 70. Gerburtstag*, ed. J. Friedrich, W. Pöhlmann, and P. Stuhlmacher, 185-98. Tübingen: Mohr; Göttingen: Vandenhoeck & Ruprecht, 1976.

— "The Signs of an Apostle: Paul's Miracles." In *The Unknown Paul: Essays on Luke-Acts and Early Christian History*, trans. Roy A. Harrisville, 77-95. Minneapolis: Augsburg, 1984.

Johnson, Dennis E. "Jesus against the Idols: The Use of Isaianic Servant Songs in the Missiology of Acts." *Westminster Theological Journal* 52 (1990): 343-53.

Johnson, Lewis. "The Pauline Letters from Caesarea." *The Expository Times* 68 (1956-57): 24-26.

Judge, Edwin. "The Teacher as Moral Exemplar in Paul and in the Inscriptions of Ephesus." In *In the Fullness of Time: Biblical Studies in Honour of Archbishop Donald Robinson*, ed. David Peterson and John Pryor, 185-201. Homebush West,

NSW [Australia]: Lancer, 1992.

Kaiser, Walter C., Jr. "The Current Crisis in Exegesis and the Apostolic Use of Deuteronomy 25:4 in 1 Corinthians 9:8-10." *Journal of the Evangelical Theological Society* 21 (1978): 3-18.

Kasdorf, Hans. "Gustav Warneck 1834-1910: Founder of the Scholarly Study of Missions." In *Mission Legacies: Biographical Studies of Leaders of the Modern Missionary Movement*, ed. Gerald H. Anderson, Robert T. Coote, Norman A. Horner, James M. Phillips, 373-82. Maryknoll, NY: Orbis, 1994.

— "Gustav Warneck: His Life and Labor." *Missiology* 8 (1980): 269-84.

Käsemann, Ernst. "Epheser 4, 11-16." In *Exegetische Versuche und Besinnungen*. Vol. 1. Göttingen: Vandenhoeck & Ruprecht, 1960.

— "Die Legitimität des Apostels. Eine Untersuchung zu II Korinther 10-13." *Zeitschrift für die neutestamentliche Wissenschaft* 41 (1942): 33-71.

— "'The Righteousness of God' in Paul." In *New Testament Questions of Today*. Translated by W. J. Montague. Philadelphia: Fortress, 1969.

Kee, Howard Clark. "The Linguistic Background of 'Shame' in the New Testament." In *On Language, Culture, and Religion: In Honor of Eugene A. Nida*, ed. Matthew Black and William A. Smalley, 133-47. The Hague: Mouton, 1974.

Kirk, J. Andrew. "Apostleship Since Rengstorf: Towards a Synthesis." *New Testament Studies* 21 (1975): 249-64.

Knox, John. "Romans 15:14-33 and Paul's Conception of His Apostolic Mission." *Journal of Biblical Literature* 83 (1964): 1-11.

Kodell, Jerome. "'The Word of God Grew': The Ecclesial Tendency of Λόγος in Acts 1,7; 12,24; 19,20." *Biblica* 55 (1974): 505-19.

Köstenberger, Andreas J. "The Challenge of a Systematized Biblical Theology of Mission: Missiological Insights from the Gospel of John." *Missiology* 23 (1995): 445-64.

— "The Place of Mission in New Testament Theology: An Attempt to Determine the Significance of Mission Within the Scope of the New Testament's Message as a Whole." *Missiology* 27 (1999): 347-62.

Kubo, Sakae "I Corinthians VII. 16: Optimistic or Pessimistic?" *New Testament Studies* 24 (1978): 539-44.

Kurz, William S. "Kenotic Imitation of Paul and of Christ in Philippians 2 and 3." In *Discipleship in the New Testament*, ed. Fernando F. Segovia, 103-26. Philadelphia: Fortress, 1985.

Lambrecht, J. "A Call to Witness by All: Evangelisation in 1 Thessalonians." In *Teologie in Konteks*, ed. J. H. Roberts, W. S. Vorster, J. N. Vorster, and J. G. van der Watt, 321-43. Johannesburg: Orion, 1991.

— "The Nekrōsis of Jesus: Ministry and Suffering in 2 Cor 4, 7-15." In *L'Apôtre Paul: Personnalité, Style et Conception du Ministère*, Bibliotheca ephemeridum theologicarum lovaniensium 73, ed. A. Vanhoye, 120-43. Leuven: Leuven University Press, 1986.

Lampe, G. W. H. "Miracles in the Acts of the Apostles." In *Miracles: Cambridge Studies in their Philosophy and History*, ed. C. F. D. Moule, 163-78. London: A. R. Mowbray, 1965.

Larkin, William J., Jr. "Introduction." In *Mission in the New Testament: An Evangelical Approach*, American Society of Missiology Series 27, ed. William J. Larkin, Jr. and Joel F. Williams, 1-7, Maryknoll, NY: Orbis, 1998.

— "Mission." In *Evangelical Dictionary of Theology*, ed. Walter E. Ewell, 534-38. Grand Rapids: Baker, 1996.

Larsson, Edvin. "μιμέομαι...." In *Exegetical Dictionary of the New Testament*. Edited by Horst Balz and Gerhard Schneider. Grand Rapids: Eerdmans, 1991.

Latourette, K. S. "The Light of History in Christian Missionary Methods." *International Review of Missions* 42 (1953): 137-43.

Lee, E. Kenneth. "Words Denoting 'Pattern' in the New Testament." *New Testament Studies* 8 (1961-62): 166-73.

Lillie, William. "The Pauline House-tables." *Expository Times* 86 (1974-75): 179-83.

Link, Hans-Georg, and Colin Brown, "Sacrifice, First Fruits...," "ἀπαρχή." In *The New International Dictionary of New Testament Theology*. Edited by Colin Brown. Exeter: Paternoster; Grand Rapids: Zondervan, 1986.

Lips, Hermann von. "Die Haustafel als 'Topos' im Rahmen der urchristlichen Paränese: Beobachtungen anhand des 1. Petrusbriefes und des Titusbriefes." *New Testament Studies* 40 (1994): 261-80.

Lumpe, A. "Exemplum." In *Reallexikon für Antike und Christentum*, vol. 6, ed. Theodor Klauser, 1229-57. Stuttgart: Anton Hiersemann, 1966.

Luther, Martin. "Lectures on Titus." In *Luther's Works*, vol. 29, ed. and trans. Jaroslav Pelikan, 1-90. St. Louis: Concordia, 1968.

Luz, Ulrich. "Überlegungen zum Epheserbrief und seiner Paränese." In *Neues Testament und Ethik*, ed. Helmut Merklein, 376-96. Freiburg: Herder, 1989.

Madvig, Donald H. "The Missionary Preaching of Paul: A Problem in New Testament Theology." *Journal of the Evangelical Theological Society* 20 (1977): 147-55.

Marshall, I. Howard. "Dialogue with Non-Christians in the New Testament." *Evangelical Review of Theology* 16 (1992): 28-47.

— "Who Were the Evangelists?" In *The Mission of the Early Church to Jews and Gentiles*. Wissenschaftliche Untersuchungen zum Neuen Testament 127, ed. Jostein Ådna and Hans Kvalbein, 251-63. Tübingen: Mohr Siebeck, 2000.

McCasland, S. Vernon. "Signs and Wonders." *Journal of Biblical Literature* 76 (1957): 149-52.

McKenzie, John L. "The Word of God in the Old Testament." *Theological Studies* 21 (1960): 183-206

McKnight, Scot. "Gentiles, Gentile Mission." In *Dictionary of the Later New Testament and Its Developments*, ed. Ralph P. Martin and Peter H. Davids, 388-94. Downers Grove: InterVarsity, 1997.

Meecham, H. G. "The Use of the Participle for the Imperative in the New Testament." *Expository Times* 58 (1946-47): 207-08.

Meeks, Wayne A. "The Circle of Reference in Pauline Morality." In *Greeks, Romans, and Christians: Essays in Honor of Abraham J. Malherbe*, ed. David L. Balch, Everett Ferguson, and Wayne A. Meeks, 305-17. Minneapolis: Fortress, 1990.

Merk, Otto. "Nachahmung Christi: Zu ethischen Perspektiven in der paulinischen Theologie." In *Neues Testament und Ethik*, ed. Helmut Merklein, 172-206. Freiburg: Herder, 1989.

Merklein, Helmut. "Die Ekklesia Gottes. Der Kirchenbegriff bei Paulus und in Jerusalem." In *Studien zu Jesus und Paulus*. Wissenschaftliche Untersuchungen zum Neuen Testament 43. Tübingen: Mohr, 1987.

Michaelis, W. "μιμέομαι...." In *Theological Dictionary of the New Testament*. Vol. 4. Edited by Gerhard Kittel. Translated and Edited by Geoffrey W. Bromiley, 659-74.

Grand Rapids: Eerdmans, 1967.

Michel, Otto. "οἶκος...." In *Theological Dictionary of the New Testament*. Vol. 5. Edited by Gerhard Friedrich. Translated and Edited by Geoffrey W. Bromiley, 119-59. Grand Rapids: Eerdmans, 1967.

Mitchell, Stephen. "The Imperial Cult." In *Anatolia: Land, Men, and Gods in Asia Minor*. Vol. 1, *The Celts in Anatolia and the Impact of Roman Rule*. Oxford: Clarendon, 1993.

Mosbech, Holger. "Apostolos in the New Testament." *Studia Theologica* 2 (1948): 166-200.

Mott, Stephen Charles. "Greek Ethics and Christian Conversion: The Philonic Background of Titus II 10-14 and III 3-7." *Novum Testamentum* 20 (1978): 22-48.

Munck, Johannes. "La vocation de l'Apôtre Paul." *Studia Theologica* 1 (1947): 131-57.

Murphy, Edward F. "The Missionary Society as an Apostolic Team." *Missiology* 4 (1976): 103-18.

Murphy-O'Connor, Jerome. "Freedom or the Ghetto (*I Cor.*, VIII, 1-13; X, 23-XI, 1)." *Revue Biblique* 85 (1978): 543-74.

— "Paul and Macedonia: The Connection Between 2 Corinthians 2.13 and 2.14." *Journal for the Study of the New Testament* 25 (1982): 99-103.

Neirynck, Frans. "The Miracle Stories in the Acts of the Apostles: An Introduction." In *Les Actes des Apôtres: Traditions, rédaction, théologie*, Bibliotheca ephemeridum theologicarum lovaniensium 48, ed. J. Kremer, 169-213. Gembloux: Ducolot; Leuven: Leuven University Press, 1979.

Nellessen, E. "Die Presbyter der Gemeinden in Lykaonien und Pisidien (Apg 14, 23)." In *Les Actes des Apôtres: Traditions, rédaction, théologie*, Bibliotheca ephemeridum theologicarum lovaniensium 48, ed. J. Kremer, 493-98. Gembloux: Ducolot; Leuven: Leuven University Press, 1979.

Newport, John P. "The Purpose of the Church." In *The People of God: Essays on the Believers' Church*, ed. Paul Basden and David S. Dockery, 19-40. Broadman: Nashville, 1991.

Noonan, John T., Jr. "The Muzzled Ox." *Jewish Quarterly Review* 70 (1979-80): 172-75.

Norris, Frederick W. "Strategy for Mission in the New Testament." In *Exploring Church Growth*, ed. Wilbert R. Shenk, 260-76. Grand Rapids, Eerdmans, 1983.

O'Brien, Peter T. "Church." In *Dictionary of Paul and His Letters*, ed. Gerald F. Hawthorne, Ralph P. Martin, and Daniel G. Reid, 123-31. Downers Grove: InterVarsity, 1993.

— "The Church as a Heavenly and Eschatological Entity." In *The Church in the Bible and the World: An International Study*, ed. D. A. Carson, 88-119. Exeter: Paternoster; Grand Rapids: Baker, 1987.

— "The Gospel and Godly Models in Philippians." In *Worship, Theology and Ministry in the Early Church: Essays in Honor of Ralph P. Martin*, Journal for the Study of the New Testament Supplement Series 87, ed. Michael J. Wilkins and Terence Paige, 273-84. Sheffield: Sheffield Academic Press, 1992.

— "Mystery." In *Dictionary of Paul and His Letters*, ed. Gerald F. Hawthorne, Ralph P. Martin, and Daniel G. Reid, 621-23. Downers Grove: InterVarsity, 1993.

— "Thanksgiving and the Gospel in Paul." *New Testament Studies* 21 (1974-75): 144-55.

Oepke, Albrecht "ὅπλον...." In *Theological Dictionary of the New Testament*. Vol 5.

Edited by Gerhard Friedrich. Edited and translated by Geoffrey W. Bromiley, 292-315. Grand Rapids: Eerdmans, 1967.

O'Toole, Robert F. "'Luke's Notion of 'Be Imitators of Me as I Am of Christ,' in Acts 25-26." *Biblical Theology Bulletin* 8 (1978): 155-61.

Ong, Walter J. "Mimesis and the Following of Christ." *Religion and Literature* 26 (1994): 73-77.

Padgett, Alan. "The Pauline Rationale for Submission: Biblical Feminism and the *hina* Clauses of Titus 2:1-10." *Evangelical Quarterly* 59 (1987): 39-52.

Piper, John. "The Supremacy of God in Missions Through Prayer." In *Let the Nations Be Glad! The Supremacy of God in Missions*, 41-70. Grand Rapids: Baker, 1993.

Plummer, Robert L. "The Great Commission in the New Testament." In *The Challenge of the Great Commission: Essays on God's Mandate for the Local Church*, ed. Chuck Lawless and Thom S. Rainer, 33-47. N.p.: Pinnacle, 2005.

— "Imitation of Paul and the Church's Missionary Role in 1 Corinthians." *Journal of the Evangelical Theological Society* 44 (2001): 219-35.

— "A Theological Basis for the Church's Mission in Paul." *Westminster Theological Journal* 64 (2002): 253-71.

Pocock, Michael. "Focus and Balance in Missionary Outreach." *Evangelical Missions Quarterly* 32 (1996): 160-64.

Polhill, John B. "Paul: Theology Born of Mission." *Review and Expositor* 78 (1981): 233-47.

Poythress, Vern Sheridan. "'Hold Fast' versus 'Hold Out' in Philippians 2:16." *Westminster Theological Journal* 63 (2002): 45-53.

Praeder, Susan Marie. "Miracle Worker and Missionary: Paul in the Acts of the Apostles." In *Society of Biblical Literature 1983 Seminar Papers*, ed. Kent Harold Richards, 107-29. Chico, CA: Scholars Press, 1983.

Proudfoot, C. Merrill. "Imitation or Realistic Participation? A Study of Paul's Concept of 'Suffering With Christ.'" *Interpretation* 17 (1963): 140-60.

Quinn, Jerome D. "Apostolic Ministry and Apostolic Prayer." *Catholic Biblical Quarterly* 33 (1971): 479-91.

Rapske, Brian. "Opposition to the Plan of God and Persecution." In *Witness to the Gospel: The Theology of Acts*, ed. I. Howard Marshall and David Peterson, 235-56. Grand Rapids: Eerdmans 1998.

Rebell, Walter. "Gemeinde als Missionsfaktor im Urchristentum: I Kor 14,24f. als Schlüsselsituation." *Theologische Zeitschrift* 44 (1988): 117-34.

Reinhartz, Adele. "On the Meaning of the Pauline Exhortation: '*mimētai mou ginesthe*—Become Imitators of Me.'" *Studies in Religion/Sciences Religieuses* 16 (1987): 393-403.

Rengstorf, Karl Heinrich. "ἀποστέλλω." In *Theological Dictionary of the New Testament*. Vol. 1. Edited by Gerhard Kittel. Translated and Edited by Geoffrey W. Bromiley, 398-447. Grand Rapids: Eerdmans, 1964.

— "σημεῖον...." In *Theological Dictionary of the New Testament*. Vol. 7. Edited by Gerhard Friedrich. Translated and Edited by Geoffrey W. Bromiley, 200-69. Grand Rapids: Eerdmans, 1971.

— "τέρας." In *Theological Dictionary of the New Testament*. Vol. 8. Edited by Gerhard Friedrich. Translated and Edited by Geoffrey W. Bromiley, 113-26. Grand Rapids: Eerdmans, 1972.

Reumann, John. "Colossians 1:24 ('What is Lacking in the Afflictions of Christ'):

History of Exegesis and Ecumenical Advance." *Currents in Theology and Mission* 17 (1990): 454-61.

Richardson, Peter. "Pauline Inconsistency: I Corinthians 9:19-23 and Galatians 2:11-14." *New Testament Studies* 26 (1979-80): 347-62.

Richardson, Peter, and Paul W. Gooch. "Accommodation Ethics." *Tyndale Bulletin* 29 (1978): 89-142.

Rigsby, Richard O. "First Fruits." In *The Anchor Bible Dictioinary.* Vol. 2. Edited by David Noel Freedman, 796-97. New York: Doubleday, 1992.

Robinson, D. W. B. "Who Were 'The Saints'?" *Reformed Theological Review* 22 (1963): 45-53.

Roloff, Jürgen. "ἐκκλησία." In *Exegetical Dictionary of the New Testament.* Edited by Horst Balz and Gerhard Schneider. Grand Rapids: Eerdmans, 1991.

Rosner, Brian S. "The Progress of the Word." In *Witness to the Gospel: The Theology of Acts,* ed. I. Howard Marshall and David Peterson, 215-33. Grand Rapids: Eerdmans 1998.

Sanders, Boykin. "Imitating Paul: 1 Cor 4:16." *Harvard Theological Review* 74 (1981): 353-63.

Schippers, Reinier. "Fullness," "πληρόω." In *The New International Dictionary of New Testament Theology.* Edited by Colin Brown. Exeter: Paternoster; Grand Rapids: Zondervan, 1986.

Schlink, Edmund. "Christ and the Church." *Scottish Journal of Theology* 10 (1957): 1-23.

Schmidt, K. L. "καλέω...." In *Theological Dictionary of the New Testament.* Vol. 3. Edited by Gerhard Kittel. Translated and edited by Geoffrey W. Bromiley, 487-536. Grand Rapids: Eerdmans, 1965.

Schmidt, W. H. "דבר." In *Theological Dictionary of the Old Testament.* Vol. 3. Edited by G. Johannes Botterweck and Helmer Ringgren. Translated by John T. Willis and Geoffrey W. Bromiley, 84-125. Grand Rapids: Eerdmans, 1978.

Schnabel, Eckhard J. "Israel, the People of God, and the Nations." Paper Presented in the Biblical Theology Group at the annual meeting of the Evangelical Theological Society Annual Meeting, Nashville, TN, November 2000.

— "Jesus and the Beginnings of the Mission to the Gentiles." In *Jesus of Nazareth, Lord and Christ: Essays on the Historical Jesus and New Testament Christology,* ed. Joel B. Green and Max Turner, 37-58. Grand Rapids: Eerdmans, 1994.

— "Mission, Early Non-Pauline." In *Dictionary of the Later New Testament and Its Developments,* ed. Ralph P. Martin and Peter H. Davids, 752-75. Downers Grove: InterVarsity, 1997.

Schnackenburg, Rudolf. "Apostles Before and During Paul's Time." In *Apostolic History and the Gospel: Biblical and Historical Essays Presented to F. F. Bruce on His 60th Birthday,* ed. W. Ward Gasque and Ralph P. Martin, trans. Manfred Kwiran and W. Ward Gasque, 287-303. Grand Rapids: Eerdmans, 1970.

Schnepel, Erich. "Missionarischer Dienst und Gemeindewerdung." In *Sammlung und Sendung: Vom Auftrag der Kirche in der Welt,* ed. Joachim Heubach and Heinrich-Hermann Ulrich, 59-71. Berlin: Christlicher Zeitschriftenverlag, 1958.

Schrage, Wolfgang. "Leid, Kreuz und Eschaton: Die Peristasenkataloge als Merkmale paulinischer theologia crucis und Eschatologie." *Evangelische Theologie* 34 (1974): 141-75.

Schulz, Anselm. "Leidenstheologie und Vorbildethik in den paulinischen Hauptbriefen."

In *Neutestamentliche Aufsätze: Festschrift für Prof. Josef Schmid zum 70. Geburtstag*, ed. J. Blinzler, O. Kuss, and F. Mußner, 265-69. Regensburg: Friedrich Pustet, 1963.

Schweizer, E. "The Church as the Missionary Body of Christ." *New Testament Studies* 8 (1961-62): 1-11.

— "Die Kirche als Leib Christi in den paulinischen Antilegomena." *Theologische Literaturzeitung* 86 (1961): 241-56.

Scobie, Charles H. H. "Israel and the Nations: An Essay in Biblical Theology.*" Tyndale Bulletin* 43 (1992): 283-305.

— "Jesus or Paul? The Origin of the Universal Mission of the Christian Church." In *From Jesus to Paul: Studies in Honour of Francis Wright Beare*, ed. Peter Richardson and John C. Hurd, 47-60. Waterloo, Ontario: Wilfrid Laurier University Press, 1984.

Sims, David C. "The Gospel of Matthew and the Gentiles." *Journal for the Study of the New Testament* 57 (1995): 19-48.

Ska, Jean-Louis. "La sortie d' Égypte (Ex 7-14) dans le récit sacerdotal (P^g) et la tradition prophétique." *Biblica* 60 (1979): 191-215.

Sloan, Robert B. "Images of the Church in Paul." In *The People of God: Essays on the Believers' Church*, ed. Paul Basden and David S. Dockery, 148-65. Nashville: Broadman, 1991.

Spencer, William David. "The Power in Paul's Teaching (1 Cor 4:9-20)." *Journal of the Evangelical Theological Society* 32 (1989): 51-61.

Stanley, David M. "'Become Imitators of Me': The Pauline Conception of Apostolic Tradition." *Biblica* 40 (1959): 859-77.

— "Imitation in Paul's Letters: Its Significance for His Relationship to Jesus and to His Own Christian Foundations." In *From Jesus to Paul: Studies in Honour of Francis Wright Beare*, ed. Peter Richardson and John C. Hurd, 127-41. Waterloo, Ontario: Wilfrid Laurier University Press, 1984.

Stendahl, Krister. "Paul at Prayer." *Interpretation* 34 (1980): 240-49.

Stenschke, Christoph. "Mission in the New Testament: New Trends in Research. A Review Article." *Missionalia* 31 (2003): 355-83.

— "Neuere Arbeiten und Tendenzen zur Mission im Neuen Testament." *European Journal of Theology* 12 (2003): 5-20.

Stettler, Hanna. "An Interpretation of Colossians 1:24 in the Framework of Paul's Mission Theology." In *The Mission of the Early Church to Jews and Gentiles*. Wissenschaftliche Untersuchungen zum Neuen Testament 127, ed. Jostein Ådna and Hans Kvalbein, 185-208. Tübingen: Mohr Siebeck, 2000.

Strickland, Wayne G. "Isaiah, Jonah, and Religious Pluralism." *Bibliotheca Sacra* 153 (1996): 24-33.

Stolz, Fritz. "Zeichen und Wunder: Die prophetische Legitimation und ihre Geschichte." *Zeitschrift für Theologie und Kirche* 69 (1972): 125-44.

Strauss, Steve. "Missions Theology in Romans 15:14-33." *Bibliotheca Sacra* 160 (2003): 457-74.

Strecker, Georg. "εὐαγγέλιον." In *Exegetical Dictionary of the New Testament*. Edited by Horst Balz and Gerhard Schneider. Grand Rapids: Eerdmans, 1991.

Sundkler, Bengt. "Jésus et les païens." *Revue d'Histoire et de Philosophie Religieuses* 16 (1936): 462-99.

Thiselton, Anthony C. "The Supposed Power of Words in the Biblical Writings."

Journal of Theological Studies 25 (1974): 283-99.

Thysman, R. "L'Éthique de l'Imitation du Christ dans le Nouveau Testament: Situation, Notations et Variations du Thème." *Ephimerides Theologicae Lovanienses* 42 (1966): 138-75.

Towner, Philip. "Paradigms Lost: Mission to the *Kosmos* in John and David Bosch's Biblical Models of Mission." *Evangelical Quarterly* 67 (1995): 99-119.

Trocmé, Étienne. "L'Épître aux Romains et la Méthode Missionaire de l'Apôtre Paul." *New Testament Studies* 7 (1960-61): 148-53.

Troeltsch, Ernst. "Missionsmotiv, Missionsaufgabe und neuzeitliches Humanitätschristentum." *Zeitschrift für Missionskunde und Religionswissenschaft* 22 (1907): 129-39, 161-66.

Turlington, Henry. "Paul's Missionary Practice." *Review and Expositor* 51 (1954): 168-86.

Twelftree, G. H. "Signs, Wonders, and Miracles." In *Dictionary of Paul and His Letters*, ed. Gerald F. Hawthorne, Ralph P. Martin, and Daniel G. Reid, 875-77. Downers Grove: InterVarsity, 1993.

Vanhoozer, Kevin. "God's Mighty Speech-Acts: The Doctrine of Scripture Today." In *A Pathway into the Holy Scripture*, ed. Philip E. Satterthwaite and David F. Wright, 143-81. Grand Rapids: Eerdmans, 1994.

Vielhauer, Philipp. "On the 'Paulinism' of Acts." In *Studies in Luke-Acts*, ed. Leander E. Keck and J. Louis Martyn, 33-50. Nashville: Abingdon, 1966.

Ware, James. "The Thessalonians as a Missionary Congregation: 1 Thessalonians 1, 5-8." *Zeitschrift für die neutestamentliche Wissenschaft* 83 (1992): 126-31.

Watson, Duane F. "1 Corinthians 10:23-11:1 in the Light of Greco-Roman Rhetoric: The Role of Rhetorical Questions." *Journal of Biblical Literature* 108 (1989): 301-18.

Weber, Otto. "Kirchenmission? Eine Mission in gegliederter Vielfalt." *Evangelische Missions-Zeitschrift für Missionswissenschaft und evangelische Religionskunde* 17 (1960): 129-40.

Weiser, Alfons. "Titus 2 als Gemeindeparänese." In *Neues Testament und Ethik*, ed. Helmut Merklein, 397-414. Freiburg: Herder, 1989.

Wickert, Ulrich. "Einheit und Eintracht der Kirche im Präskript des ersten Korinther-briefes." *Zeitschrift für die neutestamentliche Wissenschaft* 50 (1959): 73-82.

Wild, Robert A. "'Be Imitators of God': Discipleship in the Letter to the Ephesians." In *Discipleship in the New Testament*, ed. Fernando F. Segovia, 127-43. Philadelphia: Fortress, 1985.

Willert, Niels. "The Catalogues of Hardships in the Pauline Correspondence: Background and Function." In *The New Testament and Hellenistic Judaism*, ed. Peder Borgen and Søren Giversen, 217-43. Aarhus, Denmark: Aarhus University Press, 1995.

Winter, Bruce W. "Dangers and Difficulties for the Pauline Missions." In *The Gospel to the Nations: Perspectives on Paul's Mission*, ed. Peter Bolt and Mark Thompson, 285-95. Downers Grove: InterVarsity, 2000.

Winter, Ralph D. "The Two Structures of God's Redemptive Mission." *Missiology* 2 (1974): 121-39.

Wolter, Michael. "Der Apostel und seine Gemeinden als Teilhaber am Leidensgeschick Jesu Christi: Beobachtungen zur paulinischen Leidenstheologie." *New Testament Studies* 36 (1990): 535-57.

Woodhouse, John. "Signs and Wonders in the Bible." In *Signs & Wonders and Evangelicals: A Response to the Teaching of John Wimber*, ed. Robert Doyle, 17-35. Homebush West, NSW [Australia]: Lancer, 1987.

Wulf, Friedrich. "'Seid meine Nachahmer, Brüder!' (Phil 3,17)." *Geist und Leben* 34 (1961): 241-47.

Zeller, Dieter. "Theologie der Mission bei Paulus." In *Mission im neuen Testament*, ed. Karl Kertelge, 164-89. Freiburg: Herder, 1982.

Theses and Dissertations

Barram, Michael D. "'In Order That They May Be Saved': Mission and Moral Reflection in Paul." Ph.D. diss., Union Theological Seminary and Presbyterian School of Christian Education, 2001.

Bowers, Paul. "Studies in Paul's Understanding of His Mission." Ph.D. diss., University of Cambridge, 1976.

Brotherton, Dennis Othel. "An Examination of Selected Pauline Passages Concerning the Vocational Missionary: An Interpretive Basis for Critiquing Contemporary Missiological Thoughts." Ph.D. diss., Southwestern Baptist Theological Seminary, 1986.

Chambers, Stephen Lionel. "Paul, His Converts, and Mission in 1 Corinthians." Ph.D. diss., St. Michael's College (Canada), 2004.

Dickson, John. "Promoting the Gospel: 'Mission-Commitment' in the Churches of Paul Against its Jewish Background." Ph.D. diss., Macquarie University, 2001.

Fiore, Benjamin. "The Function of Personal Example in the Socratic and Pastoral Epistles." Ph.D. diss., Yale University, 1982.

Hanges, James Constantine. "Paul, Founder of Churches: A Study in Light of the Evidence for the Role of 'Founder-Figures' in the Hellenistic-Roman Period." Ph.D. diss., University of Chicago, 1999.

Hopper, Mark Edward. "The Pauline Concept of Imitation." Ph.D. diss., Southern Baptist Theological Seminary, 1983.

Little, Christopher. "Mission in the Way of Paul: With Special Reference to Twenty-First Century Christian Mission." Ph.D. diss., Fuller Theological Seminary, 2003.

Merkle, Benjamin Lee. "The Elder and Overseer: One Office in the Early Church." Ph.D. diss., Southern Baptist Theological Seminary, 2000.

Merritt, James Gregory. "Evangelism for Discipleship in the Gospel of Luke: Implications for Modern Day Evangelism." Ph.D. diss., Southern Baptist Theological Seminary, 1982.

Plummer, Robert Lewis. "The Church's Missionary Nature: The Apostle Paul and His Churches." Ph.D. diss., Southern Baptist Theological Seminary, 2001.

Schmidt, Norbert. "The Apostolic Band—A Paradigm for Modern Missions?" Th.M. thesis, Trinity Evangelical Divinity School, 1985.

Ware, James Patrick. "'Holding Forth the Word of Life': Paul and the Mission of the Church in the Letter to the Philippians in the Context of Second Temple Judaism." Ph.D. diss., Yale University, 1996.

Williams, Donald Manly. "The Imitation of Christ in Paul with Special Reference to Paul as Teacher." Ph.D. diss., Columbia University, 1967.

Scripture Index

Genesis
1:3 51
1:6 51
15:1 51
15:4 51

Exodus
3:20 108
7:3 108
7:8-8:18 109
7:9 108
8:23 108
9:20-21 51
10:1-2 108
11:9-10 108
15:11 108
23:16 64
23:19 64
34:22 64
34:26 64

Leviticus
2:12 64
2:14 64
23:10 64
23:17 64
23:20 64

Numbers
3:16 51
3:51 51
11:23 51
14:22 108
15:31 51
18:13 64
24:13 51
28:26 64
36:5 51

Deuteronomy
4:10 44
4:34 108

5:5 51
6:22 108
7:19 108
9:5 51
9:10 44
11:3 108
13:1-5 109
18:4 64
18:16 44
18:22 51
23:2-4 44
23:9 44
26:8 108
26:10-11 64
29:3 108
31:30 44
34:5 51
34:11 108

Joshua
3:5 108
8:27 51
24:17 108

Judges
2:17 85

1 Samuel
8:3-5 85
10:10 68, 142

1 Kings
2:27 59

2 Chronicles
3:6 100

Ezra
2:68 78
3:3 78

Nehemiah
9:10 108

Esther
1:6 100

Psalms
10:17 78
65:9 78
78:43 108
89:14 78
105:27 108
135:9 108
147:15 51

Proverbs
2:13 85
3:23 85

Ecclesiastes
1:15 100
7:13 100

Isaiah
6:6 45
6:8 45
9:7 45
40-55 34
40:8b 51
40:9 26
42:6 76
51:22-23 79
52:1-12 79
52:5 103
52:7 26, 79
52:7-12 79
52:10 79
52:13-53:12 79
54:1 79
55:10f 51
55:10-11 50, 51, 141
55:11 92

61:1 26

Jeremiah
4:30 100
12:16 120
20:7-9 51, 141
23:29 50, 51, 141
29:10 51
32:20-21 108

Ezekiel
2:2 68, 142
16:11 100
16:13 100
16:58 100
23:41 100
36:20-36 103

Daniel
4:2-3 108
6:27 108
11:7 78
11:20 78
11:21 78
12:1 132

Hosea
1:1 68, 142

Joel
2:28-32 68, 142

Micah
6:9 100

Nahum
1:8 79
1:14 79
1:15-2:3 79
2:1-2 79
2:3 78
3:18 79

Zephaniah
1:14-15 132

Zechariah
2:12 45

2:13 45
6:15 45
5:11 78

Matthew
1:22 59
2:15 59
2:17 59
2:23 59
4:14 59
5:10-12 122, 125
5:14-16 102
5:16 76
8:17 59
10:23 138
10:25 122, 125
11:20-24 111
12:17 59
12:30 92
12:44 100
13:35 59
14:6 89
16:18 120
18:15-17 88
23:29 100
24:8 125
24:9 125, 138
24:15-22 138
24:24 109
25:7 100
28:18-20 6, 7, 48, 66, 142
28:19 30

Mark
6:22 89
8:31-35 90
8:34-35 122
10:45 90
13:5-8 132
13:9 122, 137
13:9-11 125
13:22 109
13:27 19
14:49 59
16:5 142
16:15 66

Luke
1:20 59
4 4
4:21 59
6:13 46
7:3 45
7:10 45
9:23-27 123, 137
11:25 100
12:4-12 137
14:7 75
16:8 76
19:10 90
21:5 100
21:5-11 132
21:12-13 137
21:12-19 122
21:16 125
21:17 125
24:46-49 66
24:47 142

John
5:19 83
5:36-38 45
8:39 83
8:44 83
12:25 122
12:36 76
15:18-19 124
15:20 122
17:14 124
17:16 124
17:20-21 39
20:21 39, 40, 66, 142

Acts
1:2-3 46
1:7 65
1:8 7, 49, 65, 66, 68, 110, 111, 142
1:16 59
1:21 56
1:21-22 47
1:22 46, 47
1:24 47
2:16-21 68, 142
2:19 110

2:22 110, 111
2:23 138
2:41 65
2:43 47, 110, 143
2:43-47 105, 143
3:1-4:22 110, 143
3:5 75
3:18 59
3:18-19 138
4:4 65, 110
4:10 138
4:23-31 127
4:27-28 138
4:29 65
4:29-30 110-11, 143
4:29-31 49, 65, 142
4:31 65
4:33 46
5 38
5:11-13 110
5:12 110
5:14 110
5:28 138
6:1 118
6:2 65
6:4 65
6:7 57, 65, 66, 127
6:7-10 111, 143
6:8 110
6:10 49, 65, 142
7:3 56
7:4 56
7:7 56
7:36 108
8:1-4 35, 127
8:4 10, 29-30, 122
8:4-24 122
8:5-14 111, 143
8:6 110
8:13 110
8:14 65
8:25 65
8:29 49, 65, 142
8:39-40 49, 65, 142
9:4 124
9:4-5 124, 133
9:15-16 85, 122
9:16 122

9:31 122
10:19-20 49, 65, 142
10:23 56
10:36 65
10:36-39 111
10:37 65
10:44 65
10:44-47 49, 65, 142
11:1 65
11:12 49, 65, 142
11:19 65
11:19-21 127
11:25 56
11:29 118
12:1-19 122
12:24 57, 65, 66, 127
13:2-4 49, 65, 142
13:4-12 110
13:5 65
13:7 65
13:44 65
13:46 65
13:48 65
13:48-52 122
13:49 30, 65, 127
14:1-4 47
14:3 65, 110
14:5-6 122
14:8-18 110
14:8-20 110
14:19-20 122
14:21-22 110
14:22 122
14:23 20
14:25 65
15:7 65
15:12 110
15:35 65, 127
15:36 65
16:1 56
16:3 10
16:5 127
16:6 65
16:6-7 49, 65, 142
16:16-18 110
16:25-40 122
16:32 65
17:5-9 128

17:10 122
17:11 65
17:13 65
17:13-15 122
18:1-3 95
18:1-8 56
18:2 14
18:9-11 122
18:11 65
18:17 95
18:17-26 96
18:18-26 95
18:19 56
18:24 56
18:24-28 69
18:27 70
19:1-20 122
19:10 30, 35, 65, 127
19:11-12 110
19:18-20 127
19:20 30, 57, 65, 66
19:22 75
20:7-12 110
19:28-41 128
20:15 56
20:17-38 38
20:17-28:31 122
20:22-23 49, 65, 142
20:22-24 122
20:23 122
20:23-24 85
20:27 66
20:30 88
20:32 65
20:35 81
21:7 56
21:8 27
21:13 122
22:25-29 137
24:16 89
25-26 137
25:1-26:32 137
25:13 56
28:1-9 110

Romans
1-3 124

1:1 1, 45, 46, 47, 51, 54,
    74, 96
1:1-7 55
1:1-17 32
1:8 12, 24, 25, 73, 113,
    143
1:8-10 112
1:9 51, 74, 96
1:15 39, 96, 121
1:16 52-54, 55, 57, 92,
    141
1:16-32 124
2:12 88
2:17-20 34, 76
2:19f. 13
2:24 103
3:8 127
3:21-26 132
3:23-24 131
5:3-5 138
5:6 91
5:17 131
6:4 123
6:9-10 132
8:1 29
8:3 132
8:4 65, 66
8:11 66
8:14-17 66
8:16-17 122, 125, 143
8:17 124
8:18-19 138
8:22-23 64
8:29-30 55, 64
8:29f. 55
8:31-39 123
8:35 129
8:36 85
9:6 51
9:16-18 126
9:24 66
10:1 113, 116, 143
10:8 51
10:8-15 73, 123
10:9-10 123
10:14-15 64
10:14-17 55
10:15 30, 79

11:13 45
11:16 64
11:25 19
12:17-21 29
13:1-8 29
13:1ff. 115
13:11-12 20
13:11-14 76
14:15 88
14:19 120
14:20 120
14:21 88
15:1 86
15:1-3 120
15:1-7 90
15:2 120
15:3 29
15:5-6 112
15:7-13 113, 120
15:13 112, 143
15:14 117, 143
15:14-33 3, 31
15:16 96
15:18-19 47, 58, 108,
    141, 143
15:18-32 29
15:19 12, 58-59, 96
15:19-20 59
15:19-23 19
15:20 1, 58, 96
15:20-21 118
15:20ff. 120
15:22-23 39
15:23f. 19
15:26 74
15:28-33 20
15:30-32 24
15:30-33 116
15:33 112
16:1 69
16:3 62
16:4 44
16:5 64, 141
16:7 47
16:16 44
16:19 25
16:20 112
16:21 62

16:25 51
16:25-26 133

1 Corinthians
1:1 45, 46, 95, 96
1:2 44, 62, 88, 95
1:10-4:13 84
1:11 88
1:12 69, 70
1:17 1, 39, 54, 96
1:17-18 54
1:17-25 54-56, 57
1:18 51, 85, 88, 94, 127,
    141
1:18-25 124
1:18-31 132
1:19 88
1:20-21 124
1:21 95
1:23 54, 73, 123
1:23-24 54-55, 85
1:24 64
1:26-29 55
1:27-30 66
2:1 73, 123, 133
2:1-5 56, 131
2:2 85
2:4 143
2:4-5 55, 109
2:7 133
2:9-13 65
3:4-6 69
3:4-9 70
3:5 69
3:5-9 66
3:5-10 56
3:7 57
3:8-9 62
3:9 45, 119, 143
3:9-7 120
3:9-11 118
3:9-15 25
3:13-15 62
3:22 69
4:6 84, 120
4:8-13 84, 85
4:9 45
4:9-13 122, 143

4:9-20 85
4:10-13 129
4:14 84, 117, 143
4:14-17 83-84
4:15 1, 58, 123, 141
4:16 29, 32, 81, 82, 83-85, 143
4:17 85, 88, 117, 143
5 38
5:5 103
5:9-10 120
5:9-13 47
5:11 88
6:2 45
6:3 84
6:9 95
6:9-11 88
6:11 95
7:6-7 81
7:10-12 47
7:12-16 83, 93-94, 95, 143
7:15 55
7:16 35, 92, 93, 95
7:17 44, 88
7:25-28 47
7:28 124
7:26-31 20
8-10 86
8:1 120
8:1-9 86
8:1-11:1 127
8:10-11 86
8:11 88
8:11-13 86
8:13 86
9 92
9:1 45, 46, 62
9:1-27 86
9:2 45
9:6 47
9:11 84
9:11-12 57
9:12 1, 56, 80, 84, 91, 92, 141
9:14 73, 96, 123
9:16 1, 39, 96
9:19 33

9:19-23 29, 32, 87, 91-92
9:22 126
9:23 51, 57, 74
10 87
10-11 25
10:1-13 87
10:14-22 87
10:21 71
10:23 90
10:23-24 120, 143
10:23-30 87
10:31 87, 89
10:31-33 120, 143
10:31-11:1 32, 36, 81, 87, 92, 95, 105
10:32 91
10:32-11:1 92
10:33 33, 90, 91
11:1 29, 81, 82, 83, 85-92, 143
11:5-16 29
11:16 44, 62, 88
11:17-34 71
11:26 123
11:32 95
12-14 65
12:3 65
12:5 118
12:9-10 111, 143
12:9-30 109
12:10 109
12:13 68, 142
12:27-28 118
12:28 39, 44, 96
12:28-29 109
12:28-30 111, 143
12:30 109
13:1-13 95
14 120
14:1-26 119, 143
14:3 90, 120
14:4 120
14:5 120
14:12 120
14:17 120
14:23-24 83

14:23-25 30, 89, 94-96, 119, 120, 143
14:23-26 110, 111
14:24 109
14:24-25 90, 95
14:26 120
14:33 44, 62, 88
14:34 44
14:36 56, 80, 141
15 94
15:1 96
15:1-2 63-64, 141
15:3 95
15:3-11 94
15:7 47
15:7-9 46
15:9 45
15:10 62
15:12 73, 123
15:20 64
15:23 64
15:30-32 85, 120, 143
15:50-58 95
15:58 85
16:1 44
16:8 95
16:8-9 85, 122, 143
16:9 29
16:10 62, 85
16:12 69
16:15 64, 118, 141
16:15-18 29, 69
16:19 44, 95, 96

2 Corinthians
1:1 45, 46, 88
1:3-10 122, 143
1:3-11 130
1:5 124
1:6-7 137
1:8-9 85
1:8-11 116, 137
1:9 134
1:11 24, 85
1:19 73, 123
1:21-22 66
2:1-11 47, 130
2:12 1, 29, 51, 74, 96

2:14 131, 134
2:14-15 124
2:14-17 122, 137, 143
2:14-3:3 85
2:15 88
2:17 51, 130
3:1 130
3:1-3 29, 70
3:2 24, 25
3:5 130
3:13-16 126
3:14 124
4:1-12 129
4:2-5 131
4:3 88, 130
4:4 124
4:5 73, 123
4:6 130
4:7 108
4:7-12 85, 122, 132
4:7-15 121, 129, 130-
    131, 132, 133, 138
4:8-9 129
4:8-12 137, 143
4:10 123, 124
4:10-12 130
4:11 134
4:13 131
4:15 137, 138
5:16-21 132
6:3-7 97
6:3-10 138
6:4 130
6:4-10 85, 122, 129
6:6-7 97
6:7 108
6:13 83
6:16-18 38
8-9 62
8:1 44
8:9 90
8:16-19 29
8:18-19 69
8:19 44
8:23 44, 45
8:23-24 69
8:24 44
9:1-5 69

9:12 118
9:13 74
9:14 115, 143
10:13-16 46, 118
10:14 51, 56, 74
10:15 62
10:16 1, 96
11:4 73, 123
11:7 96
11:7-9 24
11:8 44
11:22-28 122
11:23-29 129
11:23-33 85
11:23-12:10 138
11:26 124
11:28 44
12:7 124
12:9-10 131
12:10 129
12:12 47, 143
12:13 44
12:14 83
12:19 118, 143
13:10 118, 143
13:12 45

Galatians
1:1 45, 46, 48
1:2 44
1:4 131, 132
1:6 51
1:6-9 123
1:8 96
1:8-9 47
1:10 89
1:11 96
1:12 46
1:15-16 46
1:16 1
1:19 47
1:22 44
1:23 1
1:23-24 29
2 91
2:2 51, 96
2:7 51, 74
2:7-9 46

2:11-14 83, 91
2:11-21 47
2:20 132
3:1 124, 130
3:2 65
3:3 65
3:5 109, 143
3:10-14 124
3:13 127
4:6-7 65
4:8-9 29
4:11 62
4:12-20 81
4:13 124, 130
4:19 83
5:2-3 47
5:11 130
6:12 123, 124, 143
6:12-15 124
6:16 112
6:17 122, 130
6:18 112, 122

Ephesians
1-3 77
1:1 45, 46, 115
1:3 80
1:9-10 133
1:13 51
1:13-14 65
1:16-19 112
1:20-23 80
1:22 44
1:22-23 123
2:14-17 80
2:15-22 65
2:19-22 25, 38, 118
2:20 39
3-6 77
3:1 84
3:1-13 126
3:2-7 47
3:6-7 59
3:7 108
3:8 1
3:8-9 133
3:10 44, 144
3:13 84, 132

3:21 44
4:7 119
4:11 27, 29, 39
4:11-16 118-19, 120,
   143
4:12 118-19
4:16 25
4:29 120
5:1 81
5:1-2 90
5:2 29
5:6-16 98, 105
5:8-16 76
5:14 30
5:21-6:9 101
5:22-24 104
5:23-24 44
5:25 44
5:27 44
5:29 44
5:32 44
6:10-18 124
6:10-20 33, 36, 77
6:12-13 80
6:15 27, 29, 31, 33, 48,
   77-80, 116, 128
6:15-17 143
6:17 33, 80
6:18 115
6:18-20 80, 143
6:19 1, 96, 115, 133
6:19-20 116
6:21-22 29
6:23 30

Philippians
1 25, 134
1:1 20, 88
1:3-5 113, 143
1:3-10 112
1:5 24, 29, 33, 39, 51,
   73, 74
1:5-6 81
1:7 96
1:10 89
1:11 57
1:12 29, 73, 92
1:12-14 35, 84

1:12-18 1, 59, 72-76,
   123, 128, 143
1:14 27, 29, 58, 73, 77,
   122, 135, 143
1:14-18 33, 48, 85
1:18 74
1:19 24, 116, 137
1:19-20 77
1:20-30 20
1:22 62
1:23-25 138
1:27 29, 31, 33
1:27-30 77, 122, 143
1:28 136
1:28-30 77
1:29 137
1:29-30 122, 134, 137,
   138
1:30 33
2:5-11 29, 90
2:14-16 76-77
2:14-17 36
2:15 29
2:15-17 27
2:16 33, 34, 48, 58, 62,
   74, 75, 76, 77, 128,
   143
2:22 29, 51, 74, 83
2:25 24, 39, 46
2:30 62
3:1-21 47
3:2-3 124
3:3-10 124
3:7-9 124, 133
3:10 122, 124, 134
3:17 29, 32, 62, 81
4:2 47
4:5 20, 77
4:9 81
4:10 29
4:10-18 39
4:12 129
4:15 51, 73, 74
4:22 45

Colossians
1:1 45, 46
1:3 112

1:3-8 132
1:4 133
1:5-6 2, 32, 92, 96
1:5-7 57, 141
1:6 12
1:7 127
1:9 133
1:10 57
1:18 44, 123
1:23 1, 59, 132
1:24 44, 84, 133
1:24-25 29, 121, 122,
   124, 131-34, 143
1:25 59, 80, 141
1:26-29 133
1:28 73, 117, 123, 143
1:29 108
2:13-14 132
3:12 45
3:13 29
3:16 117, 143
3:16-17 2, 63, 141
3:18-4:1 101
4:2-4 29, 80, 116, 143
4:3 85, 122
4:3-4 73, 123, 133
4:4-6 29
4:5-6 24, 29, 31, 80, 89,
   116
4:6 143
4:7-9 29
4:16 44, 88

1 Thessalonians
1:1 44
1:1-8 77
1:2-8 112, 113, 143
1:3 61-62
1:4-5 55
1:4-8 81
1:5 1, 32, 56, 96, 109,
   141
1:5-8 32, 34, 36, 92, 96
1:6 29, 32, 81, 124
1:6-8 50, 61-63, 80, 82,
   85, 135
1:7 32, 62

1:8 2, 9, 10, 12, 24, 25,
    27, 30, 35, 39, 48, 60-
    62, 128, 141
1:8-9 29
1:9 61, 124
1:9-10 62-63, 127, 128
2:1-2 60, 135
2:2 73, 96, 123
2:2-9 1
2:4 96
2:5-12 97-98
2:7 45, 83
2:9 96
2:11 83
2:12 55
2:13 47, 60, 61, 80, 96
2:13-14 62, 92
2:13-16 2, 59-60, 137,
    141
2:14 81
2:14-16 85, 122, 135,
    143
2:18 124
3:1 137
3:2 62
3:2-4 85
3:3-4 122, 136, 143
3:5 62
3:9-13 112
3:12 113, 143
4:5 29
4:11-12 89, 98
4:12 29, 105, 143
4:13-5:3 20
5:4-5 76
5:9 29
5:11 120
5:12 117, 143
5:23-24 112
5:23-25 66
5:25 29, 116

2 Thessalonians
1-2 124
1:4 29
1:4-8 124
1:4-10 85, 136, 137
1:5 137

1:5-8 29
1:5-9 137
1:5-11 138
1:8 136
1:8-10 29
1:11 112
2:1-12 124
2:9 109
2:10 88, 136
2:11-12 124
2:12 136
2:13 32
2:15 117, 143
2:16-17 80, 112, 116
3:1 2, 30, 60, 61, 62, 80,
    92, 96, 137, 141
3:1-2 32, 80, 116, 143
3:5 112
3:7 81
3:7-9 32, 62, 98, 105
3:9 81
3:14-15 102
3:15 117, 143
3:16 112

1 Timothy
1:1 45, 46, 100
1:2 83
1:15-17 81
1:18 83
1:19-20 103
1:20 102
2:1-3 30
2:1-4 98, 114-15, 137,
    143
2:3 100
2:7 45, 46, 47
2:9 100
2:11-15 104
2:12 117
3:1-13 20, 71
3:7 98, 102, 105
3:8-9 133
3:15 38
4:10 100
4:16 75
5:1-2 101
6:1 100, 103, 105, 143

6:20 48

2 Timothy
1:1 45, 46
1:1-2 48
1:2 69, 83
1:3 112
1:5 63
1:8 85, 122, 123, 137,
    143
1:10-11 47
1:11 45, 46, 96
1:11-12 122, 134
1:13 81
1:15 29
1:16 112
1:18 112
2:1 83
2:2 38, 81, 117
2:3 85, 122, 143
2:8 96
2:8-9 57, 141
2:8-11 122, 138
2:9 64, 92, 102
2:10 45, 84
2:24-25 98
3:10 81
3:10-12 85
3:10-15 122
3:12 122, 123, 125, 143
4:5 27, 85, 98
4:10 29
4:16 112
4:17 59, 96, 141

Titus
1:1 45, 104
1:3 100
1:4 69, 83
1:5 48
1:5-9 71
1:9 98
1:10-16 99
2 99, 101
2:1-10 98-105, 143
2:5 29
2:8 29
2:10 29, 35, 48

2:10-14 100-01
2:11 101, 104
2:11-15 104
2:13 100
3:1-2 29, 98
3:3-7 100-01
3:4 100
3:12 48

Philemon
2 44
4-6 112
10 83
22 116

Hebrews
2:4 111
6:12 81
10:32-34 128
13:3 128
13:7 81
13:12-14 122

James
2:23 59

1 Peter
2:9-12 29, 98, 105, 143
2:11 29
2:12 102
2:13ff. 115
2:18-3:7 101
2:20-23 122
3:1 35, 93, 98
3:1-2 105, 143
3:1-8 104
3:5 100
3:8-9 122
3:13-19 29
3:16 102
4:1 122
4:4 127
4:1-5 124
4:7 21
4:12-19 122
4:13 125
4:14 125, 127
4:16 29, 125
5:3 62
5:14 30

2 Peter
2:1 88

2:2 103
3:2 38
3:15 38
3:15-16 47, 88

1 John
3:13 124
4:4-6 124
5:16 88

3 John
1-15 38
11 81

Revelation
1:9 125
2:1-3:22 38
2:2-3 126
2:9-10 126
2:13 126
2:19 118, 126
3:8-9 126
13:13-14 109
14:4 64
21:2 100
21:19 100

Modern Author Index

Abbott, T. K. 63, 78
Adeney, David H. 126
Ahern, Barnabas Mary 134
Allen, Roland 5, 8-11, 13, 30, 39, 49
Althaus, Paul 19, 58, 117
Argyle, A. W. 49
Arnold, Clinton E. 78
Aus, Roger D. 19
Balz, Horst 99
Banks, Robert J. 43
Barnett, Paul W. 131
Barram, Michael D. 20
Barrett, C. K. 19, 40, 47, 58, 77, 84,
    93, 94, 98, 101, 114, 117, 120
Barth, Markus 119
Baudraz, Francis 88, 93
Bauer, Bran 110
Baur, Ferdinand Christian 6
Beale, G. K. 37-38
Beare, F. W. 75
Becker, Ulrich 51, 53
Beker, J. Christiaan 94
Belleville, Linda L. 82, 84, 90
Berger, Klaus 43
Best, Ernest 3, 81, 82, 83, 128, 131
Betz, Hans Dieter 82
Blauw, Johannes 68, 78
Blinzler, Josef 93
Blomberg, Craig 95
Bloomquist, Gregory L. 134, 135
Boer, Harry R. 6, 7, 9, 10, 49
Boice, James M. 111
Bolt, Peter G. 32, 112, 124, 130
Bornkamm, Günther 3, 12, 58, 91
Bosch, David J. 1, 4, 6, 8, 13, 17, 18,
    25, 135
Bowen, Clayton R. 72
Bowers, W. Paul 20, 24-25, 27, 30,
    35-36, 39, 41, 47, 61-62, 73, 83, 89,
    113, 116-17
Branner, John E. 9
Brant, Jo-Ann A. 60, 81, 82, 85, 136

Bratcher, Robert G. 118
Brown, Colin 64
Brox, Norbert 101
Bruce, F. F. 75, 93, 118
Brunt, John C. 86
Bultmann, Rudolf 67, 129
Burchard, C. 93
Burini, Clara 104
Buscarlet, Amalric F. 78
Caird, G. B. 118, 119
Calvin, John 21, 93
Carey, William 6, 48
Carson, D. A. 83, 91, 98, 108, 111-12, 113
Casson, Lionel 124
Castelli, Elizabeth A. 82, 83, 84
Cerfaux, Lucien 43, 46-47
Chambers, Stephen 27-28, 83
Chevallier, Raymond 124
Clarke, Andrew D. 61, 82
Clowney, Edmund P. 41
Coenen, Lothar 43, 44, 55
Collins, John J. 87
Collins, Raymond F. 84, 93
Conzelmann, Hans 82, 84, 85, 87, 93, 98,
    100, 101
Cowen, Andrew 81
Crafer, T. W. 110
Cranfield, C. E. B. 21, 51, 53-54, 58
Dahl, Nils Alstrup 2, 58, 112
Danker, F. W. 51
Daube, David 91,
De Boer, Willis Peter 81, 82, 85
Deissmann, Adolf 72
Delling, Gerhard 44
Dibelius, Martin 58, 75, 89, 98, 100, 101
Dickson, John P. 1, 26-27, 39, 78, 121
Dittenberger, W. 46
Dockx, S. 72
Donaldson, Terence L. 24, 28
Doohan, Helen 43
Doyle, Robert 111
Dunn, James D. G. 52, 53

Eadie, John 75
Eckert, Jost 55
Ehrhardt, Arnold 40, 41
Eicken, Erich von 45
Ellicott, Charles J. 101
Ellis, E. Earle 69, 98
Ernst, Josef 78
Fee, Gordon D. 82, 84, 86, 87, 93, 99, 101
Feldman, L. H. 26
Fenton, John 110
Fiore, Benjamin 82, 83
Fiorenza, Elisabeth Schüssler 3
Fishwick, Duncan 126
Fitzgerald, John T. 129
Fitzmyer, Joseph A. 51, 53
Flemington, W. F. 132
Fowl, Stephen E. 83
Friedländer, Ludwig 8, 9
Friedrich, Gerhard 54
Fung, Ronald Y. K. 43
Furnish, Victor Paul 83, 122, 131
Garland, David 95
Garrett, Susan R. 129
Garrison, David 134
Gebauer, Roland 112
Geisler, Norman L. 108
Gensichen, Hans-Werner 8, 22, 23
Gilliland, Dean S. 7, 10, 49
Glasser, Arthur F. 40
Glombitza, Otto 75
Gnilka, Joachim 74
Godet, Frederic Louis 88, 93
Gooch, Peter D. 86, 90-91, 127
Goodman, Martin 12
Gordon, A. J. 10
Grassi, Joseph A. 3
Green, Michael 3, 5, 9, 15-16, 32, 49, 65
Greeven, Heinrich 22, 23, 58
Grether, Oskar 51
Griffin Jr., Hayne P. 99
Griffiths, Michael C. 41
Grudem, Wayne 104
Grundmann, Walter 108
Guerra, Manuel 88
Gundry Volf, Judith M. 50, 57, 92
Guthrie, Donald 44, 98

Gutiérrez, Pedro 82, 83, 85
Güttgemann, Erhardt 132
Haenchen, Ernst 65
Hafemann, Scott J. 121-22, 130, 131, 132, 133, 138
Hahn, Ferdinand 4, 5, 119
Hardon, John A. 110
Harnack, Adolf von 2, 5, 7, 8, 11-15, 20, 35, 58, 128
Hass, Odo 83
Hatch 100
Hauck, Friedrich 74
Haupt, Erich 74
Hawthorne, Gerald F. 74, 75
Hays, Richard B. 56
Heim, Karl 91
Heinrici, Georg 88, 93
Hendriksen, William 78
Hengel, Martin 11, 12
Henneken, Bartholomaüs 61
Herbert, A. S. 79
Héring, Jean 86, 93
Hinson, E. Glenn 3
Hodge, Charles 88
Hodgson, Robert 129
Hofius, Otfried 53
Holtz, Gottfried 102
Hooker, Morna D. 49, 57
Hopper, Mark Edward 82, 87
Horsley, G. H. R. 45
Horsley, Richard A. 93
Hort, Fenton John Anthony 44
House, Paul R. 122
Howell Jr., Don N. 9, 49
Hultgren, Arland J. 19
Hunt, Arthur S. 46, 100
Hunter, W. B. 112
Hurtado, Larry W. 90
Jeremias, Joachim 68, 93, 101
Jervell, Jacob 108, 109, 110
Johnson, Lewis 72
Johnson, Luke Timothy 98
Judge, Edwin 82
Kähler, Martin 6
Kaiser Jr., Walter C. 68
Kanda, S. H. 110
Karris, Robert J. 99
Kasdorf, Hans 6
Käsemann, Ernst 19, 53, 67, 108, 109, 118

Kee, Howard C. 102
Kelly, J. N. D. 98
Kirk, J. Andrew 2
Kleinknecht, Karl Theodor 129
Knight III, George W. 99, 102, 103, 104, 105
Knox, John 3
Kodell, Jerome 65
Köstenberger, Andreas J. 3, 31, 32, 33, 49, 68
Kremer, Jacob 131
Kubo, Sakae 93
Kümmel, Werner G. 13, 16, 17, 71, 72, 95
Küng, Hans 41
Lambrecht, J. 49, 50, 61, 62, 131, 137
Lampe, G. W. H. 108
Larkin Jr., William J. 4
Larsson, Edvin 75, 81
Latourette, K. S. 11
Legrand, Lucien 19-20
Liechtenhan, Rudolf 23
Lietzmann, D. Hans 19
Lightfoot, J. B. 74, 75, 88, 93
Lillie, William 101
Lincoln, Andrew T. 77, 78, 80
Lindner, Helgo 45
Link, Hans-Georg 64
Lippert, Peter 22, 23, 98, 101
Lips, Hermann von 101
Little, Christopher R. 37
Lock, Walter 98, 119
Loh, I-Jin 75
Lohmeyer, Ernst 75
Lohse, Eduard 57
Louw, Johannes P. 59, 81
Luther, Martin 103
MacMullen, Ramsay 86, 127
Malherbe, Abraham J. 81, 82, 135
Manson, T. W. 41
March, F. A. 127
Marshall, I. Howard 21, 32, 35-36, 65, 75, 99, 101, 102, 122
Martin, Chalmers 7
McCasland, S. Vernon 108
McKenzie, John L. 51, 53, 59
McKnight, Scot 12, 34, 68
Meecham, H. G. 77
Merk, Otto 75
Merkle, Benjamin J. 20
Merklein, Helmut 43, 99

Meyer, Heinrich August Wilhelm 78
Meyer, Regina Pacis 119
Michael, J. Hugh 74
Michaelis, W. 81
Michel, Otto 3, 118, 120
Miller, M. H. 110
Minear, Paul Sevier 45
Mitchell, Stephen 126
Mitton, C. Leslie 119
Molland, Einar 50, 57
Moo, Douglas M. 98
Morgenthaler, Robert 112
Morris, Leon 54, 78, 93, 98
Mott, Stephen Charles 100
Mounce, Robert H. 52
Mounce, William D. 69, 98, 99, 101, 104, 114
Munck, Johannes 19-20, 58
Murphy, Edward F. 41
Murphy-O'Connor, Jerome 82, 90
Mußner, Franz 119
Neill, Stephen 2, 11
Neirynck, Frans 110
Nellessen, E. 20
Newport, John P. 41
Newton, Derek 82
Nida, Eugene A. 59, 75, 81, 118
Nissen, Johannes 23
O'Brien, Peter T. 1, 3, 27, 31-33, 36, 42, 44, 49-51, 56-57, 68, 72, 74-75, 83, 90, 92, 96-97, 108, 112, 131
Oepke, Albrecht 78
Ollrog, Wolf-Henning 23-24, 27, 69
Orr, William F. 93
O'Toole, Robert F. 137
Padgett, Alan 99, 104
Peerbolte, J. L. Lietaert 12, 26
Peters, George W. 41-42, 66
Pierson, Arthur T. 10
Piper, John 37, 104, 116, 133, 134-35
Plummer, Alfred 56, 88, 89, 93
Plummer, Robert L. 27, 36, 48, 81
Pobee, John S. 121, 122, 129
Poland, Franz 86, 127
Poythress, Vern Sheridan 74
Praeder, Susan Marie 109
Proudfoot, C. Merrill 132
Quinn, Jerome D. 98, 112
Rahlf, Alfred 100

Ramsay, William M. 8-9, 13-14
Rapske, Brian 122
Rebell, Walter 94, 120
Redpath 100
Reinhartz, Adele 81, 82
Renan, Ernest 5, 18-21, 58, 117
Rengstorf, Karl Heinrich 45, 47, 108
Reumann, John 131
Richarson, Peter 89, 90-91
Ridderbos, Herman 30, 31, 120
Riesner, Rainer 26
Ritchel, Frank 51
Robertson, Archibald 56, 88, 89, 93
Robinson, J. Armitage 118
Robinson, O. F. 126
Roels, Edwin D. 77, 78, 118
Roloff, Jürgen 43, 44
Rosner, Brian S. 65
Sanders, Boykin 84, 85
Sanders, E. P. 20
Saß, Gerhard 132
Senior, Donald 3, 119
Schärer, Hans 7, 8
Schenk, Wolfgang 75
Schippers, Reinier 59
Schlier, Heinrich 78
Schlink, Edmund 119
Schlunk, D. Martin 2
Schmidlin, Julius 6
Schmidt, K. L. 43, 44, 55
Schmidt, Norbert 38-42, 138
Schmidt, W. H. 51
Schmithals, Walter 40, 86, 137
Schnabel, Eckhart J. 1, 35-36, 68
Schnackenburg, Rudolf 40
Schrage, Wolfgang 93, 94, 129
Schreiner, Thomas R. 52, 53, 55, 58
Schulz, Anselm 82
Schütz, John Howard 49, 61, 82, 92,
    96
Schweitzer, Albert 20
Schweizer, E. 119
Seifrid, Mark A. 53
Seesemann, Heinrich 74
Sherwin-White, A. N. 126
Silva, Moisés 75
Ska, Jean-Louis 108
Spencer, William David 84-85

Spicq, Ceslas 46, 47, 82
Stanley, David M. 61, 82, 112, 113
Stendahl, Kirster 112
Stenschke, Christoph 4
Stettler, Hanna 131
Stolz, Fritz 108
Stott, John 99
Strauss, Steve 31
Strecker, Georg 55
Stuhlmacher, Peter 51, 53
Stuhlmueller, Carroll 3, 119
Swigchem, Douwe van 23, 27, 28-31, 32,
    61, 78, 83, 134
Teinonen, Seppo A. 6, 8
Thiselton, Anthony C. 51, 84, 88, 93
Thrall, Magaret E. 130-131
Tinsley, E. J. 82
Towner, Philip H. 99, 101, 114, 115
Troeltsch, Ernst 7, 48
Twelftree, G. H. 108
Vanhoozer, Kevin 51
Verkuyl, Johannes 31
Wallace, Daniel B. 52, 77
Walther, James Arthur 93
Ware, James Patrick 4, 12, 27, 32, 33-36,
    42, 49, 61, 62, 74-5, 76, 77
Warneck, Gustav 5-8, 13, 48
Warneck, Johannes 6, 7, 8
Weber, Otto 78
Weiser, Alfons 99
Weiss, Johannes 86, 88
Weizsäcker, Carl von 5, 13-15, 20
Wernle, Paul 5, 13, 16-18, 20
Westcott, Brooke Foss 118
Wette, Wilhelm Martin Leberecht de 6
Wickert, Ulrich 89
Wiles, Gordon P. 112
Willert, Niels 129
Williams, Donald Manly 82, 83
Willis, Wendell Lee 86, 127
Windisch, Hans 132
Winter, Bruce W. 124, 126, 127
Winter, Ralph D. 40-41
Woodhouse, John 108
Wrede, William 5, 9, 17, 18-21, 58, 117
Zeller, Dieter 23
Ziesler, John 3

Paternoster Biblical Monographs

(All titles uniform with this volume)
Dates in bold are of projected publication

Joseph Abraham
Eve: Accused or Acquitted?
A Reconsideration of Feminist Readings of the Creation Narrative Texts in Genesis 1–3

Two contrary views dominate contemporary feminist biblical scholarship. One finds in the Bible an unequivocal equality between the sexes from the very creation of humanity, whilst the other sees the biblical text as irredeemably patriarchal and androcentric. Dr Abraham enters into dialogue with both camps as well as introducing his own method of approach. An invaluable tool for any one who is interested in this contemporary debate.

2002 / 0-85364-971-5 / xxiv + 272pp

Octavian D. Baban
Mimesis and Luke's on the Road Encounters in Luke-Acts
Luke's Theology of the Way and its Literary Representation

The book argues on theological and literary (mimetic) grounds that Luke's on-the-road encounters, especially those belonging to the post-Easter period, are part of his complex theology of the Way. Jesus' teaching and that of the apostles is presented by Luke as a challenging answer to the Hellenistic reader's thirst for adventure, good literature, and existential paradigms.

2005 / 1-84227-253-5 / approx. 374pp

Paul Barker
The Triumph of Grace in Deuteronomy

This book is a textual and theological analysis of the interaction between the sin and faithlessness of Israel and the grace of Yahweh in response, looking especially at Deuteronomy chapters 1–3, 8–10 and 29–30. The author argues that the grace of Yahweh is determinative for the ongoing relationship between Yahweh and Israel and that Deuteronomy anticipates and fully expects Israel to be faithless.

2004 / 1-84227-226-8 / xxii + 270pp

Jonathan F. Bayes
The Weakness of the Law
God's Law and the Christian in New Testament Perspective

A study of the four New Testament books which refer to the law as weak (Acts, Romans, Galatians, Hebrews) leads to a defence of the third use in the Reformed debate about the law in the life of the believer.

2000 / 0-85364-957-X / xii + 244pp

Mark Bonnington
The Antioch Episode of Galatians 2:11-14 in Historical and Cultural Context

The Galatians 2 'incident' in Antioch over table-fellowship suggests significant disagreement between the leading apostles. This book analyses the background to the disagreement by locating the incident within the dynamics of social interaction between Jews and Gentiles. It proposes a new way of understanding the relationship between the individuals and issues involved.

2005 / 1-84227-050-8 / approx. 350pp

David Bostock
A Portrayal of Trust
The Theme of Faith in the Hezekiah Narratives

This study provides detailed and sensitive readings of the Hezekiah narratives (2 Kings 18–20 and Isaiah 36–39) from a theological perspective. It concentrates on the theme of faith, using narrative criticism as its methodology. Attention is paid especially to setting, plot, point of view and characterization within the narratives. A largely positive portrayal of Hezekiah emerges that underlines the importance and relevance of scripture.

2005 / 1-84227-314-0 / approx. 300pp

Mark Bredin
Jesus, Revolutionary of Peace
A Non-violent Christology in the Book of Revelation

This book aims to demonstrate that the figure of Jesus in the Book of Revelation can best be understood as an active non-violent revolutionary.

2003 / 1-84227-153-9 / xviii + 262pp

Robinson Butarbutar
Paul and Conflict Resolution
An Exegetical Study of Paul's Apostolic Paradigm in 1 Corinthians 9

The author sees the apostolic paradigm in 1 Corinthians 9 as part of Paul's unified arguments in 1 Corinthians 8–10 in which he seeks to mediate in the dispute over the issue of food offered to idols. The book also sees its relevance for dispute-resolution today, taking the conflict within the author's church as an example.

2006 / 1-84227-315-9 / approx. 280pp

Daniel J-S Chae
Paul as Apostle to the Gentiles
His Apostolic Self-awareness and its Influence on the Soteriological Argument in Romans

Opposing 'the post-Holocaust interpretation of Romans', Daniel Chae competently demonstrates that Paul argues for the equality of Jew and Gentile in Romans. Chae's fresh exegetical interpretation is academically outstanding and spiritually encouraging.

1997 / 0-85364-829-8 / xiv + 378pp

Luke L. Cheung
The Genre, Composition and Hermeneutics of the Epistle of James

The present work examines the employment of the wisdom genre with a certain compositional structure and the interpretation of the law through the Jesus tradition of the double love command by the author of the Epistle of James to serve his purpose in promoting perfection and warning against doubleness among the eschatologically renewed people of God in the Diaspora.

2003 / 1-84227-062-1 / xvi + 372pp

Youngmo Cho
Spirit and Kingdom in the Writings of Luke and Paul

The relationship between Spirit and Kingdom is a relatively unexplored area in Lukan and Pauline studies. This book offers a fresh perspective of two biblical writers on the subject. It explores the difference between Luke's and Paul's understanding of the Spirit by examining the specific question of the relationship of the concept of the Spirit to the concept of the Kingdom of God in each writer.

__2005__ / 1-84227-316-7 / approx. 270pp

Andrew C. Clark
Parallel Lives
The Relation of Paul to the Apostles in the Lucan Perspective

This study of the Peter-Paul parallels in Acts argues that their purpose was to emphasize the themes of continuity in salvation history and the unity of the Jewish and Gentile missions. New light is shed on Luke's literary techniques, partly through a comparison with Plutarch.

2001 / 1-84227-035-4 / xviii + 386pp

Andrew D. Clarke
Secular and Christian Leadership in Corinth
A Socio-Historical and Exegetical Study of 1 Corinthians 1–6
This volume is an investigation into the leadership structures and dynamics of first-century Roman Corinth. These are compared with the practice of leadership in the Corinthian Christian community which are reflected in 1 Corinthians 1–6, and contrasted with Paul's own principles of Christian leadership.
2005 / 1-84227-229-2 / 200pp

Stephen Finamore
God, Order and Chaos
René Girard and the Apocalypse
Readers are often disturbed by the images of destruction in the book of Revelation and unsure why they are unleashed after the exaltation of Jesus. This book examines past approaches to these texts and uses René Girard's theories to revive some old ideas and propose some new ones.
2005 / 1-84227-197-0 / approx. 344pp

David G. Firth
Surrendering Retribution in the Psalms
Responses to Violence in the Individual Complaints
In *Surrendering Retribution in the Psalms*, David Firth examines the ways in which the book of Psalms inculcates a model response to violence through the repetition of standard patterns of prayer. Rather than seeking justification for retributive violence, Psalms encourages not only a surrender of the right of retribution to Yahweh, but also sets limits on the retribution that can be sought in imprecations. Arising initially from the author's experience in South Africa, the possibilities of this model to a particular context of violence is then briefly explored.
2005 / 1-84227-337-X / xviii + 154pp

Scott J. Hafemann
Suffering and Ministry in the Spirit
Paul's Defence of His Ministry in II Corinthians 2:14–3:3
Shedding new light on the way Paul defended his apostleship, the author offers a careful, detailed study of 2 Corinthians 2:14–3:3 linked with other key passages throughout 1 and 2 Corinthians. Demonstrating the unity and coherence of Paul's argument in this passage, the author shows that Paul's suffering served as the vehicle for revealing God's power and glory through the Spirit.
2000 / 0-85364-967-7 / xiv + 262pp

Scott J. Hafemann
Paul, Moses and the History of Israel
The Letter/Spirit Contrast and the Argument from Scripture in 2 Corinthians 3
An exegetical study of the call of Moses, the second giving of the Law (Exodus 32–34), the new covenant, and the prophetic understanding of the history of Israel in 2 Corinthians 3. Hafemann's work demonstrates Paul's contextual use of the Old Testament and the essential unity between the Law and the Gospel within the context of the distinctive ministries of Moses and Paul.
2005 / 1-84227-317-5 / xii + 498pp

Douglas S. McComiskey
Lukan Theology in the Light of the Gospel's Literary Structure
Luke's Gospel was purposefully written with theology embedded in its patterned literary structure. A critical analysis of this cyclical structure provides new windows into Luke's interpretation of the individual pericopes comprising the Gospel and illuminates several of his theological interests.
2004 / 1-84227-148-2 / xviii + 388pp

Stephen Motyer
Your Father the Devil?
A New Approach to John and 'The Jews'
Who are 'the Jews' in John's Gospel? Defending John against the charge of antisemitism, Motyer argues that, far from demonising the Jews, the Gospel seeks to present Jesus as 'Good News for Jews' in a late first century setting.
1997 / 0-85364-832-8 / xiv + 260pp

Esther Ng
Reconstructing Christian Origins?
The Feminist Theology of Elizabeth Schüssler Fiorenza: An Evaluation
In a detailed evaluation, the author challenges Elizabeth Schüssler Fiorenza's reconstruction of early Christian origins and her underlying presuppositions. The author also presents her own views on women's roles both then and now.
2002 / 1-84227-055-9 / xxiv + 468pp

Robin Parry
Old Testament Story and Christian Ethics
The Rape of Dinah as a Case Study

What is the role of story in ethics and, more particularly, what is the role of Old Testament story in Christian ethics? This book, drawing on the work of contemporary philosophers, argues that narrative is crucial in the ethical shaping of people and, drawing on the work of contemporary Old Testament scholars, that story plays a key role in Old Testament ethics. Parry then argues that when situated in canonical context Old Testament stories can be reappropriated by Christian readers in their own ethical formation. The shocking story of the rape of Dinah and the massacre of the Shechemites provides a fascinating case study for exploring the parameters within which Christian ethical appropriations of Old Testament stories can live.

2004 / 1-84227-210-1 / xx + 350pp

Ian Paul
Power to See the World Anew
The Value of Paul Ricoeur's Hermeneutic of Metaphor in Interpreting the Symbolism of Revelation 12 and 13

This book is a study of the hermeneutics of metaphor of Paul Ricoeur, one of the most important writers on hermeneutics and metaphor of the last century. It sets out the key points of his theory, important criticisms of his work, and how his approach, modified in the light of these criticisms, offers a methodological framework for reading apocalyptic texts.

2006 / 1-84227-056-7 / approx. 350pp

Robert L. Plummer
Paul's Understanding of the Church's Mission
Did the Apostle Paul Expect the Early Christian Communities to Evangelize?

This book engages in a careful study of Paul's letters to determine if the apostle expected the communities to which he wrote to engage in missionary activity. It helpfully summarizes the discussion on this debated issue, judiciously handling contested texts, and provides a way forward in addressing this critical question. While admitting that Paul rarely explicitly commands the communities he founded to evangelize, Plummer amasses significant incidental data to provide a convincing case that Paul did indeed expect his churches to engage in mission activity. Throughout the study, Plummer progressively builds a theological basis for the church's mission that is both distinctively Pauline and compelling.

2006 / 1-84227-333-7 / approx. 324pp

David Powys
'Hell': A Hard Look at a Hard Question
The Fate of the Unrighteous in New Testament Thought
This comprehensive treatment seeks to unlock the original meaning of terms and
phrases long thought to support the traditional doctrine of hell. It concludes that
there is an alternative—one which is more biblical, and which can positively
revive the rationale for Christian mission.

1997 / 0-85364-831-X / xxii + 478pp

Sorin Sabou
Between Horror and Hope
Paul's Metaphorical Language of Death in Romans 6.1-11
This book argues that Paul's metaphorical language of death in Romans 6.1-11
conveys two aspects: horror and hope. The 'horror' aspect is conveyed by the
'crucifixion' language, and the 'hope' aspect by 'burial' language. The life of
the Christian believer is understood, as relationship with sin is concerned ('death
to sin'), between these two realities: horror and hope.

2005 / 1-84227-322-1 / approx. 224pp

Rosalind Selby
The Comical Doctrine
The Epistemology of New Testament Hermeneutics
This book argues that the gospel breaks through postmodernity's critique of
truth and the referential possibilities of textuality with its gift of grace. With a
rigorous, philosophical challenge to modernist and postmodernist assumptions,
Selby offers an alternative epistemology to all who would still read with faith
and with academic credibility.

2005 / 1-84227-212-8 / approx. 350pp

Kiwoong Son
Zion Symbolism in Hebrews
Hebrews 12.18-24 as a Hermeneutical Key to the Epistle
This book challenges the general tendency of understanding the Epistle to the
Hebrews against a Hellenistic background and suggests that the Epistle should
be understood in the light of the Jewish apocalyptic tradition. The author
especially argues for the importance of the theological symbolism of Sinai and
Zion (Heb. 12:18-24) as it provides the Epistle's theological background as well
as the rhetorical basis of the superiority motif of Jesus throughout the Epistle.

2005 / 1-84227-368-X / approx. 280pp

Kevin Walton
Thou Traveller Unknown
The Presence and Absence of God in the Jacob Narrative
The author offers a fresh reading of the story of Jacob in the book of Genesis through the paradox of divine presence and absence. The work also seeks to make a contribution to Pentateuchal studies by bringing together a close reading of the final text with historical critical insights, doing justice to the text's historical depth, final form and canonical status.
2003 / 1-84227-059-1 / xvi + 238pp

George M. Wieland
The Significance of Salvation
A Study of Salvation Language in the Pastoral Epistles
The language and ideas of salvation pervade the three Pastoral Epistles. This study offers a close examination of their soteriological statements. In all three letters the idea of salvation is found to play a vital paraenetic role, but each also exhibits distinctive soteriological emphases. The results challenge common assumptions about the Pastoral Epistles as a corpus.
2005 */ 1-84227-257-8 / approx. 324pp*

Alistair Wilson
When Will These Things Happen?
A Study of Jesus as Judge in Matthew 21–25
This study seeks to allow Matthew's carefully constructed presentation of Jesus to be given full weight in the modern evaluation of Jesus' eschatology. Careful analysis of the text of Matthew 21–25 reveals Jesus to be standing firmly in the Jewish prophetic and wisdom traditions as he proclaims and enacts imminent judgement on the Jewish authorities then boldly claims the central role in the final and universal judgement.
2004 / 1-84227-146-6 / xxii + 272pp

Lindsay Wilson
Joseph Wise and Otherwise
The Intersection of Covenant and Wisdom in Genesis 37–50
This book offers a careful literary reading of Genesis 37–50 that argues that the Joseph story contains both strong covenant themes and many wisdom-like elements. The connections between the two helps to explore how covenant and wisdom might intersect in an integrated biblical theology.
2004 / 1-84227-140-7 / xvi + 340pp

Stephen I. Wright
The Voice of Jesus
Studies in the Interpretation of Six Gospel Parables
This literary study considers how the 'voice' of Jesus has been heard in different
periods of parable interpretation, and how the categories of figure and trope may
help us towards a sensitive reading of the parables today.
2000 / 0-85364-975-8 / xiv + 280pp

Paternoster
9 Holdom Avenue,
Bletchley,
Milton Keynes MK1 1QR,
United Kingdom
Web: www.authenticmedia.co.uk/paternoster

Paternoster Theological Monographs

(All titles uniform with this volume)
Dates in bold are of projected publication

Emil Bartos
Deification in Eastern Orthodox Theology
An Evaluation and Critique of the Theology of Dumitru Staniloae
Bartos studies a fundamental yet neglected aspect of Orthodox theology: deification. By examining the doctrines of anthropology, christology, soteriology and ecclesiology as they relate to deification, he provides an important contribution to contemporary dialogue between Eastern and Western theologians.

1999 / 0-85364-956-1 / xii + 370pp

Graham Buxton
The Trinity, Creation and Pastoral Ministry
Imaging the Perichoretic God
In this book the author proposes a three-way conversation between theology, science and pastoral ministry. His approach draws on a Trinitarian understanding of God as a relational being of love, whose life 'spills over' into all created reality, human and non-human. By locating human meaning and purpose within God's 'creation-community' this book offers the possibility of a transforming engagement between those in pastoral ministry and the scientific community.

***2005** / 1-84227-369-8 / approx. 380 pp*

Iain D. Campbell
Fixing the Indemnity
The Life and Work of George Adam Smith
When Old Testament scholar George Adam Smith (1856–1942) delivered the Lyman Beecher lectures at Yale University in 1899, he confidently declared that 'modern criticism has won its war against traditional theories. It only remains to fix the amount of the indemnity.' In this biography, Iain D. Campbell assesses Smith's critical approach to the Old Testament and evaluates its consequences, showing that Smith's life and work still raises questions about the relationship between biblical scholarship and evangelical faith.

2004 / 1-84227-228-4 / xx + 256pp

Tim Chester
Mission and the Coming of God
Eschatology, the Trinity and Mission in the Theology of Jürgen Moltmann
This book explores the theology and missiology of the influential contemporary theologian, Jürgen Moltmann. It highlights the important contribution Moltmann has made while offering a critique of his thought from an evangelical perspective. In so doing, it touches on pertinent issues for evangelical missiology. The conclusion takes Calvin as a starting point, proposing 'an eschatology of the cross' which offers a critique of the over-realised eschatologies in liberation theology and certain forms of evangelicalism.
2006 / 1-84227-320-5 / approx. 224pp

Sylvia Wilkey Collinson
Making Disciples
The Significance of Jesus' Educational Strategy for Today's Church
This study examines the biblical practice of discipling, formulates a definition, and makes comparisons with modern models of education. A recommendation is made for greater attention to its practice today.
2004 / 1-84227-116-4 / xiv + 278pp

Darrell Cosden
A Theology of Work
Work and the New Creation
Through dialogue with Moltmann, Pope John Paul II and others, this book develops a genitive 'theology of work', presenting a theological definition of work and a model for a theological ethics of work that shows work's nature, value and meaning now and eschatologically. Work is shown to be a transformative activity consisting of three dynamically inter-related dimensions: the instrumental, relational and ontological.
2005 / 1-84227-332-9 / xvi + 208pp

Stephen M. Dunning
The Crisis and the Quest
A Kierkegaardian Reading of Charles Williams
Employing Kierkegaardian categories and analysis, this study investigates both the central crisis in Charles Williams's authorship between hermetism and Christianity (Kierkegaard's Religions A and B), and the quest to resolve this crisis, a quest that ultimately presses the bounds of orthodoxy.
2000 / 0-85364-985-5 / xxiv + 254pp

Keith Ferdinando
The Triumph of Christ in African Perspective
A Study of Demonology and Redemption in the African Context
The book explores the implications of the gospel for traditional African fears of occult aggression. It analyses such traditional approaches to suffering and biblical responses to fears of demonic evil, concluding with an evaluation of African beliefs from the perspective of the gospel.
1999 / 0-85364-830-1 / xviii + 450pp

Andrew Goddard
Living the Word, Resisting the World
The Life and Thought of Jacques Ellul
This work offers a definitive study of both the life and thought of the French Reformed thinker Jacques Ellul (1912-1994). It will prove an indispensable resource for those interested in this influential theologian and sociologist and for Christian ethics and political thought generally.
2002 / 1-84227-053-2 / xxiv + 378pp

David Hilborn
The Words of our Lips
Language-Use in Free Church Worship
Studies of liturgical language have tended to focus on the written canons of Roman Catholic and Anglican communities. By contrast, David Hilborn analyses the more extemporary approach of English Nonconformity. Drawing on recent developments in linguistic pragmatics, he explores similarities and differences between 'fixed' and 'free' worship, and argues for the interdependence of each.
2006 / 0-85364-977-4 / approx. 350pp

Roger Hitching
The Church and Deaf People
A Study of Identity, Communication and Relationships with Special Reference to the Ecclesiology of Jürgen Moltmann
In *The Church and Deaf People* Roger Hitching sensitively examines the history and present experience of deaf people and finds similarities between aspects of sign language and Moltmann's theological method that 'open up' new ways of understanding theological concepts.
2003 / 1-84227-222-5 / xxii + 236pp

John G. Kelly
One God, One People
The Differentiated Unity of the People of God in the Theology of
Jürgen Moltmann
The author expounds and critiques Moltmann's doctrine of God and highlights the systematic connections between it and Moltmann's influential discussion of Israel. He then proposes a fresh approach to Jewish–Christian relations building on Moltmann's work using insights from Habermas and Rawls.

2005 / 0-85346-969-3 / approx. 350pp

Mark F.W. Lovatt
Confronting the Will-to-Power
A Reconsideration of the Theology of Reinhold Niebuhr
Confronting the Will-to-Power is an analysis of the theology of Reinhold Niebuhr, arguing that his work is an attempt to identify, and provide a practical theological answer to, the existence and nature of human evil.

2001 / 1-84227-054-0 / xviii + 216pp

Neil B. MacDonald
Karl Barth and the Strange New World within the Bible
Barth, Wittgenstein, and the Metadilemmas of the Enlightenment
Barth's discovery of the strange new world within the Bible is examined in the context of Kant, Hume, Overbeck, and, most importantly, Wittgenstein. MacDonald covers some fundamental issues in theology today: epistemology, the final form of the text and biblical truth-claims.

2000 / 0-85364-970-7 / xxvi + 374pp

Keith A. Mascord
Alvin Plantinga and Christian Apologetics
This book draws together the contributions of the philosopher Alvin Plantinga to the major contemporary challenges to Christian belief, highlighting in particular his ground-breaking work in epistemology and the problem of evil. Plantinga's theory that both theistic and Christian belief is warrantedly basic is explored and critiqued, and an assessment offered as to the significance of his work for apologetic theory and practice.

2005 / 1-84227-256-X / approx. 304pp

Gillian McCulloch
The Deconstruction of Dualism in Theology
With Reference to Ecofeminist Theology and New Age Spirituality
This book challenges eco-theological anti-dualism in Christian theology, arguing that dualism has a twofold function in Christian religious discourse. Firstly, it enables us to express the discontinuities and divisions that are part of the process of reality. Secondly, dualistic language allows us to express the mysteries of divine transcendence/immanence and the survival of the soul without collapsing into monism and materialism, both of which are problematic for Christian epistemology.
2002 / 1-84227-044-3 / xii + 282pp

Leslie McCurdy
Attributes and Atonement
The Holy Love of God in the Theology of P.T. Forsyth
Attributes and Atonement is an intriguing full-length study of P.T. Forsyth's doctrine of the cross as it relates particularly to God's holy love. It includes an unparalleled bibliography of both primary and secondary material relating to Forsyth.
1999 / 0-85364-833-6 / xiv + 328pp

Nozomu Miyahira
Towards a Theology of the Concord of God
A Japanese Perspective on the Trinity
This book introduces a new Japanese theology and a unique Trinitarian formula based on the Japanese intellectual climate: three betweennesses and one concord. It also presents a new interpretation of the Trinity, a co-subordinationism, which is in line with orthodox Trinitarianism; each single person of the Trinity is eternally and equally subordinate (or serviceable) to the other persons, so that they retain the mutual dynamic equality.
2000 / 0-85364-863-8 / xiv + 256pp

Eddy José Muskus
The Origins and Early Development of Liberation Theology in Latin America
With Particular Reference to Gustavo Gutiérrez
This work challenges the fundamental premise of Liberation Theology, 'opting for the poor', and its claim that Christ is found in them. It also argues that Liberation Theology emerged as a direct result of the failure of the Roman Catholic Church in Latin America.
2002 / 0-85364-974-X / xiv + 296pp

Jim Purves
The Triune God and the Charismatic Movement
A Critical Appraisal from a Scottish Perspective
All emotion and no theology? Or a fundamental challenge to reappraise and
realign our trinitarian theology in the light of Christian experience? This study
of charismatic renewal as it found expression within Scotland at the end of the
twentieth century evaluates the use of Patristic, Reformed and contemporary
models of the Trinity in explaining the workings of the Holy Spirit.
2004 / 1-84227-321-3 / xxiv + 246pp

Anna Robbins
Methods in the Madness
Diversity in Twentieth-Century Christian Social Ethics
The author compares the ethical methods of Walter Rauschenbusch, Reinhold
Niebuhr and others. She argues that unless Christians are clear about the ways
that theology and philosophy are expressed practically they may lose the ability
to discuss social ethics across contexts, let alone reach effective agreements.
2004 / 1-84227-211-X / xx + 294pp

Ed Rybarczyk
Beyond Salvation
Eastern Orthodoxy and Classical Pentecostalism on Becoming Like Christ
At first glance eastern Orthodoxy and classical Pentecostalism seem quite
distinct. This ground-breaking study shows they share much in common,
especially as it concerns the experiential elements of following Christ. Both
traditions assert that authentic Christianity transcends the wooden categories of
modernism.
2004 / 1-84227-144-X / xii + 356pp

Signe Sandsmark
Is World View Neutral Education Possible and Desirable?
A Christian Response to Liberal Arguments
(Published jointly with The Stapleford Centre)
This book discusses reasons for belief in world view neutrality, and argues that
'neutral' education will have a hidden, but strong world view influence. It
discusses the place for Christian education in the common school.
2000 / 0-85364-973-1 / xiv + 182pp

Hazel Sherman
Reading Zechariah
The Allegorical Tradition of Biblical Interpretation through the Commentary of
Didymus the Blind and Theodore of Mopsuestia
A close reading of the commentary on Zechariah by Didymus the Blind
alongside that of Theodore of Mopsuestia suggests that popular categorising of
Antiochene and Alexandrian biblical exegesis as 'historical' or 'allegorical' is
inadequate and misleading.
2005 / 1-84227-213-6 / approx. 280pp

Andrew Sloane
On Being a Christian in the Academy
Nicholas Wolterstorff and the Practice of Christian Scholarship
An exposition and critical appraisal of Nicholas Wolterstorff's epistemology in
the light of the philosophy of science, and an application of his thought to the
practice of Christian scholarship.
2003 / 1-84227-058-3 / xvi + 274pp

Damon W.K. So
Jesus' Revelation of His Father
A Narrative-Conceptual Study of the Trinity with Special Reference to
Karl Barth
This book explores the trinitarian dynamics in the context of Jesus' revelation of
his Father in his earthly ministry with references to key passages in Matthew's
Gospel. It develops from the exegeses of these passages a non-linear concept of
revelation which links Jesus' communion with his Father to his revelatory words
and actions through a nuanced understanding of the Holy Spirit, with references
to K. Barth, G.W.H. Lampe, J.D.G. Dunn and E. Irving.
2005 / 1-84227-323-X / approx. 380pp

Daniel Strange
The Possibility of Salvation Among the Unevangelised
An Analysis of Inclusivism in Recent Evangelical Theology
For evangelical theologians the 'fate of the unevangelised' impinges upon
fundamental tenets of evangelical identity. The position known as 'inclusivism',
defined by the belief that the unevangelised can be ontologically saved by Christ
whilst being epistemologically unaware of him, has been defended most
vigorously by the Canadian evangelical Clark H. Pinnock. Through a detailed
analysis and critique of Pinnock's work, this book examines a cluster of issues
surrounding the unevangelised and its implications for christology, soteriology
and the doctrine of revelation.
2002 / 1-84227-047-8 / xviii + 362pp

Scott Swain
God According to the Gospel
Biblical Narrative and the Identity of God in the Theology of Robert W. Jenson
Robert W. Jenson is one of the leading voices in contemporary Trinitarian theology. His boldest contribution in this area concerns his use of biblical narrative both to ground and explicate the Christian doctrine of God. *God According to the Gospel* critically examines Jenson's proposal and suggests an alternative way of reading the biblical portrayal of the triune God.
2006 / 1-84227-258-6 / approx. 180pp

Justyn Terry
The Justifying Judgement of God
A Reassessment of the Place of Judgement in the Saving Work of Christ
The argument of this book is that judgement, understood as the whole process of bringing justice, is the primary metaphor of atonement, with others, such as victory, redemption and sacrifice, subordinate to it. Judgement also provides the proper context for understanding penal substitution and the call to repentance, baptism, eucharist and holiness.
2005 / 1-84227-370-1 / approx. 274 pp

Graham Tomlin
The Power of the Cross
Theology and the Death of Christ in Paul, Luther and Pascal
This book explores the theology of the cross in St Paul, Luther and Pascal. It offers new perspectives on the theology of each, and some implications for the nature of power, apologetics, theology and church life in a postmodern context.
1999 / 0-85364-984-7 / xiv + 344pp

Adonis Vidu
Postliberal Theological Method
A Critical Study
The postliberal theology of Hans Frei, George Lindbeck, Ronald Thiemann, John Milbank and others is one of the more influential contemporary options. This book focuses on several aspects pertaining to its theological method, specifically its understanding of background, hermeneutics, epistemic justification, ontology, the nature of doctrine and, finally, Christological method.
2005 / 1-84227-395-7 / approx. 324pp

Graham J. Watts
Revelation and the Spirit
*A Comparative Study of the Relationship between the Doctrine of Revelation
and Pneumatology in the Theology of Eberhard Jüngel and of
Wolfhart Pannenberg*
The relationship between revelation and pneumatology is relatively unexplored.
This approach offers a fresh angle on two important twentieth century
theologians and raises pneumatological questions which are theologically crucial
and relevant to mission in a postmodern culture.
2005 / 1-84227-104-0 / xxii + 232pp

Nigel G. Wright
Disavowing Constantine
*Mission, Church and the Social Order in the Theologies of John Howard Yoder
and Jürgen Moltmann*
This book is a timely restatement of a radical theology of church and state in the
Anabaptist and Baptist tradition. Dr Wright constructs his argument in dialogue
and debate with Yoder and Moltmann, major contributors to a free church
perspective.
2000 / 0-85364-978-2 / xvi + 252pp

Paternoster:
thinking faith

Paternoster
9 Holdom Avenue,
Bletchley,
Milton Keynes MK1 1QR,
United Kingdom
Web: www.authenticmedia.co.uk/paternoster